THE HISTORY OF AL-ṬABARĪ

AN ANNOTATED TRANSLATION

VOLUME XXI

The Victory of the Marwānids

A.D. 685–693/A.H. 66–73

The History of al-Ṭabarī

Editorial Board

Ihsan Abbas, University of Jordan, Amman

C. E. Bosworth, The University of Manchester

Franz Rosenthal, Yale University

Ehsan Yar-Shater, Columbia University (*General Editor*)

SUNY

SERIES IN NEAR EASTERN STUDIES

Said Amir Arjomand, Editor

The preparation of this volume was made possible in part by a grant from the National Endowment for the Humanities, an independent federal agency.

Bibliotheca Persica
Edited by Ehsan Yar-Shater

The History of al-Ṭabarī

(Ta'rīkh al-rusul wa'l-mulūk)

VOLUME XXI

The Victory of the Marwānids

translated and annotated
by

Michael Fishbein
University of California, Los Angeles

State University of New York Press

Published by
State University of New York Press, Albany

Printed in the United States of America

For information, address State University of New York Press, State University Plaza, Albany, N.Y., 12246

Library of Congress Cataloging-in-Publication Data

Ṭabarī, 838?–923.
[Ta'rīkh al-rusul wa-al-mulūk. English. Selections]
The victory of the Marwānids/translated and annotated by Michael Fishbein.
p. cm.—(The history of al-Ṭabarī = Ta'rīkh al-rusul wa'l-mulūk; v. 21) (Bibliotheca Persica) (SUNY series in Near Eastern studies)
Translation of extracts from: Ta'rīkh al-rusul wa-al-mulūk.
Includes index.
Bibliography: p.
ISBN 0-7914-0221-5.—ISBN 0-7914-0222-3 (pbk.)
1. Islamic Empire—History—661–750. I. Fishbein, Michael. II. Title. III. Series: Ṭabarī, 838?–923. Ta'rīkh al-rusul wa-al-mulūk. English; v. 21. IV. Series: Bibliotheca Persica (Albany, N.Y.) V. Series: SUNY series in Near Eastern studies.
DS38.2.T313 1985 vol. 21
[DS38.5] 89-4518
909'.097671—dc20 CIP

10 9 8 7 6 5 4 3 2 1

Preface

THE HISTORY OF PROPHETS AND KINGS (*Ta'rīkh al-rusul wa'l-mulūk*) by Abū Ja'far Muḥammad b. Jarīr al-Ṭabarī (839–923), here rendered as the *History of al-Ṭabarī*, is by common consent the most important universal history produced in the world of Islam. It has been translated here in its entirety for the first time for the benefit of non-Arabists, with historical and philological notes for those interested in the particulars of the text.

Ṭabarī's monumental work explores the history of the ancient nations, with special emphasis on biblical peoples and prophets, the legendary and factual history of ancient Iran, and, in great detail, the rise of Islam, the life of the Prophet Muḥammad, and the history of the Islamic world down to the year 915. The first volume of this translation will contain a biography of al-Ṭabarī and a discussion of the method, scope, and value of his work. It will also provide information on some of the technical considerations that have guided the work of the translators.

The *History* has been divided here into 38 volumes, each of which covers about two hundred pages of the original Arabic text in the Leiden edition. An attempt has been made to draw the dividing lines between the individual volumes in such a way that each is to some degree independent and can be read as such. The page numbers of the original in the Leiden edition appear in the margins of the translated volumes.

Al-Ṭabarī very often quotes his sources verbatim and traces the chain of transmission (*isnād*) to an original source. The chains of transmitters are, for the sake of brevity, rendered by only a dash (—) between the individual links in the chain. Thus, "According to Ibn Ḥumayd—Salamah—Ibn Isḥāq" means that al-Ṭabarī received the report from Ibn Ḥumayd, who said that he was told by Salamah, who said that he was told by Ibn Isḥāq, and so on. The numerous subtle and important differences in the original Arabic wording have been disregarded.

The table of contents at the beginning of each volume gives a brief survey of the topics dealt with in that particular volume. It also includes the headings and subheadings as they appear in al-Ṭabarī's text, as well as those occasionally introduced by the translator.

Well-known place names, such as, for instance, Mecca, Baghdad, Jerusalem, Damascus, and the Yemen, are given in their English spellings. Less common place names, which are the vast majority, are transliterated. Biblical figures appear in the accepted English spelling. Iranian names are usually transcribed according to their Arabic forms, and the presumed Iranian forms are often discussed in the footnotes.

Technical terms have been translated wherever possible, but some, such as dirham and imām, have been retained in Arabic forms. Others that cannot be translated with sufficient precision have been retained and italicized as well as footnoted.

The annotation aims chiefly at clarifying difficult passages, identifying individuals and place names, and discussing textual difficulties. Much leeway has been left to the translators to include in the footnotes whatever they consider necessary and helpful.

The bibliographies list all the sources mentioned in the annotation.

The index in each volume contains all the names of persons and places referred to in the text, as well as those mentioned in the notes as far as they refer to the medieval period. It does not include the names of modern scholars. A general index, it is hoped, will appear after all the volumes have been published.

For further details concerning the series and acknowledgments, see Preface to Volume I.

Ehsan Yar-Shater

Contents

Preface / v

Abbreviations / xi

Translator's Foreword / xiii

The Events of the Year 66 (cont'd) (685/686) / 1

[Al-Mukhtār Acts against the Slayers of al-Ḥusayn] / 1
Why He Seized Them; Names of Those He Killed and of Those Who Fled and Eluded His Grasp / 2
[The Kūfan *Ashrāf* Rise against al-Mukhtār] / 11
[Al-Mukhtār Acts against the Murderers of al-Ḥusayn] / 31
[The Swearing of Allegiance to al-Mukhtār in al-Baṣrah] / 45
[Al-Mukhtār Sends an Army to Trick Ibn al-Zubayr] / 53
Al-Mukhtār's Motive in Sending This Army; What Befell Them / 53
[The Khashabiyyah Perform the Pilgrimage] / 59
Why the Khashabiyyah Came to Mecca / 59
[The Siege of the Banū Tamīm in Khurāsān] / 62
[Those in Office during the Year] / 66
[Ibrāhīm b. al-Ashtar Goes to Fight ʿUbaydallāh b. Ziyād] / 67
An Explanation of the Chair Whereby al-Mukhtār and His Companions Prayed for Assistance / 69

The Events of the Year 67 (686/687) / 74

The Death of ʿUbaydallāh b. Ziyād / 74
[Muṣʿab b. al-Zubayr Becomes Governor of al-Baṣrah] / 83
[Muṣʿab b. al-Zubayr Defeats al-Mukhtār] / 85
Why Muṣʿab Marched against Him; an Account of al-Mukhtār's Death / 85
[Ibn al-Zubayr Removes Muṣʿab from al-Baṣrah] / 118
[Those in Office during the Year] / 121

The Events of the Year 68 (687/688) / 122

[The Azāriqah Return from Fārs to Iraq] / 122
An Account of Them, Their Departure, and Their Return to Iraq / 123
[Events in Syria] / 134
[The Death of ʿUbaydallāh b. al-Ḥurr] / 134
His Death; the Circumstances That Brought It upon Him / 135
[Four Separate Banners at the Pilgrimage] / 151
[Those in Office during the Year] / 153

The Events of the Year 69 (688/689) / 154

[The Revolt and Death of ʿAmr b. Saʿīd in Damascus] / 154
[A Khārijite Killed at the Pilgrimage] / 167
[Those in Office during the Year] / 168

The Events of the Year 70 (689/690) / 169

[ʿAbd al-Malik and the Byzantines] / 169
[Muṣʿab b. al-Zubayr Visits Mecca] / 169
[Those in Office during the Year] / 170

The Events of the Year 71 (690/691) / 171

[Khālid b. ʿAbdallāh Raises Support for ʿAbd al-Malik in al-Baṣrah] / 172
[ʿAbd al-Malik Attacks Muṣʿab; the Death of Muṣʿab] / 178
[ʿAbd al-Malik Enters al-Kūfah] / 188
[Khālid b. ʿAbdallāh Becomes Governor of al-Baṣrah] / 193
[Ibn al-Zubayr's Governors during This Year] / 194
[The Pilgrimage] / 194

[Ibn al-Zubayr's Sermon after the Death of Muṣʿab] / 194
[ʿAbd al-Malik's Banquet at al-Khawarnaq] / 195

The Events of the Year 72 (691/692) / 198

[ʿAbd al-Malik and the Khārijites] / 198
[ʿAbd al-Malik Sends al-Ḥajjāj to Fight Ibn al-Zubayr] / 206
[ʿAbd al-Malik and ʿAbdallāh b. Khāzim] / 209
[Those in Office during the Year] / 212
A Chapter in Which We Mention the Secretaries since the Beginning of Islam / 213

The Events of the Year 73 (692/693) / 224

A Description of [the Death of Ibn al-Zubayr] / 224
[ʿAbd al-Malik and the Khārijites] / 232
[Bishr b. Marwān Becomes Governor of al-Baṣrah] / 233
[Campaigns against the Byzantines] / 233
[Those in Office during the Year] / 234

Bibliography of Cited Works / 235

Index / 239

Abbreviations

BSOAS: Bulletin of the School of Oriental and African Studies
EI[1]: *Encyclopaedia of Islam.* 1st edition. Leiden: 1913–1934
EI[2]: *Encyclopaedia of Islam.* 2nd edition. Leiden: 1960–
JNES: Journal of Near Eastern Studies
ZDMG: Zeitschrift der Deutschen Morgenländischen Gesellschaft

Translator's Foreword

Volume XXI of the History of al-Ṭabarī spans a period extending from the year 66 (685/686) to the year 73 (692/693), corresponding to series II, pages 642–854 of the Leiden edition. The events chronicled in the volume cover the resolution of what historians have come to call the Second Civil War and the reestablishment of Umayyad hegemony over the Islamic world. In the course of the period, the major anti-Umayyad forces—the Shīʿites of Iraq and the rival caliphate of ʿAbdallāh b. al-Zubayr in Mecca—collapsed, leaving ʿAbd al-Malik b. Marwān, in the year 73, as ruler over a dynastic kingdom similar in extent to the one Muʿāwiyah had governed from Damascus before the dissolution of Umayyad authority following the death of Yazīd.

To understand the complex events of the years A.H. 66–73, one must go back to the crisis of the Umayyad caliphate after the death of Yazīd b. Muʿāwiyah in 64/683. Having earned the implacable hatred of the Shīʿah by causing the death of al-Ḥusayn and the hatred of influential elements in the Ḥijāz by his use of force to compel Mecca and Medina to acknowledge his rule, Yazīd bequeathed his caliphate to a thirteen-year-old boy, Muʿāwiyah, who survived his father by only forty days. Yazīd's two other surviving sons, even younger, obviously could not rule; the people of al-Kūfah and al-Baṣrah expelled their Umayyad governor, ending Umayyad authority in Iraq; the Ḥijāz was under the control of ʿAbdallāh b. al-Zubayr; and Syria itself was rent by tribal factionalism. The situation seemed so bad that the senior member of the Umayyad family, Marwān b. al-Ḥakam, was ready to acknowledge the authority of ʿAbdallāh b. al-Zubayr. Only the vigorous intervention of ʿUbaydallāh b. Ziyād, the Umayyad governor of Iraq, seems to have instilled new confidence into the Umayyad family. Under the leadership of Marwān, who was succeeded as head of the family the following year by his son, ʿAbd al-Malik, the Umayyads began the process that would end in 73/692 with the reestablishment of a single central authority, which, if not universally acknowledged, was accepted by the consensus of the Islamic community, and which had no obvious rival in the conduct of the affairs of the Islamic state.

Roughly, the process involved three steps. The hostility of pro-Zubayrid Arab groups in Syria had to be overcome; Iraq, itself a battleground between Zubayrid and Shīʿi loyalties, had to be brought within the Umayyad orbit; and finally ʿAbdallāh b. al-Zubayr himself had to be overcome in the Ḥijāz. By 66/685, Syrian opposition to Umayyad rule, while by no means eliminated, was well on its way to elimination. The surviving text of al-Ṭabarī gives little detail about the final collapse of pro-Zubayrid forces in Syria and al-Jazīrah; more can be gleaned from al-Balādhurī, or from the much later Ibn al-Athīr. In Iraq, the Umayyads were aided by a situation in which their opponents weakened each other. In Rabīʿ I 66 (October 685), al-Mukhtār b. Abī ʿUbayd, formerly a supporter of Ibn al-Zubayr, but now leading the Kūfan Shīʿah, led an uprising that forced Ibn al-Zubayr's governor to leave al-Kūfah and retreat to al-Baṣrah. In keeping with the Shīʿi nature of the revolt, the *ashrāf* (tribal dignitaries) of al-Kūfah pledged allegiance to al-Mukhtār, not as "Commander of the Faithful," but as the "helper" (*wazīr*) of Muḥammad b. al-Ḥanafiyyah, a surviving son of ʿAlī. Later in the year, the same *ashrāf* turned against al-Mukhtār and tried to expel him, but were defeated; many of them left for al-Baṣrah. Al-Mukhtār, who had come to power promising to avenge the death of al-Ḥusayn, lost no time in killing anyone he could capture who had been in any way connected with the death of al-Ḥusayn. Then he tried to expand his power. To the north, he was successful in two campaigns (both in 66), during the second of which the Umayyad commander ʿUbaydallāh b. Ziyād, the architect of the death of al-Ḥusayn, died in combat against Ibrāhīm b. al-Ashtar. To the south, al-Mukhtār's efforts to attract support failed. Realizing how much was at stake, Ibn al-Zubayr sent his own brother, Muṣʿab b. al-Zubayr, to govern al-Baṣrah and to deal with al-Mukhtār. Muṣʿab defeated the forces of al-Mukhtār at the Battle of al-Madhār; al-Mukhtār retreated to al-Kūfah, was besieged, and died in combat in Ramaḍān 67 (April 687).

ʿAbd al-Malik now faced Ibn al-Zubayr. On each side, the years 68, 69, 70, and 71 presented certain internal threats to be overcome before there could be a final confrontation. Al-Ṭabarī's account of events in Syria is very brief for these years. The Damascus revolt of ʿAmr b. Saʿīd al-Ashdaq in 69 or 70 is covered in some detail. The difficulties of the Zubayrids are presented rather fully. The Zubayrid governors of al-Baṣrah were continuously threatened by the Azāriqah, a Khārijite sect, who in 68/687 carried their depredations into the heartland of Iraq, and who drained off military resources that otherwise might have been used against the Umayyads. Also, there seems to have been widespread rural brigandage led by such figures as ʿUbaydallāh b. al-Ḥurr, whose picaresque biography appears under the year 68.

The decisive events that reestablished Umayyad primacy came in 71 (or 72) and 73. In each case, much was due to the Umayyad sense of politics—the ability to persuade potential opponents that more was to be gained by going over to the Umayyad side than by opposition, and that the stability and security of Iraq could best be served by an Umayyad victory. Muṣʿab b. al-Zubayr's support melted under the sun of Umayyad promises to his erstwhile supporters; the treachery of many of Muṣʿab's supporters at Dayr al-Jāthalīq in 71 (or 72) sealed his fate. ʿAbd al-Malik was then free to deal, through his commander, al-Ḥajjāj b. Yūsuf, with ʿAbdallāh b. al-Zubayr.

Al-Ṭabarī's brief account of al-Ḥajjāj's siege of Mecca and the defeat and death of Ibn al-Zubayr in 73/692 (more external details of the battles are to be found in al-Balādhurī) centers on a portrait of the heroic death of Ibn al-Zubayr, whose brave, but hopeless, fight earned the admiration of even al-Ḥajjāj's second-in-command, who pronounced the following judgment: "Women have borne none manlier [than ʿAbdallāh b. al-Zubayr]." ʿAbd al-Malik, we are told, seconded the judgment.

Thus, ʿAbd al-Malik was left in virtually uncontested possession of the title "Commander of the Faithful." (The Khārijites formed a significant exception to recognition of his claim.) More than settling the possession of a title, the end of the Second Civil War settled important questions about the nature of authority over the Muslim state. The Umayyads, in the person of ʿAbd al-Malik, reestablished a caliphate based on a family dynasty and a strong military base in the Syrian Arab army. The principle of a single strong authority was reasserted over the various centrifugal forces at work among the Arabs. Had Ibn al-Zubayr prevailed, a much weaker caliphate would have been the result. However, the Umayyad triumph by no means put an end to alternative ideas about authority in Islam. Indeed, for the Shīʿah, the years of the Second Civil War witnessed the development of many tendencies that would bear fruit only much later. In particular, the revolt of al-Mukhtār, with its idea of an Imām living in retirement, his cause energetically furthered in political action by a "wazīr" or "helper," foreshadowed a constellation of ideas important for the genesis of the ʿAbbāsid revolution. Furthermore, Khārijite ideas about the free election of a leader by the community certainly did not die out with the triumph of ʿAbd al-Malik.

A Note on the Text

The translation follows the text of the Leiden edition, which appeared in installments between 1879 and 1898 under the overall editorship of M. J. De Goeje. The task of editing Part II, pages 580–1340 (A.H. 65–99), was assigned to the Italian scholar Ignazio Guidi. For establishing the text of the section here translated (II, 642–854), Guidi had five manuscripts at his disposal:[1]

1. Constantinople, Köprülü 1047 (Siglum Co). This was a composite manuscript. The older portion, which Guidi singled out for special praise, was copied in A.D. the eleventh or perhaps the tenth century. It ended at

1. See ed. Leiden, *Introductio*, pp. LV–LXIII.

II, 706, and was followed by a section in a later hand, perhaps of the thirteenth century, much less carefully executed, and apparently from an original of a different family. This manuscript formed the based text for the edition.

2. Oxford, Bodleian, Uri 650 (Siglum O).[2]
3. Berlin, Petermann II, 635 (Siglum Pet). Beginning with II, 674, a fourth manuscript could be used:
4. Constantinople, Köprülü 1044 (Siglum C). Finally, from II, 789, a fifth manuscript was available:
5. Berlin, Ms. Or. Fol. 69 (Siglum B).[3]

Guidi divided these manuscripts into two families: an "older and much superior" family including Co (older hand), Pet, and C; and a more recent family including B, Co (younger hand), and O. (Ibn al-Athīr used a manuscript of this family.) Thus, throughout the section here translated, textual witnesses from two families were available.

To the five manuscripts used by Guidi, the 1960 Egyptian edition of Muḥammad Abū al-Faḍl Ibrāhīm adds only one additional authority for establishing the text of the section here translated: Ms. Istanbul, Ahmet III, 2929. Its readings, occasionally preferable to any that were available to Guidi, are given in the notes of the Cairo edition; otherwise, the Cairo text is the same as the Leiden text, apart from differences of punctuation and vocalization.

For the events of these years, there are important parallel accounts in al-Balādhurī's *Ansāb al-Ashrāf*, Ibn Saʿd's *Kitāb al-Ṭabaqāt al-Kabīr*, al-Dīnawarī's *Kitāb al-Akhbār al-Ṭiwāl*, al-Iṣbahānī's *Kitāb al-Aghānī*, and Ibn Aʿtham al-Kūfī's *Kitāb al-Futūḥ*. The notes to the translation indicate some of these parallels, particularly when they involve interesting differences or further information, but the notes are not intended to provide an exhaustive listing of parallels.

The translator wishes to thank Professors Moshe Perlmann,

---

2. Described by M. J. De Goeje, *ZDMG* XVI, 759.
3. See Ahlwardt, *Berlin Catalogue*, IX, 36, n. 9419.

Seeger A. Bonebakker, and Michael G. Morony, all of the University of California, Los Angeles, for their continued support and encouragement.

Michael Fishbein

The Events of the Year 66 (cont'd)

(AUGUST 8, 685–JULY 27, 686)

[*Al-Mukhtār Acts against the Slayers of al-Ḥusayn*]

According to Abū Jaʿfar [sc. al-Ṭabarī]: In this year, al-Mukhtār[1] seized the slayers of al-Ḥusayn[2] who were in al-Kūfah[3] and those who were accomplices in his murder. He killed those of them over whom he gained power; some, however, fled from al-Kūfah and eluded his grasp. [642]

---

1. The Shīʿī leader al-Mukhtār b. Abī ʿUbayd b. Masʿūd al-Thaqafī seized al-Kūfah earlier in 66/685 as the self-proclaimed "assistant" or "helper" (*wazīr*) of ʿAlī's son, Muḥammad b. al-Ḥanafiyyah. See Ṭabarī, II, 598–642; *EI*[1], s.v.

2. Al-Ḥusayn, the grandson of the Prophet, was the son of ʿAlī b. Abī Ṭālib by Muḥammad's daughter, Fāṭimah. The Shīʿah, supporters of the right of ʿAlī and his family to political and spiritual leadership, considered his death at the hands of Umayyad forces at Karbalāʾ on 10 Muḥarram 61 (October 10, 680) a martyrdom and demanded vengeance against the Umayyads. See *EI*[2], s.v. al-Ḥusayn b. ʿAlī.

3. The Muslim garrison city (*miṣr*) and provincial capital of al-Kūfah was founded ca. 17/638 in the caliphate of ʿUmar on the Euphrates near the older city of al-Ḥīrah. It grew rapidly and in 36/657 became ʿAlī's capital. ʿAlī was assassinated outside the city's great mosque in 40/661, and al-Kūfah became a focus of pro-ʿAlid Shīʿī activity. See *EI*[2], s.v.; Le Strange, *Lands*, 74ff.

Why He Seized Them; Names of Those He Killed and of Those Who Fled and Eluded His Grasp

According to Hishām b. Muḥammad [al-Kalbī][4]—ʿAwānah b. al-Ḥakam:[5] The reason for this was as follows. When Syria had become completely obedient to him, Marwān b. al-Ḥakam[6] sent out two armies. One of them was sent to the Ḥijāz under Ḥubaysh b. Duljah al-Qaynī, and we have previously mentioned him and how he perished.[7] The other was sent to Iraq under ʿUbaydallāh b. Ziyād, and we have mentioned what took place between him and the Tawwābūn[8] of the Shīʿah[9] at ʿAyn al-Wardah. When Marwān sent ʿUbaydallāh b. Ziyād to Iraq, he granted him [the

---

4. Hishām b. Muḥammad b. al-Sāʾib al-Kalbī (b. ca. 120/737, d. 204/819 or 206), often called "Ibn al-Kalbī" after his father (d. 146/763), who was himself a genealogist, historian, geographer, and Qurʾān commentator, was a Shīʿī native of al-Kūfah who wrote prolifically on many subjects. The *isnād* here is introduced by *dhakarahū Hishām*, indicating that Ṭabarī used one of Ibn al-Kalbī's books, but without authorization from a scholar who had studied with Ibn al-Kalbī. Technically, such a procedure was called "*wijādah.*" See EI^2, s.v. al-Kalbī; F. Sezgin, *GAS*, I, 268–271.

5. ʿAwānah b. al-Ḥakam b. ʿAwānah al-Kalbī (d. 147/764 or 158) was a blind Kūfan whose interests included history of the Umayyad period, genealogy, and poetry. The *Fihrist* of Ibn al-Nadīm lists two books of his: a *Kitāb al-Tārīkh*, and a *Kitāb Sīrat Muʿāwiyah wa-Banī Umayyah* on the life of Muʿāwiyah and the Banū Umayyah. Ṭabarī's material from ʿAwānah was probably obtained indirectly through the works of Ibn al-Kalbī and al-Madāʾinī. See EI^2, s.v.; F. Sezgin, *GAS*, I, 307–8.

6. The Umayyad caliph Marwān b. al-Ḥakam ruled for nine months in 64–65 (683–684). He began to reassemble the empire that his cousin Muʿāwiyah, the first Umayyad caliph, had ruled and that had fallen away from Umayyad allegiance during the reigns of Yazīd and Muʿāwiyah II. He was succeeded by his son, ʿAbd al-Malik, in Ramaḍān 65 (April 685). See EI^1, s.v.

7. This army was sent in 65/684 to take Medina from Ibn al-Zubayr, but was defeated when an army from al-Baṣrah reinforced the Zubayrid forces in the Ḥijāz. See Ṭabarī, II, 578–79.

8. The Tawwābūn ("penitents") were a Shīʿī group. Blaming their own inaction for having caused the death of al-Ḥusayn, they vowed to expiate their guilt by exacting vengeance. Their revolt after the death of Yazīd ended in defeat at the battle of ʿAyn al-Wardah on 22 Jumādā I, 65 (January 4, 685). Sulaymān b. Ṣurad, their leader, was killed, and the Tawwābūn were routed by the forces of ʿUbaydallāh b. Ziyād. See Ṭabarī, II, 497ff.; EI^1 s.v. Sulaimān b. Ṣurad al-Khuzāʿī; Dixon, *Umayyad Caliphate*, 35–37; and Jafri, *Origins*, 159.

9. Literally, "the followers, group, associates, or partisans," the word *shīʿah* came to refer to those who supported the rights of ʿAlī b. Abī Ṭālib and his descendants to political leadership of the Muslim community and to a special spiritual leadership (the imamate). See EI^1, s.v.; Jafri, *Origins*, 1–23

governance of] whatever he conquered and commanded him to sack al-Kūfah, if he overcame its people, for three days. [643]

ʿAwānah said: ʿUbaydallāh passed through the land of al-Jazīrah[10] and was delayed there. Qays ʿAylān [tribesmen][11] were there, obedient to Ibn al-Zubayr.[12] Marwān had inflicted heavy losses on the Qays at the battle of Marj Rāhiṭ,[13] when they were on the side of al-Ḍaḥḥāk b. Qays,[14] opposing Marwān and his son ʿAbd al-Malik, [who ruled] after him. ʿUbaydallāh remained preoccupied with them and unable to turn his attention to Iraq for about a year. Then he proceeded to al-Mawṣil.[15] Al-Mukhtār's governor of al-Mawṣil, ʿAbd al-Raḥmān b. Saʿīd b. Qays, wrote to al-Mukhtār:

> To proceed: I hereby inform you, O commander (*amīr*), that ʿUbaydallāh b. Ziyād has entered the territory of al-Mawṣil and has turned his horsemen and foot soldiers toward me. I have withdrawn to Takrīt[16] until your opinion and command reach me. Peace be upon you.[17]

---

10. Al-Jazīrah ("the island" or "peninsula") was the Arabic name for upper Mesopotamia. It included as its principal towns al-Mawṣil, al-Raqqah, and Āmid. See Le Strange, *Lands*, 86–114; *EI*², s.v. al-Djazīra.

11. Qays ʿAylān, or Qays (sometimes called "Muḍar"), were a group of northern Arab clans from the Ḥijāz and western Arabia. They formed the bulk of the men involved in the first conquests in Syria under Abū Bakr and were rewarded with lands in al-Jazīrah. Because Muʿāwiyah relied on the support of rival Kalb (Yemeni) tribes, and also because Yazīd, Muʿāwiyah's heir, had a Kalbī mother, many of the Qays supported Ibn al-Zubayr. Muʿāwiyah's opening of al-Jazīrah to immigration from unrelated Arab clans may also have been a factor. See *EI*², s.v. Ḳays ʿAylān; Shaban, *Islamic History*, I, 82–84, 92.

12. ʿAbdallāh b. al-Zubayr ruled the Ḥijāz at this time as a rival caliph and was recognized by opponents of the Umayyads in Syria, Egypt, southern Arabia, and al-Kūfah. See *EI*², s.v.

13. A plain near Damascus where Marwān defeated forces loyal to Ibn al-Zubayr at the end of 64 (July 684). See Yāqūt, *Muʿjam*, s.v.; Ṭabarī, II, 474ff.; *EI*², s.v.

14. Al-Ḍaḥḥāk b. Qays al-Fihrī, leader of the Qays and at first a loyal supporter of the Umayyads against ʿAlī, went over to Ibn al-Zubayr after the death of Muʿāwiyah II in 64/684. He was defeated and killed by Marwān at Marj Rāhiṭ. See *EI*², s.v.

15. Al-Mawṣil, on the upper Tigris River, was a principal town of al-Jazīrah. See Le Strange, *Lands*, 87–89.

16. Takrīt lay south of al-Mawṣil on the Tigris, on the Iraq side of the border between al-Jazīrah and Iraq. See Le Strange, *Lands*, 25, 57; *EI*¹, s.v.

17. Cf. the longer version in Balādhurī, *Ansāb*, V, 230: "ʿAbd al-Raḥmān b. Saʿīd b. Qays wrote informing al-Mukhtār that the horsemen of ʿUbaydallāh b. Ziyād were approaching al-Mawṣil, and that he, having neither horses nor men, feared he would be too weak to deal with him."

Al-Mukhtār wrote to him:

> To proceed: Your letter has reached me, and I have understood all you said in it. You did well to withdraw to Takrīt. Remain where you are until my command reaches you, God willing. Peace be upon you.

According to Hishām [b. al-Kalbī]—Abū Mikhnaf[18]—Mūsā b. ʿĀmir:[19] When ʿAbd al-Raḥmān b. Saʿīd's letter reached al-Mukhtār, he summoned Yazīd b. Anas[20] and said to him,[21] "Yazīd b. Anas, one who knows is not like one who is ignorant; truth is not like falsehood. I tell you the report of one who has not lied and has not been called a liar, who has not disobeyed or wavered. We are the believers, the fortunate ones; the victorious, the sound ones. You are the master of horses whose quivers you draw[22] and whose tails you plait, until you bring them to water in olive groves, their eyes sunken, their bellies lank.[23] Go out to al-Mawṣil and encamp in its vicinity. I will provide you with men followed
[644] by even more men." Yazīd b. Anas said to him, "Send with me three thousand horsemen whom I shall choose, and leave me to take care of the region to which you send us. If I need men, I will write to you." Al-Mukhtār said to him, "Go out and choose, in the name of God, whomever you like."

Yazīd b. Anas went out and chose three thousand horsemen.

---

18. Abū Mikhnaf Lūṭ b. Yaḥyā b. Saʿīd b. Mikhnaf al-Azdī (b. ca. 70/689, d. 157/775) was a late Umayyad composer of historical monographs, about forty of which can be identified from Ibn al-Nadīm's *Fihrist* and other works. His books, mediated through Ibn al-Kalbī, were one of Ṭabarī's major sources of information about events of the Umayyad period, particularly those centered around al-Kūfah. See EI^2, s.v.; F. Sezgin, *GAS*, I, 308–9; and U. Sezgin, *Abū Miḫnaf*, 40–47.

19. Mūsā b. ʿĀmir Abū al-Ashʿar al-Juhanī al-ʿAdawī identifies himself (Ṭabarī, II, 646) as having been in the army of Yazīd b. Anas. All his reports, mediated through Abū Mikhnaf, deal with A.H. 66. See U. Sezgin, *Abū Miḫnaf*, 213.

20. Yazīd b. Anas b. Kilāb al-Asadī, an early supporter of al-Mukhtār, was influential in drawing Ibrāhīm b. al-Ashtar to al-Mukhtār's cause and commanded part of al-Mukhtār's forces in the seizure al-Kūfah in 66/685. See Ṭabarī, II, 599–630, passim.

21. The speech is in rhymed prose (*sajʿ*), on which see EI^1, s.v. Sadjʿ.

22. The meaning of *tajurru jiʿābahā* is problematic. Ed. Leiden, *Glossarium*, p. CLXV: "probably metaphorical for the sheath of the penis of a horse. Horses' *jiʿāb* are drawn (or slit?) and tails plaited when they are to make a very long journey." No source for this meaning of *jiʿāb* or further explanation is given.

23. I.e., from long and strenuous traveling.

He put al-Nu'mān b. 'Awf b. Abī Jābir al-Azdī in charge of the fourth[24] of Medina, 'Āṣim b. Qays b. Ḥabīb al-Hamdānī in charge of the fourth of Tamīm and Hamdān, Warqā' b. 'Āzib al-Asadī in charge of Madhḥij and Asad, and Si'r b. Abī Si'r al-Ḥanafī in charge of the fourth of Rabī'ah and Kindah. Then he set out from al-Kūfah, and al-Mukhtār and the people went out with him to escort him. When he reached Dayr Abī Mūsā,[25] al-Mukhtār said goodbye to him and turned back, saying, "When you encounter your enemy, grant them no respite. When opportunity presents itself, do not delay. Let me have a report from you every day. If you need assistance, write to me, although I will assist you even if you do not ask for it; for it will give your arm more strength, make your army more powerful, and put more fear into your enemy." Yazīd b. Anas said to him, "Assist me only with your prayer; that will be enough assistance." The people said to him, "May God accompany you! May He convey you and aid you!" Then they said goodbye to him. Yazīd said to them, "Pray to God on my behalf for martyrdom! I swear by God, if I meet them and victory escapes me, martyrdom shall not escape me, God willing."

Al-Mukhtār wrote to 'Abd al-Raḥmān b. Sa'īd b. Qays:

> To proceed: Let Yazīd [b. Anas] deal with the territory—God willing! Peace be upon you.

Having marched forth with the men, Yazīd b. Anas spent the night at Sūrā.[26] The next day he marched with them and spent the night at al-Madā'in.[27] The men complained to him that they were suffering from the speed of the march, so he stayed there a day [645]
and a night. Then he took them along the territory of Jūkhā,[28]

---

24. The fourths (*rub'*, pl. *arbā'*) were divisions of the Kūfan army, in accordance with a system created by Ziyād b. Abīhi.

25. Apparently the same as Dayr Mūsā, a place near al-Kūfah on the way to Sūrā. See *EI*², s.v. Dayr Mūsā.

26. At Sūrā, a town on the upper Nahr Sūrā (modern Shaṭṭ Hindiyyah branch of the Euphrates), the main road from al-Kūfah to al-Madā'in crossed the Euphrates by bridge. See Yāqūt, *Mu'jam*, s.v.; Le Strange, *Lands*, 26, 70–72.

27. Al-Madā'in ("the cities," so named because it consisted of a number of separate towns linked by a floating bridge across the Tigris) was the former Sasanian winter capital about 20 miles south of Baghdad. See *EI*², s.v.

28. Jūkhā was a district east of al-Madā'in, extending along the Diyālā River. See Yāqūt, *Mu'jam*, s.v. Jūkhā; Le Strange, *Lands*, 42; Morony, *Iraq*, 137–141.

brought them out in the Rādhān [districts],[29] and crossed with them into the territory of al-Mawṣil, encamping at Banāt Talā.[30] His location and the place at which he had encamped were reported to ʿUbaydallāh b. Ziyād, who asked about their number. His spies told him that three thousand horsemen had left al-Kūfah with him. ʿUbaydallāh said, "I will dispatch two thousand for every thousand." He summoned Rabīʿah b. al-Mukhāriq al-Ghanawī and ʿAbdallāh b. Ḥamlah al-Khathʿamī and dispatched them, each with three thousand men. He sent Rabīʿah b. al-Mukhāriq first, waited a day, and then sent ʿAbdallāh b. Ḥamlah after him. Then he wrote to them, saying, "Whichever of you arrives first is to be the commander over his fellow. If you both arrive together, the older of you is to be commander over his fellow and the entire force." [Continuing,] he[31] said: Rabīʿah b. al-Mukhāriq arrived first and encamped by Yazīd b. Anas while he was at Banāt Talā. Yazīd b. Anas came out to [fight] him sick and exhausted.

According to Abū Mikhnaf—Abū al-Ṣalt[32]—Abū Saʿīd al-Ṣayqal,[33] who said: Yazīd b. Anas came out to us sick and mounted on a donkey. Men walked with him, holding him on his right and

---

29. Upper and Lower Rādhān were subdistricts of Jūkhā. The town of Rādhān lay on the east side of the old bed of the Tigris between the ʿAdhaym and Diyālā Rivers. See Le Strange, *Lands*, 35, 80; Yāqūt, *Muʿjam*, s.v.; Morony, *Iraq*, 138–39.

30. Vocalization and location uncertain. The mss. show much uncertainty about the dotting of the consonants of the name. Ibn al-Athīr, *Kāmil*, IV, 229 reads "Bātilī," with variants such as "Māyilī" and "Mātilī."

31. One is tempted to omit in translation this peculiar feature of the reports collected in Ṭabarī's history—namely, the frequent interruption of narratives by *qāla*, "he said." Normally, "he" refers to the earliest source in the previous *isnad*. One might thus translate: "[Mūsā b. ʿĀmir continued,] saying. . . ." However, in some cases it is not easy to determine whether the text after *qāla* resumes the words of the earliest informant or begins a passage of summary by Abū Mikhnaf or even Hishām b. al-Kalbī. I have therefore thought it best to preserve the ambiguity of the Arabic. On the other hand, these repeated *qāla*s should not be omitted. An argument can be made that they mark places where an account has been shortened through the omission of material. See U. Sezgin, *Abū Miḥnaf*, 91–92, for a discussion of the problem.

32. Abū al-Ṣalt al-Taymī is perhaps to be identified with the Kūfan scholar Zāʾidah b. Qudāmah al-Thaqafī (d. 160/776), author of various works on *ḥadīth* and Qurʾān readings and a kinsman and friend of al-Mukhtār. See Dixon, *Umayyad Caliphate*, 39–40; and U. Sezgin, *Abū Miḥnaf*, 149, 226–7.

33. Abū Saʿīd al-Ṣayqal, an eyewitness, was a *mawlā* who had fought on al-Mukhtār's side at the seizure of al-Kūfah. See Ṭabarī, II, 623. For *mawlā*, see n. 49.

on his left by his legs, arms, and sides. He stopped at each fourth and said, "O choice army (*shurṭah*) of God, be steadfast, and you shall be rewarded; vie with your enemy in steadfastness, and you shall be victorious![34] 'Fight you against the friends of Satan; surely the guile of Satan is ever feeble.'[35] If I perish, your commander is Warqā' b. ʿĀzib al-Asadī. If he perishes, your commander is ʿAbdallāh b. Ḍamrah al-ʿUdhrī. If he perishes, your commander is Siʿr b. Abī Siʿr al-Ḥanafī." [Continuing,] he said: I, by God, was among those who walked with him and held his arm and hand, and I saw by his face that death had descended upon him. [646]

[Continuing,] he said: Yazīd b. Anas put ʿAbdallāh b. Ḍamrah al-ʿUdhrī in charge of his right wing, and Siʿr b. Abī Siʿr in charge of his left wing. He put Warqā' b. ʿĀzib al-Asadī in charge of the horsemen. He himself dismounted and was placed on a litter among the men. He said to them, "Go forth to encounter them in the open field. Put me in front among the men. Then, if you will, fight for your commander; or, if you will, flee and leave him." [Continuing,] he said: We brought him out in the month of Dhū al-Ḥijjah, on the Day of ʿArafah of the year 66.[36] Sometimes we held him by his back, and he would say, "Do this, do this, and do this," giving his order. Before long the pain would overcome him and he would be set down for a while. The men were fighting. It was the morning twilight, before sunrise. [Continuing,] he said: Their left wing attacked our right wing, and their fighting became fierce. Our left wing attacked their right wing and put it to flight. Warqā' b. ʿĀzib al-Asadī attacked with the horsemen and put them to flight. By midmorning we had put them to flight and taken their camp.

According to Abū Mikhnaf—Mūsā b. ʿĀmir al-ʿAdawī, who said: We reached Rabīʿah b. al-Mukhāriq, their commander. His forces had been put to flight, leaving him, and he had dismounted

34. Cf. Qur'ān 3:200, "O believers, be patient, and vie you in patience." An alternate translation would be, "Show endurance (or steadfastness)... vie with your enemy in endurance (or steadfastness)."

35. Qur'ān 4:76.

36. July 7, 686: The ninth day of Dhū al-Ḥijjah is called "the day of ʿArafah" (or ʿArafāt) because it is the day when pilgrims gather on the plain of ʿArafāt, about 15 miles east of Mecca, for the *wuqūf* ("standing," or "station") that climaxes the Ḥajj (pilgrimage). See *EI*[2], s.vv. ʿArafa and Ḥadjdj.

and was calling out, "O supporters of the truth, O people who hear and obey, come to me! I am Ibn al-Mukhāriq." [Continuing,] Mūsā [b. ʿĀmir al-ʿAdawī] said: As for me, I was a young lad, so I was frightened and halted. ʿAbdallāh b. Warqāʾ al-Asadī and ʿAbdallāh b. Ḍamrah al-ʿUdhrī attacked him and killed him.

[647] According to Abū Mikhnaf—ʿAmr b. Mālik Abū Kabshah al-Qaynī,[37] who said: I was a lad who had just reached adolescence and was with one of my paternal uncles in that army. When we encamped by the army of the Kūfans, Rabīʿah b. al-Mukhāriq set us in order, and he did so with care. He put his brother's son in charge of his right wing and ʿAbd Rabbih al-Sulamī in charge of his left wing. He himself went forth with the horsemen and foot soldiers and said, "People of Syria, you are fighting only runaway slaves and men who have abandoned Islam and departed from it. They have no remnant [of strength][38] and do not speak Arabic!"[39] [Continuing,] he said: By God, I supposed it to be so until we fought with them.

[Continuing,] he said: By God, as soon as the men began to fight, one of the Iraqis stood in the way of the men with his sword, saying:

I have disavowed the religion of the *Muḥakkimūn*;[40]
in respect to religion, that is the worst religion among us.

---

37. He was an eyewitness on the Umayyad side. See U. Sezgin, *Abū Miḥnaf*, 198.

38. Following MS Pet, as suggested by ed. Leiden, *Addenda*, p. DCLXX, and reading *baqiyyah*. For the idiomatic meanings of *baqiyyah*—"remnant of strength, firmness of spirit, excellence" or "mercy, indulgence"—see ed. Leiden, *Glossarium*, p. CXXXIX. The original Leiden text has *taqiyyah*, which, if correct, can be understood as a synonym for *taqwā*, "piety, fear of God."

39. Although Ṭabarī's account of al-Mukhtār (mostly from Abū Mikhnaf) does not pass over the role of non-Arabs, it does not emphasize it as much as some other accounts. Cf. Dīnawarī, *Akhbār*, 296: "Most of those who responded to al-Mukhtār were [Arabs] from the tribe of Hamdān and Persians who were in al-Kūfah and whom Muʿāwiyah had enrolled in the military. They were called al-Ḥamrāʾ ('fair-skinned')."

40. The *Muḥakkimūn* (from *ḥakkama*, "to pronounce a formula containing the word *ḥukm*") were the Khārijites, who abandoned ʿAlī when he agreed to arbitration with Muʿāwiyah. Their slogan was *lā ḥukma illā li-llāh*, "Judgment [belongs] to God alone!" See Lane, *Lexicon*, II, 618.

There was fierce fighting between them and us for an hour of the day. By midmorning they had put us to flight. They killed our leader and took our camp. We went away in flight, until ʿAbdallāh b. Ḥamlah met us an hour's journey from the village called Banāt Talā and turned us back. We went with him until he encamped by Yazīd b. Anas. We spent the night keeping watch by turns. The next day, we prayed the daybreak prayer and went forth in good order. He put al-Zubayr b. Khuzaymah[41] from [the tribe of] Khathʿam in charge of his right wing, Ibn Uqayṣir al-Quḥāfī from Khathʿam in charge of his left wing, and advanced with the horsemen and foot soldiers. It was the Day of Sacrifice.[42] We fought fiercely with them. They badly defeated us, slew many of us, and took our camp. We made our way to ʿUbaydallāh b. Ziyād and told him what we had encountered. [648]

According to Abū Mikhnaf—Mūsā b. ʿĀmir [al-ʿAdawī], who said: ʿAbdallāh b. Ḥamlah al-Khathʿamī advanced toward us. He met the defeated troops of Rabīʿah b. al-Mukhāriq al-Ghanawī, turned them back, and then came and encamped at Banāt Talā. The next day, both they and we went forth early. The two troops of horsemen attacked each other from the beginning of daylight. Both they and we then withdrew until after we had prayed the noon prayer, at which time we went forth and fought, defeating them. [Continuing,] he said: ʿAbdallāh b. Ḥamlah dismounted and called out to his forces, saying, "After wheeling round, return to the fight, O people who hear and obey!" He was attacked and killed by ʿAbdallāh b. Qurād al-Khathʿamī, and we took their camp and what was in it. Three hundred prisoners were brought to Yazīd b. Anas, who was dying. He gestured with his hand that they should be beheaded, so they were killed to the last man.[43]

---

41. Following the reading of Ms. Ahmet III, adopted in ed. Cairo. The various manuscripts show so much uncertainty about the dotting of the consonants on this name, that ed. Leiden omits all dots.

42. The tenth of Dhū al-Ḥijjah, when pilgrims sacrifice an animal at Minā in memory of Abraham's sacrifice. See *EI*², s.v. Ḥadjdj.

43. Cf. Balādhurī, *Ansāb*, V, 231 (from Hishām b. al-Kalbī): "Prisoners were brought to Yazīd b. Anas al-Asadī, who was on the verge of death. He kept saying, 'Kill! Kill!' until his tongue became heavy. Then he began to signal with his hand, until his hand became heavy. Then he began to signal with his eyebrows, until he died in that condition."

Yazīd b. Anas said, "If I perish, your commander is Warqā' b. 'Āzib al-Asadī." Yazīd died by evening, and Warqā' b. 'Āzib prayed [the funeral prayer] over him and buried him. When his companions saw that, they were bewildered, and their spirits were broken by his death. After they buried Yazīd, Warqā' said to them, "Men, what do you think best? I have been told that 'Ubaydallāh b. Ziyād is coming at us with eighty thousand Syrians." They therefore began to slip away and go back. Warqā' then summoned the heads of the fourths and the most skillful horsemen among his forces and said to them, "Men, what do you think about what I have told you? I am only one of you, and not the best among you in regard to counsel. Advise me. Ibn Ziyād has come at you with the great army of the Syrians— their greatest men, horsemen, and *ashrāf*.[44] I do not think we and you have power to deal with them
[649] under these circumstances. Yazīd b. Anas, our commander, has died. Part of our forces have dispersed. If we turn back today of our own accord before we encounter them and before we reach them, so that they know that only the death of our commander turned us back, they will continue to fear us because we have killed their commander and because we can plead the death of our commander as an excuse for our withdrawal. But, if we meet them today, we run a risk. If we are defeated today, our having defeated them previously will be of no use to us." They said, "Your idea is excellent; turn back, and may God have mercy on you!" So he turned back. Their having turned back was reported to al-Mukhtār and the people of al-Kūfah. Not knowing how things had turned out, people spread alarming rumors that Yazīd b. Anas had been killed and the men defeated.

Then al-Mukhtār's governor of al-Madā'in sent al-Mukhtār one of his spies, a Nabatæan from the Sawād,[45] who gave him a report. Al-Mukhtār summoned Ibrāhīm b. al-Ashtar[46] and put

---

44. The *ashrāf* (plural of *sharīf*), literally, "eminent or distinguished men," were the tribal dignitaries.

45. "Nabatæan" refers to any of the Aramaic-speaking peasantry of the agricultural lands (*sawād*, meaning "the black," i.e., alluvial soil) of Iraq.

46. Ibrāhīm b. al-Ashtar, son of the famous Mālik b. al-Ḥārith al-Nakha'ī, had become one of al-Mukhtār's most important military aides earlier in this year and played a leading role in driving Ibn al-Zubayr's governor, Ibn Muṭī', out of al-Kūfah. See Ṭabarī, II, 609–30; and *EI*², s.v.

him in command of seven thousand men, saying to him, "Go, and, when you meet the army of Ibn Anas, turn them around with you, and go meet your enemy and fight it out with them." Ibrāhīm went out and encamped at Ḥammām Aʿyan.[47]

[The Kūfan Ashrāf *Rise against al-Mukhtār]*

According to Abū Mikhnaf—Abū Zuhayr al-Naḍr b. Ṣāliḥ,[48] who said: When Yazīd b. Anas died, the *ashrāf* in al-Kūfah met and told disturbing stories about al-Mukhtār. They said that Yazīd b. Anas had been killed, and did not believe he had died [a natural death]. They began to say, "By God, this man has made himself commander over us without our consent. He has drawn our *mawālī*[49] near to himself, mounted them on horses, given them stipends,[50] and assigned our *fay'*[51] to them. Our slaves have disobeyed us, and our orphans and widows have thus been despoiled." They settled on the house of Shabath b. Ribʿī[52] and said, "We will meet in the house of our shaykh." (Shabath was a man who

---

47. "Aʿyan's Hot Spring," near al-Kūfah, named for Aʿyan, the *mawlā* of Saʿd b. Abī Waqqāṣ. See Yāqūt, *Muʿjam*, s.v.

48. Abū Zuhayr al-Naḍr b. Ṣāliḥ b. Ḥabīb b. Zuhayr al-ʿAbsī, an eyewitness of events from 61 to 77, also transmits information about earlier events through informants. He introduces one of his reports for 77/696 by saying that he was a young man in the prime of youth at the time. See U. Sezgin, *Abū Miḥnaf*, 70, 80–81, 214.

49. *Mawlā*, pl. *mawālī*, "client(s), or freedmen," referred to non-Arabs, frequently of Persian origin, who, upon conversion to Islam, were put under the protection of an Arab tribe or a tribal leader as a way of incorporating them into the Arab social system. For a discussion of the social status of *mawālī* at this time, see Dixon, *Umayyad Caliphate*, 48–49; and *EI*², s.v.

50. Literally, "given them *ʿaṭā'*," the stipend paid from the treasury on a regular basis to Arab soldiers registered in the *dīwān* (military roll). See *EI*², s.v. ʿAṭā'.

51. *Fay'*, "permanent booty," was the tribute or tax income from which the stipends of Muslim soldiers were paid. See *EI*², s.v.

52. Shabath b. Ribʿī al-Tamīmī headed the Banū Ḥanẓalah (a powerful clan of the Tamīm) in al-Kūfah. During al-Mukhtār's uprising in 66/685, he supported Ibn al-Zubayr's governor, Ibn Muṭīʿ, but advised Ibn Muṭīʿ to withdraw gracefully when al-Mukhtār's victory appeared inevitable. On his role in the events of 66, see Ṭabarī, II, 614–30, esp. 623 (an incident illustrating his prejudice against *mawālī*) and 630. See also Dīnawarī, *Akhbār*, 223, 243; and Ṭabarī, I, 1919, 3270, 3349, 3380, 3388.

had lived both in the Time of Ignorance[53] and in the time of Islam.) They gathered and came to his house. After he had led his
[650] companions in prayer, they began to discuss the subject among themselves. [Continuing,] he said: Among al-Mukhtār's innovations concerning them, none was more grievous than his having appointed a share of the *fay'* for the *mawālī*.

Shabath said to them, "Leave me until I meet with him." He went and met with him and left unmentioned none of the things his companions found objectionable. Whenever he mentioned a practice, al-Mukhtār said to him, "I will satisfy them regarding this practice and do everything they like." [Continuing,] he said: Shabath mentioned the slaves (*mamālīk*). Al-Mukhtār said, "I will return their slaves (*ʿabīd*) to them." Shabath mentioned the *mawālī* to him, saying, "You have had recourse to our *mawālī*, who are a *fay'* that God has made permanent booty, together with these lands, for us all. We have freed them, and for that we hope for remuneration, reward, and thanks. But you, not satisfied with this for them, have made them our partners in our *fay'*." Al-Mukhtār said to them, "If I leave you your *mawālī* and give your *fay'* to you, will you fight on my side against the Umayyads and Ibn al-Zubayr and give me a promise and covenant by God to fulfill this, together with oaths that I can trust?" Shabath replied, "I do not know, until I go to my companions and talk to them about it." He left and did not return to al-Mukhtār. [Continuing,] he said: The *ashrāf* of al-Kūfah decided to fight al-Mukhtār.

According to Abū Mikhnaf—Qudāmah b. Ḥawshab, who said: Shabath b. Ribʿī, Shamir b. Dhī al-Jawshan, Muḥammad b. al-Ashʿath, and ʿAbd al-Raḥmān b. Saʿīd b. Qays came before Kaʿb b. Abī Kaʿb al-Khathʿamī.[54] Shabath spoke. Having praised and extolled God, he told Kaʿb that they had decided to fight al-Mukhtār, and he asked him to concur with them in the matter. Berating al-Mukhtār, Shabath said, "He has made himself commander over us without our consent. He has alleged that Ibn

53. *Jāhilī*, someone who has lived in the *Jāhiliyyah*, the "Time of Ignorance," before the coming of Islam. See *EI*², s.v. Djāhiliyya.

54. These men had supported Ibn al-Zubayr's governor, Ibn Muṭīʿ, against al-Mukhtār. See Ṭabarī, II, 614, 629, 631.

al-Ḥanafiyyah[55] sent him to us, but we have found out that Ibn al-Ḥanafiyyah did not do so. He has assigned our *fay'* to our *mawālī* [651] and taken our slaves, despoiling our orphans and widows by means of them. He and his Saba'iyyah[56] have openly disavowed our righteous predecessors."[57] [Continuing,] he said: Ka'b b. Abī Ka'b welcomed them and responded favorably to their call.

According to Abū Mikhnaf—my[58] father, Yaḥyā b. Sa'id: The *ashrāf* of al-Kūfah came before 'Abd al-Raḥmān b. Mikhnaf [al-Azdī] and called upon him to concur with them in fighting al-Mukhtār. He said to them, "Men, if you insist on rebelling, I will not fail you; but, if you listen to me, you will not rebel." "Why?" they asked. He said, "Because I fear you will become divided, disagree among yourselves, and abandon each other. By God, your own valiant men and skilled horsemen are on the man's side. Are not so-and-so and so-and-so with him? Your slaves and *mawālī* are also on his side, and they are of one mind. Your slaves and *mawālī* are more angry with you than your enemy. So he will fight you with the courage of the Arabs and the hostility of the Persians. But, if you leave him alone for a while, the arrival of the Syrians or the coming of the Baṣrans will spare you the trouble of dealing with him; you will have been spared dealing with him by others and will not have set your strength among yourselves." They said, "We implore you by God not to differ with us or spoil our plan and the consensus our group has reached." "I am one of you," he replied; "if you will, rebel." They went among them-

---

55. Muḥammad b. al-Ḥanafiyyah was 'Alī's son by a woman of the Banū Ḥanīfah who had been brought to Medina as a prisoner. Despite his reluctance to involve himself in politics and the fact that he was not directly descended from the Prophet, he became a focus of Shī'ī attention after al-Ḥasan's abdication and al-Ḥusayn's death at Karbalā'. See *EI*[1], s.v.; Dixon, *Umayyad Caliphate*, 40; and Jafri, *Origins*, 228–29, 235–37, 239–42.

56. Saba'iyyah ("followers of ['Abdallāh b.] Saba'") is used here as an abusive epithet for Shī'ī extremists (*ghulāt*). 'Abdallāh b. Saba' is said to have founded "heterodox" Shī'ism by attributing supernatural character to 'Alī, refusing to recognize his death, and condemning the first two caliphs in addition to 'Uthmān. See *EI*[2], s.v. 'Abd Allāh b. Saba'; Jafri, *Origins*, 300f.; cf. Ṭabarī, II, 623.

57. *Aslāfinā al-ṣāliḥīn*: specifically including Abū Bakr, 'Umar, and 'Uthmān. See Lane, *Lexicon*, IV, 1408.

58. I.e., Abū Mikhnaf's father.

selves and said, "Wait until Ibrāhīm b. al-Ashtar goes away from him."

[Continuing,] he said: They delayed until Ibn al-Ashtar had reached Sābāṭ[59] and then rose against al-Mukhtār. [Continuing,] he said: ʿAbd al-Raḥmān b. Saʿīd b. Qays al-Hamdānī went out with [men of] Hamdān to Jabbānat al-Sabīʿ.[60] Zaḥr b. Qays al-Juʿfī and Isḥāq b. Muḥammad b. al-Ashʿath went out to Jabbānat Kindah.

[652] According to Hishām [b. al-Kalbī]—Sulaymān b. Muḥammad al-Ḥaḍramī, who said: Jubayr al-Ḥaḍramī went out to the two[61] and said to them, "Get out of our cemetery; we do not want to be involved in trouble." Isḥāq b. Muḥammad asked him, "And is it your cemetery?" "Yes," he said. So they left him.[62]

Kaʿb b. Abī Kaʿb al-Khathʿamī went out to Jabbānat Bishr,[63] and Bishr[64] b. Jarīr b. ʿAbdallāh went out to them with [men of the tribe of] Bajīlah. ʿAbd al-Raḥmān b. Mikhnaf went out to Jabbānat Mikhnaf. Isḥāq b. Muḥammad and Zaḥr b. Qays went to ʿAbd al-Raḥmān b. Saʿīd b. Qays at Jabbānat al-Sabīʿ. [The tribes of] Bajīlah and Khathʿam went to ʿAbd al-Raḥmān b. Mikhnaf, who was with the [tribe of] Azd. Word reached the men in Jabbānat al-Sabīʿ that al-Mukhtār had mustered horsemen to advance on them. They sent messengers, one after the other, to Azd, Bajīlah, and Khathʿam, asking them for the sake of God and kinship to hasten to them. So they went to them, and all gathered in Jabbānat al-Sabīʿ. When word reached al-Mukhtār, he was glad they had gathered in one place.

---

59. Sābāṭ, on the west bank of the Tigris at the confluence of the Nahr al-Malik, was one of the seven cities that formed al-Madā'in. See *EI*², s.v. al-Madā'in.

60. The *jabbānāt*, or tribal cemeteries of al-Kūfah, also served as places of assembly, mobilization, and taking up arms. See *EI*², s.v. al-Kūfa. The most recent attempt to map the topography of Umayyad al-Kūfah is Hichem Djaït, *Al-Kūfa, naissance de la ville islamique*. See especially pp. 227–41, on the battles connected with al-Mukhtār, and the map, p. 302.

61. I.e., Zaḥr b. Qays al-Juʿfī and Isḥāq b. Muḥammad b. al-Ashʿath, who had assembled their men in Jabbānat Kindah.

62. Ms. O: it.

63. Jabbānat Bishr, named after Bishr b. Rabīʿah, a hero of the battle of Qādisiyyah, belonged to the tribe of Khathʿam. See Djaït, *Al-Kūfa*, 238.

64. Reading "Bishr," instead of "Bashīr," here and at 656, 13. Cf. Ṭabarī, II, 857; Ibn al-Athīr, *Kāmil*, IV, 297; and al-Mubarrad, *Kāmil*, 664, 4 (ed. Leiden, *Addenda*, p. DCLXX).

Shamir b. Dhī al-Jawshan went out and encamped in Jabbānat Banī Salūl with [the tribe of] Qays. Shabath b. Ribʿī, Ḥassān b. Fā'id al-ʿAbsī, and Rabīʿah b. Tharwān al-Ḍabbī encamped with [tribesmen of] Muḍar[65] in al-Kunāsah.[66] Ḥajjār b. Abjar and Yazīd b. al-Ḥārith b. Ru'aym encamped with those of Rabīʿah between al-Tammārīn[67] and al-Sabakhah.[68] ʿAmr b. al-Ḥajjāj al-Zubaydī encamped in Jabbānat Murād with the men who had followed him from [the tribe of] Madhḥij. The Yemenis sent to them asking that he come to them, but he refused to do so, saying to them, "Strive earnestly, and it will be as if I had come to you."

[Continuing,] he said: That very day, al-Mukhtār sent a messenger named ʿAmr b. Tawbah to ride at a gallop to Ibrāhīm b. [653] al-Ashtar at Sābāṭ and say, "Do not put this letter down until you are on your way to me with every man you have." [Continuing,] he said: That day, al-Mukhtār sent to them, saying, "Tell me what you want, and I will do everything you like." They said, "We want you to depart from us. You alleged that Ibn al-Ḥanafiyyah had sent you, but he did not send you." Al-Mukhtār sent word to them, saying, "Send a delegation to him on your behalf, and I will send him one on my behalf, and then wait until you have clarified the matter." With this proposal, he wanted to delay them so that Ibrāhīm b. al-Ashtar could reach him. He commanded his forces, and they restrained their hands. Meanwhile, the people of al-Kūfah

65. I.e., men from the tribes of Tamīm (Shabath's tribe), ʿAbs (Ḥassān's tribe), and Ḍabbah (Rabīʿah's tribe), each of which belonged to a larger grouping called "Muḍar." In pre-Islamic times, Muḍar and Rabīʿah were large, powerful combinations of North Arabian tribes. Prominent Muḍar tribes included Qays ʿAylān, Hudhayl, Khuzaymah, Asad, Kinānah, Quraysh, Dabbah, and Tamīm. Prominent Rabīʿah tribes included ʿAnazah, ʿAbd al-Qays, and the two Wā'il tribes (Bakr and Taghlib). By Umayyad times, the terms had shifted meaning, as new political conditions caused new alliances among tribes. Muḍar meant especially the tribes of Tamīm and Qays; Rabīʿah meant especially Bakr, Taghlib, and the allied Yemeni tribes of Azd and Quḍāʿah (Kalb). See *EI*[1] Suppl., s.v. Rabīʿa and Muḍar.

66. "The Place of the Sweepings," originally a dumping ground west of al-Kūfah, later became an unloading place for caravans from Arabia, a livestock market, a place of execution, and a poets' fair similar to al-Baṣrah's Mirbad. See Le Strange, *Lands*, 74–5; *EI*[2], s.v. al-Kūfa; and Djaït, *Al-Kūfa*, 230.

67. The Street or Market of Date Sellers (See Djaït, *Al-Kūfa*, 236).

68. *Sabakhah* means a salt marsh or salty ground with sparse vegetation (Lane, *Lexicon*, IV, 1292). The term was applied to the open space between the built-up area of al-Kūfah and the Euphrates River to the east. See Djaït, *Al-Kūfa*, 231.

blocked the mouths of the streets against them, so that no water was reaching al-Mukhtār and his forces, except for a paltry amount that escaped the people's notice.

[Continuing,] he said: ʿAbdallāh b. Sabīʿ went out into the square. The [men of the tribe of] Shākir fought violently with him.[69] ʿUqbah b. Ṭāriq al-Jushamī came and fought on his side for a time until he had turned the attackers away from him. Then both of them betook themselves to their defense lines. ʿUqbah b. Ṭāriq encamped with Qays in Jabbānat Banī Salūl, and ʿAbdallāh b. Sabīʿ encamped with the Yemenis in Jabbānat al-Sabīʿ.

According to Abū Mikhnaf—Yūnus b. Abī Isḥāq:[70] Shamir b. Dhī al-Jawshan went to the Yemenis and said to them, "If you gather in a place where we can form two wings and fight in one direction, I am your companion; otherwise, I am not. By God, I will not fight in a place like this, in narrow streets, where we shall be attacked from all sides." So he went off to the main body of his people in Jabbānat Banī Salūl.

[Continuing,] he said: When al-Mukhtār's messenger left to go
[654] to Ibn al-Ashtar, he reached him the same day in the evening. Ibn al-Ashtar announced to the men, "Return to al-Kūfah." He marched the rest of that evening and encamped when night fell. His forces ate their evening meal and rested their mounts very briefly. Then Ibn al-Ashtar called them. He marched all that night, prayed the morning prayer at Sūrā, marched that day, and prayed the afternoon prayer of the following day by Bāb al-Jisr.[71] Then he went and spent the night at the mosque, accompanied by his strongest and bravest forces. The morning of the third day after his enemies had taken the field against him, al-Mukhtār went out [to the mosque] and ascended the pulpit.

According to Abū Mikhnaf—Abū Janāb al-Kalbī:[72] Shabath b.

---

69. On the loyalty of the clan of Shākir (part of the tribe of Hamdān) to al-Mukhtār, see Ṭabarī, II, 619–20. Al-Mukhtār's chief of police, ʿAbdallāh b. Kāmil, was from this tribe.

70. Yūnus b. Abī Isḥāq ʿAmr b. ʿAbdallāh al-Hamdānī al-Sabīʿī (d. 159/775 in al-Kūfah) is known as a *muḥaddith* who transmitted *ḥadīth* from his father. See U. Sezgin, *Abū Miḥnaf*, 225–26.

71. The Gate of the (Pontoon) Bridge.

72. Abū Janāb Yaḥyā b. Abī Ḥayyah al-Kalbī al-Kūfī (d. 147/764 or 150) was a

Rib'ī sent his son 'Abd al-Mu'min to al-Mukhtār. 'Abd al-Mu'min said to him, "We are your kinfolk and the palm of your right hand. No, by God, we will not fight you. Trust this from us." His plan was to fight al-Mukhtār, but he deceived him.

When the Yemenis assembled in Jabbānat al-Sabī', the time for prayer came, and each chief of the Yemenis disliked having his fellow take precedence over him.[73] 'Abd al-Raḥmān b. Mikhnaf said to them, "This is the beginning of disagreement. Set in front [of you] the man who is well regarded,[74] for among your kinfolk is the master of this city's Qur'ān reciters (*qurrā'*); let Rifā'ah b. Shaddād al-Fityānī from Bajīlah lead you in prayer."[75] They did so, and he continued to be their leader in prayer until the battle took place.

According to Abū Mikhnaf—Wāzi' b. al-Sarī: Anas b. 'Amr al-Azdī went forth and entered among the Yemenis. He heard them saying, "If al-Mukhtār goes to [fight] our brothers from Muḍar, we will go to [help] them; and if he goes to [fight] us, they will go to [help] us." Having heard them say this, a certain man went swiftly, climbed up to al-Mukhtār on the pulpit,[76] and told him what they [655]
had said. Al-Mukhtār said, "As for the Yemenis, if I go to [fight] Muḍar, they are indeed likely to go to [help] them. But I bear witness that if I go to [fight] the Yemenis, Muḍar will not go to [help] them." (Later, al-Mukhtār used to invite that man and honor him.) Al-Mukhtār came down from the pulpit, mustered his forces in the market (in those days the building that is now in the market did not exist), and said to Ibrāhīm b. al-Ashtar, "Against which of the two groups do you prefer to march?" He replied, "Against whichever of the two groups you like." Being a man of discernment, al-Mukhtār considered. He disliked the idea of

---

muḥaddith also known to have collected materials about the Battle of Ṣiffīn and the death of al-Ḥusayn. See U. Sezgin, *Abū Miḥnaf*, 223f.

73. Literally, "place himself before him," i.e., to lead the prayer.

74. *Riḍā*, a man "with whom one is pleased, well pleased, contented, or satisfied; regarded with good will, or favor; liked, or approved." Lane, *Lexicon*, III, 1100.

75. The presence of Rifā'ah b. Shaddād, an early supporter of al-Mukhtār (Ṭabarī, II, 599–600), among the opposition to al-Mukhtār is noteworthy. Cf. Balādhurī, *Ansāb*, V, 233, for Rifā'ah's account of how he became angered by al-Mukhtār's lies and broke with him.

76. Ms. O: and came to al-Mukhtār, who had climbed into the pulpit.

having Ibn al-Ashtar go to fight his own kin[77] and not do his utmost in fighting them. So he said, "Go to fight Muḍar in al-Kunāsah. Shabath b. Rib'ī and Muḥammad b. 'Umayr b. 'Uṭārid are their leaders. I will go to the Yemenis." [Continuing,] he said: Al-Mukhtār is still known for his rigor and lack of mercy toward the Yemenis and others when he was victorious.

Ibrāhīm b. al-Ashtar went to al-Kunāsah; al-Mukhtār went to Jabbānat al-Sabī'. Al-Mukhtār halted at the house of 'Umar b. Sa'd b. Abī Waqqāṣ[78] and sent Aḥmar b. Shumayṭ al-Bajalī al-Aḥmasī and 'Abdallāh b. Kāmil al-Shākirī ahead. He said to Ibn Shumayṭ, "Stay on this street until you come out upon the people in Jabbānat al-Sabī' from among the houses of your kinfolk." He said to 'Abdallāh b. Kāmil, "Stay on this street until you come out at Jabbānat al-Sabī' from the house of the family of al-Akhnas b. Sharīq." He summoned the two of them and confided in them, saying, "[The tribe of] Shibām has sent word to me that they have come at the people from behind." The two men went forward along the two streets that al-Mukhtār had commanded them to take.

When the Yemenis learned that these two men were advancing
[656] on them, they divided the two streets among themselves: 'Abd al-Raḥmān b. Sa'īd b. Qays al-Hamdānī, Isḥāq b. al-Ash'ath, and Zaḥr b. Qays stood in the street behind the Mosque of Aḥmas; 'Abd al-Raḥmān b. Mikhnaf, Bishr b. Jarīr b. 'Abdallāh, and Ka'b b. Abī Ka'b stood in the street beside the Euphrates. Then the two sides fought as fiercely as men have ever fought. The forces of Aḥmar b. Shumayṭ as well as those of 'Abdallāh b. Kāmil were routed. Al-Mukhtār was surprised when the defeated men came back to him. He asked, "What has happened to you?" They said, "We have been defeated." He asked, "What has happened to Aḥmar b. Shumayṭ?" They said, "When we left him, he had dis-

77. Ibn al-Ashtar's clan, Nakha', a division of the tribe of Madhḥij, belonged to the Yemeni group (*Lisān*, s.v.; Wüstenfeld, *Genealogische Tabellen*, 8).

78. 'Umar b. Sa'd b. Abī Waqqāṣ, the son of the military leader who had founded al-Kūfah, was particularly hated by the Shī'ah because he had commanded the Umayyad army that the Umayyad governor of al-Kūfah, 'Ubaydallāh b. Ziyād, had sent to prevent al-Ḥusayn from reaching al-Kūfah.

mounted [to fight] by the Mosque of al-Quṣṣāṣ."[79] (They meant the Mosque of Abū Dāwūd in [the tribal district of] Wādi'ah. The people of that time frequented this mosque to tell stories.) "Some of his companions had dismounted with him." The companions of 'Abdallāh [b. Kāmil] said, "We do not know what happened to Ibn Kāmil." Al-Mukhtār shouted to them, "Turn back!" He went with them until he reached the house of Abū 'Abdallāh al-Jadalī. He sent out 'Abdallāh b. Qurād al-Khath'amī, who was at the head of four hundred men, companions of his, saying, "Take your forces to Ibn Kāmil. If he has perished, you are in his place; fight the enemy with your forces and his. If you find him alive and well, take a hundred of your companions, all of them skilled horsemen, and give him the rest of your forces. Order them to exert themselves on his behalf and serve him loyally, for they will thereby be serving me loyally; and whoever serves me loyally, let him rejoice! Then advance with the hundred men until you come upon the people in Jabbānat al-Sabī' from the direction of the Bath of Qaṭan b. 'Abdallāh."

'Abdallāh b. Qurād al-Khath'amī went forth. He found Ibn Kāmil standing by the Bath of 'Amr b. Ḥurayth. With him were some of his forces who had held firm; he was fighting the enemy. 'Abdallāh b. Qurād gave him three hundred of his companions [657] and continued on toward Jabbānat al-Sabī'. Then he turned into those streets, until he reached the Mosque of 'Abd al-Qays, where he halted. He asked his companions, "What do you think?" They replied, "We will follow what you say." (All who were gathered with him were from his kinfolk; they were a hundred.) He said to them, "By God, I want al-Mukhtār to be victorious. Yet, by God, I do not want the *ashrāf* of my people to perish today. By God, I would rather die than that death descend on them by my hands. But stop for a moment; I have heard people say that Shibām will come at them from behind. Perhaps Shibām will do it, and we shall be spared having to do it." His companions said, "As you think best." So he stayed by the Mosque of 'Abd al-Qays.

---

79. As the parenthetical remark explains, the word *quṣṣāṣ* (pl. of *qāṣṣ*) means "storytellers."

Al-Mukhtār sent out Mālik b. ʿAmr al-Nahdī with two hundred men (he was a man of the greatest prowess) and sent out ʿAbdallāh b. Sharīk al-Nahdī with two hundred skilled horsemen to Aḥmar b. Shumayṭ. The latter had remained in the same place. When they reached him, the enemy had gained the upper hand and were overwhelming him, so they fought as hard as they could. Ibn al-Ashtar went and encountered Shabath b. Ribʿī, who had many men from Muḍar with him, among them Ḥassān b. Fā'id al-ʿAbsī. Ibrāhīm [b. al-Ashtar] said to them, "Woe unto you! Go back, for I do not want anyone from Muḍar to be killed by my hands. Do not bring ruin upon yourselves." However, they refused and fought with him. Ibn al-Ashtar defeated them. Ḥassān b. Fā'id was carried away to his family and died when he was brought into their presence. On his deathbed, he regained consciousness briefly and said, "By God, I do not want to recover from this wound of mine. I do not want my death to be from anything but the thrust of a javelin or the blow of a sword." He spoke not a word afterward until he died.

[658] The good news reached al-Mukhtār from Ibrāhīm concerning the defeat of Muḍar. Al-Mukhtār sent the news on to Aḥmar b. Shumayṭ and Ibn Kāmil. The men were in the same state in which they had been, with the people of each street defending what was beside it.

[Continuing,] he said: The men of Shibām assembled. They had made Abū al-Qalūṣ their leader and had agreed and decided to come at the Yemenis from behind. But then they said to each other, "By God, it would be better if you directed your efforts against opponents who are not from your own tribal group.[80] March upon Muḍar or Rabīʿah, and fight them." Their shaykh, Abū al-Qalūṣ, fell silent and did not speak. They said, "Abū al-Qalūṣ, what do you think best?" He said, "God, may His praise be exalted, has said, 'O believers, fight the unbelievers who are near to you, and let them find in you a harshness.'[81] Arise!" They rose up; he led them two or three spear lengths,[82] and then said to them, "Sit down." They sat down. He led them a little farther and

80. Shibām was a subdivision (*ḥayy*) of Hamdān, a Yemeni tribe.
81. Qur'ān 9:123.
82. A spear length (*rumḥ*) was about five cubits (Lane, *Lexicon*, III, 1153).

made them sit down. Then he said to them, "Get up!" The third time, he led them a little farther and then made them sit down. "Abū al-Qalūṣ," they said to him, "by God, we consider you the bravest of the Arabs. What is causing you to do what you are doing?" He replied, "An experienced man is not like one who is untried. I wanted your hearts to return to you, and that you should prepare your minds for fighting; I did not want to rush you into battle while you were in a state of bewilderment." They said, "You are most clearsighted in what you have done."

As the men of Shibām came out toward Jabbānat al-Sabīʿ, al-Aʿsar al-Shākirī met them at the mouth of the street. Al-Junduʿī and Abū al-Zubayr b. Kurayb attacked him, threw him down, and [659] entered the Jabbānah. The men entered the Jabbānah after them, shouting, "Vengeance for al-Ḥusayn!" Ibn Shumayṭ's forces answered them with "Vengeance for al-Ḥusayn!" When Yazīd b. ʿUmayr b. Dhī Murrān from Hamdān heard this, he said, "Vengeance for ʿUthmān!"[83] Rifāʿah b. Shaddād said to them, "What have we to do with ʿUthmān? I will not fight alongside men who seek vengeance for the blood of ʿUthmān." Some of his kinfolk said to him, "You brought us, and we obeyed you. And now that we have seen our people being slain by the sword, you tell us, 'Go back and leave them!'" So he attacked [the enemy], saying:

I am Ibn Shaddād; I follow the religion of ʿAlī.
No friend am I to ʿUthmān, the son of Arwā.[84]
Today, I will take the heat amidst those who are tested
in war's hottest flame, without flagging.

He fought until he was killed.

Yazīd b. ʿUmayr b. Dhī Murrān was also killed, as were al-

---

83. "Vengeance for ʿUthmān!" was the rallying cry of the Umayyads, who demanded that ʿAlī punish the murderers of their kinsman, the third caliph, and who withheld their allegiance when he did not do so. Both Yazīd b. ʿUmayr and Rifāʿah b. Shaddād are inside Jabbānat al-Sabīʿ; the episode illustrates the disunity of the defenders.

84. Arwā, the mother of ʿUthmān, is mentioned because through her ʿUthmān was distantly related through the female line to the Prophet. Arwā's mother was Umm Ḥakīm, daughter of ʿAbd al-Muṭṭalib, Muḥammad's grandfather. The line contrasts ʿAlī, whose relation to the Prophet (first cousin and son-in-law) was very close, and ʿUthmān, whose relation was remote. See Ṭabarī, I, 3055.

Nuʿmān b. Ṣuhbān al-Jarmī al-Rāsibī, who was an ascetic,[85] and Rifāʿah b. Shaddād b. ʿAwsajah al-Fityānī at the Bath of al-Mahbadhān at al-Sabakhah. He, too, was an ascetic. Al-Furāt b. Zaḥr b. Qays al-Juʿfī was killed, and Zaḥr b. Qays was carried away wounded. ʿAbd al-Raḥmān b. Saʿīd b. Qays was killed, as was ʿUmar b. Mikhnaf. ʿAbd al-Raḥmān b. Mikhnaf fought until he was carried away wounded; the men carried him away unconscious, while men of Azd were fighting around him. Ḥumayd b. Muslim[86] said:

In defense of Abū Ḥakīm,[87] I will strike
the heads of slaves and nobles.

[660] And Surāqah b. Mirdās al-Bāriqī[88] said:

O my soul, if you are not steadfast, you will commit a
blameworthy action;
do not turn away from Abū Ḥakīm.

Five hundred prisoners were taken from the houses of the [tribe of] Wādiʿah.[89] They were brought to al-Mukhtār with their hands bound behind their backs. A man from the Banū Nahd, one of al-Mukhtār's chief companions, ʿAbdallāh b. Sharīk by name, whenever he encountered an Arab, would set him free. This was reported to al-Mukhtār by Dirham, a *mawlā* of the Banū Nahd. Al-Mukhtār said to him, "Bring the prisoners before me; watch for any of them who was present at the murder of al-Ḥusayn, and let me know about him." So whenever a man who had been present at the murder of al-Ḥusayn was led before him, he was

---

85. Al-Nuʿmān b. Ṣuhbān was "a Shīʿī ascetic (*nāsik*) who had come from al-Baṣrah to fight on the side of the Shīʿah and avenge the death of al-Ḥusayn. When he heard al-Mukhtār say things he found objectionable, he fought against him with the people in Jabbānat al-Sabīʿ and was killed" (Balādhurī, *Ansāb*, V, 233).

86. Ḥumayd b. Muslim was a major source for Abū Mikhnaf's account of the fight against al-Ḥusayn, in which he was a participant, to his later regret. He was a friend of Ibrāhīm b. al-Ashtar (Ṭabarī, II, 613), and later composed an elegy for ʿAbd al-Raḥmān b. Mikhnaf (Ṭabarī, II, 878). See U. Sezgin, *Abū Miḥnaf*, 218.

87. The *kunyah* (agnomen) of ʿAbd al-Raḥmān b. Mikhnaf.

88. The poet Surāqah b. Mirdās al-Bāriqī, later a supporter of al-Farazdaq in his rivalry with Jarīr, appears here fighting beside the Azdī leader ʿAbd al-Raḥmān b. Mikhnaf. The poet's family, the Banū Bāriq, were a clan of the Azd. See F. Sezgin, *GAS*, II, 327–8; Hahn, *Surâqa b. Mirdâs*.

89. Wādiʿah was a group associated with Hamdān. See *Lisān*, s.v.

told, "This is one of those who were present at his murder," and he had him brought forward and beheaded. Before he left the place, he killed two hundred and forty-eight men.

Whenever al-Mukhtār's companions saw a man who had annoyed them, quarreled with them, or harmed them, they took him aside and killed him. Many of these men were killed without al-Mukhtār's knowledge. When al-Mukhtār was informed of this afterward, he summoned the remaining prisoners and freed them, making them swear not to aid any enemy against him or seek to do him or his companions mischief. Surāqah b. Mirdās al-Bāriqī was an exception; [al-Mukhtār] ordered him to be led with him to the mosque. [Continuing,] he said: Al-Mukhtār's crier proclaimed, "Anyone who closes his door will be safe, except for any man who participated in shedding the blood of the family of Muḥammad."

According to Abū Mikhnaf—al-Mujālid b. Sa'īd[90]—'Āmir al-Sha'bī:[91] Yazīd b. al-Ḥārith b. Yazīd b. Ru'aym and Ḥajjār b. Abjar[92] sent out messengers, saying to them, "Be close to the Yemenis. If you see that they have gained the upper hand, let the first of you who reaches us say '*ṣarafān*.' If they have been defeated, let him say '*jumzān*.'" When the Yemenis were defeated, their messengers came to them, and the first who reached them said "*jumzān*." So the two men arose and said to their people, "Go back to your houses." So they went back. [661]

'Amr b. al-Ḥajjāj al-Zubaydī, who was one of those who had been present at the murder of al-Ḥusayn, left [his house], mounted his camel, and rode away, taking the road to Sharāf and Wāqiṣah.[93]

90. Mujālid b. Sa'īd b. 'Umayr al-Hamdānī Abū 'Amr Abū Sa'īd al-Kūfī (d. 144/762) transmitted *ḥadīth* from al-Sha'bī, was a *rāwiyah* (prolific transmitter) of *akhbār* (historical reports), and was credited with the composition of a biography of the Prophet. See U. Sezgin, *Abū Miḥnaf*, 210–11.

91. Abū 'Amr 'Āmir b. Sharaḥīl al-Sha'bī (b. 19/640, d. 103/721) was a Kūfan-born jurist, collector of poetry, and transmitter of *ḥadīth*, in addition to his interest in history. He served as a special ambassador to the Byzantines for 'Abd al-Malik, and as *qāḍī* under 'Umar b. 'Abd al-'Azīz. Later historians considered him very trustworthy and often used him as a source. See *EI*[1], s.v. al-Sha'bī; F. Sezgin, *GAS*, I, 277; and U. Sezgin, *Abū Miḥnaf*, 136–37.

92. See above, Ṭabarī, II, 652. They were encamped with members of the Rabī'ah tribes "between al-Tammārīn and al-Sabakhah."

93. Sharāf and Wāqiṣah are two watering places about 110 miles south of al-Kūfah on the road to Najd. See Yāqūt, *Mu'jam*, s.v. Sharāf.

He was never seen again, and no one knows whether the earth swallowed him up or the sky rained stones on him.[94]

When Furāt b. Zaḥr b. Qays was killed, ʿĀʾishah bint Khalīfah b. ʿAbdallāh al-Juʿfiyyah, who had been the wife of al-Ḥusayn b. ʿAlī, sent and asked al-Mukhtār to allow her to bury his body. He did so, and she buried it.

Al-Mukhtār sent a lad (*ghulām*)[95] of his named Zirbī to pursue Shamir b. Dhī al-Jawshan.

According to Abū Mikhnaf—Yūnus b. Abī Isḥāq—Muslim b. ʿAbdallāh al-Ḍabābī, who said: Al-Mukhtār's lad Zirbī followed us and overtook us. We had left al-Kūfah on lean[96] horses of ours. He approached us, riding at a fast gait. When he came near us, Shamir said to us, "Run, and get away from me. Perhaps the slave wants [to take] me." [Continuing,] he said: We ran and distanced ourselves. The slave wanted to take Shamir, but Shamir wheeled round to draw him away. When the slave had been separated from his companions, Shamir attacked him and broke his back. When word of this was brought to al-Mukhtār, he said, "Alas for Zirbī! Had he asked my advice, I would not have commanded him to go out after Abū al-Sābighah."

According to Abū Mikhnaf—Abū Muḥammad[97] al-Hamdānī—Muslim b. ʿAbdallāh al-Ḍabābī, who said: When Shamir b. Dhī al-Jawshan keft [al-Kūfah], I was with him. (This was at the time
[662] when al-Mukhtār defeated us, killed the Yemenis at Jabbānat al-Sabīʿ, and sent his lad Zirbī to seek Shamir, with the result

94. Cf. Dīnawarī, *Akhbār*, 310: "ʿAmr b. al-Ḥajjāj [printed text reads Ḥajjāḥ], one of the chief murderers of al-Ḥusayn, fled for al-Baṣrah. However, he was afraid the people would gloat over his misfortune; so he turned toward Sarāf. The people of the watering place told him to leave, since they did not feel safe from al-Mukhtār. After he rode away, they chided each other, saying, 'We have behaved badly.' A group of them rode in search of him, to bring him back; but when he saw them from afar, he thought they were al-Mukhtār's men and turned onto the sand at a place called al-Buyayḍah, between the villages of Kalb and those of Ṭayyiʾ. It was the heat of summer. He fell asleep there at midday, and he and his companions died of thirst." Cf. also Balādhurī, *Ansāb*, V, 240.

95. *Ghulām* means "a young lad"; that Zirbī was in fact a slave is shown by the use of the word *ʿabd* ("slave") to refer to him in the next paragraph.

96. *Ḍāmir*, "lean and lank in the belly," was applied to a horse that was fattened and then put on short rations so that it lost weight and became faster for purposes of racing. See Lane, *Lexicon*, V, 1804.

97. Perhaps the *kunyah* of Yūnus b. Abī Isḥāq. See U. Sezgin, *Abū Miḫnaf*, 109, 189.

that Shamir killed the lad.) Shamir went on until he reached Sātīdamā.[98] Then he went and encamped next to a village called "al-Kalbāniyyah,"[99] on a riverbank beside a hill. He sent to the village, took a native peasant, beat him, and said, "Hurry with this letter of mine to al-Muṣʿab b. al-Zubayr."[100] He wrote the address of the letter, "To the Commander, al-Muṣʿab b. al-Zubayr, from Shamir b. Dhī al-Jawshan." [Continuing,] he said: The native went until he entered a village in which there were some houses. Abū ʿAmrah[101] was there, having been sent to that village in those days by al-Mukhtār to be an armed guard [over the road] between him and the people of al-Baṣrah.[102] That native met a native of that village and started complaining to him of what he had suffered at the hands of Shamir. While they were talking, one of Abū ʿAmrah's men passed and saw the letter in the possession of the native, with its address, "To Muṣʿab, from Shamir." They asked the native where he was, and he told them. It turned out that only three *farsakh*s[103] lay between them and him. [Continuing,] he said: So they set out toward him.

---

98. The location is unknown. Ms. O omits the phrase; Mss. Pet and Co leave the word undotted. Ed. Leiden reads "Sātīdamā" on the basis of Yāqūt, *Muʿjam*, which mentions that the word occurs in poetry and lists several possible identifications, none likely in this context. Le Strange, *Lands*, 111, places the Sātīdamā River near Mayyāfāriqīn. The context indicates that Shamir is apprehended somewhere between al-Kūfah and al-Baṣrah. Dīnawarī, *Akhbār*, 308, reads, "He encamped near al-Baṣrah, in a place called Sādamāh."

99. Yāqūt, *Muʿjam*, gives al-Kaltāniyyah, a village between al-Sūs (in Khūzistān) and al-Ṣaymarah (near al-Baṣrah), as the place where Shamir was killed. The mss. of Ṭabarī read "al-Kalbāniyyah," which ed. Leiden originally emended to agree with Yāqūt. However, ed. Leiden, *Addenda*, p. DCLXX, restores "al-Kalbāniyyah." De Goeje's reasons can be found in his edition of Ibn Rustah, *Kitāb al-aʿlāq al-nafīsah*, 188d. Morony, *Iraq*, 198, refers to a place of this name in western Khūzistān.

100. Muṣʿab b. al-Zubayr was governor of al-Baṣrah for his brother, the anti-Umayyad caliph ʿAbdallāh b. al-Zubayr. See EI^1, s.v.; Ṭabarī, II, 602, 665.

101. Kaysān Abū ʿAmrah, a *mawlā* of ʿUraynah, was in charge of al-Mukhtār's personal guard (*ḥaras*). See EI^2, s.v. Kaysān; Ṭabarī, II, 634. On the use of Kaysāniyyah ("followers of Kaysān") to designate the followers of al-Mukhtār, see EI^2, s.v. Kaysāniyya.

102. Al-Baṣrah was a Muslim Arab garrison city (*miṣr*) and provincial capital near the Tigris-Euphrates estuary in lower Iraq, just south of the modern city. See Le Strange, *Lands*, 44–46; EI^2, s.v.

103. A *farsakh*, from Persian *farsang*, was originally the distance that could be covered on foot in an hour's march. In Islamic times, it was standardized at three Arab miles, each of 1000 *bāʿ* (fathoms), each of four canonical ells of 49.875 cm.; or 5.985 km/3.717 miles. See EI^2, s.v.

According to Abū Mikhnaf—Muslim b. ʿAbdallāh, who said: By God, I was with Shamir that night. We said to him, "If only you would take us away from this place, for we are apprehensive in it." He replied, "And all this from fear of the great liar? By God, I will not move from here for three days. God has filled your hearts with panic." [Continuing,] he said: There were many locusts
[663] in the place where we were. By God, I was between waking and sleeping when I heard the sound of horses' hooves. I said to myself that it was the sound of the locusts. Then I heard it louder, so I roused myself and rubbed my eyes. "No, by God," I said, "it is not locusts." [Continuing,] he said: I went to get up, and suddenly I saw them looking down at us from the hill. With a shout of "*Allāhu akbar* [God is most great]!" they surrounded our tents. We went out, running on foot, and left our horses. [Continuing,] he said: I passed Shamir. He had wrapped the lower part of his body in a cloak with a colored pattern. He was suffering from leprosy, and I can still see the white of his flanks above the cloak. He was thrusting at them with a lance, for they had rushed him before he could put on his sword and his clothes. We went on and left him. [Continuing,] he said: I had been running only a short time when I heard, "*Allāhu akbar*! God has slain the villain."

According to Abū Mikhnaf—al-Mishraqī[104]—ʿAbd al-Raḥmān b. ʿUbayd Abū al-Kanūd,[105] who said: By God, I was the man who got the letter. I saw it with the native and took it to Abū ʿAmrah, and I killed Shamir. [Al-Mishraqī] said: I asked [Abū al-Kanūd], "Did you hear him say anything that night?" "Yes," he replied, "he came out toward us and tried to thrust at us with his lance for a time. Then he threw down his lance, went into his tent, got his sword, and came out at us, saying:

You have aroused a bold lion from his covert,
    a grim-faced one who breaks the back [of his prey].
Never has he been seen to shrink from a foe,
    but rather fighting or killing,
Striking them with force and quenching the spear's thirst."

---

104. Al-Ḍaḥḥāk b. ʿAbdallāh al-Mishraqī, see U. Sezgin, *Abū Miḥnaf*, 200–1.

105. Abū al-Kanūd ʿAbd al-Raḥmān b. ʿUbayd al-Azdī al-Kūfī (born in pre-Islamic times, d. after 70/689) transmitted traditions from ʿAlī. In 50, he was Ziyād b. Abīhi's agent (*ʿāmil*) at al-Kūfah, according to Ṭabarī, II, 101. See Ibn Ḥajar, *Tahdhīb*, XII, 213 (who gives a different *ism*); and U. Sezgin, *Abū Miḥnaf*, 218.

According to Abū Mikhnaf—Yūnus b. Abī Isḥāq: When al-Mukhtār left Jabbānat al-Sabīʿ and went to the palace, Surāqah b. Mirdās began to call to him at the top of his voice:[106] [664]

Be gracious to me today, O best of Maʿadd;[107]
O best of those who dwell at Shiḥr and al-Janad;[108]
O best of those who greet with the Muslim greeting, perform the pilgrimage, and bow in worship.[109]

Al-Mukhtār had him sent to prison and held for a night. The next morning, he sent and had him taken out. He summoned Surāqah. As the latter approached al-Mukhtār, he recited:

Tell Abū Isḥāq[110] that we
leapt a leap[111] that was to our harm.
We revolted, thinking the poor[112] were nothing;
but our revolt was insolence and death.
We thought them[113] few in their ranks;
but when we met they were like locusts.
We took the field when we saw them; and when
we saw that the people had come out toward us,
We suffered at their hands strong blows
and well-aimed thrusts, so that we turned back.
You were aided against your enemy every day
by squadrons each of which was mourning al-Ḥusayn;
Even as Muḥammad was aided on the day of Badr

---

106. The *Dīwān* of Surāqah preserves a fuller version of the poet's encounter with al-Mukhtār. See Hahn, *Surâqa b. Mirdâs*, 19–29, 31–33; and Jumaḥī, *Tabaqāt al-shuʿarāʾ*, 105.

107. Maʿadd, the son of ʿAdnān, and father of Nizār, was an ancestor of the northern Arabian tribes, to which al-Mukhtār's tribe of Thaqīf belonged.

108. Shiḥr, on the south coast of the Arabian peninsula, and al-Janad, in the highlands, are two places in Yemen. Al-Mukhtār is being praised as the best of the northern and southern Arabs.

109. I.e., best of all Muslims. Use of the greeting *al-salāmu ʿalaykum* (cf. Qurʾān 6:54, and 7:46) was a mark of the Muslim and was believed to mirror the greeting of those in Paradise. "Perform the pilgrimage": the Arabic means, literally, "say the formula beginning *labbayka*," which is used by pilgrims to Mecca.

110. I.e., al-Mukhtār, whose *kunyah* was Abū Isḥāq.

111. I.e., made an attack, revolted. The verb *nazā* also suggests rashness, succumbing to base instincts, or greed.

112. Al-Mukhtār invoked defense of the poor (*ḍuʿafāʾ*) along with vengeance for al-Ḥusayn as reasons for his revolt. Cf. Ṭabarī, II, 606–7, 609–10.

113. *Dīwān*: You would think them.

and on the day of the gorge when he reached Ḥunayn.[114]
Having obtained your object, grant pardon; had we obtained our object,
We would have acted unjustly in governing and transgressed.
Accept my repentance; as for me,
I will be thankful if you make the cash a debt.[115]

When he reached al-Mukhtār, he said to him, "May God preserve you, commander! Surāqah b. Mirdās swears by God, other than Whom there is no god,[116] that he saw the angels fighting on piebald horses between heaven and earth."[117] Al-Mukhtār said to him, "Go up into the pulpit and let the Muslims know about it." So he went up and told them of it; then he came down. Al-Mukhtār took him aside and said, "I know indeed that you did
[665] not see the angels. But I know what you wanted: that I should not kill you. Go away from me, wherever you wish, and don't corrupt my companions for me."

According to Abū Mikhnaf—al-Ḥajjāj b. ʿAlī al-Bāriqī[118]—Surāqah b. Mirdās, who said: "In no oath I ever swore did I lie more vigorously or outrageously than in this oath of mine, when I swore to them that I had seen the angels fighting on their side."

They set Surāqah b. Mirdās free, and he fled and joined ʿAbd al-Raḥmān b. Mikhnaf in the entourage of al-Muṣʿab b. al-Zubayr in al-Baṣrah. The *ashrāf* of al-Kūfah and leading men left and joined Muṣʿab b. al-Zubayr in al-Baṣrah. As Surāqah b. Mirdās was leaving al-Kūfah, he recited:

---

114. The Qur'ān says that God gave the Prophet supernatural assistance at the Battle of Badr, in A.H. 2, at which the infant Muslim community defeated a much larger Meccan force, and the Battle of Ḥunayn, in A.H. 8, at which a coalition of tribes was turned back near al-Ṭā'if. See Qur'ān 8:9, 17 (Badr) and 9:25–27 (Ḥunayn). The *Sīrah* literature elaborates upon these incidents. See *EI*², s.vv. Badr and Ḥunayn.

115. The sense is, "I will be thankful if you make my obligation, which ought to be paid immediately in cash, payable as a debt in the future." The *Dīwān* adds another line: "Thus you will find Surāqah; so be kind to him, for he will make your foes ever more contemptible."

116. Qur'ān 59:22.

117. In Ibn Hishām's biography of the Prophet, enemy spies before the Battle of Ḥunayn come back terrified at having seen "white men on piebald horses." See Ibn Hishām, *Sīrah*, IV, 891.

118. See U. Sezgin, *Abū Miḥnaf*, 204.

Tell Abū Isḥāq that I
saw that the piebald horses were black and of one color!
I deny your revelation, and I have bound myself by vow
to fight you to the death.
I make my eyes see what they did not perceive;
both of us are experts in lies!
When they speak, I say to them, "You have lied."
And when they come out, I gird on my weapon for them.[119]

According to Abū al-Sā'ib Salm b. Junādah—Muḥammad b. Barrād (one of the descendants of Abū Mūsā al-Ashʿarī)—a shaykh, who said: When Surāqah al-Bāriqī was taken prisoner, he said, "Was it you who took me prisoner? No, I was taken prisoner by men wearing white garments and riding piebald horses." [Continuing,] he said: Al-Mukhtār said, "Those were the angels!" And he released him. Then Surāqah recited:

Tell Abū Isḥāq that I
saw that the piebald horses were black and of one color!
I make my eyes see what they did not see;
both of us are experts in lies!

According to Abū Mikhnaf—ʿUmayr b. Ziyād: ʿAbd al-Raḥmān b. Saʿīd b. Qays al-Hamdānī said on the day of the Battle of Jabbānat al-Sabīʿ, "Alas for you! Who are these who have come [666]
at us from behind?" When he was told that they were men from Shibām, he said, "O the wonder of it! One who has no kindred fights me by means of my kindred!"

According to Abū Mikhnaf—Abū Rawq:[120] Shuraḥbīl b. Dhī Buqlān, a member of the Nāʿiṭ,[121] was killed that day. He was one of the nobility[122] of [the tribe of] Hamdān. That day, before he was killed, he said, "What a way of killing! How misguided

119. The *Dīwān* adds: "When al-Mukhtār learned of his having gone to al-Baṣrah and of these verses of his, he tore down Surāqah's house. Muṣʿab rebuilt it after al-Mukhtār was killed."

120. Full name: ʿAṭiyyah b. al-Ḥārith Abū Rawq al-Hamdānī. He is known as a traditionist and Qur'ānic commentator, in addition to his activity as a historian. See U. Sezgin, *Abū Miḫnaf*, 199.

121. Nāʿiṭ was a clan (*baṭn*) of the tribe of Hamdān.

122. Arabic, *buyūtāt*, "the [noble] houses."

those who were slain! A fight without a leader! A fight without a purpose! A hastening of the separation from loved ones! Even if we kill them, we shall not be safe from them. 'Surely we belong to God, and to Him we return.'[123] By God, I went out only to share the lot of my people, fearing that they would be oppressed. I swear by God that I have not escaped from that, neither have they been saved. I have been of no avail to them, neither have they availed anything." [Continuing,] he said: A man named Aḥmar b. Hadīj, from the Fā'ish [clan] of Hamdān, shot him with an arrow and killed him.

[Continuing,] he said: Three men fought with 'Abd al-Raḥmān b. Sa'īd b. Qays al-Hamdānī: Si'r b. Abī Si'r al-Ḥanafī, Abū al-Zubayr al-Shibāmī, and another man. Si'r said, "I hit him with a thrust [of the lance]." Abū al-Zubayr said, "But I struck him ten blows [with the sword], or more, and his son said to me, 'Abū al-Zubayr, will you kill 'Abd al-Raḥmān b. Sa'īd, the lord (*sayyid*) of your people?' I said to him, 'Thou shalt not find any people who believe in God and the Last Day who are loving to anyone who opposes God and His Messenger, not though they were their fathers, or their sons, or their brothers, or their clan.'"[124] Al-Mukhtār said, "You all did well." The battle left seven hundred and eighty of his people slain.

According to Abū Mikhnaf—al-Naḍr b. Ṣāliḥ: At that time, there was great slaughter among the Yemenis. Of the people of
[667] Muḍar in al-Kunāsah a dozen or so were struck down. They then went and passed by the men of Rabī'ah, whereupon Ḥajjār b. Abjar, Yazīd b. al-Ḥārith b. Ru'aym, Shaddād b. al-Mundhir (the brother of Ḥuḍayn[125]) and 'Ikrimah b. Rib'ī retreated, all of them returning to their homes. 'Ikrimah attacked the enemy and fought violently with them, but retreated from them wounded. He came to his house and entered it. Then he was told that horsemen had passed by the quarter of the tribe. He went out of the house and tried to jump from the wall of his house to another house beside it, but was unable to do so until a [slave] lad of his lifted him up.

123. Qur'ān 2:156.
124. Qur'ān 58:22.
125. Corrected by ed. Leiden, *Addenda*, p. DCLXX, from "Ḥuṣayn."

The battle of Jabbānat al-Sabīʿ took place on Wednesday, six days before the end of Dhū al-Ḥijjah, 66.[126]

[Al-Mukhtār Acts against the Murderers of al-Ḥusayn]

[Continuing,] he said: The *ashrāf* left and reached al-Baṣrah.[127] Al-Mukhtār turned his attention to the murderers of al-Ḥusayn. He said, "It is no part of our religion to leave people who murdered al-Ḥusayn walking alive in this world and safe. What a bad avenger[128] of the family of Muḥammad I should then be in this world! I should then be the liar they have called me. I take God as my helper against them. Praise be to God, Who has made me a sword whereby He has smitten them, a lance whereby He has thrust at them, the avenger of the family of Muḥammad, and the upholder of their right! Verily, God's right it is to slay those who slew them and humble those who ignored their right. Name them to me, and follow them until you annihilate them."

According to Abū Mikhnaf—Mūsā b. ʿĀmir: Al-Mukhtār said to them, "Seek me out the murderers of al-Ḥusayn; food and drink will have no savor for me until I purify the earth and cleanse the city of them."

According to Abū Mikhnaf—Mālik b. Aʿyan al-Juhanī:[129] ʿAbdallāh b. Dabbās (he was the man who killed Muḥammad b. ʿAmmār b. Yāsir, of whom the poet said:

Slain by Ibn Dabbās; he hit the back of his head) [668]

was the man who guided al-Mukhtār to some of the men who had murdered al-Ḥusayn, among them ʿAbdallāh b. Usayd b. al-Nazzāl al-Juhanī from [the clan] of Ḥuraqah, Mālik b. al-Nusayr al-Baddī,

---

126. Literally, "six nights remaining," i.e., 23 Dhū al-Ḥijjah 66 A.H. (July 21, 686), which, however, fell on Saturday, not Wednesday.

127. Cf. Balādhurī, *Ansāb*, V, 237: "After the men had been defeated at the Battle of Jabbānat al-Sabīʿ, the Kūfan *ashrāf* left and joined Muṣʿab b. al-Zubayr, who had come to al-Baṣrah as governor of the two provinces of Iraq."

128. *Nāṣir*, literally, "helper," but for this meaning see Lane, *Lexicon*, VIII, 2802, s.v. *naṣara*.

129. Perhaps to be identified with the Abū Manṣūr al-Juhanī who passed on a collection of ʿAlī's sermons collected by Zayd b. Wahb al-Juhanī. See U. Sezgin, *Abū Miḥnaf*, 209.

and Ḥamal b. Mālik al-Muḥāribī. Al-Mukhtār sent one of his chief companions, Abū Nimrān[130] Mālik b. ʿAmr al-Nahdī, after them. He came upon them while they were in al-Qādisiyyah,[131] took them, and brought them back to al-Mukhtār in the evening.

Al-Mukhtār said to them, "Enemies of God, enemies of His Book, enemies of His Messenger and the family of His Messenger! Where is al-Ḥusayn, the son of ʿAlī? Deliver al-Ḥusayn to me. You killed him whom you were commanded to bless during prayer." They replied, "May God have mercy on you. We were sent unwillingly. Be gracious to us and spare us." Al-Mukhtār said, "Why were you not gracious to al-Ḥusayn, the son of your prophet's daughter? Why did you not spare him and give him drink?" Then al-Mukhtār said to al-Baddī, "You took his hood?"[132] ʿAbdallāh b. Kāmil said to him, "Yes, he is the very man." Al-Mukhtār said, "Cut off his hands and feet, and leave him. Let him thrash about until he dies." This was done to him. He was left and continued bleeding until he died.[133] [Al-Mukhtār] gave orders for the other two. They were brought forward. ʿAbdallāh b. Kāmil killed ʿAbdallāh al-Juhanī, and Siʿr b. Abī Siʿr killed Ḥamal b. Mālik al-Muḥāribī.

According to Abū Mikhnaf—Abū al-Ṣalt al-Taymī—Abū Saʿīd al-Ṣayqal: Al-Mukhtār was guided to some of the murderers of al-Ḥusayn by Siʿr al-Ḥanafī. [Continuing,] he said: Al-Mukhtār sent ʿAbdallāh b. Kāmil. We went out with him. He passed through the Banū Ḍubayʿah[134] and took from them a man named Ziyād b. Mālik [Continuing,] he said: Then he went to [the clan of]
[669] ʿAnazah[135] and took from them a man named ʿImrān b. Khālid. [Continuing,] he said: Then he sent me, together with some of his

---

130. Ed. Leiden, *Addenda*, pp. DCLXIX–DCLXX, emends ms. "Abū Nimr" to "Abū Nimrān" on the basis of Ṭabarī, II, 727.

131. Al-Qādisiyyah, 19 miles southwest of al-Kūfah, was a large hamlet at the first stage on the road to Mecca. In 14/635, the Muslims had won their first great victory over the Persians near it. See EI^2, s.v. al-Ḳādisiyya; Yāqūt, *Muʿjam*, s.v.; and Le Strange, *Lands*, 76.

132. *Burnus*, which at first meant a long, pointed hat or hood, later was applied to any cloak with a hood attached. See Lane, *Lexicon*, I, 196.

133. Cf. the equally graphic account in Balādhurī, *Ansāb*, V, 239, where Mālik is gradually dismembered, with each limb being thrown into a fire.

134. A clan of the tribe of Bakr b. Wā'il, or from the Rabīʿah group. See *Lisān*, s.v.

135. A tribe from the Rabīʿah group. See *Lisān*, s.v.

men who were called "the investigators,"[136] to a house in the Persian section.[137] 'Abd al-Raḥmān b. Abī Khushkārah al-Bajalī and 'Abdallāh b. Qays al-Khawlānī were in it. We brought them back to [al-Mukhtār]. He said to them, "Murderers of the righteous! Murderers of the lord of the youth of Paradise! Do you not see that God has retaliated against you today? The *wars*[138] came to you on an unlucky day." (They had taken some *wars* that had been in al-Ḥusayn's possession.) "Take them out to the market and behead them." This was done to them. They were four men.

According to Abū Mikhnaf—Sulaymān b. Abī Rāshid[139]—Ḥumayd b. Muslim, who said: Al-Sā'ib b. Mālik al-Ash'arī[140] came with al-Mukhtār's horsemen to take us. I went our toward [the tribe of] 'Abd al-Qays, and 'Abdallāh and 'Abd al-Raḥmān, the two sons of Ṣalkhab,[141] went out following me. The arrest of the two diverted al-Mukhtār's men from me, so I escaped. Taking the two men, they passed by the house of a man named 'Abdallāh b. Wahb b. 'Amr, a cousin of A'shā Hamdān,[142] from the Banū

---

136. *Dabbābah*, from the verb "to creep," could mean either (as collective pl. of *dabbāb*) "those much given to creeping about," or (as a *nomen instrumenti*) "a machine for creeping." In the latter sense, it was applied to a siege engine (Latin *testudo*) used to protect men advancing to breach the walls of a city. Either sense could be extended to give the meaning suggested by the Leiden edition glossary.

137. Literally, "in [the section of] al-Ḥamrā'. The Ḥamrā' ("fair or light-complexioned people") were originally a group of Persian soldiers who went over to the Arab side at the Battle of Qādisiyyah. Later, some of them were settled at al-Kūfah with the Muslim army. They included some 4,000 Daylamīs, who became allies of the Banū Tamīm and had their own chief (*naqīb*) and mosque. See Morony, *Iraq*, 197–98.

138. *Wars* is a bright yellow dye derived from a plant grown in Yemen. Mixed with oil, it makes an ointment still used in parts of the Arabian peninsula to protect against sunburn. The Arabic rhymes and has a proverbial ring to it: *jā'akumu-l-wars bi-yawmi naḥs*.

139. He mediated reports on the deaths of 'Alī and al-Ḥusayn and on the campaign of Sulaymān b. Ṣurad. See U. Sezgin, *Abū Miḥnaf*, 217.

140. One of al-Mukhtār's early supporters and chief companions, al-Sā'ib b. Mālik had spoken out in opposition to Ibn al-Zubayr's governor of al-Kūfah before al-Mukhtār's seizure of the city and had been present when al-Mukhtār approached Ibrāhīm b. al-Ashtar seeking his support. See Ṭabarī, II, 601, 603, 612.

141. Variant in P, "Ṣalḥab"; Ibn Athīr has "Ṣalḥat."

142. A'shā Hamdān ('Abd al-Raḥmān b. 'Abdallāh Abū al-Muṣabbiḥ), of the Jusham clan of the South Arabian tribe of Hamdān, was a major poet. He was consistently hostile to the Umayyads and was to meet his death in 83/702 for his part in Ibn al-Ash'ath's rebellion against al-Ḥajjāj. See *EI*^{2}, s.v.; F. Sezgin, *GAS*, II, 345–46.

ʿAbd, and took him. They brought these men to al-Mukhtār; he gave orders concerning them, and they were killed in the market. They were three men.

When he escaped from al-Mukhtār's men, Ḥumayd b. Muslim said:

Have you not seen me in dismay?
I escaped, but almost did not escape.
The hope for God saved me;
I hope for nothing but Him.

According to Abū Mikhnaf—Mūsā b. ʿĀmir al-ʿAdawī from [the tribe of] Juhaynah (Shahm b. ʿAbd al-Raḥmān al-Juhanī also knew this report), who said: Al-Mukhtār sent ʿAbdallāh b. Kāmil
[670] to [take] ʿUthmān b. Khālid b. Usayr al-Duhmānī from Juhaynah and Abū Asmāʾ Bishr b. Sawṭ al-Qābiḍī. Both men were among those who had been present at the murder of al-Ḥusayn and had participated in shedding the blood of ʿAbd al-Raḥmān b. ʿAqīl b. Abī Ṭālib[143] and in taking his spoils. About the time of the mid-afternoon prayer, ʿAbdallāh b. Kāmil surrounded the mosque of the Banū Duhmān and said [to us], "If ʿUthmān b. Khālid b. Usayr is not brought to me, upon me be sins like those of the Banū Duhmān from the day they were created until the day on which they shall be resurrected, if I do not behead you to your last man." "Give us time," we said to him, "and we will seek him." So the men went out with horses to seek him. They found the two men sitting in the cemetery (*jabbānah*), about to leave for al-Jazīrah. They were brought to ʿAbdallāh b. Kāmil, who said, "Praise be to God, Who 'spared the believers a fight!'[144] Had they not found this man together with that one, it would have put us to the bother of going to his house to seek him. Praise be to God, Who has brought the time of calamity upon you, so that it has overpowered you." He took them away to the site of Biʾr al-Jaʿd and beheaded them. Then he returned and gave al-Mukhtār a report about them. The latter ordered him to go back to them and burn them with fire, saying, "They shall not be buried until they are burned." These were two men.

---

143. Al-Ḥusayn's cousin, killed at Karbalāʾ. See Ṭabarī, II, 357, 387.
144. Qurʾān 33:25.

Aʿshā Hamdān recited the following verses as an elegy for ʿUthmān al-Juhanī:

Weep, my eye, for the most valiant of young men, ʿUthmān;
O young man of the family of Duhmān, do not go afar.
Recall a glorious young man of beautiful character;
there is no horseman like him among the people of Hamdān.[145]

[Continuing,] Mūsā b. ʿĀmir said: Al-Mukhtār sent out Muʿādh b. Hāni' b. ʿAdī al-Kindī, the son of Ḥujr's brother,[146] and Abū [671] ʿAmrah, the head of his bodyguard. They went and surrounded the house of Khawalī b. Yazīd al-Aṣbaḥī, the man who had taken al-Ḥusayn's head and brought it [to al-Kūfah]. Khawalī concealed himself in the latrine.[147] When Muʿādh ordered Abū ʿAmrah to seek him in the house, Khawalī's wife came out to them. They asked her. "Where is your husband?" She said, "I do not know where he is." But she pointed with her hand to the latrine. They went in and found him—he had put a basket over his head. They brought him out. Al-Mukhtār was walking in al-Kūfah and going to see his companions. Abū ʿAmrah sent him a messenger, and al-Mukhtār received the messenger at the house of Abū Bilāl.[148] Ibn Kāmil was with him. The messenger told him the news. Al-Mukhtār went to meet them and took charge of Khawalī. He brought him back and killed him in the presence of his family. Then he called for fire and burned him, not leaving until the body had turned to ashes; then he departed. Khawalī's wife (she was from Ḥaḍramawt and was named al-ʿAyūf bint Mālik b. Nahār b. ʿAqrab) had become hostile to Khawalī when he had brought al-Ḥusayn's head [to al-Kūfah].

---

145. *Dīwān* (ed. Geyer), poem no. 48; translation in von Goutta, *Der Agānīartikel über 'Aʿšā von Hamdān*, 50.

146. In 51/671, the Kūfan Shīʿī leader Ḥujr b. ʿAdī al-Kindī and his associates revolted against Muʿāwiyah and the governor of Iraq, Ziyād b. Abīhi. Ziyād arrested Ḥujr and sent him to Syria, where he was beheaded. See Ṭabarī, II, 111–55; *EI*², s.v. Ḥudjr b. ʿAdī al-Kindī; and Jafri, *Origins*, 159–66.

147. *Makhraj* ("exit") also means "a place in the open air where one satisfies the needs of nature" (Dozy, *Supplément*, I, 360). The context suggests an enclosed outhouse.

148. Probably to be read "Bilāl," without "Abū," as at Ṭabarī, II, 735. See ed. Leiden, *Addenda*, p. DCLXX.

According to Abū Mikhnaf—Mūsā b. ʿAmir Abū al-Ashʿar: One day while al-Mukhtār was talking to his companions, he said, "Tomorrow I will kill a man with big feet, sunken eyes, and prominent eyebrows. His death will gladden believers and the angels stationed near [God]." [Continuing,] he said: Al-Haytham b. al-Aswad al-Nakhaʿī was close to al-Mukhtār when he heard this statement. It occurred to him that the man whom al-Mukhtār
[672] meant was ʿUmar b. Saʿd b. Abī Waqqāṣ; so when he returned to his house, he called his son al-ʿUryān and said, "Meet Ibn Saʿd tonight and tell him about such-and-such a matter. Tell him, 'Take care, for he means no one else but you.'" [Continuing,] he said: The son went to ʿUmar b. Saʿd, took him aside, and told him what had been said. ʿUmar b. Saʿd said to him, "God reward your father for his brotherly behavior! How could he intend to do such a thing to me after the promises and covenants he has given me?" Now when al-Mukhtār had first achieved victory, he had behaved in the best and friendliest possible manner toward people. ʿUmar b. Saʿd had spoken to ʿAbdallāh b. Jaʿdah b. Hubayrah (one of the men most honored by al-Mukhtār because of his closeness to ʿAlī) and had said to him, "I do not feel safe from this man"—meaning al-Mukhtār. "Get me a guarantee of safety (*amān*) from him." ʿAbdallāh had done so.[149]

[Continuing,] he said: I saw his guarantee of safety and read it:

> In the name of God, the Merciful, the Compassionate: This is a guarantee of safety from al-Mukhtār b. Abī ʿUbayd for ʿUmar b. Saʿd b. Abī Waqqāṣ. You are safe, with God's protection for yourself, your property, your family, and the people of your house and your children. You will not be taken to task for any offense committed by you in the past, so long as you heed and obey and keep close to your domicile,[150] your family, and your city. Whosoever encounters ʿUmar b. Saʿd, whether one of the police (*shurṭat Allāh*), the supporters (*Shīʿah*) of the

149. Cf. Balādhurī, *Ansāb*, V, 237, according to which ʿUmar b. Saʿd had gone into hiding after al-Mukhtār's victory and had come out only after obtaining an *amān*.

150. *Raḥl*, "a man's dwelling, or habitation" (Lane, *Lexicon*, III, 1054): ʿUmar was not to leave al-Kūfah for any of his other properties.

family of Muḥammad, or anyone else, let him do him only good.

Witnessed by: al-Sā'ib b. Mālik, Aḥmar b. Shumayṭ, ʿAbdallāh b. Shaddād, and ʿAbdallāh b. Kāmil. And al-Mukhtār has taken upon himself an oath and covenant by God to uphold for ʿUmar b. Saʿd the guarantee of safety he has given him, unless he cause some offense. He has made God his witness—"and God suffices for a witness."[151] [673]

[Continuing,] he said: Abū Jaʿfar Muḥammad b. ʿAlī[152] used to say, "As for al-Mukhtār's guarantee of safety for ʿUmar b. Saʿd, 'unless he cause some offense,' he meant by it: 'if he enters the privy and causes offense!'"[153]

[Continuing,] he said: When al-ʿUryān had brought him this message, ʿUmar b. Saʿd left under cover of that night. Having come to Ḥammām [ʿUmar],[154] he said to himself, "I will go and stay in my house." So he returned to it, passing al-Rawḥā',[155] and reaching his house in the morning. He told a *mawlā* of his what had happened concerning his guarantee of safety and what had been planned for him. His *mawlā* said, "What offense is greater than what you have done? You have left your residence and your family and come here. Go back to your residence [in al-Kūfah]. Do not give the man a way against you." So he returned to his home. His departure was reported to al-Mukhtār, who said, "No, indeed. On his neck there is a chain that will bring him back even if he does his utmost to depart." [Continuing,] he said: The next morning, al-Mukhtār sent Abū ʿAmrah to him and ordered him to bring ʿUmar to him. Abū ʿAmrah went before ʿUmar and said,

---

151. Qur'ān 4:79.

152. I.e., Abū Jaʿfar Muḥammad b. ʿAlī b. al-Ḥusayn, called Muḥammad al-Bāqir (d. 113/731), the fifth Imām according to both the Twelvers and the Ismāʿīlīs.

153. Al-Mukhtār tricked ʿUmar by an equivocation. Arabic *aḥdatha ḥadathan*, "he caused an incident," was a euphemism for "he voided excrement."

154. Ḥammām ʿUmar (the text reads "his *ḥammām*," but the context requires a place name, not "his bath") was a village on the Nars Canal, some 40 miles northeast of al-Kūfah. See Le Strange, *Lands*, 73; Djaït, *Al-Kūfa*, 282. Morony, *Iraq*, 269–70, places it at the village of Bitrī, across the Euphrates from al-Kūfah. Ṭabarī, II, 910, locates it between Qaṣr Hubayrah and Qubbīn.

155. A village of al-Rawḥā' near al-Sindiyyah on the Nahr ʿĪsā close to Baghdad is mentioned by Yāqūt, *Muʿjam*, s.v.

"Obey the commander!" ʿUmar got up, but tripped over his coat (*jubbah*), and Abū ʿAmrah struck him with his sword and killed him. He brought the head, wrapped in the lower part of his tunic (*qabā'*), and set it before al-Mukhtār. Al-Mukhtār said to the man's son, Ḥafṣ b. ʿUmar b. Saʿd, who was sitting in his presence, "Do you recognize this head?" [Ḥafṣ] exclaimed, "Surely we belong to God, and to Him we return!"[156] and said, "Yes, and there is no good in life after his death." "You are right," al-Mukhtār said to him, "for you shall not live after him." He gave orders concerning him; he was killed, and his head was with his father's. Al-Mukhtār said, "This one is for Ḥusayn, and that one for ʿAlī b. Ḥusayn! But there is no equivalence; by God, if I killed three-fourths of Quraysh[157] in requital for Ḥusayn, they would not measure up to one of his fingernails!"

Ḥumaydah, the daughter of ʿUmar b. Saʿd, recited the following, lamenting her father:

[674] Had someone other than a brother of Qasiyy[158] deceived him,
or other than one of Yemen, or other than a Persian,
That would have consoled me somewhat. Know
this concerning him (and a patrician is not like a most base man):
In the scroll, he gave Ibn Saʿd and his son
a promise that even a speckled snake would treat him gently.

When al-Mukhtār killed ʿUmar b. Saʿd and his son, he sent their heads with Musāfir b. Saʿīd b. Nimrān al-Nāʿiṭī and Ẓabyān b. ʿUmārah al-Tamīmī, who brought the heads to Muḥammad b. al-Ḥanafiyyah. Al-Mukhtār wrote Ibn al-Ḥanafiyyah a letter concerning the matter.

According to Abū Mikhnaf—Mūsā b. ʿĀmir, who said: What aroused al-Mukhtār to kill ʿUmar b. Saʿd was the fact that Yazīd b. Sharāḥīl al-Anṣārī had come to Muḥammad b. al-Ḥanafiyyah; after greetings, the conversation had turned to the subject of al-

156. Qur'ān 2:156, traditionally said in times of misfortune.

157. Quraysh, as the Prophet's tribe, was the most prestigious and "valuable" tribe.

158. Qasiyy b. Munabbih was the brother of Thaqīf, the ancestor of al-Mukhtār's tribe, and Qasiyy became a nickname for the entire tribe. There is an allusion here to the derivation of the name from *qasā* "he was cruel." See *Lisān*, s.v.

Mukhtār, his rebellion, and his call for avenging the blood of the people of the Prophet's family.[159] Muḥammad b. al-Ḥanafiyyah said, "To his least important messengers he alleges that he is a partisan (*shīʿah*) of ours, yet the murderers of al-Ḥusayn are his table companions, seated on chairs, and conversing with him." [Continuing,] he said: The other man noted what he had said. When he came to al-Kūfah, he went to al-Mukhtār and greeted him. Al-Mukhtār asked him, "Did you meet the Mahdī?"[160] He replied, "Yes." Al-Mukhtār asked, "What did he say to you and what did he discuss with you?" [Continuing,] he said: So he gave him a report.

[Continuing,] he said: Al-Mukhtār therefore lost no time in killing ʿUmar b. Saʿd and his son and then sent their heads to Ibn al-Ḥanafiyyah with the two messengers named above. He sent the following letter with them to Ibn al-Ḥanafiyyah: [675]

> In the name of God, the Merciful, the Compassionate. To the Mahdī, Muḥammad b. ʿAlī, from al-Mukhtār b. Abī ʿUbayd. Peace be upon you, O Mahdī! I praise God to you, the God save Whom there is no god. To proceed: God has sent me as a vengeance upon your enemies. They have either been killed or imprisoned, or are outcasts and fugitives. Praise be to God, who has slain those who slew you and assisted those who helped you. I have sent you the head of ʿUmar b. Saʿd and his son. We have killed whoever participated in [shedding] the blood of al-Ḥusayn and his household—God's mercy upon them!—all those over whom we have gained power. Those who remain will not escape from God. I will not cease from them, until no vestige of them on the face of the earth is reported to me. Write to me, O Mahdī, giving your opinion, and I will follow it and conform to it. Peace be upon you, O Mahdī, and God's mercy and blessings!

---

159. *Ahl al-bayt*, means literally, "people of the house." I have translated it as "people of the Prophet's family." The phrase occurs in Qur'ān 33:33 in a passage referring to Fāṭimah, ʿAlī, and their sons. Jafri, *Origins*, 9ff., argues that even before Islam the phrase was used to honor the Banū Hāshim as hereditary keepers of the Kaʿbah, and that the Shīʿī use of the phrase reflects the idea that the pre-Islamic eminence of this family climaxed in the appearance of the prophetic office in it. See *EI*[2], s.v.

Then al-Mukhtār sent ʿAbdallāh b. Kāmil to [take] Ḥakīm b. Ṭufayl al-Ṭāʾī al-Sinbisī, who had taken the spoils of al-ʿAbbās b. ʿAlī[161] and shot Ḥusayn with an arrow. (He used to say, "My arrow caught in his coat of mail[162] and did not harm him.") ʿAbdallāh b. Kāmil came, seized him, and led him away. Ḥakīm's family went and sought help from ʿAdī b. Ḥātim.[163] The latter overtook the men in the street and spoke to ʿAbdallāh b. Kāmil about Ḥakīm. ʿAbdallāh b. Kāmil said, "I have nothing to do with his affair. It is a matter for the commander, al-Mukhtār." ʿAdī b. Ḥātim said, "I will go to him." ʿAbdallāh b. Kāmil said, "Then go to him—and may you take the right way!"[164] So ʿAdī went to al-Mukhtār. Now al-Mukhtār had already accepted ʿAdī's intercession for a group of his tribesmen taken prisoner on the day of Jabbānat al-Sabīʿ who had said nothing concerning al-Ḥusayn or the members of his family. The Shīʿah therefore said to Ibn Kāmil, "We are afraid that the commander will accept the intercession of ʿAdī b.
[676] Ḥātim for his villain, whose guilt you know. Let us kill him." He said, "Do what you want with him." They took him with his hands bound to the place where the tribe of ʿAnazah lived and set him up as a target. Then they said to him, "You despoiled ʿAlī's son of his clothing; by God, we will despoil you of your clothes while you are alive and watching." So they stripped off his clothes. Then they said to him, "You shot Ḥusayn and used him as a

---

160. *Mahdī*, "the rightly guided one," was in the early days of Islam used as an honorific epithet in poems praising the Prophet, ʿAlī, and various Umayyad rulers. Sometime during the Second Civil War, the term developed the sense of a restorer of religion and justice after a period of injustice such as saw the martyrdom of al-Ḥusayn. Al-Mukhtār was not the first to apply the term to ʿAlī and his descendants. Sulaymān b. Ṣurad, the leader of the Tawwābūn, had used it in reference to al-Ḥusayn (Ṭabarī, II, 546), calling him "the Mahdī, son of the Mahdī." The novelty, if one can call it that, in al-Mukhtār's use of the term lay in the application of it to Muḥammad b. al-Ḥanafiyyah. See *EI*², s.v. al-Mahdī; and Dixon, *Umayyad Caliphate*, 36.

161. Al-ʿAbbās b. ʿAlī, the half-brother of al-Ḥusayn, was killed at Karbalāʾ. See Ṭabarī, II, 386.

162. *Sirbāl*, which can mean either "shirt" or "coat of mail." See Lane, *Lexicon*, IV, 1343; and ed. Leiden, *Glossarium*, p. CCXC.

163. ʿAdī b. Ḥātim al-Ṭāʾī was the leader of the powerful tribe of Ṭayyiʾ and an old supporter of ʿAlī. See *EI*², s.v.

164. Literally, "Go to him, taking the right way, or being well guided (*rāshidan*)." The phrase is based on an idiom: "One says to the traveller, *rashidta*, 'Mayest thou take, or follow, the right way.'" (Lane, *Lexicon*, IV, 1089).

target for your arrows, and you said, 'My arrow caught in his coat of mail and did not harm him.' We swear to God that we will shoot you the way you shot him with arrows, and let what sticks in you be sufficient for you!" [Continuing,] he said: They shot him with one volley of arrows, many of which hit him, and he fell dead.

According to Abū Mikhnaf—Abū al-Jārūd[165]—someone who saw him dead: He had so many arrows in him that he looked like a hedgehog.

When ʿAdī b. Ḥātim came before al-Mukhtār, the latter gave him a seat with him in the place he was sitting. ʿAdī told al-Mukhtār why he had come, and al-Mukhtār said to him, "Abū Ṭarīf,[166] do you think it permissible to petition for the murderers of al-Ḥusayn?" ʿAdī replied, "He has been falsely accused, God preserve you!" Al-Mukhtār said, "Then we leave him to you." [Continuing,] he said: Before long Ibn Kāmil entered. Al-Mukhtār said to him, "What has happened to the man?" He replied, "The Shīʿah have killed him." Al-Mukhtār, who would not have been pleased had he not killed him, said, "What made you hurry to kill him before bringing him to me? ʿAdī, here, has come for him, and he is a man whose intercession deserves to be accepted and whose wish should be carried out." Ibn Kāmil said, "By God, the Shīʿah overcame me." ʿAdī said to him, "You are lying, enemy of God! You thought someone better than you was going to accept my intercession for him, so you forestalled me and killed him, and you had no nobility[167] to restrain you from what you did." [Continuing,] he said: Ibn Kāmil cursed him roundly, but al-Mukhtār put his finger on his mouth, commanding Ibn Kāmil to be still [677]
and leave ʿAdī alone. So ʿAdī arose satisfied with al-Mukhtār and angry with Ibn Kāmil, about whom he complained to any of his tribesmen he encountered.

165. Abū al-Jārūd Ziyād b. al-Mundhir (d. between 150/767 and 160/776), a famous student of Abū Jaʿfar al-Bāqir and, after the latter's death, a follower of al-Bāqir's brother Zayd. The Jārūdiyyah (a Zaydī Shīʿite group) took their name from him. See Ibn Ḥajar, *Tahdhīb*, III, 386–387; Shahrastānī, *Milal*, 161; *EI*², s.v. al-Djārūdiyya; and U. Sezgin, *Abū Miḥnaf*, 227.

166. ʿAdī's *kunyah*.

167. On *khaṭar* as "eminence, nobility, dignity" see Lane, *Lexicon*, II, 764; and ed. Leiden, *Glossarium*, p. CCXXVI.

Al-Mukhtār sent ʿAbdallāh b. Kāmil to [take] the slayer of ʿAlī b. al-Ḥusayn. This was a man from ʿAbd al-Qays named Murrah b. Munqidh b. al-Nuʿmān al-ʿAbdī. He was a brave man; when Ibn Kāmil came for him and surrounded his house, he came out to meet them, lance in hand, and mounted on a swift horse. He thrust at ʿUbaydallāh b. Nājiyah al-Shibāmī and threw him down, but did not injure him. [Continuing,] he said: Ibn Kāmil would strike him with his sword, and he would ward it off with his left hand. Soon the sword had cut into it, but the horse spirited him away. He escaped and joined Muṣʿab, but his arm was paralyzed after that.

[Continuing,] he said: Al-Mukhtār also sent out ʿAbdallāh al-Shākirī to [take] a man from Janb[168] called Zayd b. Ruqād, who used to say, "I shot one of their young men with an arrow: he was holding his hand on his forehead, warding off the arrows, and I pinned his hand to his forehead, so that he could not remove his hand from his forehead."

According to Abū Mikhnaf—Abū ʿAbd al-Aʿlā al-Zubaydī: The young man was ʿAbdallāh b. Muslim b. ʿAqīl.[169] When his hand was pinned to his forehead, he said, "O God, they have despised and humiliated us; slay them, O God, as they have slain us, and humiliate them, as they have humiliated us." Then Zayd b. Ruqād hit the young man with another arrow and killed him. Zayd said, "I came to him when he was dead and pulled out of his body my arrow with which I had killed him. I kept working the arrow in his forehead back and forth until I pulled it out, but the arrowhead remain fixed in his forehead; I could not pull it out."

[Continuing,] he said: When Ibn Kāmil came to Zayd b. Ruqād's
[678] house, he surrounded it, and the men rushed in to seize him. Zayd, who was a brave man, came out to meet them with his sword drawn. Ibn Kāmil said, "Do not strike him with the sword or thrust at him with the lance; shoot him with arrows and pelt him with stones." They did this, and he fell. Ibn Kāmil said, "If there is still a last gasp of life in him, bring him out." They brought him

168. Janb was a Yemeni tribal group of uncertain affiliation. See *Lisān*, s.v.
169. In the account of the death of ʿAbdallāh b. Muslim b. ʿAqīl b. Abī Ṭālib in Ṭabarī, II, 357, the man who shot him is identified as ʿAmr b. Ṣubayḥ al-Ṣudāʾī.

out; there was still life in him. Ibn Kāmil called for fire, and they burned him alive, before he had given up the ghost.[170]

Al-Mukhtār sought out Sinān b. Anas, who claimed to have killed al-Ḥusayn. Finding that he had fled to al-Baṣrah, he tore down his house.

Al-Mukhtār sought out ʿAbdallāh b. ʿUqbah al-Ghanawī. Finding that he had fled and reached al-Jazīrah, he tore down his house. This al-Ghanawī had killed one of the young men [of the family of al-Ḥusayn], and another man, of the Banū Asad (his name was Ḥarmalah b. Kāhil), had also killed a man from al-Ḥusayn's family. Ibn Abī ʿAqib al-Laythī recited the following about these two men:

Amongst [the tribe of] Ghanī there is a drop of our blood;
and amongst [the tribe of] Asad there is another [drop] to be counted and remembered.

Al-Mukhtār sought out a man from Khathʿam called ʿAbdallāh b. ʿUrwah al-Khathʿamī, who said that he had shot twelve arrows at them unsuccessfully. When ʿAbdallāh eluded him and joined Muṣʿab, al-Mukhtār tore down his house.

Al-Mukhtār sought out a man from [the tribe of] Ṣudāʾ[171] named ʿAmr b. Ṣubayḥ, who said, "I thrust at some of them and wounded them, but killed none of them."[172] They came to get him at night, after people were at rest. He was on his roof, unaware, though [679]
with his sword under his head. When they grabbed him and took his sword, he said, "God damn you, sword; so close, yet so far!" He was brought to al-Mukhtār, who imprisoned him with him in the palace. The next morning, he gave audience to his companions, and it was announced, "Let anyone who wants to enter enter." The people came in, and ʿAmr was brought in, bound. He said, "You band of infidels and liars, if my sword were in my hand, you would know that I do not tremble or quake at the blade of a sword. Since it is my fate to be killed, I want no one but you

170. Cf. Balādhurī, *Ansāb, V*, 239, for a version in which he is flayed alive.
171. Ṣudāʾ was a Yemeni tribe (*Lisān*, s.v.).
172. "But some said that he was the man who had shot ʿAbdallāh b. Muslim in the forehead, while Zayd b. Ruqād had pierced his heart" (Balādhurī, *Ansāb*, V, 239).

to kill me. I know you are the worst of God's creatures. But I wish there were a sword in my hand so that I could strike you with it for a time." Then he lifted his hand and slapped Ibn Kāmil, who was beside him, in the eye. Ibn Kāmil laughed, grabbed his hand, and held it. Then he said, "He claims to have wounded and thrust at some of the family of Muḥammad. Give us your command concerning him." Al-Mukhtār said, "Bring me lances!" They were brought. "Thrust at him," he said, "until he dies." So he was thrust with lances until he died.

According to Abū Mikhnaf—Hishām b. ʿAbd al-Raḥmān[173] and his son al-Ḥakam b. Hishām: Al-Mukhtār's companions passed by the house of the sons of Abū Zurʿah b. Masʿūd, who shot at them from atop the house. So they went into the house and killed al-Hibyāṭ[174] b. ʿUthmān b. Abī Zurʿah al-Thaqafī and ʿAbd al-Raḥmān b. ʿUthmān b. Abī Zurʿah al-Thaqafī. ʿAbd al-Mālik b. Abī Zurʿah escaped from them with a blow on his head. He went swiftly and came before al-Mukhtār, who gave orders to his wife, Umm Thābit bint Samurah b. Jundab, who nursed the
[680] wound. Then al-Mukhtār called him and said, "I am not at fault. You shot at the men and angered them."

Muḥammad b. al-Ashʿath b. Qays[175] was at the village of al-Ashʿath next to al-Qādisiyyah. To take him, al-Mukhtār sent out Ḥawshab, the Keeper of the Chair,[176] with a hundred men, saying, "Set out after him. You will find him diverting himself hunting, or standing cringing with fear, or afraid and turning this way and that in confusion, or lurking hidden. If you overpower him, bring me his head." Ḥawshab went out, reached Muḥammad b. al-Ashʿath's palace, and surrounded it. The latter left and joined Muṣʿab. The men stayed by the palace, thinking that he was in it. When they entered and learned that he had eluded them, they returned to al-Mukhtār, who sent and had the house town down.

---

173. Hishām b. ʿAbd al-Raḥmān al-Thaqafī; see U. Sezgin, *Abū Miḥnaf*, 204.

174. Ms. O, al-Himyāṭ.

175. Muḥammad b. al-Ashʿath b. Qays al-Kindī, a descendant of the kings of Kindah, was the father of the ʿAbd al-Raḥmān (often called simply "Ibn al-Ashʿath"), who in 81/700 led a major revolt against al-Ḥajjāj in Iraq.

176. On the Chair that al-Mukhtār exhibited as a relic of ʿAlī, see below, Ṭabarī, II, 702–06.

With the adobe bricks and clay he [re]built the house of Ḥujr b. ʿAdī al-Kindī, which Ziyād b. Sumayyah[177] had torn down.

[The Swearing of Allegiance to al-Mukhtār in al-Baṣrah]

According to Abū Jaʿfar [sc. al-Ṭabarī]: In this year, al-Muthannā b. Mukharribah al-ʿAbdī summoned the people of al-Baṣrah to swear allegiance to al-Mukhtār.

According to Aḥmad b. Zuhayr[178]—ʿAlī b. Muḥammad [al-Madāʾinī][179]—ʿAbdallāh b. ʿAṭiyyah al-Laythī and ʿĀmir b. al-Aswad: Al-Muthannā b. Mukharribah al-ʿAbdī was among those who had witnessed [the Battle of] ʿAyn al-Wardah with Sulaymān b. Ṣurad. Afterwards, he returned with the surviving Tawwābūn who returned to al-Kūfah. Al-Mukhtār was then being detained. Al-Muthannā waited until al-Mukhtār came out of prison and then swore allegiance to him secretly. Al-Mukhtār said to him, "Make your way back to your territory in al-Baṣrah and summon the people, keeping your activity secret." Al-Muthannā went to al-Baṣrah and received a favorable response from some of his tribesmen and others.

When al-Mukhtār evicted Ibn Muṭīʿ from al-Kūfah and prevented ʿUmar b. ʿAbd al-Raḥmān b. al-Ḥārith b. Hishām from entering al-Kūfah, al-Muthannā b. Mukharribah went out and [681]
took possession of a mosque. His tribesmen gathered round

177. The governor Ziyād b. Abīhi, whose paternity was notoriously unclear, is in this form of his name given a *nisbah* to his mother Sumayyah, a notorious prostitute of al-Ṭāʾif. Ms. O adds, "May God curse him!"

178. Abū Bakr Aḥmad b. Abī Khaythamah Zuhayr b. Ḥarb al-Nasāʾī (b. 185/801, d. 279/892) was a Baghdad traditionist, historian, and literary scholar, probably of Khurasanian origin. He was a student of al-Madāʾinī and a teacher of al-Ṭabarī. See F. Sezgin, *GAS*, I, 319–20; Rotter, "Zur Überlieferung einiger historischer Werke Madāʾinīs," 110.

179. Abū al-Ḥasan ʿAlī b. Muḥammad b. ʿAbdallāh b. Abī Sayf al-Madāʾinī (b. 135/752, d. ca. 228/843), a historian of the generation following Abū Mikhnaf, was active al-Baṣrah (his birthplace), al-Madāʾin, and Baghdad, and was credited with over 200 works on history and literature, most of which survive only as quoted in the works of later authors. See *EI*², s.v.; Rotter, "Zur Überlieferung einiger historischer Werke Madāʾinīs"; and Schoeler, "Die Frage der schriftlichen oder mündlichen Überlieferung."

him,[180] and he propagandized for al-Mukhtār. Then he went to the provision depot[181] and encamped by it. (Food was stored and camels were slaughtered in "the city.") Against them, al-Qubā'[182] dispatched 'Abbād b. Ḥuṣayn, the head of his police, and Qays b. al-Haytham with police and soldiers. Turning into the street of the *mawālī*, they came out into al-Sabakhah and halted. People remained in their houses; no one came out. 'Abbād kept waiting to see someone he might question. Seeing no one, he said, "Isn't there any man here from the Banū Tamīm?" Khalīfah al-A'war, a *mawlā* of the Banū 'Adī ('Adī al-Ribāb),[183] replied, "This is the house of Warrād, a *mawlā* of the Banū 'Abd Shams." "Knock on the door," he said. So Khalīfah knocked on the door, and Warrād came out to him. 'Abbād cursed him, saying, "Woe unto you! Here I am standing, and you did not come out to me." Warrād replied, "I did not know what would please you." "Put on your sword," he said, "and get your mount." He did so. They waited. Al-Muthannā's forces came and stood opposite them. 'Abbād said to Warrād, "Stay where you are with Qays." Qays b. al-Haytham and Warrād stayed where they were. While the men waited in al-Sabakhah, 'Abbād went back and turned into al-Dhabbāḥīn[184] Street until he reached al-Kallā'.[185] Now the supply depot had four gates: one adjoining al-Baṣrah, one toward al-Khallālīn,[186] one toward the mosque, and one toward the quarter from which the north wind blows. 'Abbād came to the gate facing the river,

180. Ms. O: "some of his tribesmen gathered around him in it." Al-Muthannā's tribe was 'Abd al-Qays (*nisbah*, "al-'Abdī").

181. *Madīnat al-rizq* "the city of provisions." After the Arab conquest, a supply depot was set up at Zābūqah, one of the abandoned Sasanian fortresses at the site of al-Baṣrah. It had a courtyard and was called a "village of provisions" (*qaryat al-arzāq*). It was rebuilt and enlarged by Ziyād b. Abīhi and his son 'Ubaydallāh, so that it resembled a city and had four iron gates. See Morony, *Iraq*, 62–63; Yāqūt, *Mu'jam*, s.v. Rizq.

182. Al-Ḥārith b. 'Abdallāh b. Abī Rabī'ah al-Qurashī al-Makhzūmī al-Qubā', one of the first men to have sworn allegiance to Ibn al-Zubayr as caliph in 64/683, was Ibn al-Zubayr's governor for al-Baṣrah. See Madelung, "'Abd Allāh b. al-Zubayr and the Mahdī," 295; Ṭabarī, II, 601.

183. Since several tribes or clans had the name 'Adī, his tribe is further defined as the 'Adī of the al-Ribāb confederation, which included the tribes of Ḍabbah, Thawr, 'Ukl, Taym, and 'Adī. See *Lisān*, s.vv. *'Adī* and *Ribāb*.

184. Butchers' Street.

185. Al-Kallā' ("the place where boats are drawn up") was a riverside market.

186. The street or section of vinegar makers or sellers.

next to the people who deal with rubbish.[187] It was a small gate. There he halted and called for a ladder, which he placed against the wall of the depot. Thirty men climbed up. He told them, "Stay on top. When you hear the shout of '*Allāhu akbar*,' shout '*Allāhu akbar*' on the roof." 'Abbād then went back to Qays b. al-Haytham and said to Warrād, "Incite the men to attack." Warrād attacked al-Muthannā's forces. The fighting became confused. [682] Forty of al-Muthannā's men and one of 'Abbād's men were killed. Hearing the tumult and the shouts of "*Allāhu akbar*," the men on the roof of the supply depot[188] shouted "*Allāhu akbar*." Those who were in the depot fled. Hearing shouts of "*Allāhu akbar*" behind them, al-Muthannā and his forces took to flight. 'Abbād and Qays b. al-Haytham ordered the men to stop pursuing them. They took the supply depot and its contents, while al-Muthannā and his forces went to [the tribal district of] 'Abd al-Qays. When 'Abbād and Qays and their forces returned to al-Qubā', he sent them to the 'Abd al-Qays district. Qays b. al-Haytham approached from the direction of the bridge; 'Abbād came at them from the Mirbad[189] road, and they met.

While al-Qubā' was in the mosque, sitting on the pulpit, Ziyād b. 'Amr al-'Atakī[190] came to him. Ziyād entered the mosque on his horse and said, "Turn your horsemen away from our brothers,[191] man, or we will fight them." Al-Qubā' sent al-Aḥnaf b. Qays[192]

---

187. *Saqaṭ*, which can mean rubbish, household goods of small value, or the offal of slaughtered animals (Lane, *Lexicon*, IV, 1381).

188. Here the term is *Dār al-rizq*, rather than *Madīnat al-rizq*.

189. Al-Mirbad ("the Kneeling Place for Camels"), near the western gate of al-Baṣrah, was the place where desert caravans halted and one of the busiest parts of the city. See Le Strange, *Lands*, 45; and *EI*², s.v.

190. Ziyād, a member of the 'Atīk, a division of the powerful Yemeni tribe of Azd, had become the leader of the Azd in al-Baṣrah after the assassination of the Azdī leader Mas'ūd b. 'Amr in 64/663. This assassination had provoked severe tribal conflict in al-Baṣrah between the Azd, allied with Bakr b. Wā'il (or Rabī'ah; Mālik b. Misma' was its leader) and 'Abd al-Qays, on the one hand, and Tamīm (Muḍar; al-Aḥnaf b. Qays was its leader), on the other. This tribal animosity now threatens to blaze up again. See Ṭabarī, II, 461.

191. I.e., the 'Abd al-Qays, with whom the Azd were allied.

192. Abū Baḥr Sakhr b. Qays al-Tamīmī al-Sa'dī, surnamed al-Aḥnaf ("having a misshapen foot"), headed the tribe of Tamīm in al-Baṣrah. In the tribal fighting that had racked al-Baṣrah in 64/663, he had worked for a moderate settlement and appears here again as a force for moderation. Compare the very different account of al-Aḥnaf's behavior (Balādhurī, *Ansāb*, V, 244–45), where the mediators are

and ʿUmar b. ʿAbd al-Raḥmān al-Makhzūmī to bring about a settlement. The two went to the tribal district of ʿAbd al-Qays. Al-Aḥnaf said to Bakr and Azd and to the general population (*ʿāmmah*), "Are you not in a state of allegiance to Ibn al-Zubayr?" "Yes," they said, "but we will not hand over our brothers." "Then," he said, "order them to leave for any territories they like and not disturb this city for its people who are dwelling in safety. Let them depart wherever they will." So Mālik b. Misma', Ziyād b. ʿAmr, and their most prominent companions went to al-Muthannā and said to him and his companions, "By God, we do not hold your opinion, but we do not want you to be harmed. Go join your leader,[193] for those who have responded favorably to your opinion are few; then you will be safe." Al-Muthannā accepted their proposal and advice and went away. Al-Aḥnaf
[683] returned and said, "Never have I been deficient in my judgement, except today. I went to these people and left Bakr and Azd behind me." ʿAbbād and Qays returned to al-Qubāʿ, while al-Muthannā went to al-Mukhtār in al-Kūfah with a small band of his companions.

Suwayd b. Ri'āb[194] al-Shannī and ʿUqbah b. ʿAshīrah al-Shannī fell in that fighting. The latter was killed by a man from the Banū Tamīm, who was in turn killed. The brother of ʿUqbah b. ʿAshīrah lapped up the blood of the Tamīmī and said, "My revenge!"

When al-Muthannā arrived [in al-Kūfah], he told al-Mukhtār what Mālik b. Misma' and Ziyād b. ʿAmr had done, how they had come to him and had defended him until he left al-Baṣrah. Hoping to win them to his side, al-Mukhtār wrote to them:

> To proceed: Heed and obey, and I will give you whatever you want of this world and guarantee Paradise to you.[195]

ʿUmar b. ʿAbd al-Raḥmān al-Makhzūmī and ʿAbdallāh b. Muṭīʿ, and where al-Aḥnaf resists attempts at conciliation, despite his reputation for moderation (*ḥilm*). The Balādhurī account, with al-Aḥnaf as head of Tamīm stubbornly hostile to al-Muthannā's tribe of ʿAbd al-Qays and its allies (Bakr and Azd) better explains al-Mukhtār's hostile letter to al-Aḥnaf (below, Ṭabarī, II, 683–84). See *EI*², s.v. al-Aḥnaf b. Ḳays.

193. I.e., al-Mukhtār.

194. Ms. O: Ziyād. Shann was a clan (*ḥayy*) of the tribe of ʿAbd al-Qays. See *Lisān*, s.v. *Shann*.

195. Cf. the longer version, in rhymed prose (*saj'*), in Balādhurī, *Ansāb*, V, 245.

Mālik said to Ziyād, "O Abū al-Mughīrah,[196] Abū Isḥāq has given us a great deal: this world and the next!" Ziyād replied jestingly to Mālik, "O Abū Ghassān,[197] as for me, I do not fight on credit; if someone gives me cash, I fight for him."

Al-Mukhtār wrote to al-Aḥnaf b. Qays:

> From al-Mukhtār to al-Aḥnaf and those who are with him. May you be at peace! To proceed: Woe to the mother of Rabī'ah from Muḍar![198] Al-Aḥnaf is taking his tribesmen to drink of Saqar,[199] whence he cannot bring them forth. I have no power over what has been written in the divine dispensation. I have been told that you call me a liar. The prophets were called liars before me, and I am no [684] better than many of them.[200]

He also wrote to al-Aḥnaf:

If you buy a horse with your money
  and take a shield in your left hand,
Make sharp sword fighting your concern.[201]

According to Abū al-Sā'ib Salm b. Junādah—al-Ḥasan b. Ḥammād—Ḥabbān[202] b. 'Alī—al-Mujālid—al-Sha'bī, who said: I entered al-Baṣrah and sat down by a circle of men among whom was al-Aḥnaf b. Qays.[203] One of the men said to me, "Who are

---

196. The *kunyah* of Ziyād b. 'Amr.
197. The *kunyah* of Mālik b. Misma'.
198. Cf. the variant below, Ṭabarī, II, 685: "Woe to the mother of Rabī'ah *and* Muḍar!" This makes better sense, since al-Mukhtār has reason to condemn both Muḍar (al-Aḥnaf's tribe) for opposing al-Muthannā and Rabī'ah for sending al-Muthannā back to al-Kūfah. Balādhurī, *Ansāb*, V, 245, reads "Rabī'ah and Muḍar."
199. A Qur'ānic name for hell.
200. Cf. Qur'ān 3:184. "But if they cry lies to thee, lies were cried to messengers before thee." Al-Mukhtār's language is ambiguous about whether he lays claim to being among the prophets. Cf. Balādhurī's version (*loc. cit.*): "By my life, if you fight me and call me a liar, those who were before me were called liars; and I am not the best of them."
201. The text is difficult and the manuscripts show many variants. My translation assumes the following text: *Idhā shtarayta farasan min mālikā/thumma akhadhta l-jawba fī shimālikā/fa-j'al misā'an ḥadhiman min bālikā.*
202. Ms. Ḥayyān, corrected in ed. Leiden on the basis of Dhahabī, *Mīzān* (Lucknow, 1301/1883–4), I, 182.
203. The context makes it clear that the conversation took place after the defeat and death of al-Mukhtār. Cf. al-Balādhurī, *Ansāb*, V, 245.

you?" "A Kūfan," I said. He said, "You are *mawālī* of ours." "How so?" I asked. "We saved you," he said, "from the hands of your slaves, the forces of al-Mukhtār." "Do you know," I said, "what the shaykh of Hamdān[204] said about us and about you?" Al-Aḥnaf b. Qays asked, "And what did he say?" I said, "He said:

Will you boast, if you killed slaves
and once defeated unarmed people?
If you view with us for glory, remember
what we did to you on the Day of the Camel:[205]
Both old man with dyed beard
and young man, white, bright-faced, in long garments.
He came to us tottering[206] in a long coat of mail,
and we slaughtered him in the morning as one slaughters a lamb.
We gave, but you forgot our giving;
you were ungrateful for the bounty of God the Most High.
You killed members of the Khashabiyyah[207] instead of them—
the worst of substitutions on the part of your people!"

[685] Al-Aḥnaf became angry and said, "Boy, bring that scroll here!" A scroll was brought. It contained:

> In the name of God, the Merciful the Compassionate. From al-Mukhtār b. Abī ʿUbayd to al-Aḥnaf b. Qays. To proceed: Woe to the mother of Rabīʿah and Muḍar! Al-Aḥnaf is taking his tribesmen to drink of Saqar, whence

---

204. I.e., the poet Aʿshā Hamdān. Another version of the incident is found in *Aghānī*, V, 157–58.

205. Cf. the explanation in Balādhurī, *Ansāb*, V, 245: "We spared (or pardoned) you, but you gave no thanks." At the Battle of the Camel (36/656), reinforcements from al-Kūfah helped ʿAlī dislodge the rebels Ṭalḥah and Zubayr from al-Baṣrah. See *EI*², s.v. al-Djamal.

206. *Yahdiju*: *Aghānī* reads *yarfulu*, walking proudly.

207. An alternative translation would be, "You killed members of the Khashabiyyah instead—from your own kinsmen—the worst of substitutions." The term *Khashabiyyah* (from *khashabah*, a piece of wood, club) was applied disparagingly to al-Mukhtār's followers because some of the *mawālī* were armed with clubs, rather than swords. Other explanations connect the name with the rescue of Ibn al-Ḥanafiyyah narrated below (Ṭabarī, II, 693), either because al-Mukhtār's men used clubs in order not to violate the prohibition on drawing swords in the Meccan sanctuary or because they took the wood Ibn al-Zubayr had prepared for burning Ibn al-Ḥanafiyyah. See Balādhurī, *Ansāb*, V, 231; also *EI*², s.v. Khashabiyya.

they cannot come forth. I have been informed that you call me a liar. If I am called a liar, messengers were called liars before me, and I am not better than they.

"Is this [man] one of us or one of you?" al-Aḥnaf asked.

According to Hishām b. Muḥammad [al-Kalbī]—Abū Mikhnaf—Manīʿ b. al-ʿAlāʾ al-Saʿdī: Miskīn[208] b. ʿĀmir b. Unayf b. Shurayḥ b. ʿAmr b. ʿUdas was among those who fought al-Mukhtār. When the men were defeated, he joined Muḥammad b. ʿUmayr b. ʿUṭārid in Ādharbayjān[209] and said:

Dukhtanūs[210] marveled when she saw
that a veil of gray hair had come over me.
She raised her voice and cried out.
[I said to her:] Do not be frightened that my beard has turned gray.
If you see that the vigor of my youth has departed
and that ages have passed since my birth,
[I am] a man of fifty-two years;
what lifetime is there that does not have turns of fortune?
Would that she had had my sword and I her dress
the day she said, 'Is there no generous man who is indignant?"
Would that we had died before that day,
or had done what free men do.
But, like men from whom the good flees, [686]
we did not fight, but the brave man fought.
I turned away from them, and they were stricken;
disgrace and shame have exiled me from them.
O the sadness of my spirit for "the meteor of Quraysh,"[211]
the day his head was brought to al-Mukhtār!

---

208. Known as Miskīn al-Dārimī (from the Dārim clan of the tribe of Tamīm), he wrote poems in praise of Muʿāwiyah and Yazīd and an elegy upon the death of Ziyād b. Abīhi. He is said to have died in 89/708. See F. Sezgin, *GAS*, II, 323.

209. Ādharbayjān was the province in northwestern Iran with its capital at Ardabīl. See *EI*[2], s.v.; Le Strange, *Lands*, 158 ff.

210. Dukhtanūs was a pre-Islamic poetess of the Dārimī clan of Tamīm (*Dīwān Miskīn al-Dārimī*, 42).

211. The "Meteor of Quraysh" refers to ʿUmar b. Saʿd b. Abī al-Waqqāṣ (*Dīwān Miskīn al-Dārimī*, 43).

Al-Mutawakkil[212] said:

They killed Ḥusayn; then they lament his death.
    Verily, time brings changes to people!
Do not be far away at al-Ṭaff,[213] O slain ones who have been left untended,
    whose heads' resting places have been soaked by rains.
The picked troops of al-Dajjāl[214] under his banner
    are not more astray than those whom al-Mukhtār has deceived.
O Banū Qasiyy,[215] bind fast your Dajjāl,
    and the [obscuring] dust will clear away; you will be free.
If your fellow tribesman had had knowledge of the unseen,
    the learned[216] would have agreed with you about him,
And it would have been a clear matter,
    related in the past by prophecies and reports.
I hope that thrusts that break your lances and a siege
    will prove that your inspiration is a lie,
And that to you will come men whose swords
    in their hands under the dust of battle are like fire.
They will not retreat when they meet you,
    until the heads of your armored men are broken in pieces.

---

212. Al-Mutawakkil b. ʿAbdallāh b. Nahshal Abū Juhmah al-Laythī was a poet from the tribe of Layth b. Bakr (Kinānah) who lived in al-Kūfah and visited Damascus, where he wrote poems in praise of Muʿāwiyah and Yazīd. See F. Sezgin, *GAS*, II, 322.

213. Al-Ṭaff is the desert region west of al-Kūfah along the alluvial plain of the Euphrates. It is higher than the low-lying ground by the river and forms the transition to the central Arabian plateau. The area contains a number of springs and was the site of a number of Sasanian border forts. Karbalāʾ, where al-Ḥusayn was killed, was located within it. See EI^1, s.v.; Yāqūt, *Muʿjam*, III, 359. The translation given here amends the vocalization of the Leiden text from *lā tabʿadan* (energetic second person singular) to *lā tabʿadun* (energetic second person plural). "Do not be far away" was a ritualized expression of mourning. Cf. the poem quoted in the *Lisān*, s.v. *baʿuda*: "As they bury me, they shall say, 'Do not be far away!' But where is there a place of [greater] remoteness than my place?"

214. Al-Dajjāl ("the Liar") is an apocalyptic figure similar to the Antichrist; see EI^2, s.v. al-Dadjdjāl.

215. I.e., al-Mukhtār's tribe of Thaqīf.

216. *Aḥbār*, pl. of *ḥabr* or *ḥibr*: a Jewish scholar, or one who has become a Muslim (Lane, *Lexicon*, II, 498). Such scholars were often credited with an ability to predict the future. See below, Ṭabarī, II, 786, and note 572 on Kaʿb al-Aḥbār.

[Al-Mukhtār Sends an Army to Trick Ibn al-Zubayr]

According to Abū Ja'far [sc. al-Ṭabarī]: In this year, al-Mukhtār dispatched an army to Medina to trick Ibn al-Zubayr. He pretended to Ibn al-Zubayr that he had sent the army to help him fight the army that 'Abd al-Malik b. Marwān[217] had sent to fight him and that had encamped in Wādī al-Qurā.[218]

Al-Mukhtār's Motive in Sending This Army; What Befell Them

According to Hishām b. Muḥammad [al-Kalbī]—Abū Mikhnaf—Mūsā b. 'Āmir, who said: Having been expelled by al-Mukhtār from al-Kūfah, Ibn Muṭī' went to al-Baṣrah. Not wishing to proceed to Ibn al-Zubayr in Mecca in a state of defeat and flight, he stayed in al-Baṣrah until 'Umar b. 'Abd al-Raḥmān b. al-Ḥārith b. Hishām came to him. Thus, both of them were in al-Baṣrah. [687]

The reason for 'Umar's coming to al-Baṣrah: When al-Mukhtār came into the open in al-Kūfah and met with success in his enterprise (the Shī'ah thought he was merely propagandizing for Ibn al-Ḥanafiyyah and seeking to avenge the blood of the members of the Prophet's family), he set out to deceive Ibn al-Zubayr and wrote to him as follows:

> To proceed: You know my sincere advice to you and my effort against the people hostile to you and what you for your part gave to me, on condition that I do this. But when I satisfied you and carried out my obligation to you, you stood me up and did not fulfill what you had promised me, although you saw on my part that which you saw. If you wish to return to me, I will return to you; if you want my sincere advice, I will advise you.

By this means, al-Mukhtār wanted to keep Ibn al-Zubayr at arm's length until the success of his own enterprise. He told the Shī'ah

---

217. 'Abd al-Malik b. Marwān (b. 23/643 or 26/646, d. 86/705) succeeded his father Marwān b. al-Ḥakam as Umayyad caliph upon the latter's death in 65/684. See *EI*², s.v.

218. Wādī al-Qurā ("the Valley of the Villages") was a fertile valley stretching north from Medina on the road to Syria. See *EI*¹, s.v. Wādī 'l-Ḳurā; Yāqūt, *Mu'jam*, s.vv. Qurā and Wādī al-Qurā.

nothing about the matter; if anything about it reached them, he pretended to them that he was of all men the most remote from such a thing.

[Continuing,] he said: Desiring to know whether it was war or peace, Ibn al-Zubayr summoned ʿUmar b. ʿAbd al-Raḥmān b. al-Ḥārith b. Hishām al-Makhzūmī and said to him, "Make ready to go to al-Kūfah, for we have appointed you its governor (*wālī*)." "How can that be," he asked, "when al-Mukhtār is there?" Ibn al-Zubayr said, "He claims that he heeds and obeys." [Continuing,] he said: ʿUmar b. ʿAbd al-Raḥmān outfitted himself at a cost of between thirty and forty thousand dirhams and set out for al-Kūfah. [Continuing,] he said: Al-Mukhtār's spy came from Mecca and reported the news. Al-Mukhtār asked, "At that cost did he outfit himself?" The spy answered, "Between thirty and forty thousand [dirhams]."

[688] [Continuing,] he said: Al-Mukhtār summoned Zā'idah b. Qudāmah and said to him, "Take seventy thousand dirhams with you—twice what he spent on his journey to us—and meet him in the desert. Take Musāfir b. Saʿīd b. Nimrān al-Nāʿiṭī with you, with five hundred skilled horsemen armed with chain mail, lances, and helmets, and say to ʿUmar b. ʿAbd al-Raḥmān, 'Take this sum, which is twice your expense, for we have learned how much you spent to outfit yourself and do not want you to lose money. Take it and go back.' If he does, [good]; if not, show him the horsemen, and say to him, 'Behind them are a hundred squadrons like them!'" [Continuing,] he said: Zā'idah took the money and went out with the horsemen. He met ʿUmar b. ʿAbd al-Raḥmān in the desert, offered him the money, and commanded him to go back. ʿUmar said to him, "The Commander of the Faithful appointed me governor of al-Kūfah, and his order must be carried out." Zā'idah summoned the horsemen, whom he had kept hidden out of sight. When ʿUmar saw them coming, he said, "This furnishes me more of an excuse and makes me look better. Hand over the money!" Zā'idah said to him, "He has sent it to you only on account of [the relation] between you and him." Then he paid him the money. ʿUmar took it and retreated toward al-Baṣrah. There he met with Ibn Muṭīʿ. It was during the time when al-Ḥārith b. ʿAbdallāh b. Abī Rabīʿah was in command, before the

uprising of al-Muthannā b. Mukharribah al-ʿAbdī in al-Baṣrah.[219]

According to Abū Mikhnaf—Ismāʿīl b. Nuʿaym:[220] Having been informed that the Syrians were approaching Iraq, al-Mukhtār knew he would be the first [to be attacked]. Therefore, fearing that the Syrians would come at him from the west and Muṣʿab b. al-Zubayr would come at him from al-Baṣrah, he sought a reconciliation with Ibn al-Zubayr, beguiling him and deceiving him. ʿAbd al-Malik b. Marwān had sent ʿAbd al-Malik b. al-Ḥārith b. al-Ḥakam b. Abī al-ʿĀṣ to Wādī al-Qurā. Deceiving and beguiling Ibn al-Zubayr, al-Mukhtār wrote to him: [689]

> To proceed: I have been informed that ʿAbd al-Malik b. Marwān has sent an army against you. If you want me to provide you with help, I will help you.

ʿAbdallāh b. al-Zubayr wrote to him:

> To proceed: If you are in a state of obedience to me, I am not averse to your sending the army to my territories and having the men swear allegiance to me before you. When news of your having sworn allegiance reaches me, I will believe what you say and withdraw my soldiers from your territories. Hurry and dispatch to me the army you are sending. Command them to march against the soldiers of Ibn Marwān who are in Wādī al-Qurā and fight them. Peace!

Al-Mukhtār summoned Shuraḥbīl b. Wars, from Hamdān, and sent him with three thousand men, mostly *mawālī*, with only seven hundred Arabs among them. He said to him, "Go and enter Medina. When you have entered it, write to me, so that I can give you my command." His intention was that, when they had entered Medina, he would send a commander to be over them in his name[221] and would order Ibn Wars to advance on Mecca, besiege

---

219. Cf. Balādhurī, *Ansāb*, V, 244: "It was during the governorship of al-Qubāʿ (al-Ḥārith b. ʿAbdallāh b. Abī Rabīʿah), and before the coming of Muṣʿab b. al-Zubayr to al-Baṣrah."

220. Full name: Ismāʿīl b. Nuʿaym al-Namarī al-Bursumī, see U. Sezgin, *Abū Miḫnaf*, 209.

221. I.e., he would replace Ibn Zubayr's governor of Medina with his own man.

Ibn al-Zubayr, and fight him there. Shuraḥbīl left for Medina. Ibn al-Zubayr, however, afraid that al-Mukhtār was merely deceiving him, sent ʿAbbās b. Sahl b. Saʿd from Mecca to Medina with two thousand men and ordered him to seek aid from the Bedouin Arabs. Ibn al-Zubayr said to him, "If you see that the men are obedient to me, welcome them. If not, use deceit against them until you have destroyed them."

This, then, is what they did. ʿAbbās b. Sahl went and met Ibn Wars at al-Raqīm.[222] Ibn Wars had deployed his forces: In charge of his right wing he had placed Salmān b. Ḥimyar al-Thawrī from Hamdān; in charge of his left wing he had placed ʿAyyāsh b. Jaʿdah al-Jadalī. His entire cavalry was in his right and left wings.
[690] [ʿAbbās] approached and greeted him. [Ibn Wars] had dismounted to walk with the foot soldiers. ʿAbbās and his forces came separated from each other and not drawn up in order. He found Ibn Wars encamped by the watering place, with his forces drawn up for battle. He approached and greeted them. Then he said, "Come apart with me here." Ibn Wars went apart with him. ʿAbbās said to him, "God have mercy on you! Aren't you under obedience to Ibn al-Zubayr?" Ibn Wars replied, "Yes." "Then," he said, "march with us against this enemy of his in Wādī al-Qurā; Ibn al-Zubayr has told me that your master[223] has made you journey here only to attack them." Ibn Wars said, "I was not commanded to obey you. I was only commanded to go to Medina and, having reached it, to follow my own judgment." ʿAbbās b. Sahl said to him, "If you are under obedience to Ibn al-Zubayr, he has ordered me to march with you and your forces against our enemy in Wādī al-Qurā." Ibn Wars said to him, "I was not ordered to obey you, nor will I follow you, until I enter Medina and write to my master for his orders." When ʿAbbās b. Sahl saw his obstinacy, he realized his disobedience. Not wishing to let him know that he saw through him, he said, "Your opinion is better; do what seems best to you. As for me, I will march to Wādī al-Qurā."

ʿAbbās b. Sahl then came and encamped by the water. He sent

222. Ms. Pet. and Balādhurī, *Ansāb*, V, 246, read "al-Raqam," which Yāqūt, *Muʿjam*, gives as a place near Medina. The reading "al-Raqīm" may reflect the Qurʾānic "al-Raqīm," the place associated with the Men of the Cave (Sūrah 18).

223. I.e., al-Mukhtār.

Ibn Wars some camels fattened for slaughter that he had brought and gave them to him as a gift. He also sent him flour and sheep that had been skinned. Ibn Wars and his men had been perishing of hunger. 'Abbās b. Sahl sent a sheep for each ten of them. So they slaughtered the sheep and busied themselves with them. They mixed with each other at the watering place; the men left their battle array and felt safe with each other. When 'Abbās b. Sahl saw how they had busied themselves, he gathered about a thousand of his bravest and most courageous men and went to the tent of Shuraḥbīl b. Wars. When Ibn Wars saw them coming toward him, he called for his men. Before a hundred men had come to him, 'Abbās b. Sahl reached him. Shuraḥbīl was saying, "O picked troops (*shurṭah*) of God, come to me! Come to me! Fight those who hold it permissible to shed innocent blood[224] and are friends of Satan, the accursed. You are followers of truth and right guidance; they have betrayed and acted wickedly." [691]

According to Abū Mikhnaf—Abū Yūsuf:[225] 'Abbās b. Sahl reached them while he was reciting:

I am the son of Sahl, a skilled horseman, no weakling who
    commits matters to others!
    Exciting admiration, bold to advance when the leader turns
    aside!
I smite the head of the celebrated hero,
    with sword on the day of battle, so that it is severed.

[Continuing,] he said: We had hardly fought for any time at all before Ibn Wars was skilled, together with seventy of the guards. 'Abbās b. Sahl raised a banner of safety for Ibn Wars's companions; they went over to it, except for about three hundred men who retreated with Salmān b. Ḥimyar al-Hamdānī and 'Ayyāsh b. Ja'dah al-Jadalī. When they fell into the hands of 'Abbās b. Sahl, he gave orders and they were killed. However, about two hundred men were released because some of the men into whose custody

224. *Al-muḥillīn*: literally, "those who make [the illicit] licit," i.e., shedders of innocent blood. Here, the word designates those who had shed, or had allowed to be shed, the blood of al-Ḥusayn. For al-Mukhtār's use of the word, see Ṭabarī, II, 599.

225. Full name: Muḥammad b. Yūsuf b. Thābit al-Anṣārī al-Khazrajī Abū Yūsuf, see U. Sezgin, *Abū Miḥnaf*, 212.

they had been placed were unwilling to kill them. They went back, but most of them died along the way.

When al-Mukhtār learned what had happened to them, and those who came back returned, he stood up to preach and said: "Verily, the wicked libertines have killed the excellent pious ones. Verily, it was a thing fulfilled and a decree decreed."

Al-Mukhtār sent Ṣāliḥ b. Mas'ūd al-Khath'amī with the following letter to Ibn al-Ḥanafiyyah:

[692] In the name of God, the Merciful, the Compassionate. To proceed: I sent you an army to humble your enemies for you and take possession of the country for you. They marched toward you, until, having approached Ṭaybah,[226] they were met by the army of the blasphemer. The latter deceived them by appeal to God and beguiled them by a promise in the name of God. When they felt at ease with them and trusted them because of this, they rose up against them and killed them. If you deem that I should send to the people of Medina a densely mustered army from me, while you send them messengers[227] from you, so that the people of Medina may know that I am under obedience to you and only sent the army at your order, do so. Then you shall find most of them readier to acknowledge your right and show pity toward you, the members of the Prophet's family, than they are toward the family of al-Zubayr, the wrongdoers and blasphemers. Peace be upon you!

Ibn al-Ḥanafiyyah wrote to him:

To proceed: When your letter reached me, I read it and took cognizance of the veneration in which you hold me and of how you intend to render me joyful. Verily, the most pleasing of all things to me is that wherein obedience is showed to God. So obey God as much as you can in what you do openly and what you do secretly. Know that

226. Ṭaybah, meaning "the fragrant," is an epithet for Medina. See Yāqūt, *Mu'jam*, s.v. Ṭaybah.

227. Ms. O: a man.

> if I wanted fighting, I would find men hastening to me and my helpers to be many. But I am keeping apart from them and waiting patiently until God judges in my favor; and He is the best of judges.[228]

Ṣāliḥ b. Mas'ūd came to Ibn al-Ḥanafiyyah, who said farewell to him, wished him peace, and gave him the letter, saying, "Tell al-Mukhtār to fear God and turn away from blood." [Continuing,] he said: I[229] said to him, "May God preserve you! Have you not written to him saying so?" Ibn al-Ḥanafiyyah said, "I have ordered him to obey God. Obedience to God gathers together all that is [693] good and prohibits all that is evil." When Ibn al-Ḥanafiyyah's letter reached al-Mukhtār, the latter proclaimed to the people: "I have been commanded with an order that gathers together piety and ease and casts away unbelief (*kufr*) and betrayal."

[The Khashabiyyah Perform the Pilgrimage]

According to Abū Ja'far [sc. al-Ṭabarī]: In this year the Khashabiyyah[230] came to Mecca and performed the pilgrimage. Their leader (*amīr*) was Abū 'Abdallāh al-Jadalī.

Why the Khashabiyyah Came to Mecca

According to Hishām [b. al-Kalbī]—Abū Mikhnaf and 'Alī b. Muḥammad [al-Madā'inī]—Maslamah b. Muḥārib, the reason was as follows: 'Abdallāh b. al-Zubayr imprisoned Muḥammad b. al-Ḥanafiyyah and those members of his family who were with him, together with seventeen notables from al-Kūfah, at Zamzam.[231] Unwilling to swear allegiance to someone upon whom the community (*ummah*) had not united in agreement,

228. Cf. Qur'ān 7:87, 10:109, and 12:80.

229. Leiden note suggests that one should read "He said...."

230. For the origin of the name, see note 207.

231. Zamzam was the sacred well within the Meccan sanctuary (*ḥaram*). See *EI*[1], s.v. Ibn al-Athīr, *Kāmil*, IV, 250, explains Ibn al-Zubayr's motive as follows: "After al-Mukhtār gained control of al-Kūfah and the Shī'ah began propagandizing for Ibn al-Ḥanafiyyah, Ibn al-Zubayr feared that people would unite in approval of Ibn al-Ḥanafiyyah. So he pressured the latter and his companions to swear allegiance to him."

they had fled to the sacred precinct (*ḥaram*). [Ibn al-Zubayr] threatened to kill them and burn them. He swore an oath to God that, if they did not swear allegiance, he would carry out his threat to them; and he set them a deadline.

Some of those with Ibn al-Ḥanafiyyah counseled him to send al-Mukhtār and the Kufans a messenger to inform them of their condition, the condition of those with them, and of Ibn al-Zubayr's threat. And so, while the guards at the door of Zamzam slept, Ibn al-Ḥanafiyyah sent three Kūfans with a letter to al-Mukhtār and the people of al-Kūfah, informing them of his condition, the condition of those with him, and of Ibn al-Zubayr's threat to kill them and burn them with fire; he asked them not to fail him, as
[694] they had failed al-Ḥusayn and the members of his family. The messengers came to al-Mukhtār and gave him the letter. He summoned the people and read them the letter, saying, "This is the letter of your Mahdī, the pure descendant of the family of your Prophet. They have been left penned up like sheep, waiting all night and all day to be killed and burned in the fire. I am not Abū Isḥāq if I do not aid them effectively and send them troop after troop of horsemen, as one torrent follows another, until woe descends on the son of the woman from the tribe of Kāhil."[232]

Al-Mukhtār sent Abū ʿAbdallāh al-Jadalī with seventy riders, men of strength. He sent Ẓabyān b. ʿUthmān,[233] a member of the Banū Tamīm, with four hundred men, Abū al-Muʿtamir with one hundred, Hāni' b. Qays with one hundred, ʿUmayr b. Ṭāriq with forty, and Yūnus b. ʿImrān with forty.

Al-Mukhtār wrote to Muḥammad b. ʿAlī[234] by way of al-Ṭufayl b. ʿĀmir and Muḥammad b. Qays about the sending of the armies to him. The men set out, one group on the heels of the other. Abū ʿAbdallāh [al-Jadalī] came to Dhāt ʿIrq[235] and encamped with seventy riders. Then ʿUmayr b. Ṭāriq overtook him with forty

---

232. This refers to Ibn al-Zubayr, whose great-grandfather, Khuwaylid, was the son of a woman (Zuhrah bint ʿAmr) from the Banū Kāhil b. Asad b. Khuzaymah. See Ibn al-Athīr, *Kāmil*, IV, 250.

233. Cf. Ṭabarī, II, 674, above (Ẓabyān b. ʿUmārah), which is probably the correct reading (ed. Leiden, *Addenda*, p. DCLXXI).

234. I.e., Muḥammad b. al-Ḥanafiyyah.

235. Dhāt ʿIrq lay two days' march northeast of Mecca, at the intersection of the two pilgrim roads from Mesopotamia to the Ḥijāz—one from al-Kūfah, the other from al-Baṣrah. See Le Strange, *Lands*, 83.

riders, and Yūnus b. ʿImrān with forty riders, so that they numbered one hundred and fifty in all. Abū ʿAbdallāh led them until they entered the sacred mosque, carrying clubs[236] and proclaiming, "Vengeance for al-Ḥusayn!" Finally they reached Zamzam. With two days remaining until the deadline, Ibn al-Zubayr had already prepared the wood to burn the prisoners. Al-Mukhtār's men chased away the guards, broke the wooden bolts (*aʿwād*) of Zamzam, went inside to Ibn al-Ḥanafiyyah, and said to him, "Leave us free to deal with God's enemy, Ibn al-Zubayr." Ibn al-Ḥanafiyyah said to them, "I do not deem it lawful to fight in God's sacred precinct." [695] Ibn al-Zubayr said, "Do you think I will release them without the pledge of allegiance from him and them?[237] Abū ʿAbdallāh al-Jadalī replied, "By the Lord of the Corner[238] and the Station,[239] the Lord of what is permitted and what is forbidden, you shall set him free, or we will contest it with you by our swords in fighting that will make the followers of falsehood doubt."[240] Ibn al-Zubayr replied, "By God, they are paltry in number.[241] If I gave my forces permission, their heads would be plucked before an hour had passed." Qays b. Mālik said to him, "By God, if you try it, I expect you will be reached before you see done to us what you want to do." Ibn al-Ḥanafiyyah restrained his companions and cautioned them against discord (*fitnah*).

Then Abū al-Muʿtamir arrived with one hundred men, Hāni' b. Qays with one hundred, and Ẓabyān b. ʿUmārah with two hundred men and the money.[242] Having entered the mosque, they shouted,

---

236. *Kāfirkūbāt*: from Arabic *kāfir*, infidel, and Persian *kūb*, smash, pound, i.e. "infidel smashers." Cf. Balādhurī, *Ansāb*, V, 231, and Ibn al-Athīr, *Kāmil*, IV, 251, on their unwillingness to carry swords in the sacred precinct.

237. Ms. O reads "you," instead of "them."

238. I.e., the corner (*rukn*) of the Kaʿbah, where the Black Stone kissed by pilgrims is affixed to the building.

239. I.e., the Station or Standing Place (*maqām*) of Abraham: according to Qur'ān 2:125 and 3:97, the Kaʿbah in Mecca was located at the place where Abraham had prayed. A stone on which Abraham stood is said still to show the imprint of his feet. See von Grunebaum, *Muhammadan Festivals*, 19.

240. Cf. Qur'ān 29:48. The meaning is that the fighting will be so violent that because of it those who follow falsehood (i.e., those who follow Ibn al-Zubayr) will doubt their allegiance.

241. Literally, "they are eaters of a head," i.e., so few that they could satisfy their stomachs with a single sheep. See Lane, *Lexicon*, I, 73.

242. Al-Mukhtār had sent 400,000 dirhams. See Ibn al-Athīr, *Kāmil*, IV, 250.

"Vengeance for al-Ḥusayn!" When Ibn al-Zubayr saw them, he was frightened of them. Muḥammad b. al-Ḥanafiyyah and those with him departed for Shiʿb ʿAlī. They were reviling Ibn al-Zubayr and asking Ibn al-Ḥanafiyyah for permission to go to fight him, but he continued to refuse. Four thousand men gathered with Muḥammad b. ʿAlī at Shiʿb [ʿAlī], and he divided the money among them.[243]

[The Siege of the Banū Tamīm in Khurāsān]

According to Abū Jaʿfar [sc. al-Ṭabarī]: In this year ʿAbdallāh b. Khāzim[244] besieged the men of Banū Tamīm in Khurāsān in order to kill those of them who had killed his son Muḥammad.

According to ʿAlī b. Muḥammad [al-Madā'inī]—al-Ḥasan b. Rushayd al-Jūzjānī[245]—al-Ṭufayl b. Mirdās al-ʿAmmī,[246] who
[696] said: When the Banū Tamīm dispersed in Khurāsān during the days of Ibn Khāzim, a number of their skilled horsemen—between seventy and eighty—went to the fortress of Fartanā.[247] They made ʿUthmān b. Bishr b. al-Muḥtafiz al-Muzanī[248] their leader, and with him were Shuʿbah b. Ẓahīr al-Nahshalī, Ward b. al-Falaq al-ʿAnbarī, Zuhayr b. Dhu'ayb al-ʿAdawī, Jayhān b. Mashjaʿah al-Ḍabbī, al-Ḥajjāj b. Nāshib al-ʿAdawī, and Raqabah b. al-Ḥurr, with the skilled horsemen of the Banū Tamīm. [Continuing,] he said: Ibn Khāzim came against them. He besieged them and dug a fortified trench. [Continuing,] he said: The Banū Tamīm would come out to fight him and then return to the fortress.

[Continuing,] he said: One day Ibn Khāzim came out of his

243. Except for mentioning his presence at the pilgrimage in 68 (see Ṭabarī, II, 782, below), Ṭabarī does not record the subsequent fate of Ibn al-Ḥanafiyyah. See Ibn al-Athīr, *Kāmil*, IV, 251–54; Ibn Saʿd, *Ṭabaqāt*, V, 66–86.

244. ʿAbdallāh b. Khāzim al-Sulamī was the governor of Khurāsān province. For the events leading up to the siege, see Ṭabarī, II, 488–96, 593–97; also *EI*[2], s.v. ʿAbd Allāh b. Khāzim.

245. See Rotter, "Zur Überlieferung einiger historischer Werke Madā'inīs," 127; Dhahabī, *Mīzān*, I, 228.

246. The Banū ʿAmm were a subtribe of the Tamīm. See Rotter, op. cit., 119–20.

247. The fortress of Fartanā was located at Marw al-Rūdh. See Yāqūt, *Muʿjam*, s.v.

248. His *nisbah* is given as al-Māzinī below (Ṭabarī, II, 700). The latter may be correct, since the Banū Māzin were a subtribe of Tamīm, while the Muzaynah (*nisbah*, al-Muzanī) were a separate Muḍar tribe (*Lisān*, s.v.).

trench with six thousand men in battle order, and the men from the fortress came out to meet him. ʿUthmān b. Bishr b. al-Muḥtafiz said to the Banū Tamīm, "Avoid Ibn Khāzim today, for I do not think you have strength to prevail against him." But Zuhayr b. Dhu'ayb al-ʿAdawī swore that he would divorce his wife if he retreated before he had broken their battle lines.[249] Beside them there was a riverbed into which water came during the winter, but there was no water in it at that time. Zuhayr descended into it and advanced. None of Ibn Khāzim's men noticed him until he attacked them and pressed back those in the forefront against those in the rear. They[250] circled around. He hurried back, and they followed him on both sides of the riverbed, shouting at him, but with no one going down[251] to fight him, until he had reached the spot where he had climbed down. Coming out [of the riverbed], he attacked them, so that they got out of his way until he [697]
made his way back.

[Continuing,] he said: Ibn Khāzim said to his men. When you fight with Zuhayr, put hooks on your spears, and grapple them into his gear, if you gain the upper hand over him. One day, Zuhayr came out against them—they had attached hooks to their spears in readiness for him. They fought him and caught four spears in his armor, but he turned to attack them, and their hands became unsteady. They let go of their spears, and he went back to the fortress dragging four spears. [Continuing,] he said: Ibn Khāzim sent Ghazwān b. Jaz' al-ʿAdawī to Zuhayr, saying to him, "Say to Zuhayr, 'If I guaranteed your safety, gave you a hundred thousand [dirhams], and granted you Bāsār[252] as a means of support (*ṭuʿmah*), would you be loyal to me?'" Zuhayr replied to Ghazwān, "Woe unto you! How can I be loyal to people who killed al-Ashʿath b. Dhu'ayb?" Ghazwān let word of this slip out in the presence of Mūsā, the son of ʿAbdallāh b. Khāzim.

---

249. An oath to divorce one's wife was one of the most serious oaths that could be made.

250. Ms. O: he.

251. Ms. O: no one daring to go down.

252. Ms. "Bāsān"; Ms. O, "Maysān." Ed. Leiden, *Addenda*, p. DCLXXI, amends to "Bāsār" on the basis of Bāsārā, a city in Khurāsān mentioned by Ibn Khurradādhbih (*al-Masālik wa-al-mamālik*, 37, l. 8), and Bāsārān, mentioned by al-Yaʿqūbī (*Kitāb-al-buldān*, 289, l. 18).

[Continuing,] he said: When the siege became too long for the Banū Tamīm, they sent a message to Ibn Khāzim, saying, "Let us leave, and we will disperse." He replied, "Not unless you submit to my judgment." They said, "We will submit to your judgment." Zuhayr said to them, "May your mothers be bereft of you![253] By God, he will kill you to the last man. If you are content to die, die as honorable men. Let us all go out: Either you will all die, or some of you will escape and some will die. I swear to God that if
[698] you attack them with true bravery, they will make a way for you as broad as the road to al-Mirbad. If you wish, I will be in front of you; and, if you wish, I will be behind you." [Continuing,] he said: They refused. So he said, "Then I will show you." He and Raqabah b. al-Ḥurr went out (Raqabah had a young Turkish lad [*ghulām*] of his with him), along with Shuʿbah b. Ẓahīr.

[Continuing,] he said: They attacked with unusual vigor, so that the men made way for them and they advanced. Zuhayr, however, returned to his companions. Entering the fortress, he said to his companions, "You see! So obey me." (Raqabah and his lad and Shuʿbah continued to press forward.) But Zuhayr's companions said, "Among us there are men who are too weak for this and who desire to live."[254] Zuhayr said, "May God bring evil upon you! Will you abandon your companions? By God, I will not be the most timorous among you at the time of death!"

[Continuing,] he said: So they opened the fortress and came down. Ibn Khāzim sent someone to them and had them bound. They were brought to him one by one. He wanted to spare them, but his son Mūsā refused, saying, "By God, if you pardon them, I will fall on my sword so that it comes out of my back!" ʿAbdallāh [b. Khāzim] said to him, "By God, I know what you are ordering me to do is wrong." Then he killed all but three of them. [Continuing,] he said: One of those three was al-Ḥajjāj b. Nāshib al-ʿAdawī. He had shot Ibn Khāzim while the latter was besieging them and had broken his tooth. Ibn Khāzim had sworn that if he captured him, he would kill him or cut off his hand. Now al-Ḥajjāj was a youth, and some of the Banū Tamīm who had kept

253. This imprecation is not as strong as the literal translation suggests, but more like "You fools!"

254. Ms. O: They said, "We are too weak for this and desire to live."

aloof from ʿAmr b. Ḥanẓalah spoke to Ibn Khāzim concerning him. One of them said, "He is my cousin and a young, ignorant lad. Give him to me." [Continuing,] he said: Ibn Khāzim gave him to him, saying, "Get away, and let me not see you." [Continuing,] he said: There was also Jayhān b. Mashjaʿah al-Ḍabbī, who had thrown himself on Ibn Khāzim's son Muḥammad the day the latter was killed.[255] Ibn Khāzim said, "Let this mule that walks [on two feet] go." And there was a man from the Banū Saʿd who had said on the day they met Ibn Khāzim, "Turn back from the skilled horseman of Muḍar."

[Continuing,] he said: They brought Zuhayr b. Dhu'ayb. They [699] wanted to carry him bound, but he refused and walked with his legs shackled, until he sat down before Ibn Khāzim. The latter said to him, "What thanks will you give if I release you and give you Bāsār as a possession?" Zuhayr said, "If you did nothing but forbear to shed my blood, I would thank you." But Ibn Khāzim's son Mūsā stood up and said, "Will you kill the female hyena and leave the male? kill the lioness and leave the lion?" Ibn Khāzim said, "Woe unto you! Shall we kill a man like Zuhayr? Who will there be to fight the Muslims' enemies? who to protect the women of the Arabs?" Mūsā replied, "By God, had you—even you!—participated in shedding the blood of my brother, I would kill you." Then a man from the Banū Sulaym approached Ibn Khāzim and said, "I beseech you to be mindful of God concerning Zuhayr." But Mūsā said to him, "Use him as a stud for your daughters!" Ibn Khāzim became angry and ordered Zuhayr to be killed. Zuhayr said to him, "I have a request." "What is it?" he asked. "That you kill me separately," he said, "and not mix my blood with that of these base men; for I told them not to do what they did. I commanded them to die as honorable men and come out against you with drawn swords. By God, had they done so, they would have given this little son of yours a fright and would have made him too worried about his own life to seek vengeance for his brother. But they refused. Had they done it, not a man of them would have been killed before he had killed several men." Ibn Khāzim gave orders concerning him, and he was taken aside and killed.

---

255. He had tried to prevent the murder. See Ṭabarī, II, 594.

According to Maslamah b. Muḥārib: Whenever al-Aḥnaf b. Qays mentioned them, he said, "God curse Ibn Khāzim! As the price for his son, a foolish and stupid boy not worth anything of value,[256] he killed many men from the Banū Tamīm. Had he killed but one of them for him, he would have done enough. [Continuing,] he said: The Banū ʿAdī asserted that, when they tried to carry Zuhayr b. Dhuʾayb, he refused. Leaning on his spear
[700] and gathering his legs together, he jumped the trench.

When news of their death reached al-Ḥarīsh b. Hilāl,[257] he said:

You who find fault with me, I did nothing blameworthy in the fight with them;
my sword struck their chief and penetrated to the bone.
You who find fault with me, I did not turn away until men dispersed
and I found no place to advance.
You who find fault with me, the sword has destroyed me:
Whoever fights long with heroes returns wounded.
My eyes, if you shed tears, pour out
the blood that adheres closely to me, before pouring out any [other] blood.
After Zuhayr and the son of Bishr followed each other [in death],
and after Ward, shall I hope for any gain in Khurāsān?
You who find fault with me, how many days of war have I witnessed,
wheeling to charge again when the bad horseman drew back!

By "after Zuhayr," he meant Zuhayr b. Dhuʾayb. "The son of Bishr" is ʿUthmān b. Bishr b. al-Muḥtafiz al-Māzinī. Together with Ward b. al-Falaq al-ʿAnbarī, they were killed on that day, and Sulaymān b. al-Muḥtafiz, Bishr's brother, was also killed.

[Those in Office during the Year]

According to Abū Jaʿfar [sc. al-Ṭabarī]: ʿAbdallāh b. al-Zubayr led the pilgrimage this year. Muṣʿab b. al-Zubayr was in charge of

256. With no change of consonants, Arabic *ʿilq,* "something of value," can be read as *ʿalaq,* "a blood clot."

257. Al-Ḥarīsh b. Hilāl b. Qudāmah is mentioned as a skilled horseman of the tribe of Tamīm, famous for his exploits in Khurāsān (Ibn Durayd, *Ishtiqāq,* 257).

Medina on behalf of his brother, ʿAbdallāh. Al-Ḥārith b. ʿAbdallāh b. Abī Rabīʿah was in charge of al-Baṣrah, and Hishām b. Hubayrah was in charge of its judiciary. Al-Mukhtār controlled al-Kūfah, and ʿAbdallāh b. Khāzim Khurāsān.

[Ibrāhīm b. al-Ashtar Goes to Fight ʿUbaydallāh b. Ziyād]

In this year, Ibrāhīm b. al-Ashtar went out, heading toward ʿUbaydallāh b. Ziyād, to fight him. this took place eight nights before the end of the month of Dhū al-Ḥijjah.[258]

According to Hishām b. Muḥammad [al-Kalbī]—Abū Mikhnaf—al-Naḍr b. Ṣāliḥ (who was alive at that time), Fuḍayl b. Khadīj[259] (who witnessed the event), and one or more others, who said:[260] After al-Mukhtār finished dealing with the people of [Jabbānat] al-Sabīʿ and the people of al-Kunāsah, Ibrāhīm b. al-Ashtar re- [701] mained [in the city] only two days before al-Mukhtār sent him forth in the same direction as before to fight the Syrians. He left on Saturday, eight nights before the end of the month of Dhū al-Ḥijjah in the year 66. With him, al-Mukhtār sent his most eminent companions, skilled horsemen and valiant men who had seen and experienced war. Qays b. Ṭahfah al-Nahdī went out with him in charge of the fourth of the people of Medina.[261] He appointed ʿAbdallāh b. Ḥayyah al-Asadī commander of the fourth of Madhḥij and Asad, sent al-Aswad b. Jarād al-Kindī in charge of the fourth of Kindah and Rabīʿah, and sent Ḥabīb b. Munqidh

258. I.e., 21 (or 22, if the month had 30 days) Dhū al-Ḥijjah 66, corresponding to 19 or 20 July, 686. Balādhurī, *Ansāb*, V, 248, reads: "six (some say eight) nights into Dhū al-Ḥijjah." Neither date is consistent with the date given above (Ṭabarī, II, 668) for the battle of Jabbānat al-Sabīʿ. There is a discussion in Wellhausen, *Oppositionsparteien*, 84n.

259. Fuḍayl b. Khadīj al-Kindī, see U. Sezgin, *Abū Miḥnaf*, 201.

260. The verb *qālū* is in the plural, implying a composite account, not the words of one observer. See the discussion of Abū Mikhnaf's methods in U. Sezgin, *Abū Miḥnaf*, 68.

261. Cf. Tabari, II, 1382 (anno 101): "The people of the Highland (*al-ʿĀliyah*) included the tribes of Quraysh, Kinānah, Azd, Bajīlah, Khathʿam, all of Qays ʿAylan, and Muzaynah. In al-Kūfah, the people of al-ʿĀliyah are called 'the fourth of the people of Medina.' In al-Baṣrah, they are called 'the fifth of the Highland (*al-ʿĀliyah*).'"

al-Thawrī from Hamdān in charge of the fourth of Tamīm and Hamdān.

Al-Mukhtār went out with [Ibn al-Ashtar] to escort him. When [Ibn al-Ashtar] reached Dayr ʿAbd al-Raḥmān b. Umm al-Ḥakam,[262] al-Mukhtār's companions met him with the Chair (*al-Kursī*),[263] borne upon a gray mule on which they used to carry it. They halted for him on the bridge. The man in charge of the Chair, Ḥawshab al-Bursumī, was saying, "O Lord, preserve us alive in Thy obedience, and help us against enemies; be mindful of us, forget us not, and protect us." His companions answered, "Amen, amen." Fuḍayl continued: I heard Ibn Nawf al-Hamdānī say: Al-Mukhtār said:

By the Lord of "the loosed ones [sent out] successively,"[264]
we will kill rank after rank
And thousand upon thousand deviators.[265]

Fuḍayl continued: When al-Mukhtār and Ibn al-Ashtar reached them, they crowded together in a great throng on the bridge. Together with Ibrāhīm b. al-Ashtar, al-Mukhtār proceeded to the bridges of Ra's al-Jālūt, which are beside Dayr ʿAbd al-Raḥmān. Behold, the people with the Chair had halted on the bridges of Ra's al-Jālūt, calling [on God] for assistance.

[702] When al-Mukhtar arrived between the bridge of Dayr ʿAbd al-Raḥmān and the bridges of Ra's al-Jālūt, he halted, since he wanted to go back. He said to Ibn al-Ashtar, "Receive three charges from me: Fear God in your secret and public actions; march quickly; and, when you meet your foe, fight them as soon as you meet them. If you meet them by night, and can do so, do not wait for morning before attacking them. If you meet them by day, do not wait for night to descend on them before summoning them to the judgment of God." Then he said, "Have you committed my advice

262. Dayr ʿAbd al-Raḥmān was located about one stage north of al-Nukhaylah. See *EI*², s.v.; al-ʿAlī, *"Minṭaqat al-Kūfah,"* 240.

263. For a discussion of this cult object, see Ṭabarī, II, 702–06.

264. Qur'ān 77:1.

265. *Al-qāsiṭīn*: ʿAlī applied the word to his opponents at Ṣiffīn on the basis of Qur'ān 72:15: "Those who have surrendered sought rectitude, but as for those who have deviated, they have become firewood for Gehenna!" See Lane, *Lexicon*, VII, 2523, and Jafri, *Origins*, 96.

to memory?" Ibn al-Ashtar said, "Yes." "God accompany you," said al-Mukhtār and turned back. Ibrāhīm's army had been located at the site of Ḥammām A'yan, and from there he set forth with his army.

According to Abū Mikhnaf—Fuḍayl b. Khadīj, who said: After al-Mukhtār turned back, Ibrāhīm went on with his forces until he reached the people with the Chair. They were circling round it with hands upraised to heaven, praying for assistance. "O God," said Ibrahim, "do not take us to task for what the foolish ones have done after the manner of the Children of Israel—by Him in Whose hand my soul lies!—when they circled about their calf."[266] After Ibrāhīm and his forces crossed the bridge, the people with the Chair went back.

An Explanation of the Chair Whereby al-Mukhtār and His Companions Prayed for Assistance[267]

According to Abū Ja'far [sc. al-Ṭabarī]: Its origin was as follows, according to what I was told by 'Abdallāh b. Aḥmad b. Shabbawayh, from his father, from Sulaymān,[268] from 'Abdallāh b. al- [703]
Mubārak,[269] from Isḥāq b. Yaḥyā[270] b. Ṭalḥah, from Ma'bad b. Khālid [al-Jadalī], from Ṭufayl b. Ja'dah b. Hubayrah, who said: I was once in need of money. While in that state, I went out one day and came upon an oil merchant, a neighbor of mine, who had a chair covered with a thick [coat of] filth. It occurred to me that I should speak to al-Mukhtār about it. So I went back and sent

266. The story of the Golden Calf worshipped by the Children of Israel is found in Qur'ān 7:147ff. There is also an echo of Qur'ān 2:286 and 7:155.

267. In an article tracing the survival of Persian royal symbolism into Islam, S. Shaked has drawn a connection between the veneration of 'Alī's Chair and Persian throne symbolism. That many of al-Mukhtār's followers were Persians may support Shaked's view. On the other hand, the poem by A'shā Hamdān quoted below (Ṭabarī, II, 704) identifies the venerators of the Chair as Arabs from the tribe of Hamdān. See Shaul Shaked, "From Iran to Islam," 81–82.

268. An *isnād* in Ṭabarī, II, 208 gives the name in fuller form as Abū Ṣāliḥ Sulaymān b. Ṣāliḥ.

269. 'Abdallāh b. al-Mubārak b. Wāḍiḥ al-Ḥanẓalī al-Tamīmī Abū 'Abd al-Raḥmān (b. 118/736, d. 181/797 in Hīt) was a famous traditionist, historian, and Sufi, active both as transmitter of earlier works and as an author in his own right. See F. Sezgin, *GAS*, II, 95.

270. Ms. O: "'Abdallāh."

word to the oil merchant, saying, "Send me the chair." He sent it to me. I went to al-Mukhtār and said, "I have been concealing something from you which I do not think I ought to. It seems best that I mention it to you." "What is it?" he asked. I answered, "A chair on which [my father] Ja'dah b. Hubayrah[271] used to sit as if he thought that in regard to it there was a vestige of some knowledge."[272] [Al-Mukhtār] said, "Praise God! And you put the matter off until today? Send to him! Send to him!" [Continuing,] he said: When it was washed, it turned out to be tamarisk wood, and it shone from the oil it had absorbed. It was brought to al-Mukhtār covered. He ordered me to be paid twelve thousand [dirhams], and then he summoned to congregational prayer.

Ma'bad b. Khālid al-Jadalī continued, saying: Ṭufayl b. Ja'dah took me and Ismā'īl b. Ṭalḥah b. 'Ubaydallāh and Shabath b. Rib'ī. People were running to the mosque. Al-Mukhtār said, "Nothing has existed among past communities but that its like will exist in this community. Among the Children of Israel there was the Ark, in which there was a remnant of what the family of Moses and the family of Aaron left behind.[273] Among us, this is like the Ark. Uncover it!" When they removed its draperies, the
[704] Saba'iyyah[274] stood up, raised their hands, and shouted "God is great!" three times. Shabath b. Rib'ī stood up and said, "People of Muḍar, do not become infidels." But they pushed him aside and drove him away; they shunned him and put him out. (Isḥāq [b. Yaḥyā b. Ṭalḥah] said: "By God, I hope these words will be accounted to the credit of Shabath!") Presently, someone said, "Behold, 'Ubaydallāh b. Ziyād has encamped with the Syrians at Bājumayrā."[275] So they took the Chair out on a mule. It was covered; seven men held it on its right and seven on its left. The

---

271. Ja'dah was the nephew of 'Alī; hence, it would be plausible for him to possess some relic of 'Alī. See below, Ṭabarī, II, 705.

272. The Arabic *atharah* (*uthrah*, or *athrah*) *min 'ilm* echoes Qur'ān 46:4. The meaning is that Ja'dah used to sit upon the chair as if family tradition reported that it had belonged to 'Alī. See Lane, *Lexicon*, s.v. *atharah*. The reading in Ibn al-Athīr, *Kāmil*, IV, 258 (*atharan min* 'Alī, "a relic of 'Alī") should be rejected on textual grounds as a *lectio facilior*.

273. Cf. Qur'ān 2:248.

274. See note 56 above.

275. Bājumayrā (for which Mss. O and Pet read "Bākhumayrā") is near Takrīt. See Yāqūt, *Mu'jam*, s.v.

Syrians suffered a massacre such as they had never suffered before, and this tempted them even further; they advanced until they vied with each other in infidelity. I said, "We belong to God!"[276] and I regretted what I had done. The people spoke about the matter, and the Chair was made to disappear; I never saw it again.

According to ʿAbdallāh [b. Aḥmad b. Shabbawayh]—his father —Abū Ṣāliḥ [Sulaymān b. Ṣāliḥ]: On this subject, Aʿshā Hamdān composed the following, as I have been told on the authority of someone other than ʿAbdallāh [b. al-Mubārak]:

I bear witness against you that you are Saba'iyyah;
O picked troops of polytheism,[277] I know you well!
I swear that your Chair is no Sakīnah,[278]
even if cloths have been draped over it;
And that it is not like the Ark among us, even if [705]
Shibām, Nahd, and Khārif[279] walk around it.
I am a man who loves the family of Muḥammad;
I have followed a revelation contained in the books [of the Qur'ān].
I followed ʿAbdallāh [b. al-Zubayr],
when the hoary-headed and noble men of Quraysh, one after another, followed him.[280]

---

276. See note 156 above.

277. *Shirk*, literally "associating [other gods with Allāh]," is a sin that would render a person outside the Islamic community.

278. Arabic *sakīnah* is a loan word from Hebrew *shĕkhīnāh*, "dwelling," specifically the Divine Presence in the Tabernacle in the wilderness (Exod. 25:8) and in the temple in Jerusalem. In Qur'ān 2:248, the word occurs in a context referring to the Ark of the Covenant: a prophet (unnamed) tells the Children of Israel, skeptical about whether Saul is really a God-appointed king over them, that "The sign of his kingship is that the Ark will come to you, in it a *Sakīnah* from your Lord, and a remnant of what the folk of Moses and Aaron's folk left behind, the angels bearing it." Arabic exegesis explains the word in many ways, either abstract, "a [cause of] tranquillity" (based perhaps on the Christian notion of the Holy Spirit as *paraclētos*, "comforter"), or as some sort of physical image that inspired fear in the enemy. See *EI*^{1}, s.v.

279. Shibām, Nahd, and Khārif are clans of the tribe of Hamdān.

280. The *Dīwān* of Aʿshā Hamdān (Poem 31), adds four extra lines: "Even though the tribesmen of Shākir circle round it, touch its wood, and devise, it will not help. Because of it, we ourselves have become obedient to Ibn al-Zubayr: among us there is no deception, nor are precedents cut off. The outcome, I think, will be in favor of the family of Muḥammad; the wronged will be helped, and the fearful become secure. My Lord will gather together a community that has become fragmented, among whom wars and enmities have raged."

Also, al-Mutawakkil al-Laythī said:

Tell Abū Isḥāq, if you come to him,
that I am a nonbeliever as regards your Chair.
[The tribe of] Shibām goes leaping round its boards,
and [the tribe of] Shākir ascribes inspiration to it.
Their eyes are as red around it
as if they were swelling chickpeas.

Abū Mikhnāf, however, on the authority of certain of his shaykhs, mentions a story of this Chair different from the one that ʿAbdallāh b. Aḥmad mentions with the chain of authorities we have given going back to Ṭufayl b. Jaʿdah. We have been told Abū Mikhnaf's account according to Hishām b. Muḥammad [al-Kalbī]—[Abū Mikhnaf]—Hishām b. ʿAbd al-Raḥmān and his son, al-Ḥakam b. Hishām: Al-Mukhtar said to the family of Jaʿdah b. Hubayrah b. Abī Wahb al-Makhzūmī (Jaʿdah's mother was Umm Hāniʾ bint Abī Ṭālib, the full sister of ʿAlī b. Abī Ṭālib), "Give me the Chair of ʿAlī b. Abī Ṭālib." "No," they replied, "by God, we
[706] do not have it, nor do we know whence we can obtain it." "Do not be foolish," he said. "Go and bring it to me." [Continuing,] he said: Thereupon, the family suspected that he would accept from them any chair they would bring him, saying it was the one. So they brought a chair and said, "That is it," and he accepted it. [Continuing,] he said: Having wrapped it with silk and brocade, the men of Shibām and Shākir and the chief companions of al-Mukhtār marched out with it.

According to Abū Mikhnaf—Mūsā b. ʿĀmir Abū al-Ashʿar al-Juhanī: When Ibn al-Zubayr was told about the Chair, he said, "Why don't some of the Jundabs of Azd go to see it?"[281] [Continuing,] Abū al-Ashʿar said: When the Chair was obtained, the

---

281. For the idiom, *"ayna . . . ʿan,"* see Dozy, *Supplément*, II, 46. Cf. the parallel passage in Balādhurī, *Ansāb*, V, 242: "Ibn ʿUmar, upon being told that al-Mukhtār had sought out ʿAlī's Chair and was carrying it about on a gray mule, and that his companions were encircling it, praying for rain and victory, said, 'Why don't the Jundabs of Azd go to see it? One of *them* would not be deceived by it.'" (Read *lā yaghtarru bihī*, for the printed edition's *lā yuʿaqribuhū*.) The allusion is to a pious companion of the Prophet, Jundab b. Kaʿb al-Azdī, who was so incensed by the impostures of a sorcerer in al-Kūfah (the man had pretended to cut off his assistant's head and reattach it), that he struck off the sorcerer's head. He is supposed to have said, "If he is genuine, let him revive himself." Al-Mukhtār, in other words, needs

first person to serve as its keeper was Mūsā b. Abī Mūsā al-Ash'arī, who used to come to al-Mukhtār and serve him when [al-Mukhtār] first came, because his mother was Umm Kulthum bint al-Faḍl b. al-'Abbās b. 'Abd al-Muṭṭalib. Afterwards, he was reproved and became ashamed of it. He therefore gave it to Ḥawshab al-Bursumī, who was the man in charge of it until al-Mukhtār perished.

[Continuing,] he said: One of al-A'shā's paternal uncles was a man called Abū Umāmah. He used to come into the *majlis*[282] of his companions and say, "Today there has been established for us a [source of] inspiration the like of which men have never heard of. In it there is news of what will come to be."

According to Abū Mikhnaf—Mūsā b. 'Āmir: It was 'Abdallāh b. Nawf who used to do this for them, and he used to say, "Al-Mukhtār commanded me to do it." But al-Mukhtār disavowed him.

---

someone like Jundab to deal with his impostures. See Ibn Ḥajar, *Iṣābah*, I, 511–13; *Aghānī*, IV, 185–86.

282. The sitting place or assembly.

[707]

The Events of the Year 67

(July 28, 686–July 17, 687)

Among the events of this year was the death of ʿUbaydallāh b. Ziyād and of the Syrians who were with him.

The Death of ʿUbaydallāh b. Ziyād

According to Hishām b. Muḥammad [al-Kalbī]—Abū Mikhnaf—Abū al-Ṣalt [al-Taymī]—Abū Saʿīd al-Ṣayqal, who said: We departed with Ibn al-Ashtar, heading toward ʿUbaydallāh b. Ziyād and the Syrians who were with him. We went out quickly, not turning aside, wanting to encounter him before he entered the land of Iraq.[283] [Continuing,] he said: We arrived well before him at the borders of the land of Iraq and pushed on into the land of al-Mawṣil. Hurrying toward him and marching quickly, we met him at the Khāzir [River], beside a village called Bārʿītā, five *farsakhs* from al-Mawṣil.[284] In charge of his vanguard, Ibn al-Ashtar had

283. See above, Ṭabarī, II, 643. "Iraq" means the part of Mesopotamia south of Takrīt; al-Mawṣil constituted a separate province.

284. I.e., about 15 miles east of al-Mawṣil. The Khāzir (or Khāzar) River is a

placed al-Ṭufayl b. Laqīṭ, from the Wahbīl [clan] of [the tribe of] Nakhaʿ, a fellow tribesman of his and a brave and valiant man. Having approached Ibn Ziyād, Ibn al-Ashtar drew Ḥumayd b. Ḥurayth close to himself and began to march only in battle order. He drew all his forces close to himself, with his horsemen and foot soldiers, and began to advance with them all, not dividing them. He did, however, send al-Ṭufayl b. Laqīṭ ahead with advance forces, so that he entered that village.

[Continuing,] he said: ʿUbaydallāh b. Ziyād came and encamped near them on the bank of the Khāzir. ʿUmayr b. al-Ḥubāb [708]
al-Sulamī[285] sent word to Ibn al-Ashtar, saying, "I am on your side and want to meet you tonight." Ibn al-Ashtar sent to him, saying, "Meet me, if you wish." The whole of Qays was in al-Jazīrah and were[286] opponents of Marwān and the family of Marwān. At that time, Marwān's army was from Kalb. Their commander was Ibn Baḥdal.

ʿUmayr came to Ibn al-Ashtar at night and swore allegiance to him, informing him that he was in charge of his commander's right wing, and promising him that he would fall back with his men. Ibn al-Ashtar said, "What do you think best? Should I dig myself in and wait two or three days?" ʿUmayr b. al-Ḥubāb replied, "Don't do it! We belong to God! What do they want but this? If they keep putting you off and procrastinating, it will be better for them. They greatly outnumber you; and the few gain no advantage over the many by procrastination. Rather, attack them, for they have been filled with fear of you. Come at them; for if they draw within sight of your companions and fight them day after day and time after time, they will feel at ease with them and gain courage against them." Ibrāhīm [b. al-Ashtar] said, "Now I know you are advising me sincerely. You have spoken the truth. What you have

---

tributary of the Greater Zāb, which flows into the Tigris south of al-Mawṣil. (Yāqūt, *Muʿjam*, s.vv. Khāzir and Zāb). The mss. show uncertainty about the name of the village. Ed. Leiden, *Addenda*, p. DCLXXI, amends the Ms. Pet reading Bārbīthā to Bārʿītā on the basis of Syriac Bārʿidtā. Balādhurī, *Ansāb*, V, 248, reads "Bārītā," which Goitein argues may reflect the actual pronunciation.

285. ʿUmayr b. al-Ḥubāb's tribe, the Banū Sulaym (*nisbah* al-Sulamī), were part of the Qays ʿAylān; thus there was a tribal element in his offer. Cf. above, Ṭabarī, II, 643; and the parallel account in Dīnawarī, *Akhbār*, 301–02.

286. Mss. O and Co: some of them were.

said is the right idea; indeed, my commander recommended this idea to me and commanded me to follow it." ʿUmayr said, "Do not go against his opinion. War has tested the old man,[287] and he has experienced in it what we have not experienced.[288] Rise early and fight with the man."

ʿUmayr then went back. That night, Ibn al-Ashtar kept his
[709] guards on alert all night long, and not a wink of sleep entered his eyes. At the crack of dawn he set his men in order, formed his battalions, and gave orders to his commanders. He sent out Sufyān b. Yazīd b. al-Mughaffal al-Azdī in charge of his right wing, and ʿAlī b. Mālik al-Jushamī (the brother of Abū al-Aḥwaṣ) in charge of his left wing. He sent out ʿAbd al-Raḥmān b. ʿAbdallāh (Ibrāhīm b. al-Ashtar's half-brother by his mother) in charge of the horsemen. Since his horsemen were few, he kept them near him, so that they were in the right wing and the main part of the army. He placed al-Ṭufayl b. Laqīṭ in charge of his foot soldiers, and his banner was with Muzāḥim b. Mālik. [Continuing,] he said: When dawn broke, Ibrāhīm b. al-Ashtar led them in the morning prayer in the twilight. Then he led them out and lined them up, placing the commanders of the fourths in their positions. He made the commander of the right wing join the right wing, the commander of the left wing join the left wing, and the commander of the foot soldiers join the foot soldiers. He gathered the horsemen to himself, with ʿAbd al-Raḥmān b. ʿAbdallāh, his half-brother on his mother's side, in charge of them, so that they were in the midst of the men.

Ibrāhīm dismounted and walked. He said to the men, "March," and the men marched with him at a gentle pace, advancing little by little, until he reached the top of a great hill overlooking the enemy. There he sat down; none of the men of the enemy had yet moved. He dispatched ʿAbdallāh b. Zuhayr al-Salūlī, who rode a horse of his that shone with sleekness. Ibrāhīm said to him, "Ride your horse at a gallop and bring me a report about them." ʿAbdallāh departed. Shortly thereafter he came back and said, "The enemy have come out in a state of confusion and dismay. One of their men met me, and all he could say over and over again

---

287. Literally, "Wars have bitten into him." ʿUbaydallāh b. Ziyād is meant.
288. Another reading is, "what no one else has experienced."

was, 'O Shī'ah of Abū Turāb![289] O Shī'ah of the liar al-Mukhtār!' I said, 'The issue between you and us is too momentous for abuse.' He replied to me, 'O enemy of God, to what are you summoning us? You are fighting without an *imām*.'[290] I said to him, 'No, it is vengeance for al-Ḥusayn, the son[291] of the Messenger of God. Hand over to us 'Ubaydallāh b. Ziyād, who killed the son of the [710] Messenger of God and the lord of the youth of Paradise, so that we can kill him to avenge some of our *mawālī* whom he killed with al-Ḥusayn; for we do not consider him al-Ḥusayn's equal, that we might agree to his being retaliation for him. If you hand him over to us and we kill him for some of our *mawālī* whom he killed, we will set between you and us the Book of God or any righteous Muslim you wish as mediator.' He said to me, 'We had experience with you another time involving this sort of thing'—he meant two mediators—'and you acted treacherously.' 'How so?' I asked. He said, 'We appointed two mediators between you and us, but you were not satisfied with their decision.' I said to him, 'You have produced no proof [of treachery]. Our peace was made on condition that if both mediators agreed on a man, we would follow their decision, accept him, and swear allegiance to him. But they did not agree on one man and went each his own way. God did not direct and rightly dispose the two of them.' 'Who are you?' he asked. I told him and asked him, 'Who are you?' 'Gee up!' he said to his mule, urging it on. I said to him, 'You haven't given me my due! This is the beginning of your treachery.'"

[Continuing,] he said: Ibn al-Ashtar called for a horse of his, mounted it, and passed by all the standard-bearers, stopping beside each banner that he passed. Then he said, "O helpers of the religion [of Islam], partisans of truth, picked army of God, here is 'Ubaydallāh b. Marjānah,[292] the murderer of al-Ḥusayn, the son

---

289. Abū Turāb ("Father of Dust," or "Dusty") was a nickname given to 'Alī by Muḥammad. Accounts differ about why it was given and whether it was meant to be laudatory or pejorative. The Umayyads, as is clear from this passage, used it pejoratively, sometimes calling the Shī'ah "Turābiyyah." Shī'ī writers explain it as laudatory. See Ṭabarī, I, 1271–72 for one version of the story; full discussion in Kohlberg, "Abū Turāb," 347–52.

290. Another possible translation: "You are fighting on the side of a non-*imām*."

291. I.e., the descendant. He was Muḥammad's grandson.

292. Marjānah was the mother of 'Ubaydallāh b. Ziyād (Ibn Qutaybah, *Ma'ārif*, 347). Calling a man by his mother's name was an insult.

of ʿAlī and of Fāṭimah, the daughter of the Messenger of God. He prevented him, his daughters, his wives, and his partisans from reaching the water of the Euphrates and drinking of it when they were in sight of it. He prevented him from coming to the son of his paternal uncle[293] so as to reach a peaceful settlement with him. He prevented him from going back to his dwelling and his family. He prevented him from traveling anywhere in the wide world, until he slew him and slew the members of his family. By
[711] God, Pharaoh never did to the noble sons of the Children of Israel what the son of Marjānah did to the members of the family of the Messenger of God—God bless him and grant him peace!—people from whom God removed uncleanness and whom he truly purified.[294] God has brought him to you and has brought you to him. By God, I hope God has brought you and him together in this place only that He may give relief to your hearts through the shedding of his blood by your hands; for God knows that you have come forth in zeal for the family of your Prophet."

Ibrāhīm b. al-Ashtar went between the right wing and the left. He went among all the men, arousing their desire for holy war,[295] and urging them to fight. Then he returned and dismounted under his banner, and the enemy advanced toward him. Ibn Ziyād had placed al-Ḥuṣayn b. Numayr al-Sakūnī in charge of his right wing, ʿUmayr b. al-Ḥubāb al-Sulamī in charge of his left wing, and Shuraḥbīl b. Dhī al-Kalāʿ in charge of the horsemen. He himself walked among the foot soldiers. When the two battle lines drew near each other, al-Ḥuṣayn b. Numayr with the right wing of the Syrians attacked the left wing of the Kūfans, which was under ʿAlī b. Mālik al-Jushamī. The latter held his ground against him by himself and was killed. His banner was taken up by Qurrah, ʿAlī's son, who, together with some men of the guard, was also killed. The left wing was put to flight. The banner of ʿAlī b. Mālik al-Jushamī was taken up by ʿAbdallāh b. Warqāʾ b. Junādah al-

293. Al-Ḥusayn sent his cousin, Muslim b. ʿAqīl b. Abī Ṭālib, to al-Kūfah in response to the invitation of the Kūfan Shīʿah. Muslim was received enthusiastically and wrote to al-Ḥusayn to come to al-Kūfah. For this, Muslim was beheaded by ʿUbaydallāh b. Ziyād. See Jafri, *Origins*, 182–84.

294. Cf. Qurʾān 33:33.

295. The implication is that the enemy are unbelievers, against whom holy war (*jihād*) is an obligation.

Salūlī, the nephew of Ḥubshī b. Junādah, the companion of the Prophet. Confronting the men of the left wing as they were fleeing, he said, "To me, O picked troops of God!" Most of them went to him. He said, "Here is your commander fighting. Let us go to him." He went forward until he came to him. There he was, head uncovered, calling out, "O picked troops of God, to me! I am Ibn al-Ashtar. The best of those of you who fled are those of [712] you who turn back [to fight]: he who turns from evil is no wrongdoer."[296] So his men returned to him. He sent to the commander of the right wing, saying, "Attack their left wing," for he hoped at that time that ʿUmayr b. al-Ḥubāb would fall back before them, as he had said. The commander of the right wing, Sufyān b. Yazīd b. al-Mughaffal, attacked, but ʿUmayr b. al-Ḥubāb held his ground against him and fought him vigorously. When Ibrāhīm saw that, he said to his companions, "Head toward this main body of men; by God, if we disperse it, those of them you see to the right and the left will flee like frightened birds taking wing."

According to Abū Mikhnaf—Ibrāhīm b. ʿAbd al-Raḥmān al-Anṣārī—Warqā' b. ʿĀzib [al-Asadī], who said: We walked toward them. Having drawn near them, we fought briefly with spears and then turned to swords and maces and struck blows at each other with them for a large part of the day. By God, I can compare the sound I heard of iron on iron as we fought with each other only to that of fullers' mallets in the house of al-Walīd b. ʿUqbah b. Abī Muʿayṭ. [Continuing,] he said: Thus it was. Then God defeated them and made them turn their backs to us [in flight].

According to Abū Mikhnaf—al-Ḥārith b. Ḥaṣīrah[297]—Abū Ṣādiq:[298] Ibrāhīm b. al-Ashtar would say to his standard bearer, "Plunge into them with your banner." The standard bearer would reply to him, "May I be made your ransom! I have no room to advance." "Indeed you have," Ibn al-Ashtar would reply. "Your

---

296. Proverbial: see Freytag, II, 641 (Maydānī, II, 203).

297. Al-Ḥārith b. Ḥaṣīrah al-Azdī Abū Nuʿmān al-Kūfī was a *muḥaddith* of the sixth "class" and lived to the age of 100. The traditions related from him concern the virtues of the family of the Prophet. He was considered an extreme Shīʿī, even a *Khashabī*. See U. Sezgin, *Abū Miḥnaf*, 205.

298. Abū Ṣādiq al-Azdī al-Kūfī: his full name is variously given as Muslim b. Yazīd or ʿAbdallāh b. Nājid. See U. Sezgin, *Abū Miḥnaf*, 206.

comrades will fight[299] and, God willing, they will not flee." When his standard bearer advanced with his banner, Ibrāhīm attacked with his sword and felled every man he struck, driving the men
[713] before him as if they were sheep. Whenever he attacked with his banner, his companions attacked as one man.

According to Abū Mikhnaf—al-Mishraqī:[300] ʿUbaydallāh b. Ziyād had with him on that day a sharp sword that spared nothing it touched. When his forces were defeated, ʿUyaynah b. Asmā' picked up his sister, Hind bint Asmā' (she was the wife of ʿUbaydallāh b. Ziyād), and took her[301] away. He recited the following verse of *rajaz* poetry:[302]

If you sever our bonds, oft
in the fray will I make the courageous distinguished man perish.

According to Abū Mikhnaf—Fuḍayl b. Khadīj: When Ibrāhīm [b. al-Ashtar] attacked Ibn Ziyād and his forces, the latter were defeated after fierce fighting and many deaths on both sides. When ʿUmayr b. al-Ḥubāb saw that Ibrāhīm's men had defeated those of ʿUbaydallāh, he sent word to Ibrāhīm, saying, "Shall I come to you now?" Ibrāhīm replied, "Do not come to me until the anger of God's picked troops abates, for I fear they may do you harm."

Ibn al-Ashtar said, "I killed a man who smelled of musk.[303] His arms went to the east and feet to the west. He was under a separate banner on the bank of the Khāzir River."[304] They looked to see who he was, and it turned out to be ʿUbaydallāh b. Ziyād who had been slain: Ibrāhīm had struck him and cut him in two, so that his
[714] feet had gone to the east and his arms to the west. Sharīk b. Jadīr al-Taghlibī attacked al-Ḥuṣayn b. Numayr al-Sakūnī, supposing him

---

299. Mss. O and Co add, "behind it."

300. Full name: al-Ḍaḥḥāk b. ʿAbdallāh al-Mishraqī (U. Sezgin, *Abū Miḥnaf*, 200).

301. Possibly, "took it (i.e., the sword) away."

302. *Rajaz*, the least formal of the Arabic meters, is often used for hastily improvised verses.

303. The parallel in Balādhurī, *Ansāb*, V, 250, adds that Ibn al-Ashtar did not know for certain who the man was. Cf. also Dīnawarī, *Akhbār*, 303.

304. Mss. O and Co read: "'I killed a man under a separate banner on the bank of the Khāzir River.' So they looked for him, and I smelled the odor of musk from him. His arms had gone to the east and his feet to the west."

to be ʿUbaydallāh b. Ziyād. Each of them grasped the other, and al-Taghlibī cried out, "Kill me and the son of the whore." Ibn al-Numayr was killed.

According to ʿAbdallāh b. Aḥmad—his father—Sulaymān [b. Ṣāliḥ]—ʿAbdallāh b. al-Mubārak—al-Ḥasan b. Kathīr, who said: Sharīk b. Jadīr al-Taghlibī had been with ʿAlī (may God bless him and grant him peace) and had been injured in the eye with him.[305] When the war involving ʿAlī ended, he made his way to Jerusalem and was there when the murder of al-Ḥusayn was reported to him. He said, "I swear to God that if I am given the power to do so,"—that is, to avenge the blood of al-Ḥusayn—"I will kill Ibn Marjānah or die in the attempt." When he was told that al-Mukhtār had come out seeking vengeance for the blood of al-Ḥusayn, he went to him. [Continuing,] he said: Al-Mukhtār sent him with Ibrāhīm b. al-Ashtar, and he was placed in charge of the horsemen from [the tribal group of] Rabīʿah. He said to his companions, "Thus have I sworn to God." Three hundred men swore allegiance to him until death. When the encounter took place, he attacked and with his companions began to rip apart line after line until they reached ʿUbaydallāh. The dust rose and nothing was to be heard but the din of iron and swords. When the men separated, the two lay dead, al-Taghlibī and ʿUbaydallāh b. Ziyād, with no one between them. [Continuing,] he said: It was he who said:

All life I think loathsome,
save planting the spear firmly in the horse's shadow.

According to Hishām [b. al-Kalbī]—Abū Mikhnaf—Fuḍayl b. Khadīj, who said: Shuraḥbīl b. Dhī al-Kalāʿ was killed. Three men claimed to have killed him: Sufyān b. Yazīd b. al-Mughaffal al-Azdī, Warqāʾ b. ʿĀzib al-Asadī, and ʿUbaydallāh b. Zuhayr al-Sulamī. [715]

[Continuing,] he said: When ʿUbaydallāh's forces were defeated, Ibrāhīm b. al-Ashtar's men pursued them. Those who drowned were more than those who were slain. Their camp was taken, with all sorts of things in it. This was reported to al-Mukhtār, who had been saying to his companions, "Victory will come to you today or tomorrow, God willing, at the hands of Ibrāhīm

305. Ibn al-Athīr, *Kāmil*, IV, 264, adds: "at [the Battle of] Ṣiffīn."

b. al-Ashtar and his forces, who will have defeated the forces of ʿUbaydallāh b. Marjānah." [Continuing,] he said: Having appointed al-Sā'ib b. Mālik al-Ashʿarī as his deputy over the city, al-Mukhtār left al-Kūfah. He led the men out and encamped at Sābāṭ.

According to Abū Mikhnaf—al-Mishraqī—al-Shaʿbī, who said: My father and I were among those who went out with him. [Continuing,] he said: When we had passed beyond Sābāṭ, al-Mukhtār said to the people, "Rejoice, for God's picked troops have indeed slain them with the sword for a day until nightfall at Naṣībīn,[306] or close to Naṣībīn, and just this side of their own homes.[307] Most of them, however, are besieged at Naṣībīn."

[Continuing,] he said: We entered al-Madā'in and assembled in his presence. He ascended the pulpit. By God, even while he was preaching to us and commanding us to be earnest, hold right beliefs, exert ourselves, and be firm in obedience and in seeking vengeance for the blood of the people of [the Prophet's] family, the good news came to him, one message after another, about the death of ʿUbaydallāh b. Ziyād, the defeat of his forces, the taking of his camp, and the killing of the Syrian *ashrāf*. So al-Mukhtār
[716] said, "You picked troops of God, did I not announce this good news to you before it took place?" "Yes," they said, "you said so."

[Continuing,] he said: A certain neighbor of ours from the tribe of Hamdān said to me, "Do you believe now, O Shaʿbī?" [Continuing,] he said: I said, "What should I believe? Should I believe that al-Mukhtār knows the invisible? I will never believe it." He said, "Didn't he tell us they had been defeated?" I said to him, "He told us they had been defeated at Naṣībīn in the land of al-Jazīrah, but it was at Khāzir in the land of al-Mawṣil." He said, "By God, O Shaʿbī, you will not believe until you see 'the painful chastisement.'"[308] Al-Mishraqī said: I asked al-Shaʿbī, "Who was this man from Hamdān who was saying this to you?" He answered, "A man who, by my life, was brave and who was later

306. Naṣībīn, an important city of al-Jazīrah province, lay about 120 miles northwest of al-Mawṣil. See Yāqūt, *Muʿjam*, s.v.

307. Mss. O and Co read, "and have inherited their homes."

308. The Qur'ān speaks frequently of the "painful chastisement," i.e., the punishment in hell that awaits people who deny God's signs.

killed with al-Mukhtār at the Battle of Ḥarūrā'. He was called Salmān b. Ḥimyar, from the Thawr clan of Hamdān."

[Continuing,] he said: Al-Mukhtār returned to al-Kūfah. Ibn al-Ashtar went from his camp to al-Mawṣil and sent out his financial agents (*'ummāl*) over the territory. He sent out his brother, 'Abd al-Raḥmān b. 'Abdallāh, to be in charge of Naṣībīn, and he subdued Sinjār, Dārā, and the adjacent territory of al-Jazīrah.[309] The people of al-Kūfah whom al-Mukhtār had fought and defeated[310] went out and joined Muṣ'ab b. al-Zubayr in al-Baṣrah. Among those who went to Muṣ'ab was Shabath b. Rib'ī.

Praising Ibrāhīm b. al-Ashtar and his companions for killing 'Ubaydallāh b. Ziyād, Surāqah b. Mirdās al-Bāriqī said the following:

There came upon you a young man, one of the chiefs of [the tribe of] Madhḥij,
courageous against enemies, unflinching.
Son of Ziyād, be slain in retaliation for the greatest Mālik;[311]
taste the blade of a burnished, piercing two-edged [sword].
We smote you with the cutting of the sword in fury,[312]
when we slew a slayer in retaliation for a man slain.
May God reward the picked troops of God, for they
sated my thirst for vengeance upon 'Ubaydallāh yesterday.

[Muṣ'ab b. al-Zubayr Becomes Governor of al-Baṣrah]

In this year, 'Abdallāh b. al-Zubayr removed al-Qubā'[313] from al-Baṣrah and sent his own brother Muṣ'ab b. al-Zubayr to be in charge of it. [717]

---

309. Sinjār lies about 55 miles west of al-Mawṣil. Dārā lies about 20 miles west of Naṣībīn. See Yāqūt, *Mu'jam*, s.vv. Cf. the longer lists of agents to be found in Balādhurī, *Ansāb*, V, 251; Dīnawarī, *Akhbār*, 302.

310. I.e., the *ashrāf* whom al-Mukhtār had defeated at the Battle of Jabbānat al-Sabī' in Dhū al-Ḥijjah 66 (July 686).

311. I.e., Mālik b. al-Ḥārith al-Nakha'ī, surnamed al-Ashtar, the father of Ibrāhīm b. al-Ashtar. Appointed by 'Alī to the governorship of Egypt, he was poisoned by an agent of Mu'āwiyah. See Ṭabarī, I, 3393f.

312. Instead of "in fury," the *Dīwān*, 34, reads, "and we did no wrong."

313. Full name: Al-Ḥārith b. 'Abdallāh b. Abī Rabī'ah al-Qurashī al-Makhzūmī al-Qubā'.

According to ʿUmar b. Shabbah[314]—ʿAlī b. Muḥammad [al-Madā'inī]—al-Shaʿbī—Wāfid b. Abī Yāsir, who said: ʿAmr b. Sarḥ, a *mawlā* of al-Zubayr, used to come to us. He said to us: "By God, I was with the party that came from Mecca to al-Baṣrah with al-Muṣʿab[315] b. al-Zubayr." [Continuing,] he said: Muṣʿab came with his face muffled. Having made his camel kneel by the door of the mosque, he entered and ascended the pulpit. The people said, "Commander! Commander!"

[Continuing,] he said: When al-Ḥārith b. ʿAbdallāh b. Abī Rabīʿah, who had been the city's commander before him, came, al-Muṣʿab unveiled his face. The people recognized him and said, "Muṣʿab b. al-Zubayr!" He said to al-Ḥārith, "Come up! Come up!" So the latter ascended and sat a step below Muṣʿab on the pulpit. [Continuing,] he said: Then al-Muṣʿab stood. Having praised and extolled God (and, by God, he did not speak a great deal), he said, "'In the Name of God, the Merciful, the Compassionate. *Ṭā, Sīn, Mīm*. Those are the signs of the Manifest Book. We will recite to thee something of the tiding of Moses [and Pharaoh].'"[316] When he reached the words, "He[317] was of the workers of corruption," he pointed his hand in the direction of Syria. [Continuing to recite, he said,] "'Yet We desired to be gracious to those that were abased in the land, and to make them leaders, and to make them the inheritors.'" Here he pointed his hand in the direction of the Ḥijāz. "'And to show Pharaoh and Haman, and their hosts, what they were dreading from them.'" Here he pointed his hand in the direction of Syria.

According to ʿUmar b. Shabbah—ʿAlī b. Muḥammad [al-Madā'inī]—ʿAwānah, who said: When Muṣʿab came to al-Baṣrah, he delivered a sermon to the people and said: "People of al-Baṣrah, I have been told that you nickname your commanders. I have named myself 'al-Jazzār' (the Slaughterer)."[318]

---

314. Abū Zayd ʿUmar b. Shabbah (b. 173/789, d. 262/875), a traditionist and historian, was a pupil of al-Madā'inī. According to Ṭabarī, II, 168, Ṭabarī personally studied ʿUmar b. Shabbah's *Kitāb akhbār ahl al-Baṣrah* under the author. See F. Sezgin, *GAS*, I, 345; U. Sezgin, *Abū Miḥnaf*, 44–5; and Rotter, "Zur Überlieferung einiger historischer Werke Madā'inīs," 110.

315. Mss. O and Co, Muṣʿab

316. Qur'ān 28:1–5.

317. I.e., Pharaoh.

318. The nickname alludes to generosity (slaughtering many camels to feed

[Muṣʿab b. al-Zubayr Defeats al-Mukhtār]

During this year, Muṣʿab b. al-Zubayr marched against al-Mukhtār and killed him. [718]

Why Muṣʿab Marched against Him; an Account of Mukhtār's Death

According to Hishām b. Muḥammad [al-Kalbī]—Abū Mikhnaf—Ḥabīb b. Budayl, who said:[319] When Shabath [b. Ribʿī] came to join Muṣʿab, he was riding a female mule whose tail had been docked and the tip of whose ear had been cut. He had torn his tunic (*qabā'*) and was shouting, "Help! Help!" Someone went to Muṣʿab and told him that there was a man at the gate with his tunic torn shouting for help, and he described him. Muṣʿab said, "Yes, this is Shabath b. Ribʿī; no one else would do this. Bring him in." Shabath was brought before Muṣʿab. The Kūfan *ashrāf* came before Muṣʿab and told him how they had gathered around Shabath, what they had suffered, and how their own slaves and *mawālī* had risen against them. They complained to him and asked him to assist them and march against al-Mukhtār with them.

Muḥammad b. al-Ashʿath b. Qays also came to them. He had not been present at the fighting in al-Kūfah, having been in a fortress of his at Ṭīzanābādh, near al-Qādisiyyah. When the defeat of the men was reported to him, he prepared himself to march forth. Al-Mukhtār inquired about him, was told where he was, and sent ʿAbdallāh b. Qurād al-Khathʿamī with a hundred men to deal with him. When Muḥammad b. al-Ashʿath was told that they were marching against him and had drawn near, he went out into the desert in the direction of al-Muṣʿab, until he joined him. Having reached al-Muṣʿab, he urged the latter to go forth. Muṣʿab drew him near to himself and honored him because of his high

guests), rather than to bloodthirstiness. Cf. Dozy, *Supplément*, I, 192 (s.v. *jazūr*). In Balādhurī, *Ansāb*, V, 281, the remark occurs in the context of descriptions of Muṣʿab's generosity.

319. Ḥabīb b. Budayl al-Nahshalī was governor of al-Rayy in 131/748. See Ṭabarī, III, 2, 3.

rank. [Continuing,] he said: Al-Mukhtār sent men to the house of Muḥammad b. al-Ashʿath and destroyed it.

[719] According to Abū Mikhnaf—Yūsuf[320] b. Yazīd: When al-Muṣʿab was about to march against al-Kūfah, many men having come to him,[321] he said to Muḥammad b. al-Ashʿath, "I will not go until al-Muhallab b. Abī Ṣufrah comes to me." Al-Muṣʿab wrote to al-Muhallab, who was his governor over Fārs,[322] saying, "Come to us, so that you may be present in our enterprise, for we are about to march against al-Kūfah." However, al-Muhallab and his companions delayed, giving as reason something having to do with taxes (*kharāj*), not wishing to go forth. Muṣʿab therefore ordered Muḥammad b. al-Ashʿath, among the things he urged him to do, to go to al-Muhallab and bring him. He informed him that he would not set out unless al-Muhallab came. Muḥammad b. al-Ashʿath took al-Muṣʿab's letter to al-Muhallab. When the latter read it, he said to Muḥammad b. al-Ashʿath, "Does someone like you, Muḥammad, come as a letter carrier? Could al-Muṣʿab find no letter carrier besides you?" Muḥammad [b. al-Ashʿath] replied, "By God, I am nobody's letter carrier—except that our slaves and *mawālī* have taken our wives, children, and families from us by force!"

Al-Muhallab therefore set out. He came bringing many troops and much money with him, with such troops and in such a state of readiness as none of the people of al-Baṣrah could match. When al-Muhallab entered al-Baṣrah, he went to al-Muṣʿab's door in order to go in to meet him, having obtained permission for the men. However, the gatekeeper barred his way, not recognizing him Al-Muhallab raised his hand and broke the man's nose. The man went inside to al-Muṣʿab with his nose dripping blood. "What happened to you?" asked Muṣʿab. He answered, "A man I do not know hit me." Al-Muhallab entered. When the gatekeeper

---

320. Ed. Leiden, *Addenda*, p. DCLXXII, corrects ms. "Abū Yūsuf" to "Yūsuf."

321. The parallel in Dīnawarī, *Akhbār*, 310, puts the number of Kūfans who had left for al-Baṣrah at 10,000.

322. Arabic, *Fāris* (Persian, *Fārs* or *Pārs*): The Iranian province lying on the Persian Gulf, east of Khūzistān and west of Kirmān. Its chief city at this time was Iṣṭakhr. Shīrāz, located in it, was founded later by al-Ḥajjāj. See *EI*², s.v.; Yāqūt, *Muʿjam*, s.v.; Le Strange, *Lands*, 6, 248ff.

saw him, he said, "That's the one!" Al-Muṣʿab said to him, "Go back to your post."

Al-Muṣʿab ordered the men to encamp by the Great Pontoon Bridge (*al-Jisr al-Akbar*). Summoning ʿAbd al-Raḥmān b. Mikhnaf, he said to him, "Go to al-Kūfah and induce everyone you can to come out to me. Invite them to swear allegiance to me secretly, and induce al-Mukhtār's companions to abandon him." So ʿAbd [720] al-Raḥmān left him clandestinely and remained in his home, concealing himself, and not appearing [in public]. Al-Muṣʿab set out. He sent ʿAbbād b. al-Ḥuṣayn al-Ḥabaṭī of the Banū Tamīm ahead in charge of his vanguard. He sent ʿUmar b. ʿUbaydallāh b. Maʿmar in charge of his right wing, and al-Muhallab b. Abī Ṣufrah in charge of his left wing. He put Mālik b. Mismaʿ in charge of the Bakr b. Wā'il fifth,[323] Mālik b. al-Mundhir in charge of the ʿAbd al-Qays fifth, al-Aḥnaf b. Qays in charge of the Tamīm fifth, Ziyād b. ʿAmr al-Azdī in charge of the al-Azd fifth, and Qays b. al-Haytham in charge of the Highland[324] fifth.

This was reported to al-Mukhtār, who stood up among his companions, praised and extolled God, and said, "People of al-Kūfah! People of the religion [of Islam], upholders of the truth, helpers of the weak, and partisans of the Messenger and of the family of the Messenger! Those who have fled from you, who sought to harm you, have gone to their fellow transgressors and drawn them into error against you, that truth may cease and vanity be lifted up, and that the friends of God may be slain. By God, if you perish, God will be worshiped on earth only with lying against God and cursing against the family of His Prophet.[325] Rally to the call with Aḥmar b. Shumayṭ. If you meet them, you will slay them, God willing, as ʿĀd and Iram were slain."[326]

---

323. *Khums*, pl. *akhmās*, "fifth": The army of al-Baṣrah was divided into five divisions.

324. Arabic *al-ʿĀliyah* refers to the highlands of the Ḥijāz north and east of Medina. Yāqūt, *Muʿjam*, s.v., gives a list of tribes included in this area. See note 261.

325. A reference to the Umayyad practice of cursing ʿAlī from the pulpit.

326. ʿĀd and Iram appear in the Qur'ān as examples of nations that perished, ʿĀd because it rejected the prophet sent to it by God. The two names are juxtaposed in Qur'ān 89:7. See EI^2, s.vv.

Aḥmar b. Shumayṭ went out and encamped at Ḥammām Aʿyan. Al-Mukhtār summoned the heads of the fourths (*arbāʿ*) who had been with Ibn al-Ashtar and sent them with Aḥmar b. Shumayṭ as they had been with Ibn al-Ashtar. (They had left Ibn al-Ashtar because they thought he was making light of al-Mukhtār's enter-
[721] prise, and had departed from him.) Al-Mukhtār sent them with Ibn Shumayṭ and sent a massive army with him. Ibn Shumayṭ went out. In charge of his vanguard, he sent Ibn Kāmil al-Shākirī. Aḥmar b. Shumayṭ marched until he arrived at al-Madhār.[327] Al-Muṣʿab came and encamped near him.

Each of them mustered his army, and they advanced toward each other. Aḥmar b. Shumayṭ put ʿAbdallāh b. Kāmil al-Shākirī in charge of his right wing, ʿAbdallāh b. [Anas b.][328] Wahb b. Naḍlah al-Jushamī in charge of his left wing, Razīn ʿAbd al-Salūlī in charge of the horsemen, Kathīr b. Ismāʿīl al-Kindī (at the battle of Khāzir he had been with Ibn al-Ashtar) in charge of the foot soldiers, and Kaysān Abū ʿAmrah (a *mawlā* of ʿUraynah) in charge of the *mawālī*.

Having been put in charge of the left wing, ʿAbdallāh b. Wahb b. Anas[329] al-Jushamī came to Ibn Shumayṭ and said to him, "*Mawālī* and slaves are weaklings when it comes time to show true fortitude. Although you are walking, they have many men on horseback with them. Order them to dismount with you, for they will have an example to emulate in you. I fear that if they are assaulted for a time and attacked with spears and swords, they will flee on the backs of their horses and abandon you. However, if you make them go on foot, they will have no choice but to hold out." [ʿAbdallāh b. Anas] said this only out of rancor toward the *mawālī* and slaves, because of what they [sc. the *ashrāf*] had experienced at their hands in al-Kūfah. If the battle turned against them, he wanted them to be on foot and none of them to escape. Ibn Shumayṭ did not suspect him; believing that he only wanted to give him good advice, so that they would hold out and fight, he

327. Al-Madhār, the main city of the Maysān district, lay about 200 miles southeast of al-Kūfah and 40 miles north of al-Baṣrah, on the shore of a backwater formed by a former bed of the Tigris. See Le Strange, *Lands*, 42–3.

328. Cf. Balādhurī, *Ansāb*, V, 253 (and note).

329. Sic, except in Ms. C, which omits "b. Anas."

said, "You *mawālī,* dismount with me and fight." So they dismounted with him and walked in front of him and his banner.

Muṣʿab b. al-Zubayr came. He had put ʿAbbād b. al-Ḥuṣayn in charge of the horsemen. Having approached Ibn Shumayṭ and his forces, ʿAbbād said, "We summon you only to the Book of God, the Sunnah of His Messenger, and allegiance to the Commander of the Faithful ʿAbdallāh b. al-Zubayr." The other side said, "We summon you to the Book of God, to the Sunnah of His Messenger, to allegiance to the commander al-Mukhtār, and to our making this issue a matter to be determined by consultation (*shūrā*) among the family of the Prophet. As for any person who alleges that someone ought to rule over them,[330] we disavow him and will strive against him." ʿAbbād returned and reported to al-Muṣʿab. Al-Muṣʿab said to him, "Go back and attack them." ʿAbbād went back and attacked Ibn Shumayṭ and his forces, but none of them gave way; then he returned to his position. Al-Muhallab attacked [ʿAbdallāh] b. Kāmil. The forces [of the latter] jostled[331] each other in the fray,[332] and Ibn Kāmil dismounted. Al-Muhallab then drew back from him, and [Ibn Kāmil][333] stood his ground. They stopped [fighting] for a time; then al-Muhallab said to his forces, "Charge them with true bravery, for the enemy have given you hope by their confusion." So he made a formidable attack on them, and they retreated. Ibn Kāmil held his ground with foot soldiers from Hamdān, and al-Muhallab could hear the men's battle cry, "I am the young man of Shākir! I am the young man of Shibām! I am the young man of Thawr!" But it was only a short time before they were defeated. [722]

ʿUmar b. ʿUbaydallāh b. Maʿmar attacked ʿAbdallāh b. Anas. The latter fought for a time and then retreated. All the men together attacked [Aḥmar] b. Shumayṭ, who fought until he was killed. His men called to each other, "Men of Bajīlah and Khathʿam, be steadfast!" But al-Muhallab called to them, "Flee! Flight is safer for you today. Why will you kill yourselves on the side of these slaves? God has led your enterprise astray." Then he looked toward [723]

330. Viz., the family of the Prophet.
331. Mss. O and Co read: "They jostled each other."
332. For this meaning of *jāla*, see Blachère, *Dictionnaire*, s.v.
333. The antecedent is unclear.

his companions and said, "By God, I think the killing has been vehement today only among my men." The horsemen turned on Ibn Shumayṭ's foot soldiers, who separated and fled, taking to the desert. Al-Muṣʿab dispatched ʿAbbād b. al-Ḥuṣayn in charge of the horsemen, saying, "Behead any prisoner you take." And he sent Muḥammad b. al-Ashʿath with a large body of horsemen, Kūfan horsemen who were among the people al-Mukhtār had expelled, saying, "Take your revenge!" The Kūfans were even more severe than the Baṣrans toward those who were defeated. They killed every fleeing man they overtook and pardoned no prisoner that they took. [Continuing,] he said: Of that army, only a group of horsemen escaped; the foot soldiers perished, except for a few.

According to Abū Mikhnaf—Ibn ʿAyyāsh al-Mantūf,[334] who said: Muʿāwiyah b. Qurrah al-Muzanī[335] said [to me], "I caught up with one of them, put the head of my spear into his eye, and began mashing his eye with the head of my spear." I said to him, "You did that to him?" "Yes," he said, "we thought it more permissible to spill their blood than to kill Turks and Daylamites."[336] Muʿāwiyah b. Qurrah was a judge of the people of al-Baṣrah. Concerning [the battle at al-Madhār], al-Aʿshā[337] said:

Yea, has it reached you? Reports are told
    about what [the tribe of] Bajīlah encountered at al-Madhār.
There a strong blow was ordained for them,
    and a well-aimed thrust at the beginning of the day.
It was as if a cloud had hurled thunderbolts upon them
    and encompassed them with destruction there.
Announce humiliation to al-Mukhtār's Shīʿah,

334. ʿAbdallāh b. ʿAyyāsh b. Abī Rabīʿah al-Mantūf Abū al-Jarrāḥ (d. 158/775) was an expert in genealogy and poetry. See Sezgin, *Abū Miḥnaf*, 191.

335. Ibid., p. 191.

336. The Daylamites were an Iranian people living in the highlands of Gīlān in northern Iran. They had served the Sasanians as mercenaries and stubbornly maintained their independence despite many Muslim expeditions against them. See EI^2, s.v. Daylam.

337. I.e., Aʿshā Hamdān. The version in the *Dīwān*, 330, adds two lines at the end of the poem: "What happened to them did not displease me, whether things go badly or well for me. Rather, I was gladdened, my sleep became sweet, and I rested calmly because of their death."

if you pass by the little city[338] of al-Kūfah.
Their fallen men and the many remnants of their army
slaughtered in the deserts delighted my eye.
I did not rejoice that my people were killed,
even if they, in truth, were empowered to choose;[339]
Rather, I rejoiced at what overtook
Abū Isḥāq[340]—shame and disgrace. [724]

Al-Muṣʿab advanced across the reeds in the direction of Wāsiṭ.[341] (The present city of Wāsiṭ had not yet been built at that time.) He took the road to Kaskar,[342] and then loaded the foot soldiers, their baggage, and those who were weak onto boats and traveled by way of a canal called the Khurshādh. From that canal, he came out onto a canal called Qūsān, whence he brought his men out onto the Euphrates.

According to Abū Mikhnaf—Fuḍayl b. Khadīj al-Kindī: The people from al-Baṣrah would get out and pull their boats, saying:

Al-Muṣʿab has accustomed us to pulling hawsers
and ships long and hollow.

[Continuing,] he said: When the Persians who were with al-Mukhtār learned what had befallen their brethren with Ibn Shumayṭ, they said in Persian, "*Īn bār durōgh guft*," meaning, "This time he has lied."

According to Abū Mikhnaf—Hishām b. ʿAbd al-Raḥmān al-Thaqafī—ʿAbd al-Raḥmān b. Abī ʿUmayr al-Thaqafī, who said: By God, I was sitting by al-Mukhtār when the defeat of the men

---

338. *Al-Kuwayfah*, the diminutive of al-Kūfah, is probably being used contemptuously. There was, however, a place called Kuwayfat Ibn ʿUmar, near Bazīqiyā in the district of al-Kūfah. See Yāqūt, *Muʿjam*, s.v. al-Kuwayfah.

339. The translation follows the Leiden text (*fī khiyārī*) and von Goutta, *Aġānī-artikel*, 51. The sense would be: "even if they willingly chose to follow the error of al-Mukhtār."

340. I.e., al-Mukhtār.

341. The city of Wāsiṭ, founded in 84/703 by al-Ḥajjāj, lay on the Tigris, approximately equidistant (50 leagues) from Baghdad, al-Kūfah, al-Baṣrah, and Ahwāz. From al-Madhār, the site of Wāsiṭ lay about 100 miles to the northwest. South of Wāsiṭ, the Tigris flowed into the Great Swamp, the "reeds" to which the text refers. See Le Strange, *Lands*, 39–40; EI^1, s.v.

342. Kaskar was a town across the river from Wāsiṭ and gave its name to the surrounding district. See Le Strange, loc. cit.; EI^2, s.v.

and what had befallen them was reported to him. [Continuing,] he said: Al-Mukhtār turned to me and said, "By God, the slaves have been killed on an unheard-of scale." Then he said, "Ibn Shumayṭ and Ibn Kāmil have been killed, as well as others," and he named Arab casualties each of whom was better in war than a multitude of men. [Continuing,] he said: I said to him, "By God, this is a disaster." He said to me, "There is no escape from death, and there is no death I would rather die than one like that of Ibn Shumayṭ. How excellent the deaths of noble men!" [Continuing,] he said: Thus, I realized that the man had resolved inwardly that,
[725] if he did not attain his object, he would fight until he died.

When it was reported to al-Mukhtār that Muṣʿab's forces were coming toward him by water and by land, he took his men and encamped at al-Saylaḥīn,[343] facing the confluence of the al-Ḥīrah, al-Saylaḥīn, al-Qādisiyyah, and Yūsuf[344] canals. He dammed the Euphrates below the confluence of the canals, so that all the water of the Euphrates went into these canals, and the boats of the Baṣrans were left in the mud. When they saw this, they got out of the boats and walked. Their horsemen galloped forward, reached the dam, broke it, and headed toward al-Kūfah. When he saw this, al-Mukhtār went toward them and encamped at Ḥarūrā',[345] blocking their way to al-Kūfah. He had fortified his palace and the mosque and had brought provisions for the siege into his palace.

Al-Muṣʿab came marching toward al-Mukhtār, who was at Ḥarūrā' and had left ʿAbdallāh b. Shaddād as his agent in charge of al-Kūfah. Al-Mukhtār came out to meet Muṣʿab, having put Sulaym b. Yazīd al-Kindī in charge of his right wing and Saʿīd b. Munqidh al-Hamdānī al-Thawrī in charge of his left wing. ʿAbdallāh b. Qurād al-Khathʿamī was in charge of al-Mukhtār's picked troops (*shurṭah*) that day. Al-Mukhtār sent ʿUmar[346] b. ʿAbdallāh al-Nahdī in charge of the horsemen and Mālik b. ʿAmr[347] al-Nahdī in charge of the foot soldiers. Muṣʿab put al-Muhallab b. Abī Ṣufrah in charge of his right wing, ʿUmar b.

343. Al-Saylaḥīn (or al-Saylaḥūn) was located between al-Ḥīrah and al-Qādisiyyah. See Yāqūt, *Muʿjam*, s.v.

344. Corrected from the ms. reading "Bursuf" (ed. Leiden, *Addenda*, p. DCLXXII).

345. Ḥarūrā' was about two miles from al-Kūfah (Yāqūt, *Muʿjam*, s.v.).

346. Mss. O, Co and Ibn al-Athīr, *Kāmil*, IV, 270: "ʿAmr."

347. Mss. O, Co and Ibn al-Athīr, loc. cit., "ʿAbdallāh."

ʿUbaydallāh b. Maʿmar al-Taymī in charge of his left wing, ʿAbbād b. al-Ḥuṣayn al-Ḥabaṭī in charge of the horsemen, and Muqātil b. Mismaʿ al-Bakrī in charge of the foot soldiers. He himself dismounted to go on foot, shouldering a bow of his.

[Continuing,] he said: Muṣʿab put Muḥammad b. al-Ashʿath in charge of the Kūfans. Muḥammad came and encamped between [726] al-Muṣʿab and al-Mukhtār, moving to the west and to the right. [Continuing,] he said: When al-Mukhtār saw that, he sent one of his companions against each of the fifths of the Baṣrans. He sent Saʿīd b. Munqidh, the commander of his left wing, against the [fifth of] Bakr b. Wā'il, which was led by Mālik b. Mismaʿ al-Bakrī. He sent ʿAbd al-Raḥmān b. Shurayḥ al-Shibāmī, who was in charge of his treasury, against the [fifth of] ʿAbd al-Qays, which was led by Mālik b. al-Mundhir. He sent ʿAbdallāh b. Jaʿdah al-Qurashī al-Makhzūmī against the [fifth] of the Highlanders, who were led by Qays b. al-Haytham al-Sulamī. He sent Musāfir b. Saʿīd b. Nimrān al-Nāʿiṭī against the [fifth of] al-Azd, which was led by Ziyād b. ʿAmr al-ʿAtakī. He sent Sulaym b. Yazīd al-Kindī, the commander of his right wing, against the [fifth of] Banū Tamīm, which was led by al-Aḥnaf b. Qays. He sent al-Sā'ib b. Mālik al-Ashʿarī against Muḥammad b. al-Ashʿath. He himself halted among the rest of his forces.

The men advanced and closed with each other. Saʿīd b. Munqidh and ʿAbd al-Raḥmān b. Shurayḥ attacked [the fifths of] Bakr b. Wā'il and ʿAbd al-Qays, which were in the left wing under ʿUmar b. ʿUbaydallāh b. Maʿmar. The forces of Rabīʿah[348] fought them fiercely and held their own against them, but Saʿīd b. Munqidh and ʿAbd al-Raḥmān b. Shurayḥ did not abandon the attack: when one attacked and withdrew, the other then attacked, and sometimes both attacked together.

[Continuing,] he said: Al-Muṣʿab sent word to al-Muhallab, saying, "Why are you waiting to attack those across from you? Don't you see what these two fifths have been encountering since the day began? Attack with your forces." Al-Muhallab replied, "By my life, I am not one to make the Azd and Tamīm slaughter,

348. I.e., the forces from the tribes of Bakr b. Wā'il and ʿAbd al-Qays, both of which belonged to the grouping of Rabīʿah tribes.

for fear of the people of al-Kūfah, until I see my opportunity."[349]

[727] [Continuing,] he said: Al-Mukhtār sent word to ʿAbdallāh b. Jaʿdah, saying, "Attack those opposite you." Accordingly, he attacked the Highlanders and put them to flight, so that they came at last to al-Muṣʿab. Not being one to flee, al-Muṣʿab knelt on his knees and shot his arrows, and the men took up a position beside him. The two sides fought for a time and then separated.

[Continuing,] he said: Al-Muṣʿab sent to al-Muhallab, who was with two large and numerous fifths and the skilled horsemen, saying, "May you have no father![350] Why are you waiting to attack the enemy?" The latter waited not far away and said to his companions, "The men have fought since the day began, while you have been standing still. They have done a good job; now it remains for you to do what you ought to do. Attack! Pray for God's help, and be steadfast." [Al-Muhallab] vigorously attacked those who were near him; they crushed al-Mukhtār's forces badly and put them to flight. ʿAbdallāh b. ʿAmr al-Nahdī,[351] a veteran of Ṣiffīn,[352] said, "O God, I am in the same state of mind as I was that Thursday night at Ṣiffīn. O God, I declare to Thee that I have no part in the action of these men"—meaning his companions when they fled—"and I declare to Thee that I have no part with the souls of these men"—meaning the companions of al-Muṣʿab. He then fought with his sword until he was killed.

Mālik b. ʿAmr Abū Nimrān al-Nahdī, who was in charge of [al-Mukhtār's] foot soldiers, was brought his horse and he mounted. Al-Mukhtār's forces were in full flight, as if they were a canebrake set ablaze. Having mounted, Mālik said, "What am I going to do by mounting? By God, I would rather be killed here than be killed in my house. Where are the men of valor? Where are the men of

349. The reading in Balādhurī, *Ansab*, V, 259, is superior: "I am not one to make the Azd and Tamīm slaughter the Khashabiyyah of the people of al-Kūfah, until I see my opportunity." The words *khashyah* (fear) and *khashabiyyah* are easily confused in Arabic script.

350. *Lā abā laka*, which is more an expletive or an expression of impatience than a real curse.

351. He was commanding al-Mukhtār's cavalry. See Ṭabarī, II, 725, above.

352. At Siffīn, a plain on the right bank of the Euphrates near al-Raqqah, in 38/657, forces loyal to the caliph ʿAlī confronted those of Muʿāwiyah, the governor of Syria and leader of the party demanding vengeance for the death of the caliph ʿUthmān.

steadfastness?" About fifty men returned to him—it was toward evening—and he wheeled round to attack the forces of Muḥammad b. al-Ashʿath. Muḥammad b. al-Ashʿath was killed next to him—both he[353] and most of his companions. Some men therefore say [728] it was Abū Nimrān who killed Muḥammad b. al-Ashʿath. (Abū Nimrān was found slain next to him.) But Kindah assert that ʿAbd al-Malik b. Ashāʾah al-Kindī was the man who killed him; that when al-Mukhtār with his companions passed by Muḥammad b. al-Ashʿath lying dead, he said, "O supporters, attack the guileful foxes"; they attacked, and Abū Nimrān was killed. Khathʿam assert that ʿAbdallāh b. Qurād[354] was the man who killed [Ibn al-Ashʿath].

According to Abū Mikhnaf: I heard ʿAwf b. ʿAmr[355] al-Jushamī assert that one of their *mawālī* killed him. Four persons claimed his killing, each of them asserting to have slain him.

The forces of Saʿīd b. Munqidh retreated. He fought amid a band of his tribesmen, about seventy men, until they were killed. Salīm b. Yazīd al-Kindī fought amid ninety men, tribesmen of his and others. He fought until he was killed. Al-Mukhtār fought at the entrance of the Shabath Road.[356] He dismounted, intending not to withdraw, and fought most of that night, until the men left him. Among his companions, men of his bodyguard, who were killed with him that night were ʿĀṣim b. ʿAbdallāh al-Azdī, ʿAyyāsh b. Khāzim al-Hamdānī al-Thawrī, and Aḥmar b. Ḥadīj al-Hamdānī al-Fāyishī.

According to Abū Mikhnaf—Abū al-Zubayr:[357] The men of Hamdān called to each other that night, saying, "People of Hamdān strike them with swords and fight them as hard as you can."

When they dispersed, leaving al-Mukhtār, his companions said to him, "Commander, the men have gone away. Go back to your [729] dwelling, to the palace." Al-Mukhtār said, "By God, I did not dismount intending to go to the palace. But since they have gone

---

353. I.e., Ibn al-Ashʿath.

354. Commander of al-Mukhtar's police.

355. Mss. O and C: ʿAmr b. ʿAwf.

356. This road was probably located in the southeast part of al-Kūfah. See Djaït, *Al-Kūfa*, 241.

357. Full name: Abū al-Zubayr al-Arḥabī al-Hamdānī. See U. Sezgin, *Abū Miḥnaf*, 190.

away, let us ride in the name of God." So he came and entered the palace.

Concerning the death of Muḥammad b. al-Ash'ath, al-A'shā [Hamdān] said:[358]

To your eye its rheum returned;
    to your soul its recollection returned.
You returned to one of your nights;
    you were wakeful, though watchers sought sleep.
Not until its dawn brightened
    did the eye taste the savor of slumber.
Those who announced the death of Abū Qāsim[359] arose;
    and their weeping caused tears to flow.
It was right that for the son of al-Ashajj[360]
    eyes should not cease their flowing,
That they should continue to weep for him,
    and that their lashes be moist with tears.
For you, Muḥammad, since you have been slain,
    the lands and their trees weep.
Whenever people mention you, they weep—
    whenever a pact is betrayed by its protector.
Many a bare winter's night,
    when the *maysir*[361] players distributed nothing;
When the savage dogs did not bark,
    and there was nothing but growling and torpor [because of the cold];
When a cloak was of no benefit to the youth,
    nor the woman's close place of concealment to the lady;
On such nights, Muḥammad,
    you regarded camels as of little value and butchered them.
Your bowls remained set out,
    their edges running over with fat.

---

358. The poem can be found in the *Dīwān* (ed. Geyer), 331–32.

359. The *kunyah* of Muḥammad b. al-Ash'ath.

360. The son of al-Ashajj is Muḥammad b. al-Ash'ath. Al-Ashajj ("the man whose head was wounded") is another nickname for al-Ash'ath ("the man with dissheveled or matted hair") b. Qays al-Kindī. Cf. Ibn al-Athīr, *Usd al-ghābah*, I, 97.

361. *Maysir* was a game in which players cast lots for the pieces of a slaughtered camel; see EI^2, s.v.

The last drops in your milk skin were completely consumed [by
your guests],
when the camels whose milk was drying up were led back
from pasture.
O bestower of comely servants; [730]
if they are measured, their stature is full.
O bestower of short-haired [horses swift] as arrows:
those who display them please the battle line.
O bestower of young she-camels of good breed
that have recently foaled, and their first-born foals answer
each other.
You were like the Tigris when its current
heaps itself up and rushes into the sea.
You were bold and full of strength,
when proof of these traits was sought of you.
If a town ever came to be in tumult,
and its tyrant proclaimed war,
You sent against it men of piercing eyes,
so that reports about it came succeeding one another—
With God's permission! And the horses'
training place was prepared for that campaign.
You fed your horses swift running,
until their colts were neglected.
The stout camel cutting its first teeth
knew that you would tire it on the plain.
Oh my grief the day you encountered them,
when those who fled betrayed your men!
The horsemen came back defeated,
in distress, their backs wounded,
At the river bank of Ḥarūrā'; and there gathered
against you the *mawālī* and their beguiler.[362]
You risked your life in their defense, [731]
and the risking of it gained disaster.
Do not be far, O Abū Qāsim!
For the soul's measure will reach it;
The accidents of fortune and the passage
and succession of nights have made our lords perish.

362. I.e., al-Mukhtār.

According to Hishām [b. al-Kalbī]: My father said that al-Sā'ib came with Muṣʿab b. al-Zubayr and was killed by Warqā' al-Nakhaʿī from [the clan of] Wahbīl. Warqā' said:

Who will take a message from me to ʿUbayd, that I
have overcome his brother with a sword of Indian steel?
If you seek knowledge about him, he is
lying prostrate by the two monasteries, with no pillow for his head.
Resolutely I sought him and brought his head low with a
trenchant blade;
and I bereaved him of [his son], Sufyān, after [the death of] Muḥammad.

According to Hishām [b. al-Kalbī]—Abū Mikhnaf—Ḥaṣīrah b. ʿAbdallāh:[363] Every extremist of the Shīʿah used to gather and talk at the house of Hind bint al-Mutakallifah al-Nāʿiṭiyyah and at the house of Laylā bint Qumāmah al-Muzaniyyah. The latter's brother, Rifāʿah b. Qumāmah, was a member of the Shīʿah of ʿAlī, but, since he was a moderate, she did not like him. Abū ʿAbdallāh al-Jadalī and Yazīd b. Sharāḥīl had informed Ibn al-Ḥanafiyyah about these two women and their extremism and about Abū al-Aḥrās al-Murādī, al-Buṭayn al-Laythī, and Abū al-Ḥārith al-Kindī.

According to Hishām [b. al-Kalbī]—Abū Mikhnaf—Yaḥyā b. Abī ʿĪsā, who said:[364] Ibn al-Ḥanafiyyah had sent a letter with Yazīd b. Sharāḥīl to the Shīʿah in al-Kūfah, warning them of these people. He wrote to them:

[732] From Muḥammad b. ʿAlī to those of our Shīʿah who are at al-Kūfah. To proceed: Go forth to the assemblies and the mosques; remember God both publicly and secretly, and do not take for yourselves intimates outside the believers.[365] If you fear for your souls, beware those who speak lies against your religion. Be frequent in

---

363. Ḥaṣīrah b. ʿAbdallāh b. al-Ḥārith b. Durayd al-Azdī was born probably ca. 50/670. All his reports, mediated through Abū Mikhnaf, concern the troubles in Iraq between A.H. 66 and 72. See U. Sezgin, *Abū Miḥnaf*, 207.

364. Full name: Yaḥyā b. Abī ʿĪsā al-Azdī. See ibid., 224.

365. Cf. Qur'ān 3:118.

worship, fasting, and prayer; for no creature has power to hurt or profit anyone, except as God wills. Every soul shall be pledged for what it has earned.[366] No soul laden bears the load of another.[367] God stands over every soul for what it has earned.[368] Work righteousness, and forward goodness for your souls; and do not be among the heedless.[369] Peace be upon you.

According to Abū Mikhnaf—Ḥaṣīrah b. ʿAbdallāh: When the men went forth to Ḥarūrā', ʿAbdallāh b. Nawf came out of the house of Hind bint al-Mutakallifah, saying, "The day of Wednesday: the sky has risen aloft and judgment has descended, bringing the defeat of the enemy. Go forth then in the name of God to Ḥarūrā'."[370] He went forth. When the men encountered each other to fight, he was struck a blow on his face. As the men were retreating in defeat, ʿAbdallāh b. Sharīk al-Nahdī, who had heard his saying, met him and said to him, "Didn't you assert to us, Ibn Nawf, that we would defeat them?" ʿAbdallāh b. Nawf replied, "Have you not read in the Book of God, 'God blots out, and He establishes whatsoever He will; and with Him is the Essence of the Book.'"[371]

[Continuing,] he said: The next morning, al-Muṣʿab marched forth with the Baṣrans who were with him and the Kūfans who had gone out to him, taking them toward al-Sabakhah.[372] When

366. Cf. ibid., 74:38.
367. Ibid., 6:164.
368. Cf. ibid., 13:33.
369. Cf. ibid., 7:205.
370. The saying of ʿAbdallāh b. Nawf is in rhymed prose (*sajʿ*), the form in which pre-Islamic soothsayers delivered their predictions; see note 21, above. If the reading, "The sky has risen aloft," is correct, it is an allusion to daybreak. Ed. Leiden, *Addenda*, p. DCLXXII, suggests reading *tazabbaʿat*, "has become stormy."
371. Qur'ān 13:39. Al-Mukhtār is said to have to derived a doctrine called "*bidā'*" ("change of mind") from this verse. Muslim theology accepted the idea that God might alter or abrogate earlier commands (e.g., that He might command the Muslim community to abstain from fighting at one time, but later command it to fight). What was not accepted was the idea that God's eternal decree could at one time be one thing (victory for someone) and at another time be different (defeat for that person). This is the position the heresiographers say al-Mukhtār adopted in order to explain why some of his predictions failed to be fulfilled. See Shahrastānī, *al-Milal wa-al-niḥal*, 151.
372. See note 68. An area between al-Kūfah and the Euphrates was referred to by this name.

he passed by al-Muhallab, the latter said to him, "What a victory!
[733] What a joy it would have been, had Muḥammad b. al-Ashʿath not been killed!" Muṣʿab replied, "You are right. May God have mercy on Muḥammad!" He walked a short way and then said, "Muhallab—." "At your service, commander!" he replied. "Do you now," said Muṣʿab, "that ʿUbaydallāh b. ʿAlī b. Abī Ṭālib has been killed?" Al-Muhallab replied, "'Surely we belong to God, and to Him we return.'"[373] Al-Muṣʿab said, "Indeed, he was someone I wanted to have seen this victory. We do not consider ourselves more entitled to anything we now have than he was. Do you know who killed him?" "No," he said. Muṣʿab said, "He was killed by someone who claims to be a partisan of his father. And they killed him, knowing who he was!"[374] [Continuing,] he said: Muṣʿab then went and encamped at al-Sabakhah, cutting off water and supplies from al-Mukhtār's forces. He sent ʿAbd al-Raḥmān b. Muḥammad b. al-Ashʿath, who encamped at al-Kunāsah. He sent ʿAbd al-Raḥmān b. Mikhnaf b. Sulaym to Jabbānat al-Sabīʿ. He asked ʿAbd al-Raḥmān b. Mikhnaf,[375] "What have you done in the matter I entrusted to you?" He replied, "God make you prosper! I found the people to be of two sorts: whoever had an inclination toward you went out to you; whoever held the opinion of al-Mukhtār would not abandon him or prefer anyone over him. So I did not leave my house until you came." Muṣʿab said, "You have spoken the truth."

Muṣʿab sent ʿAbbād b. al-Ḥuṣayn to Jabbānat Kindah. All these men were cutting off water and supplies from al-Mukhtār and his companions who were in al-Mukhtār's palace. He also sent Zaḥr b. Qays to Jabbānat Murād and sent ʿUbaydallāh b. al-Ḥurr to Jabbānat al-Ṣā'idiyyīn.[376]

---

373. See note 156.

374. Cf. Dīnawarī, *Akhbār*, 312–13 (where his name is given as ʿUmar, not ʿUbaydallāh): "He had come from the Ḥijāz to al-Mukhtār. Al-Mukhtār asked him, 'Do you have Muḥammad b. al-Ḥanafiyyah's letter with you?' 'No,' said ʿUmar b. ʿAlī, 'I do not have his letter with me.' 'Then go away, wherever you wish,' said al-Mukhtār, 'for I have nothing to give you.' He therefore left al-Mukhtār and went to Muṣʿab, who met him on the way and gave him a gift of 100,000 dirhams."

375. Muṣʿab had sent ʿAbd al-Raḥmān ahead to induce as many of al-Mukhtār's partisans as possible to abandon al-Mukhtār and go over to Muṣʿab. See Ṭabarī, II, 719.

376. The problem of its location is discussed in Djaït, *Al-Kūfa*, 245f.

According to Abū Mikhnaf—Fuḍayl b. Khadīj, who said: I saw ʿUbaydallāh b. al-Ḥurr charging and fighting al-Mukhtār's horsemen in Jabbānat al-Ṣā'idiyyīn. Sometimes I saw their horsemen chase away his horsemen, while he was behind his horsemen [734] inciting their ardor; when he had reached the house of ʿIkrimah, he wheeled round and chased them until he made them reach Jabbānat al-Ṣā'idiyyīn. Sometimes I saw ʿUbaydallāh's horsemen take and beat one or more water carriers. Because of the difficulty they encountered, they would bring them water only if they gave them one or two dinars for each bag of water.

Sometimes al-Mukhtār and his companions would come out and fight feebly, inflicting no damage on their foe. Whenever horsemen of his came out, they were bombarded with stones from the housetops and doused with filthy water. The people were emboldened against them. Most of their sustenance came from their wives. A woman would leave her house carrying food, dainties, and water over which she had thrown her outer garment.[377] She would leave as if intending to go to the Great Mosque for prayers, or as if she were going to her kin and visiting a woman relative of hers. When she approached the palace, someone would open for her and she would bring in food and drink for her husband or relation. When word of this reached al-Muṣʿab and his companions, al-Muhallab, who was experienced, said to him, "Set up barricades[378] against them, so that you prevent their families and children from coming to them and so that you leave them in their stronghold until they die in it."

When the people in the palace were hard pressed by thirst, they quenched their thirst with the water of the well. Al-Mukhtār ordered honey [to be given] to them; it was poured into [the well] to alter its taste, so that they might drink from it. Most of them satisfied their thirst in this way. Muṣʿab then ordered his forces to approach the palace. ʿAbbād b. al-Ḥuṣayn al-Ḥabaṭī came and took up a position by the Mosque of Juhaynah. Sometimes he advanced until he reached the Mosque of the Banū Makhzūm,[379]

377. Literally, "over which she had put on her *liḥāf*." The *liḥāf* was an unlined sheet of cloth used as an outer wrap.

378. *Durūb*: the exact meaning is unclear; perhaps gates at the end of certain streets. See Djaït, *Al-Kūfa*, 246.

379. This mosque was named after the clan of the tribe ʿAbs to which Ḥu-

[735] so that his forces might shoot arrows at any of al-Mukhtār's men who showed themselves to them from the palace. Whenever he met a woman close to the palace, he said to her, "Who are you, where have you come from, and what do you want?" One day, he seized three women, wives of men from the tribes of Shibām and Shākir, going to their husbands in the palace and sent them to Muṣʿab. They had food with them. Muṣʿab turned them back, but did them no harm.

Muṣʿab sent out Zaḥr b. Qays, who took up a position at the [Street] of the Smiths,[380] where riding animals were hired out. Also, he sent out ʿUbaydallāh b. al-Ḥurr: his position was by the house of Bilāl. He sent out Muḥammad b. ʿAbd al-Raḥmān b. Saʿīd b. Qays: his position was by his father's house. He sent out Ḥawshab b. Yazīd, who halted by the Lane of the Baṣrans, at the mouth of the Street of the Banū Jadhīmah b. Mālik, [a clan] of the Banū Asad b. Khuzaymah. Al-Muhallab came and took up a position at the crossroads of Khunays. ʿAbd al-Raḥmān b. Mikhnaf came from the direction of Dār al-Siqāyah.[381]

Some young Kūfans and Baṣrans, inexperienced fellows with no knowledge of war, rushed to the marketplace and began to shout—they had no commander: "Son of Dawmah! Son of Dawmah!"[382] Al-Mukhtār looked out at them and said, "By God, even if the person reproaching me with the name 'Dawmah' were 'a man of moment from the two cities,'[383] he would not reproach me with it." Noting their disorganization, the state of their appearance, and how scattered they were, he felt a desire to subdue them, and said to a group of his companions, "Go out with me." About two

---

dhayfah b. al-Yamān, a famous companion of the Prophet, had belonged. See Djaït, *Al-Kūfa*, 247.

380. Djaït locates it in the southwest part of the city, not far from al-Kunāsah (*Al-Kūfa*, 248).

381. Dār al-Siqāyah: "the building for providing water."

382. Dawmah bint ʿAmr b. Wahb b. Muʿattib was al-Mukhtār's mother (Balādhurī, *Ansāb*, V, 214).

383. Referring to Qur'ān 43:31, where Muḥammad's opponents are said to have reproached the Prophet by asking, "Why was this Qur'ān not sent down upon some man of moment in the two cities?" The parallel text in Balādhurī, *Ansab*, V, 261, reads: "He whom you are reproaching is indeed the son of 'a man of moment from the two cities.'" (Goitein's note to the Balādhurī passage mentions that some commentators identified one of the men as al-Mukhtār's grandfather or great-grandfather.)

hundred of them made a sortie with him. He attacked them, wounded about a hundred of them, and put them to flight. They fled in confusion in the direction of the house of Furāt b. Ḥayyān al-ʿIjlī. [736]

Then a man from the Banū Ḍabbah, a Baṣran named Yaḥyā b. Ḍamḍam, so tall that when he rode his feet almost touched the ground, a man most deadly to other men and awesome to behold, began to attack al-Mukhtār's forces. No man toward whom he directed himself held his ground. Al-Mukhtār, seeing him, attacked him and struck him a blow on his forehead, causing his forehead and brainpan to fly off; and he fell dead.

Then those commanders and chiefs [whom Muṣʿab had stationed] advanced from all sides. Al-Mukhtār's forces had no strength to stand up to them and so entered the palace. There they stayed, and the siege tightened around them. Al-Mukhtār said to them, "Alas! The siege is only making you weaker. Let us go down and fight until we are killed as honorable men, if we are to be killed. By God, I have not lost hope that if you fight them steadfastly, God will help you." But they lacked strength and hung back. So al-Mukhtār said to them, "As for me, by God, I will not submit, neither will I allow them to pass judgment over my life." When ʿAbdallāh b. Jaʿdah b. Hubayrah b. Abī Wahb saw what al-Mukhtār wanted, he let himself down from the palace by a rope, joined some of his brothers, and went into hiding among them.

Seeing the weakness of his companions and their discouragement, al-Mukhtār determined to make a sortie against the enemy. He sent to his wife, Umm Thābit bint Samurah b. Jundab al-Fazārī, and she sent him a large quantity of perfume. He washed, sprinkled his clothes with spices,[384] and put the perfume on his head and beard. Then he went out with nineteen men. Among them was [737] al-Sāʾib b. Mālik al-Ashʿarī, who was al-Mukhtār's deputy over al-Kūfah whenever al-Mukhtār went out to al-Madāʾin. He was married to ʿAmrah bint Abī Mūsā al-Ashʿarī, who bore him a child whom he named Muḥammad. This Muḥammad was with

384. As if preparing himself for burial: Lane, *Lexicon*, II, 657, s.v. *taḥannaṭa*, refers to a tradition in which a man going into battle does this to prepare himself for death and to induce himself to endure the fight with patience.

his father in the palace. When his father was killed and those in the palace taken, he was found and released, since he was a young lad.

When al-Mukhtār left the palace, he said to al-Sā'ib, "What do you think best?" Al-Sā'ib replied, "It is for you to say. What do you think?" Al-Mukhtār said, "I think? or God thinks?" Al-Sā'ib said, "Nay, what God thinks." Al-Mukhtār said, "Alas for you! You are a fool. I am a man of the Arabs. I saw Ibn al-Zubayr seize the Ḥijāz for himself; I saw Najdah[385] seize al-Yamāmah, and Marwān[386] Syria. Not being inferior to any man among the Arabs, I took this country and was like one of them—except that I sought vengeance for the members of the Prophet's family, while the Arabs were asleep about the matter. I killed those who participated in shedding their blood and have spared no effort in the matter until this very day. Fight, then, for the glory of your name, if you have no inner intention."[387] Al-Sā'ib said, "'Surely we belong to God, and to Him we return.'[388] What have I been doing that I should fight for the glory of my name? Thereupon, al-Mukhtār quoted the verses of Ghaylān b. Salamah b. Muʿattib al-Thaqafī:[389]

---

385. In 66/685, Najdah b. ʿĀmir al-Ḥanafī became leader of a group of Khārijites who had controlled central Arabia (al-Yamāmah) since 64/683. See Ṭabarī, II, 517; Balādhurī, *Ansāb*, XI, 127–28; Dixon, *Umayyad Caliphate*, 74.

386. I.e., the Umayyad caliph, Marwān b. al-Ḥakam.

387. The exchange is more cynical in tone in Dīnawarī, *Akhbār*, 313: Al-Mukhtār says to al-Sā'ib, "Let us go out to fight for the glory of our names, not for religion's sake." Shocked, al-Sā'ib exclaims, "Abū Isḥāq, people think you undertook this enterprise as a matter of religion!" Al-Mukhtār replies, "No, by my life it was only to seek [the goods of] this world. I saw that ʿAbd al-Malik b. Marwān had seized Syria, ʿAbdallāh b. al-Zubayr the Ḥijāz, Muṣʿab al-Baṣrah, Najdah the Harūrī al-ʿArūḍ [i.e., Arabia], and ʿAbdallāh b. Khāzim Khurāsān. I am inferior to none of them. Only by advocating vengeance for the death of al-Ḥusayn, was I was able to do what I wanted." In al-Ṭabarī's version, al-Mukhtār combines Shīʿī dedication with opportunism; in Dīnawarī he is a cynical opportunist.

388. See note 156.

389. A slightly different version of the poem, together with a story that throws light on the imagery, can be found in *Aghānī*, XII, 48. The poet Ghaylān b. Salamah has accompanied Abū Sufyān b. Ḥarb and a group of Quraysh and Thaqīf on a trading caravan to Iraq. As they cross into Iraq, Abu Sufyān gathers the men, warns them of the danger of entering the kingdom of a tyrant (*jabbār*) whose country is not their accustomed place of trade, and asks who is willing to go first and receive half the profit of the entire enterprise. Ghaylān volunteers. To illustrate the value of daring, he goes to a stream bed and begins striking (shaking off?) the leaves of the trees, reciting the poem.

Were Abū Ghaylān to see me, when anxieties retired
from me because of some affair having consequence,
He would say in fright and fear that two things are joined together:
life's profit, and soul's terror and fear.[390]
Either you obtain glory and noble deeds,
or the leaves are an example for you in regard to the one whom you destroy.[391]

Al-Mukhtār went out with nineteen men. He said to Muṣ'ab's men, "Will you give me an assurance of safety, and I will go out to you?" They said, "No, except on condition of your submitting to judgment." Al-Mukhtār said, "I will never allow you to pass judgment over my life"; and he fought with his sword until he was killed. He had said to his companions when they refused to follow him out, "If I make a sortie against them and am killed, you will only become weaker and more humiliated. If you submit to their judgment, your enemies whose relatives you have killed will jump up; each of them will say about one of you, 'This one is my revenge for my kinsman,' and the man will be killed, while you watch each other being struck down. Then you will say, 'If only we had obeyed al-Mukhtār and done what he thought best.' Had you gone out with me, failing to gain victory, you would have died as honorable men; or if any of you had escaped and reached his people, his people would have protected him. At this hour tomorrow, you will be the most abject people on the face of the earth." And it came to pass as he had said. [Continuing,] he said: People have asserted that al-Mukhtār was killed at the present site of al-Zayyātīn [Street],[392] and that he was killed by two men of the Banū Ḥanīfah, brothers, one of whom was named Ṭarafah, and the other Ṭarrāf, sons of 'Abdallāh b. Dajājah of the Banū Ḥanīfah. [738]

The day after al-Mukhtār's death, Bujayr b. 'Abdallāh al-Muslī

---

390. Version in *Aghānī*: "He would say that desire and fear are joined together: the love of life, and the soul's terror and fear."

391. Version in *Aghānī*: "Either you continue in [pursuit of] glory and fame, or the leaves are an example for you as regards those who perish." As the story in *Aghānī* shows, the life of a man who dies without glory is being compared to leaves that fall.

392. I.e., the oil sellers' street.

said, "Men, yesterday your commander gave you good advice: would that you had obeyed him! Men, if you submit to the enemy's judgment, you will be slaughtered like sheep. Go forth with your swords, and fight until you die nobly." But they disobeyed him and said, "Someone with more claim to our obedience and better than you at advising us commanded us to do it, and we disobeyed him. Shall we obey you?" So the men gave themselves up and submitted to be judged. Muṣʿab sent ʿAbbād b. al-Ḥuṣayn al-Ḥabaṭī to deal with them. He brought them out with their hands tied
[739] behind their backs. ʿAbdallāh b. Shaddād al-Jushamī made a will to ʿAbbād b. al-Ḥuṣayn.[393] ʿAbdallāh b. Qurād sought a stick or a piece of iron or anything with which to fight, but found nothing; that was because he was seized with regret after they came in, took his sword, and brought him out with his hands tied. ʿAbd al-Raḥmān [b. Muḥammad b. al-Ashʿath] passed by him as he was saying:

I was not afraid that I would be seen a prisoner:
Those who disobeyed the commander
Have been humbled and utterly destroyed.

So ʿAbd al-Raḥmān b. Muḥammad b. al-Ashʿath said, "Bring this one to me. Give him to me so that I can cut off his head." ʿAbdallāh b. Qurād said, "If I didn't smite your father and kill him with my sword, then I have the same religion as your grandfather, who believed and then became a nonbeliever!"[394] ʿAbd al-Raḥmān b. Muḥammad dismounted and said, "Bring him near me." They brought him near, and ʿAbd al-Raḥmān b. Muḥammad killed him. ʿAbbād became angry and said, "You killed him, though you were not commanded to kill him."

ʿAbd al-Raḥmān passed ʿAbdallāh b. Shaddād al-Jushamī, who was a *sharīf*. ʿAbd al-Raḥmān asked ʿAbbād to detain him until he had spoken to the commander concerning him. He then went to Muṣʿab and said, "I would like you to give me ʿAbdallāh b. Shaddād so that I may kill him. It is a matter of blood revenge."

---

393. The meaning apparently is that he asked ʿAbbād to protect his children after his death. See Dozy, *Supplément*, II, 822.

394. This refers to the fact that al-Ashʿath had taken part in the Riddah, the defection of some Arab tribes from Islam after the death of Muḥammad.

Muṣʿab ordered him to be given to ʿAbd al-Raḥmān. The latter went to him, took him, and beheaded him. ʿAbbād used to say, "By God, had I known that you only wanted to kill him, I would have given him to someone else and he would have killed him. But I thought you would speak to him concerning him and would then release him."

The son of ʿAbdallāh b. Shaddād was brought, Shaddād by name. He had reached puberty, but had applied a depilatory to himself. ʿAbd al-Raḥmān said, "Uncover him. Has he matured?" They said, "No, he is still is boy." So they released him.

Al-Aswad b. Saʿīd had asked Muṣʿab to offer his brother assurance of safety, and, if he submitted, to leave him to him. Al-Aswad therefore went to him and offered him assurance of safety, but the brother refused to submit, saying, "Dying with my comrades is [740] more pleasing to me than life with you." He was named Qays, and he was brought out and killed among those who were killed.

When Bujayr b. ʿAbdallāh al-Muslī—it is said that he was a *mawlā* of theirs—was brought to Muṣʿab together with many of al-Mukhtār's men, he said to Muṣʿab, "Praise be to God, who has tested us with shackles, and tested you by your forgiving us. There are two stations: one of them is God's good pleasure, the other His wrath. Whoever forgives, God forgives him and increases him in might; whoever punishes is not safe from retaliation. Ibn al-Zubayr, we are people who turn to the same *qiblah*[395] as you and hold your creed;[396] we are not Turks or Daylamites. If we have quarreled with our brothers and fellow countrymen, either we are right and they are wrong, or we are wrong and they are right. We have fought among ourselves as the people of Syria fought among themselves, who fought each other and then drew together; or as the people of al-Baṣrah fought among themselves, who quarreled and fought among themselves and then made peace and drew together. Now that you have obtained power, be gentle; having prevailed, forgive." He kept saying this and things like it until the men felt pity for them. Muṣʿab himself felt pity for them and

---

395. The *qiblah* is the direction of the Kaʿbah in Mecca, which Muslims face in prayer. See *EI*², s.v. Ḳibla.

396. *Millah* means both a religious creed and the community that holds that creed.

wanted to free them, but ʿAbd al-Raḥmān b. Muḥammad b. al-Ashʿath arose and said, "Will you free them? Choose us, Ibn al-Zubayr; or choose them!" And Muḥammad b. ʿAbd al-Raḥmān b. Saʿīd b. Qays al-Hamdānī jumped up and said, "My father and five hundred men of Hamdān, *ashrāf* of the people, and men of the city were killed; and you set them free, while our blood still is surging in their bodies! Choose us, or choose them!" Every man and member of a family that had lost a member jumped up and said something similar.

[741] When Muṣʿab b. al-Zubayr saw this, he ordered the men to be killed. They cried out to him all together, "Ibn al-Zubayr, do not kill us! Make us your vanguard against the Syrians tomorrow; by God, neither you nor your forces will be able to do without us tomorrow, when you meet your enemy. If we are killed, we shall have weakened them for you before being killed. If we win victory over them, it will be to your advantage and to the advantage of those who are with you." But Muṣʿab refused them and followed what pleased the generality of the people. Bujayr al-Muslī said, "My request to you is that I not be killed with these men. I commanded them to come out with their swords and fight to the death as honorable men, but they disobeyed me." So he was brought forward and killed.

According to Abū Mikhnaf—his father—Abū Rawq: Musāfir b. Saʿīd b. Nimrān said to Muṣʿab b. al-Zubayr, "Ibn al-Zubayr, what will you say to God when you come before Him after having put to death a group of Muslims who made you judge over their lives?—when the right thing in regard to their lives was that you not kill a Muslim soul except for a Muslim soul. If we killed a number of your men, kill as many [of us] as we killed of you, and free the rest of us. Among us now there are many men who were not present for a single day at any battlefield of the war between you and us. They were in al-Jibāl[397] and the Sawād,[398] collecting taxes and securing the roads." But Muṣʿab did not listen to him.

397. Al-Jibāl ("the mountains") was the region known earlier as Māh or Media. It was bounded on the east by the great desert of Khurāsān, on the southeast by Fārs, on the south by Khūzistān, on the west and southwest by Iraq, on the northwest by Ādharbayjān, and on the north by the Alburz range. See *EI*², s.v. Djibāl; Le Strange, *Lands*, 185ff.

398. See note 45; and Le Strange, *Lands*, 24.

So Musāfir said, "God's curse upon people I ordered to make a night sortie against the guards of one of these roads, so that we might drive them off and join our kin, but who disobeyed me until they drove me to suffer what is most contemptible, base, and low, insisting upon dying the death of slaves! I ask you not to mix my blood with theirs." So he was brought forward and killed separately.

Al-Muṣʿab then ordered al-Mukhtār's hand to be cut off and nailed with an iron nail to the side of the mosque. There it remained until al-Ḥajjāj b. Yūsuf arrived.[399] He looked at it and said, "What is this?" They said, "Al-Mukhtār's hand." He ordered it to be taken down. [742]

Muṣʿab sent his financial agents in charge of al-Jibāl and the Sawād. Then he wrote to [Ibrāhīm] b. al-Ashtar, summoning him to obedience to him, and saying to him, "If you respond to me and become obedient to me, Syria will be yours; you shall have control of the horses and of whatever land of the west[400] you subdue, as long as the family of al-Zubayr has dominion." ʿAbd al-Malik b. Marwān also wrote to Ibn al-Ashtar from Syria, summoning him to obedience to him, and saying, "If you respond to me and become obedient to me, you shall have Iraq." Ibrāhīm [b. al-Ashtar] summoned his companions and said, "What do you think?" Some of them said, "You should become obedient to ʿAbd al-Malik." Others said, "You should become obedient to Ibn al-Zubayr." Ibn al-Ashtar said, "Had I not killed ʿUbaydallāh b. Ziyād and the leaders of the Syrians, I would follow ʿAbd al-Malik, even though I do not want to choose [the people of] another city over the people of my city, or other tribesmen over my tribesmen." He therefore wrote to Muṣʿab, and Muṣʿab wrote him to come. So he came to him in obedience.

According to Abū Mikhnaf—Abū Janāb al-Kalbī: Muṣʿab's letter came to Ibn al-Ashtar containing the following:

> To proceed: God has killed the liar al-Mukhtār and his partisans who adopted unbelief as their religion and be-

399. After being appointed governor of Iraq by ʿAbd al-Malik, al-Ḥajjāj b. Yūsuf reached al-Kūfah in Ramaḍān of A.H. 75. (December 694–January 695). See Ṭabarī, II, 872.

400. For "west" (*maghrib*), Mss. O, Co and C read "of the Arabs" (*ʿarab*).

guiled[401] with enchantment. We summon you to the Book of God, the Sunnah of His Prophet, and allegiance to the Commander of the Faithful. If you respond favorably to this, come to me. You shall have the territory of al-Jazīrah and all the territory of the west, as long as you live and as long as the dominion of the family of al-Zubayr remains.
[743] In this matter you have an oath and covenant by God, and the strictest oath or bond that God accepted from the prophets. Peace!

ʿAbd al-Malik b. Marwān wrote to him as follows:

To proceed: The family of al-Zubayr have revolted against the Imāms of guidance, have tried to wrest command from those entitled to it, and have blasphemed in the Sacred House.[402] God will give power over them,[403] and will bring an evil turn upon them.[404] I summon you to God and the Sunnah of His Prophet. If you accept and respond favorably, you shall have authority over Iraq, as long as you live and I live. You have my oath and covenant by God that I will fulfill this.

Ibn al-Ashtar called his companions, read the letter to them, and asked their advice. One said ʿAbd al-Malik; another said Ibn al-Zubayr. So he said to them, "And my opinion is to follow the Syrians; but how can I do so, when there dwells not a tribe in Syria but I have slain members of it, giving it cause to seek revenge? Also, I am not going to leave my tribesmen and the people of my city." He therefore went to Muṣʿab. When word of his arrival reached Muṣʿab, the latter sent al-Muhallab to the district where he was to serve as governor. (This was the year in which al-Muhallab took up residence in the Euphrates [district].)

According to Abū Mikhnaf—Abū ʿAlqamah al-Khathʿamī:[405]

---

401. Mss. O and Co read: "and were learned men of enchantment."

402. I.e., the Kaʿbah. Mss. O and Co add: "and have profaned the sacred precinct."

403. Cf. Qur'ān 8:71.

404. Cf. Qur'ān 9:98 and 48:6.

405. Abū ʿAlqamah ʿAbdallāh b. ʿAlqamah al-Khathʿamī died in 87/706 as the last surviving Companion of the Prophet (*ṣaḥābī*) in al-Kūfah, cf. Ibn Ḥajar, *Tahdhīb*, V, 324, 151–2; and U. Sezgin, *Abū Miḥnaf*, 191.

Al-Muṣʿab sent for Umm Thābit bint Samurah b. Jundab, al-Mukhtār's wife, and ʿAmrah bint al-Nuʿmān b. Bashīr al-Anṣārī, who was also al-Mukhtār's wife, and said to them, "What do you say about al-Mukhtār?" Umm Thābit said, "What should we say? We say about him only what you yourselves say." So they told her to go. ʿAmrah, however, said, "God's mercy upon him, if[406] he was one of God's righteous servants." Muṣʿab therefore had her taken away to prison and wrote concerning her to ʿAbdallāh b. al-Zubayr, saying that she claimed al-Mukhtār was a prophet. ʿAbdallāh wrote back that he should take her out and kill her. Muṣʿab therefore had her taken out between al-Ḥīrah and al-Kūfah after nightfall, and Maṭar gave her three strokes with the sword. (Maṭar, a servant [*tābiʿ*] of the Qafal family of the Banū Taymallāh b. Thaʿlabah, was with the police.) ʿAmrah cried out, "O my father! O my family! O my people!" One of the Anṣār heard about her—it was Abān b. al-Nuʿmān b. Bashīr—and went to Maṭar and slapped him, saying, "Son of a whore! You cut off her soul; may God cut off your right hand!" Maṭar held fast to him, until he had taken him to Muṣʿab, where Maṭar said, "My mother is a Muslim woman." He claimed that the Banū Qafal would bear witness. No one, however, bore witness to him. Muṣʿab said, "Let the young man go free, for he has seen something horrible." [744]

ʿUmar b. Abī Rabīʿah al-Qurashī[407] composed [the following verses] about Muṣʿab's killing of ʿAmrah bint al-Nuʿmān b. Bashīr:

A thing most amazing in my eyes
    is the slaying of a fair-skinned, free, graceful-necked woman.
Though without fault, she was killed in this way:[408]
    Oh what an excellent person has been killed!
Killing and fighting have been prescribed for us,
    but for chaste women the dragging of skirts.

---

406. Ed. Cairo reads, "verily, he was." Cf. Balādhurī, *Ansāb*, V, 263: "I only know that he was a Muslim, one of God's righteous servants."

407. ʿUmar b. Abī Rabīʿah, a resident of Medina, was one of the most famous early writers of *ghazal* (love poetry) in Arabic. The verses are also attributed to ʿAbdallāh b. al-Zabīr al-Asadī (Balādhurī, *Ansāb*, V, 264).

408. For "in this way," *Dīwān*, 498, reads, "in vain"; Balādhurī, *Ansāb*, loc. cit., reads, "unjustly."

[745] According to Abū Mikhnaf—Muḥammad b. Yūsuf: Muṣʿab met ʿAbdallāh b. ʿUmar,[409] and, greeting him, said, "I am your brother's son, Muṣʿab." Ibn ʿUmar replied to him, "Yes, you are the man who in a single morning killed seven thousand people who turn toward the *qiblah*. Live as long as you are able!" Muṣʿab said, "They were unbelievers, beguilers." Ibn ʿUmar said, "Had you killed their number in sheep from your father's inheritance, it would have been extravagance."

Concerning this [viz. the killing of al-Mukhtār's wife], Saʿīd b. ʿAbd al-Raḥmān b. Ḥassān b. Thābit[410] composed [the following verses]:

A rider came bringing amazing tidings:
 the killing of al-Nuʿmān's daughter, a woman of religion and nobility:
The killing of a young woman pleasing of mien, modest,
 refined in character, disposition, and lineage;
A woman most pure, a descendant of noble men
 who chose virtue in ages past.
The friend and helper of the Chosen Prophet,
 his companion in war, misfortune, and grief,
Reported to me that the blasphemers agreed
 upon killing her: may they themselves not be spared killing and plundering!
May life give no joy to the family of al-Zubayr!
 May they taste the garment of humiliation, fear, and despoliation!
[746] You would think that when they brought her out and she was cut to pieces
 by their swords, they had won the kingdom of the Arabs!
Did the people not marvel at the killing of a free woman,
 chaste[411] of religion, praiseworthy of manners:

409. ʿAbdallāh b. ʿUmar, the son of the caliph ʿUmar b. al-Khaṭṭāb, was one of the most frequently cited authorities for traditions. He was married to al-Mukhtār's sister, Ṣafiyyah, and had interceded with the Umayyad authorities on al-Mukhtār's behalf in 64/783 (Ṭabarī, II, 522–23) and with the Zubayrids in 66/685 (Ṭabarī, II, 599–600). See *EI*², s.v.

410. A Medinan poet, grandson of the Prophet's "court poet," Ḥassān b. Thābit. See F. Sezgin, *GAS*, II, 423.

411. Dīnawarī, *Akhbār*, 315, reads, "sincere of religion."

A woman of leisure, a believer free
from blame, slander, doubt, or lying?
Upon us the divine decree of slaying and valor is incumbent;
but women are to be chaste in their bridal pavilions and veils.
In the religion of her noble grandfathers and fathers,
she passed on, not shaming her kin or acting immodestly.
A bashful woman, not frequent in going forth or unseemly in speech,
one who promoted harmony, [not] envious of the neighbor not of her clan,
Nor of the neighbor who was a kinsman: she did not know what foul speech was;
she never made evil draw near, nor did she like it.
I marveled on her account, when she was wrapped in a shroud, while alive.
Verily, this affair is a most extraordinary wonder.

According to ʿAlī b. Ḥarb al-Mawṣilī[412]—Ibrāhīm b. Sulaymān al-Ḥanafī (the son of the brother of Abū al-Aḥwaṣ)[413]—Muḥammad b. Abān—ʿAlqamah b. Marthad—Suwayd b. Ghaflah, who said: While I was journeying behind al-Najaf,[414] a man overtook me and struck me from behind with his staff. When I turned to him, he [747] said, "What do you have to say concerning the shaykh?" "Which of the shaykhs?" I asked. He said, "ʿAlī b. Abī Ṭālib." I said, "I bear witness that I love him with my hearing and sight and my heart and tongue." He said, "And I make you a witness that I hate him with my hearing and sight and my heart and tongue." Then we journeyed on until we entered al-Kūfah and parted. (After this, Suwayd stayed there some years, or, he may have said, for some time.)

[Continuing,] he said: Once while I was in the Great Mosque, a man wearing a turban entered. He carefully examined the faces of

---

412. Abū al-Ḥasan ʿAlī b. Ḥarb al-Mawṣilī (b. 170/786, d. 265/879) was a traditionist, scholar of ancient Arabian history, and poet. See F. Sezgin, *GAS*, I, 145.

413. On Abū al-Aḥwaṣ, see Dhahabī, *Tadhkirat al-ḥuffāẓ*, ed. F. Wüstenfeld (Göttingen, 1833–34), 9, 71 [Leiden note].

414. Al-Najaf lies about four miles west of al-Kūfah. ʿAlī was buried there, but for security reasons the site was kept secret during this period. In 175/791, the Caliph Hārūn "discovered" the spot and ordered a shrine to be built there. See *EI*[1], s.v. al-Nadjaf.

the people and kept looking at them. Seeing no beards more foolish than those of Hamdān, he sat down with them. I therefore moved and sat down with them. They asked, "Where have you come from?" He said, "From the family of your Prophet." They said, "What news have you brought us?" "This is not the right time for it," he said and arranged to meet them the following day. When he came the next day—I came, too—he took out a letter he had with him (at the bottom of it there was a lead seal), handed it to a young lad, and since he himself was illiterate and could not write, said to him, "Read it, boy." The boy said, "'In the name of God, the Merciful, the Compassionate. This is a letter to al-Mukhtār b. Abī ʿUbayd, which the legatee[415] of the family of Muḥammad wrote to him. To proceed...,'" and so forth. The people having burst out in tears, the man said, "Boy, put your letter aside until the people pull themselves together." I said, "People of Hamdān, I bear witness by God that this man once met me behind al-Najaf," and I told them his story. But they said, "By God, you insist upon holding people back from the family of Muḥammad and commending Naʿthal, who rent the books of the Qur'ān."[416] [Continuing, he said]: I said, "People of Hamdān, I tell you only what my ears have heard and my heart remembers from ʿAlī b. Abī Ṭālib (peace be upon him!). I heard him say, 'Do not call ʿUthmān "him who ripped up the books of the Qur'ān"; by God, he ripped them up only after consultation with us, the companions of Muḥammad. Had I come across them,[417] I would have done to
[748] them as he did.'" They said, "God! You heard this from ʿAlī?" I said, "By God, I heard it from him." [Continuing, he said]: They therefore left him. He then turned to the slaves, made use of them, and plied his craft.

---

415. On ʿAlī's special role as *waṣī*, "legatee" of the Prophet, in the ideology of early Shīʿī Islam, see Jafri, *Origins*, 92f, 97, 119, 121, 153. Here the term is extended to Muḥammad b. al-Ḥanafiyyah.

416. The *Lisān*, s.v., gives two explanations for *naʿthal*. Either it means "foolish old man," or it is the name of a long-bearded Egyptian who resembled ʿUthmān. In any case, ʿUthmān's enemies applied the term abusively. The epithet *shaqqāq*, "he who ripped up (the books of the Qur'ān)," refers to ʿUthmān's attempt to impose a standard recension of the Qur'ān and suppress variant texts. Some Shīʿites accused him of altering or suppressing passages supporting the claims of ʿAlī and the family of the Prophet to leadership.

417. I.e., books containing variant texts of the Qur'ān.

According to Abū Ja'far [sc. al-Ṭabarī]: Part of what we have reported about al-Mukhtār b. Abī 'Ubayd has been related by al-Wāqidī,[418] who differs on the subject from some of the people whose reports we have given. He alleges that al-Mukhtār openly opposed Ibn al-Zubayr only when Muṣ'ab came to al-Baṣrah. When Muṣ'ab set out toward al-Mukhtār and news of his setting out reached the latter, he sent Aḥmar b. Shumayṭ al-Bajalī against Muṣ'ab, ordering him to attack him at al-Madhār and saying, "Victory is at al-Madhār." [Al-Wāqidī] continued: Al-Mukhtār said that only because it was said that, "A man from the [tribe of] Thaqīf will be granted a great victory at al-Madhār." He thought it was he, but it really had to do with al-Ḥajjāj b. Yūsuf and his fight with 'Abd al-Raḥmān b. al-Ash'ath.[419]

Muṣ'ab ordered the commander of his vanguard, 'Abbād al-Ḥabaṭī, to march toward the assembled forces of al-Mukhtār. 'Abbād advanced, and with him went 'Ubaydallāh b. 'Alī b. Abī Ṭālib. Muṣ'ab encamped at Nahr al-Baṣriyyīn, on the bank of the Euphrates. (He dug a canal there which for that reason came to be called Nahr al-Baṣriyyīn.)[420] [Al-Wāqidī] continued: Al-Mukhtār went forth with twenty thousand men and halted facing them. Muṣ'ab and his forces advanced and came upon al-Mukhtār by night ready for battle. Al-Mukhtār sent word to his forces when evening came, saying, "Let none of you leave his place until he hears a crier cry out, '*Yā Muḥammad.*' When you hear it, attack." One of al-Mukhtār's companions said, "This man, by God, is a liar against God." He and those with him went over to al-Muṣ'ab. Al-Mukhtār delayed until the moon rose and then gave orders to a crier, who cried out, "*Yā Muḥammad.*" Then they attacked Muṣ'ab and his forces, put them to flight, and made him enter his camp, and they continued fighting them until morning. In the [749]

---

418. Muḥammad b. 'Umar al-Wāqidī (b. 130/747 in Medina, d. 207/823 in Baghdad): major historian, author of *Kitāb al-maghāzī* on the early Islamic conquests. See F. Sezgin, *GAS*, I, 294–97.

419. In 81–82/701, 'Abd al-Raḥmān ibn al-Ash'ath led a revolt against the governor of Iraq, al-Ḥajjāj b. Yūsuf. Of two battles in which al-Ḥajjāj defeated Ibn al-Ash'ath (al-Zāwiyah and Dayr al-Jamājim), the former seems more likely to be meant here. Although both locations lie between al-Kūfah and al-Baṣrah, al-Zāwiyah is closer to al-Madhār. See *EI*^{2}, s.v. Ibn al-Ash'ath; Yāqūt, *Mu'jam*, s.v. al-Madhār, Dayr al-Jamājim.

420. I.e., the river or canal of the Baṣrans.

morning, al-Mukhtār, having no one with him, and with his forces having penetrated into the forces of Muṣʿab, retreated in flight and entered the palace in al-Kūfah. When al-Mukhtār's forces came in the morning, they waited for a time and, not seeing al-Mukhtār, said, "He has been killed." Those who were able fled and went into hiding in the houses of al-Kūfah; about eight thousand of them, finding no one to lead them in fighting, betook themselves to the palace. There they found al-Mukhtār, and they went inside with him. During that night, al-Mukhtār's forces had killed many men from Muṣʿab's forces, including Muḥammad b. al-Ashʿath. In the morning, Muṣʿab came and surrounded the palace. Muṣʿab continued besieging it for four months. Every day, al-Mukhtār made a sortie against them and fought them in the market of al-Kūfah from one direction, but he was unable to overcome him. Finally, al-Mukhtār was killed.

After al-Mukhtār was killed, those in the palace sent and asked for a guarantee of safe-conduct. Muṣʿab refused, until they submitted to his judgment. After they submitted to his judgment, he killed about seven hundred of the Arabs; the rest of those he killed were Persians. [Al-Wāqidī] continued: When they came out, Muṣʿab wanted to kill the Persians and spare the Arabs; but those with him spoke to him, saying, "What kind of religion is this? How do you hope for victory when you kill the Persians and spare the Arabs, though their religion is the same!" So he had the Arabs brought forward and beheaded.

According to Abū Jaʿfar [sc. al-Ṭabarī]—ʿUmar b. Shabbah—ʿAlī b. Muḥammad [al-Madāʾinī], who said: After al-Mukhtār had been killed, Muṣʿab consulted his companions about the besieged men who had submitted to his judgment. ʿAbd al-Raḥmān b.
[750] Muḥammad b. al-Ashʿath, Muḥammad b. ʿAbd al-Raḥmān b. Saʿīd b. Qays, and others like them whose kinsmen al-Mukhtār had slain said, "Kill them." [The tribe of] Ḍabbah also raised an outcry and said, "The blood of Mundhir b. Ḥassān!"[421] ʿUbayd-

421. Al-Mundhir b. Ḥassān b. Ḍirār al-Ḍabbī was a Kūfan *sharīf*. After al-Mukhtār's victory over Ibn Muṭīʿ, Ibn al-Zubayr's governor, in 66/685, al-Mundhir had gone to swear allegiance to al-Mukhtār. As he left the palace, a group of Shīʿites attacked him as "one of the chief tyrants," killing him and his son Ḥayyān, despite the attempts of their leader, Saʿīd b. Munqidh, to restrain them. See Ṭabarī, II, 633.

allāh b. al-Ḥurr said, "Commander, turn over each man you have to his people, bestowing them as a favor to them; for, if they have killed us, we have killed them. Also, we need them on our frontiers. Turn over our slaves that you have to their masters; for they belong to our orphans and widows and those who are frail, that they may return them to their work. But kill these *mawālī*; for their unbelief has become obvious, their pride great, and their thankfulness small." Muṣʿab laughed and said to al-Aḥnaf [b. Qays], "What do you think, Abū Baḥr?" Alluding to them, he replied, "Ziyād wanted me to, but I refused him."[422] Muṣʿab then gave orders concerning all the men, and they were killed. They were six thousand. ʿUqbah al-Asadī composed [the following verses]:

You killed the six thousand in cold blood,
  their hands tied behind them, in spite of a firm pledge.
You made the protection of al-Ḥabaṭī[423] a bridge
  whose back was easy for the tramplers.
The morning they were called and deceived by their pledge,
  they were not the first men to perish by their own foolishness.
I had commanded them—if only they had obeyed me!—
  to fight in the lanes, unsheathing their swords.

Al-Mukhtār was killed, it has been said, at the age of sixty-seven, on the fourteenth day of the month of Ramaḍān in the year 67 (April 3, 687).

---

422. The reference is unclear. "Ziyād" is the Leiden editor's conjecture (the mss. have "Riyād"). Apparently, al-Aḥnaf recommended mercy, alluding to a previous occasion on which he had refused to give in to pressure to kill prisoners, but his advice was rejected by Muṣʿab. Cf. Balādhurī, *Ansāb*, V, 263: "(According to ʿAbdallāh b. Ṣāliḥ al-Muqri'—al-Haytham [b. ʿAdī]—ʿAwānah) When Muṣʿab was about to kill al-Mukhtār's companions who had submitted to his judgment, he consulted al-Aḥnaf b. Qays about them. Al-Aḥnaf said, 'I think you should forgive them; forgiveness is nearer to piety.' But the Kūfan *ashrāf* said, 'Kill them,' and became unruly. After they were killed, al-Aḥnaf said, 'Now that you have taken vengeance by killing them, may there be no evil consequence in the future [or, in the world to come].'" Another report in Balādhurī, *loc. cit.*, has Muṣʿab's wife send a message recommending mercy, but the message arrives too late.

423. I.e., ʿAbbād b. al-Ḥuṣayn al-Ḥabaṭī, Muṣʿab's commander, to whom the besieged partisans of al-Mukhtār had surrendered. See Ṭabarī, II, 738f.

Having concluded the affair of al-Mukhtār and his companions, and with Ibrāhīm b. al-Ashtar having come to him, Muṣ'ab sent al-Muhallab b. Abī Ṣufrah to be in charge of al-Mawṣil, al-Jazīrah, Ādharbayjān, and Armenia; he himself resided in al-Kūfah.

[Ibn al-Zubayr Removes Muṣ'ab from al-Baṣrah]

During this year, 'Abdallāh b. al-Zubayr removed his brother Muṣ'ab from al-Baṣrah and sent his own son, Ḥamzah b. 'Abdallāh,
[751] there. Differing reasons have been given for his removal of Muṣ'ab from al-Baṣrah and of how it took place.[424] Some have said what 'Umar [b. Shabbah] told me, [as follows]:

According [to 'Umar b. Shabbah]—'Alī b. Muḥammad [al-Madā'inī], who said: Al-Muṣ'ab continued in charge of al-Baṣrah until he went from there to fight al-Mukhtār, leaving as his deputy over al-Baṣrah 'Ubaydallāh[425] b. 'Ubaydallāh b. Ma'mar. Al-Mukhtār having been killed, Muṣ'ab went to visit 'Abdallāh b. al-Zubayr, who removed him from office and detained him in his house. He excused his removing him, saying to him, "By God, I know you are worthier and more qualified than Ḥamzah, but my opinion in the matter is that of 'Uthmān concerning 'Abdallāh b. 'Āmir,[426] when he appointed him [governor] and removed Abū Mūsā al-Ash'arī."

According to 'Umar [b. Shabbah]—'Alī b. Muḥammad [al-

424. The chronology of Muṣ'ab's movements is not easy to determine. Compare the following notice in Balādhurī, *Ansāb*, V, 264–65: "(According to al-'Umarī—al-Haytham b. 'Adī—'Awānah, and others) Muṣ'ab went [to Mecca] to visit his brother 'Abdallāh three times. The first time was from al-Kūfah after the death of al-Mukhtār, and Ibrāhīm b. al-Ashtar was with him. The second time was from al-Baṣrah, bringing the tribute from Iraq; and on that occasion ['Abdallāh] removed him from [the governorship] of al-Baṣrah and appointed his son Ḥamzah." Ḥamzah having proved incompetent, 'Abdallāh removed him "and reappointed Muṣ'ab to al-Kūfah and al-Baṣrah. Finally, Muṣ'ab needed to speak face to face with his brother concerning 'Abd al-Malik, when he learned of the latter's decision to invade Iraq. He went to see him, stayed only a day, and then rode back to Iraq."

425. Mss. O and Co: 'Umar.

426. In 29/649, 'Uthmān removed Abū Mūsā al-Ash'arī from the governorship of al-Baṣrah, to which he had been appointed by 'Umar in 17/649, and replaced him with 'Abdallāh b. 'Āmir b. Kurayz, after a delegation of Baṣrans had complained about abuses allegedly committed by Abū Mūsā. See Ṭabarī, I, 2829ff; Balādhurī, *Ansāb*, V, 256; *EI*[2], s.v. al-Ash'arī.

Madā'inī], who said: Ḥamzah came to al-Baṣrah as governor. He was munificent and generous, but disorderly in his affairs: sometimes he was generous to the point of not sparing anything he possessed; sometimes he held back what someone like him [ordinarily] would not hold back. In al-Baṣrah, his unsteadiness[427] and weakness became apparent. It is said that one day he rode to the estuary[428] of al-Baṣrah. When he saw it, he said, "If they handle the matter properly, this pond will suffice them for their summer." Some time afterwards, he rode out to it and chanced to come upon it when the water had ebbed. "I have already seen this once," he said, "and I suspected it would not be sufficient for them." Al-Aḥnaf [b. Qays] said to him, "This is water that comes to us and then ebbs away from us." He set out for al-Ahwāz.[429] When he saw its mountain, he said, "This is Quʿayqiʿān," referring to the place near Mecca, and therefore they named the mountain Quʿayqiʿān. He sent to Mardānshāh[430] and urged him [to hand over] the taxes. When the latter delayed, he betook himself to him with his sword, smote him, and killed him. Al-Aḥnaf said to him, "How sharp the commander's sword is!"

According to ʿUmar [b. Shabbah]—ʿAlī b. Muḥammad [al-Madā'inī], who said: When Ḥamzah had caused such confusion in al-Baṣrah, these traits of his having become apparent, and when he was about to smite ʿAbd al-ʿAzīz b. Bishr, al-Aḥnaf wrote to [752] Ibn al-Zubayr about it and asked him to reinstate Muṣʿab. [Continuing,] he said: It was Ḥamzah who put ʿAbdallāh b. ʿUmayr al-Laythī in charge of fighting the Najdiyyah[431] in al-Baḥrayn.

According to ʿUmar [b. Shabbah]—ʿAlī b. Muḥammad [al-

427. *Khiffah* (literally, "lightness") also connotes bad judgment, as illustrated in the next paragraph.

428. The *fayḍ* of al-Baṣrah, i.e., the Tigris-Euphrates estuary, the present Shaṭṭ al-ʿArab. See Le Strange, *Lands*, 43.

429. Al-Ahwāz was a city in Khūzistān, about 70 miles northeast of al-Baṣrah. See *EI*², s.v.

430. According to Balādhurī, *Ansāb* V, 256, this was the name of the *dihqān* of al-Ahwāz. *Dihqāns* were Persian landlords in Iraq who administered subdistricts.

431. These Khārijites, followers of Najdah b. ʿĀmir al-Ḥanafī, had extended their control from Central Arabia to the coastal region of al-Baḥrayn. ʿAbdallāh b. ʿUmayr's expedition failed to dislodge them. Najdah remained in control until 72/691, when his followers deposed him and settled on Abū Fudayk as his successor. See below, Ṭabarī, II, 829; Balādhurī, *Ansāb*, XI, 133ff; Dixon, *Umayyad Caliphate*, 169ff.

Madā'inī], who said: When Ibn al-Zubayr removed Ḥamzah, the latter carried off a great deal of money from the treasury of al-Baṣrah. Mālik b. Misma' confronted him, saying, "We will not allow you to go away with our stipends."[432] However, 'Ubaydallāh b. 'Ubayd b. Ma'mar guaranteed him the stipend (*'aṭā'*) and he yielded. Ḥamzah took away the money. When Ḥamzah left his father and came to Medina, he deposited the money with some men, but they made off with it, except for a Jew with whom he had deposited money and who fulfilled his obligation. When Ibn al-Zubayr heard what Ḥamzah had done, he said, "God curse him! I wanted to vie for glory with the sons of Marwān through him, but he retreated."

Hishām b. Muḥammad [al-Kalbī], on the authority of Abū Mikhnaf, mentions a different story about Muṣ'ab and how his brother removed him from al-Baṣrah and then reinstated him. What he mentions on the subject is in the course of a report that has been related to me [as follows]:

According to [Abū Mikhnaf]—Abū al-Mukhāriq al-Rāsibī:[433] After Muṣ'ab had subdued al-Kūfah, he resided there for a year, having been removed from the governorship of al-Baṣrah. ('Abdallāh [b. al-Zubayr] had removed him and had sent his own son Ḥamzah.) Having stayed there a year, Muṣ'ab went to visit his brother 'Abdallāh in Mecca, and the latter reinstated him over al-Baṣrah.

It has also been said that when Muṣ'ab had concluded the affair of al-Mukhtār, he returned to al-Baṣrah and put al-Ḥārith b. 'Abdallāh b. Abī Rabī'ah in charge of al-Kūfah.[434]

According to Muḥammad b. 'Umar [al-Wāqidī]: After Muṣ'ab killed al-Mukhtār, he held both al-Kūfah and al-Baṣrah.

---

432. On the role of Mālik b. Misma' in leading the opposition to Ḥamzah, see Balādhurī, *Ansāb*, V, 265; Ibn al-Athīr, *Kāmil*, IV, 281; EI^2, s.v. Masāmi'a.

433. He is, according to U. Sezgin, perhaps to be identified with Abū al-Mukhāriq al-Kūfī, who belonged to the fourth "class" of traditionists. See her *Abū Miḥnaf*, 189.

434. Ibn al-Athīr, *Kāmil*, IV, 279, gives a fuller version: "It has been said that Muṣ'ab returned to al-Baṣrah after having killed al-Mukhtār. He made al-Ḥārith b. Abī Rabī'ah his agent for al-Kūfah, for both [cities] were in his governorate. Then his brother removed him from al-Baṣrah and appointed his son Ḥamzah to be its governor. He afterwards removed Ḥamzah at the petition of al-Aḥnaf and the people of al-Baṣrah and reinstated Muṣ'ab."

[Those in Office during the Year]

ʿAbdallāh b. al-Zubayr led the pilgrimage this year. His governor (*ʿāmil*) in charge of al-Kūfah was Muṣʿab. (I have mentioned how the historians[435] differ about the governor of al-Baṣrah.) ʿAbdallāh b. ʿUtbah b. Masʿūd was in charge of the judiciary of al-Kūfah. Hishām b. Hubayrah was in charge of the judiciary of al-Baṣrah. [753]
ʿAbd al-Malik b. Marwān was in Syria, and ʿAbdallāh b. Khāzim al-Sulamī was in charge of Khurāsān.

435. *Ahl al-siyar*, literally, "people concerned with biographies, stories of how men conducted themselves."

The Events of the Year 68

(July 18, 687–July 5, 688)

Among these events was ʿAbdallāh [b. al-Zubayr's] returning of his brother Muṣʿab to Iraq as commander (*amīr*). We have already mentioned why ʿAbdallāh returned his brother Muṣʿab to Iraq as commander after having removed him. Having been returned there as commander, Muṣʿab sent al-Ḥārith b. Abī Rabīʿah to be commander in charge of al-Kūfah. This was because Muṣʿab, after his removal, began his return to Iraq as commander in al-Baṣrah and went there.

[The Azāriqah Return from Fārs to Iraq][436]

In this year, the Azāriqah[437] returned from Fārs to Iraq. They came into the vicinity of al-Kūfah and entered al-Madā'in.

---

436. Parallels, often implying different chronology, in Balādhurī, *Ansāb*, XI, 110ff; Ibn al-Athīr, *Kāmil*, IV, 281ff.

437. The Azāriqah (pl. of Azraqī) were a group of Khārijites named for their leader, Nāfiʿ b. al-Azraq, who is said to have held that all his adversaries, with their wives and children, should be put to death. In 64/683, these Khārijites took

An Account of Them, Their Departure, and Their Return to Iraq

According to Hishām [b. al-Kalbī]—Abū Mikhnaf—Abū al-Mukhāriq al-Rāsibī: Muṣʿab sent ʿUmar b. ʿUbaydallāh b. Maʿmar as commander in charge of Fārs. After al-Muhallab's onslaught upon them in al-Ahwāz, the Azāriqah had gone to Fārs, Kirmān, and the neighborhood of Iṣbahān.[438] When al-Muhallab left that area and was sent as governor in charge of al-Mawṣil and its neighborhood,[439] ʿUmar b. ʿUbaydallāh b. Maʿmar being in charge of Fārs, the Azāriqah, with al-Zubayr b. al-Māḥūz, de- [754]
scended upon ʿUmar b. ʿUbaydallāh in Fārs. He met them at Sābūr,[440] fought them vigorously, and won a clear victory over them; however, not many of them were killed, and they went away as if on the defensive, having left the battle in that condition.

According to Abū Mikhnaf—a shaykh of the tribe [of Azd][441] in al-Baṣrah, who said: I heard the letter of ʿUmar b. ʿUbaydallāh being read:

> In the name of God, the Merciful, the Compassionate. To proceed: I hereby inform the commander—may God preserve him!—that I met the Azāriqah, who have strayed from the religion of Islam and followed their caprices without guidance from God. With the Muslims, I fought them most vigorously for a part of the day. God then

advantage of the disturbances in al-Baṣrah to gain temporary control of the city; they were expelled, but remained a threat centered in neighboring Khūzistān province. In 65/684, both Nāfiʿ b. al-Azraq and the Zubayrid commander Muslim b. ʿUbays were killed fighting each other in Khūzistān. The Azāriqah regrouped under ʿUbaydallāh b. al-Māḥūz and spread terror between al-Ahwāz and al-Baṣrah. In 66/685, al-Muhallab b. Abī Ṣufrah was sent from al-Baṣrah to deal with them; he defeated to Azāriqah at Sillā wa-Sillibrā, near al-Ahwāz. ʿUbaydallāh was killed, but his successor, al-Zubayr b. al-Māḥūz, retreated to Fārs and regrouped his forces. See, in addition to the parallels cited above, Balādhurī, *Ansāb*, XI, 78ff.; *EI*², s.v.

438. Iṣbahān lay north of Fārs, in the province of al-Jibāl. See *EI*², s.v.; Le Strange, *Lands*, 204–6.

439. Muṣʿab's strategy was to use al-Muhallab as a barrier between himself and the forces of ʿAbd al-Malik. See Ibn al-Athīr, *Kāmil*, IV, 282.

440. Sābūr, or Shāpūr, is a city in Fārs province, some 65 miles west of Shīrāz. See Yāqūt, *Muʿjam*, s.v.; Le Strange, *Lands*, 248, 262f.

441. I.e., of Abū Mikhnaf's own tribe. See U. Sezgin, *Abū Miḥnaf*, 100.

smote them before and behind and made them turn their backs to us. Those whom God killed suffered by failing to attain and by losing [what they hoped to gain in this world and the hereafter]—and all are [destined] for loss! I have written this letter of mine to the commander while on the back of my horse, seeking the foe, whom I hope God will exterminate, if He so wills. Peace.

ʿUmar b. ʿUbaydallāh followed them. They immediately went and encamped by Iṣṭakhr.[442] He went after them, met them at the Ṭamastān bridge, and fought them vigorously. His son was killed, but he won a victory over them. Having cut the Ṭamastān bridge,[443] the Azāriqah removed to the neighborhood of Iṣbahān and Kirmān, where they remained until they had recovered and become strong, ready, and numerous. They then passed into Fārs, where ʿUmar b. ʿUbaydallāh b. Maʿmar was, crossing its territory in an area other than the one where he was. They made their way
[755] past Sābūr and then went out through Arrajān.[444] When ʿUmar b. ʿUbaydallāh saw that the Khārijites had crossed his territory, heading toward al-Baṣrah, he became afraid that Muṣʿab b. al-Zubayr would not forgive him for this. Hastening after them, he reached Arrajān and found that they had left it, heading toward al-Ahwāz. The coming of the Azāriqah was reported to Muṣʿab, who went forth and encamped with his men at the Great Bridge.[445] He said, "By God, I don't know what I have gained by putting ʿUmar b. ʿUbaydallāh in Fārs and giving him an army whose provisions (*arzāq*) I pay every month, whose stipends (*aʿṭiyāt*) I pay in full every year, and for whom I order special grants (*maʿāwin*)[446] every

---

442. Iṣṭakhr, just north of ancient Persepolis (modern Takht-e-Jāmshīd), lay on the Pulwar River about 40 miles northeast of Shīrāz. See *EI*², s.v.; Yāqūt, *Muʿjam*, s.v.; Le Strange, *Lands*, 275ff.

443. They cut the bridge to hinder the forces pursuing them. See Ibn al-Athīr, *Kāmil*, IV, 282.

444. Arrajān, on the Ṭāb River (modern Āb-i Kurdistān or Mārūn), lay on the border between Fārs and Khūzistān. See *EI*², s.v. Arradjān; Le Strange, *Lands*, 268ff.

445. Arabic, *al-jisr al-akbar*.

446. *Maʿūnah*, pl. *maʿāwin*, referred to money given to a tribe to prepare it to make an expedition, then to a special levy made when the public treasury was depleted, and finally was extended to cover taxes in general. See Dozy, *Supplément*, II, 192; and *EI*², s.v.

year equal to the stipends! I have cut off any pretext he might have, supplied him with men, and made them strong—and the Khārijites cross his territory toward me! By God, had he fought them and then fled, it would have been more excusable for him in my eyes, even though someone who takes flight should not have his excuse accepted and has not acted in a way that deserves honor."

Led by al-Zubayr b. al-Māḥūz, the Khārijites came and encamped at al-Ahwāz. Their spies having reported to them that ʿUmar b. ʿUbaydallāh was on their heels and that Muṣʿab b. al-Zubayr had left al-Baṣrah to fight them, al-Zubayr arose among them, praised and extolled God, and said, "To proceed: For you to fall between these two forces would be bad strategy and confusion. Let us hasten toward our enemy and meet them from one direction."

He led them across the district of Jūkhā, turned toward the Nahrawān districts,[447] and followed the bank of the Tigris until he reached al-Madā'in, where Kardam b. Marthad b. Najabah al-Fazārī was. They made a raid on the people of al-Madā'in, killing children, women, and men, and ripping open pregnant women. Kardam fled. Then they went to Sābāṭ and used their swords on [756]
the people, killing a slave woman who had borne a child[448] to Rabīʿah b. Nājid, and also killing Bunānah, the daughter of Abū Yazīd b. ʿĀṣim al-Azdī. Bunānah had read the Qur'ān and was exceedingly beautiful. When they came at her with swords, she said, "Woe unto you! Have you ever heard of men killing women? Woe unto you! You kill someone who stretches out no hand against you, wishes you no harm, and has no power to help herself. Will you kill someone who grew up bedecked with ornaments and was never seen in conflict?" One of them said, "Kill her." A certain man among them said, "You should leave her." Somebody said [to him], "Her beauty pleases you, you enemy of God! You have fallen into unbelief[449] and been seduced." Then the man

447. The Nahrawān districts (Upper, Middle, and Lower) lay on a canal east of the Tigris. See Le Strange, *Lands*, 80, 57ff.

448. Literally, "an *umm walad*," i.e. a slave woman who had borne a child to her master. Such a woman was normally freed and her children recognized as legitimate after her master died. See Schacht, *Islamic Law*, 129.

449. *Kafarta*, "you have disbelieved, become a *kāfir* (nonbeliever)."

went away and left them. We thought he had left them no longer disagreeing [with him],[450] but they attacked her and killed her.

Rayṭah bint Yazīd said, "Praise God! Do you think God is pleased with what you do, killing women, children, and those who have done you no wrong?" Then she went away. They attacked her. In front of her was al-Ruwāʿ bint Iyās b. Shurayḥ al-Hamdānī, the daughter of Rayṭah's full brother. They attacked Rayṭah and struck her on the head with the sword; the point of the sword hit the head of al-Ruwāʿ, and the two fell to the ground together. Iyās b. Shurayḥ fought the attackers for a time, but was thrown down and lay among the slain; they left him, thinking they had killed him. A man from Bakr b. Wā'il, named Razīn b. al-Mutawakkil, was also injured. When the Khārijites went away from them, only Bunānah bint Abī Yazīd and the slave woman who had borne a
[757] child to Rabīʿah b. Nājid died; the rest of them recovered. They gave each other water to drink, bandaged their wounds, hired mounts, and went toward al-Kūfah.

According to Abū Mikhnaf—al-Ruwāʿ bint Iyās, who said: I never saw a man more cowardly than one who was with us. His daughter was with him; when they came at us, he put her into our hands and fled, leaving her and us. On the other hand, I never saw a man nobler than one who was with us. We did not know him, nor he us. When they came at us, he fought to protect us until he was thrown down [wounded] among us. It was Razīn b. al-Mutawakkil al-Bakrī. Afterwards, he used to visit us and befriended us. He perished during al-Ḥajjāj's term of office. The Arab tribesmen were his heirs: he was a righteous worshiper [of God].

According to Hishām b. Muḥammad [al-Kalbī]—Abū Mikhnaf—his father[451]—his paternal uncle:[452] Muṣʿab b. al-Zubayr had sent Abū Bakr b. Mikhnaf to be in charge of Upper Ustān.[453] When al-Ḥārith b. Abī Rabīʿah came,[454] he removed him. After-

450. For this meaning of *fāraqa*, see Dozy, *Supplément*, II, 259.

451. Abū Mikhnaf's father was Yaḥya b. Saʿīd b. Mikhnaf.

452. I.e., Muḥammad b. Mikhnaf b. Sulaym, the paternal uncle of Abū Mikhnaf's father. From Ṭabarī, I, 3266, one can deduce that he was born about 19/640 and was present at the Battle of Ṣiffīn. See U. Sezgin, *Abū Miḥnaf*, 224f.

453. *Ustān al-ʿāl*: Middle Persian *ōstān*, which designated Sasanian crown land, occurs in Arabic as *ustān, istān,* or *astān.* Upper Ustān was the territory controlled from al-Anbār on the middle Euphrates. See Le Strange, *Lands*, 80; Morony, *Iraq*, 145.

wards, however, he confirmed him in charge of his financial district (*ʿamal*) in the second year. When the Khārijites came to al-Madā'in, they dispatched one of their bands, led by Ṣāliḥ b. Mikhrāq, to fight him. He encountered him at Karkh,[455] fought him for a time, and then they dismounted: Abū Bakr dismounted and the Khārijites dismounted [to fight]. Abū Bakr, his *mawlā* Yasār, ʿAbd al-Raḥmān b. Abī Jiʿāl, and one of his tribesmen were killed, and the rest of his forces were put to flight. Surāqah b. Mirdās al-Bāriqī (from a subtribe of Azd) said:[456]

Help, O people, against the anxieties that visit by night!
    Against the event that has brought distress!
The death of a chieftain of noble descent; [758]
    one who was daring, a protector, and exceedingly brave!
The death of [Abū Bakr] b. Mikhnaf was reported to me just before
    [I reached] the foothills,[457]
    when the first of the flickering stars had set.
I said, "May God receive you with mercy!
    May God, the Lord of East and West, bless you!"
May God cover with shame a people who turned aside from you
    in the morning
    and did not endure steadfastly the shining, flashing [swords].
They turned their backs; in the morning they distanced
    themselves from our leader
    and master in the distressing strait.
Therefore, whenever you come to us in our houses,
    you hear wailing from women and young girls.
They weep for a man of praiseworthy nature, glorious,
    steadfast in battle for those he must defend.
Therefore my soul has become sad,
    and my hair has turned white from the burden I bear because
    of him.

---

454. I.e., when he came to al-Baṣrah to serve as governor for Ibn al-Zubayr. This happened in 66/685; see Ṭabarī, II, 601.

455. Karkh: a village that became a southwestern suburb of Baghdad. Balādhurī, *Ansāb*, XI, 115, reads "Karkh of Baghdad." See Yāqūt, *Muʿjam*, s.v.

456. See *Dīwān*, 35–36.

457. *Al-khayf* can either be a generic term or refer specifically to Khayf al-Minā, near Mecca. See Yāqūt, *Muʿjam*, s.v.

According to Abū Mikhnaf—Ḥadrah b. ʿAbdallāh al-Azdī, al-Naḍr b. Ṣāliḥ al-ʿAbsī, and Fuḍayl b. Khadīj (all of whom reported this to me): The people of al-Kūfah came to al-Ḥārith b. Abī Rabīʿah[458] and cried out to him, saying, "Go out [to fight]; behold, our enemy has drawn near us, and he has no mercy." He
[759] went out, exerting himself energetically, until he encamped at al-Nukhaylah.[459] There he stayed for several days. Ibrāhīm b. al-Ashtar jumped up before him; having praised and extolled God, he said: "To proceed: A merciless foe has come toward us, killing men, women, and children, terrorizing travelers, and laying waste to towns. Let us hasten to meet him. Order a departure." So al-Ḥārith went forth and encamped at Dayr ʿAbd al-Raḥmān. There he stayed until Shabath b. Ribʿī came before him and spoke to him as Ibn al-Ashtar had spoken. So he departed, but did not exert himself. When the people saw how slowly he was traveling, they recited this verse of *rajaz* about him:

Al-Qubāʿ has led us an arduous march:
he travels for a day and halts for a month!

They made him journey on from that place, but whenever he encamped with them, he halted until the people raised a clamor about it and cried out around his tent. It took him something over ten days to reach al-Ṣarāt.[460] When he came to al-Ṣarāt, the enemy's vanguard and first horsemen had already reached it.

When spies brought the Azāriqah word that the forces of the people of the garrison city [sc. of al-Kūfah] had come to them, they cut the bridge between them and these forces. The people began to recite this verse of *rajaz*:

Al-Qubāʿ has traveled a smooth journey:
five days between Dabīrā and Dabāhā![461]

---

458. Mss. O and Co add: "who was nicknamed al-Qubāʿ."

459. Al-Nukhaylah is close to al-Kūfah, on the road to Syria (Yāqūt, *Muʿjam*, s.v.). Al-ʿAlī, "Minṭaqat al-Kūfah," 237–38, locates it as the first stage north of al-Kūfah, close to present-day Jisr al-ʿAbbāsiyyāt.

460. There were two canals named al-Ṣarāt. The first, which is probably the one meant here, branched from the Nahr ʿĪsā between al-Anbār and Baghdad, and flowed into the Tigris. The second lay further south, was usually called the Great Ṣarāt, and flowed from the Euphrates just north of al-Ḥillah, to the Tigris. See Le Strange, *Lands*, 66, 72.

461. Dabīrā is mentioned by Yāqūt as a village near Baghdad; Dabāhā is men-

According to Abū Mikhnaf—Yūnus b. Abī Isḥāq—his father: There was a man from Sabīʿ[462] with a touch of insanity about him in a village called Jawbar, near al-Kharrārah.[463] He was named Simāk b. Yazīd. The Khārijites came to his village and took him and his daughter. His daughter they brought forward and killed. Abū al-Rabīʿ al-Salūlī stated to me that his daughter's name was Umm Yazīd and that she kept saying to them, "People of Islam, my father is afflicted;[464] do not kill him. As for me, I am only a girl. I swear to God I have never committed indecency, harmed any neighbor of mine, or been proud and conceited."[465] When they brought her forward to kill her, she started to cry out, "What is my offense? What is my offense?" She fell down in a faint or dead, and then they cut her up with their swords. Abū al-Rabīʿ said: This report was given to me by her nurse, a Christian woman from the people of al-Khawarnaq,[466] who was with her when she was killed. [760]

According to Abū Mikhnaf—Yūnus b. Abī Isḥāq—his father: The Azāriqah brought Simāk b. Yazīd with them, until they came within sight of al-Ṣarāt. [Continuing,] he said: Turning to our army and seeing the large number of men assembled, Simāk b. Yazīd began to shout to us in a loud voice, "Come over to them; they are few and wicked." Thereupon, they beheaded him and crucified him, while we were looking on at him. [Continuing,] he said: When night fell, a tribesman and I crossed over, took him down, and buried him.

---

tioned by him as a village near Baghdad in the administrative subdistrict (*tassūj*) of Nahr al-Malik. See Yāqūt, *Muʿjam*, s.vv.

462. Sabīʿ was a division of the Hamdān tribe. Note that the report is being related on the authority of Yūnus b. Abī Isḥāq ʿAmr b. ʿAbdallāh al-Hamdānī al-Sabīʿī.

463. For Jawbar, Mss. O and Co read Juwayn, which is in Khurāsān, nowhere near al-Kharrārah, a place near al-Saylaḥūn, in the district of al-Kūfah (Yāqūt). The Leiden editor corrects to Jawbar. Yāqūt, *Muʿjam*, lists a village named Jawbar in the *sawād* of Baghdad. The Nahr Jawbar canal connected the Tigris and the Euphrates just south of al-Madāʾin (Le Strange, *Lands*, 68).

464. A euphemism for "weak-minded," or "insane."

465. The verbs *taṭallaʿtu. . .tasharraftu* also have the literal sense of looking down from a high place, perhaps to spy.

466. Al-Khawarnaq Palace, built according to tradition by al-Nuʿmān, prince of al-Ḥīrah, for the Sasanian king Bahrām Gūr (reg. 421–431, or 420–438), lay a few miles south of al-Kūfah and about one mile east of Najaf. See EI^2, s.v.; Le Strange, *Lands*, 75ff; Yāqūt, *Muʿjam*, s.v.

[761] According to Abū Mikhnaf—his father: Ibrāhīm b. al-Ashtar said to al-Ḥārith b. Abī Rabī'ah, "Send the men with me, so that I can cross over to these dogs and bring you their heads right now." But Shabath b. Rib'ī, Asmā' b. Khārijah, Yazīd b. al-Ḥārith, Muḥammad b. al-Ḥārith, and Muḥammad b. 'Umayr said, "May God preserve the commander! Let them go; don't start anything with them." [Continuing,] he said: They seem to have been jealous of Ibrāhīm b. al-Ashtar.

According to Abū Mikhnaf—Ḥaṣīrah b. 'Abdallāh [b. al-Ḥārith al-Azdī] and Abū Zuhayr [al-Naḍr b. Ṣāliḥ] al-'Absī: When the Azāriqah reached the bridge of al-Ṣarāt and saw that the army of the people of the garrison city [sc. of al-Kūfah] had come out to fight them, they cut the bridge. Al-Ḥārith, taking advantage of the opportunity to delay, sat down with the men, praised and extolled God, and said: "To proceed: The first part of fighting is the shooting of arrows, then the pointing of spears, then the thrusting of them right and left; and the end of it all is the drawing of swords." [Continuing,] he said: A man stood up before him and said, "The commander—may God preserve him!—has described it well. But how long shall we keep doing this, while this river lies between us and our enemy? Order this bridge rebuilt the way it was, and lead us across to them. God will make you see a result you will like concerning them."

Al-Ḥārith therefore commanded that the bridge should be rebuilt, and the men crossed toward the Azāriqah. The latter fled until they reached al-Madā'in. When the Muslims arrived at al-Madā'in, some horsemen from the Azāriqah came and weakly charged some Muslim horsemen at the [floating] bridge and then drew back from them. Al-Ḥārith b. Abī Rabī'ah had 'Abd al-Raḥmān b. Mikhnaf pursue them with six thousand men to expel them from the territory of al-Kūfah; however, they were to let them go, if they reached the territory of al-Baṣrah. So he pursued
[762] them until they left the territory of al-Kūfah and went toward Iṣbahān; then he turned away from them, not having fought them; no fighting had taken place between him and them. The Azāriqah proceeded and encamped near 'Attāb b. Warqā', who was at Jay.[467]

467. Jay was one of two adjacent cities that together formed Iṣbahān. See Le Strange, *Lands*, 203. Ibn al-Athīr, *Kāmil*, IV, 284–87, reports that before besieging Iṣbahān, the Khārijites went to Rayy, where the local inhabitants (non-Muslims?)

They stayed there and besieged him. He made a sortie and fought them, but was unable to prevail against them. They attacked his forces, so that they went back into the city. (At that time, Iṣbahān was assigned as a grant (*ṭuʿmah*) to Ismāʿīl b. Ṭalḥah from[468] Muṣʿab b. al-Zubayr. [Ismāʿīl b. Ṭalḥah] had sent ʿAttāb to be in charge.) ʿAttāb held out against them; every day he made a sortie and fought them at the gate of the city, and they bombarded the Azāriqah from the wall with arrows and stones.

There was with ʿAttāb a man from Ḥaḍramawt[469] named Abū Hurayrah b. Shurayḥ. He used to go out with ʿAttāb and was a brave man. As he attacked the Azāriqah, he would recite:[470]

You dogs of hell! What do you think
    of the attack of Abū Hurayrah, the snarler?
He snarls at you by night and by day,
    O Ibn Abī al-Māḥūz and you evil ones.
What do you think of Jay[471] as a goal?

When his recitations had gone on too long for the Khārijites, one of them (he is supposed to have been ʿAbīdah b. Hilāl) laid wait for him. Abū Hurayrah went out one day and did as he had been doing, saying what he was accustomed to say. Suddenly, ʿAbīdah b. Hilāl attacked him and struck him a blow with the sword on the muscle[472] of his shoulder blade and threw him down. Abū Hurayrah's companions attacked ʿAbīdah b. Hilāl; they carried away Abū Hurayrah, brought him inside [the city], and treated [763]
him. Afterwards, the Azāriqah began calling at them, saying, "You

---

helped them defeat the governor, Yazīd b. al-Ḥārith b. Ru'aym, whose son Ḥawshab fled ignominiously. Muṣʿab later ordered ʿAttāb b. Warqā' to punish the inhabitants of Rayy for helping the Khārijites. ʿAttāb did so, defeating them and their leader al-Farrukhān.

468. Correcting *ibn*, "son of," to *min*, "from," as proposed in ed. Leiden, *Addenda*, p. DCLXXIII. No son of Muṣʿab named Ṭalḥah is known. On the other hand, Ismāʿīl b. Ṭalḥah b. ʿUbaydallāh is mentioned by Ibn Qutaybah, *Maʿārif*, 120, and is given the *kunyah* Abū al-Bakhtarī in Ṭabarī, II, 808.

469. Ḥaḍramawt is the extreme south of the Arabian peninsula, modern South Yemen. See *EI*², s.v.

470. The lines, in *rajaz* meter, pun on the literal meaning of "Abū Hurayrah," "father of the cat," i.e. a man fond of cats. Variants can be found in al-Mubarrad, *Kāmil*, 1096, and in Ibn ʿAbd Rabbih, *ʿIqd*, I, 219.

471. Another reading: "What do you think of fighting me..." (Mss. O, Co, and Ibn al-Athīr, *Kāmil*, IV, 285).

472. *Ḥabl* can mean muscle, nerve, or vein (Lane, *Lexicon*, II, 504f).

enemies of God! What did Abū Hurayrah, 'the snarler,' do?" They, in turn, would call out, "You enemies of God! By God, he has nothing to fear." Abū Hurayrah soon recovered and afterwards went out against them. The Azāriqah began to say, "You enemy of God! We had hopes that we had sent you to visit your mother!" He said to them, "You ungodly ones! Why do you mention my mother?" They started to say, "Indeed, he is angry on account of his mother and is going to visit her shortly!" Abū Hurayrah's companions said to him, "Woe unto you! They mean hell." Realizing what they meant, he said, "You enemies of God, how undutiful you are to your mother when you separate yourselves from her! She[473] is *your* mother and unto her you are destined to go!"

The Khārijites continued attacking them for several months, until their horses died and their food ran out; the siege had become very severe, and they were afflicted by great weariness. So ʿAttāb b. Warqā' summoned the people of Jay. Having praised and extolled God, he said, "To proceed: People, you see what weariness has befallen you. By God, naught remains save that each of you die in his bed and that his brother come to bury him, if he can. But the brother will most likely be too weak to do it; so each will die by himself and find no one to bury him or pray over him. Then fear God; for by God you are not so few in number that your strength will be contemptible to your enemy. Among you there are skilled horsemen from the garrison city, and you are the most pious among your fellow tribesmen. Let us make a sortie against these men, while there is life and strength in you, before each of you becomes unable to march toward his enemy from weariness or defend himself from a woman if she comes at him. May each man fight to protect himself; may he be steadfast and brave! By God, I have hope that if you fight bravely, God will make you victorious over them and cause you to subdue them."

[764] The people cried to him from every side, "You have gone straight to the mark. Let us make a sortie against them." So he gathered the people to himself at night and ordered them given a large evening meal. They ate the evening meal at his house. The next morning,

473. I.e., the fire of hell. ("Fire" is grammatically feminine in Arabic.)

he led them out under their banners. They came upon the enemy in their camp in the morning, when they felt safe that they would not be come upon in their camp. They attacked the enemy beside the camp and fought with them. The Khārijites cleared away from the front of the camp, so that the attackers reached al-Zubayr b. al-Māḥūz. Together with a band of his companions, he dismounted and fought until he was killed. The Azāriqah withdrew and joined Qaṭarī,[474] to whom they swore allegiance. ʿAttāb reentered his city, having taken whatever he wanted from their camp. Qaṭarī came pursuing him, apparently intending to fight him, and halted at the camp of al-Zubayr b. al-Māḥūz. The Khārijites assert that one of Qaṭarī's spies came to him and said, "I heard ʿAttāb say, 'If these men were to ride donkeys and lead horses, and if they were to sojourn today in one land and tomorrow in another, they would be more likely to survive.'" When that was reported to Qaṭarī, he went away and left them alone.

According to Abū Mikhnaf—Abū Zuhayr [al-Naḍr b. Ṣāliḥ] al-ʿAbsī (who was with them): We went forth to meet Qaṭarī the following day, on foot, with drawn swords. [Continuing,] he said: They departed; and, by God, it was the last they were encountered. [Continuing,] he said: Qaṭarī then went until he reached the area of Kirmān,[475] where he stayed until many troops had joined him. He pillaged the land,[476] appropriated the revenues, and became strong. Then he turned to the territory of Iṣbahān, came out by way of the Nāshiṭ mountain pass to Īdhaj,[477] and stayed in the territory of al-Ahwāz.

Al-Ḥārith b. Abī Rabīʿah was Muṣʿab b. al-Zubayr's governor in charge of al-Baṣrah. He wrote informing Muṣʿab that the Khārijites had descended upon al-Ahwāz and that only al-Muhallab could deal with them. Muṣʿab therefore sent to al-Muhallab, who was in charge of al-Mawṣil and al-Jazīrah, ordering him to go and fight [765]

474. On the career of Qaṭarī b. al-Fujā'ah, the last and most famous leader of the Azāriqah, see *EI*², s.v. Ḳaṭarī b. al-Fudjā'a.

475. Kirmān, major city of the province of the same name, lay about 350 miles southeast of Iṣbahān. See *EI*², s.v.

476. Literally, "He ate up the land." For this meaning, see Dozy, *Supplément*, I, 31.

477. Modern Persian, Izeh, 80 miles northeast of Ahwāz, at the foot of the Zagros Mountains. See *EI*², s.v.

the Khārijites, and sending Ibrāhīm b. al-Ashtar to [take charge of] his district. Al-Muhallab went to al-Baṣrah, chose men, and led out the men he had selected. He then headed toward the Khārijites, and they advanced toward him. They met at Sūlāf[478] and fought there for eight months in some of the hardest fighting the men had ever seen, with neither side sufficiently injuring the other through spear thrusts and sword blows to force it to yield.

[Events in Syria]

According to Abū Ja'far [sc. al-Ṭabarī]: In this year, there was severe drought in Syria, so severe that they were unable to campaign.

In this year, 'Abd al-Malik b. Marwān encamped at Buṭnān Ḥabīb in the territory of Qinnasrīn.[479] They were rained on there, and there was so much mud that they called the place "Buṭnān al-Ṭīn."[480] 'Abd al-Malik spent the winter there and then returned to Damascus.

[The Death of 'Ubaydallāh b. al-Ḥurr]

In this year, 'Ubaydallāh b. al-Ḥurr was killed.[481]

---

478. Sūlāf was a village in Khūzistān, about 20 miles north of al-Ahwāz, west of the Dujayl river and near the town of Manādhir al-Kubrā. See Yāqūt, *Mu'jam*, s.v.; Le Strange, *Lands*, p. 239.

479. Qinnasrīn is in northern Syria near Aleppo. Buṭnān Ḥabīb (the name means "the lowlands of Ḥabīb," after Ḥabīb b. Maslamah, the Muslim conqueror of the area) is a wādī about 30 kilometers east of Aleppo. See *EI*^{2}, s.v. Buṭnān; Yāqūt, *Mu'jam*, s.v. Buṭnān and Qinnasrīn.

480. I.e., "the lowland of mud."

481. 'Ubaydallāh b. al-Ḥurr al-Ju'fī: Further information on this Kūfan *sharīf*-outlaw in Dīnawarī, *Akhbār*, 243–56, 265–72; Balādhurī, *Ansāb*, V, 290–98; Ibn al-Athīr, *Kāmil*, IV, 287–95. On his activity as a poet, see F. Sezgin, *GAS*, II, 355–6. In 51/671, he witnessed the arrest in al-Kūfah of Ḥujr b. 'Adī (Ṭabarī, II, 135). In 60/680, when Mu'āwiyah died, he was present in al-Kūfah when a group of *ashrāf* invited al-Ḥusayn to come to the city; but when the governor 'Ubaydallāh b. Ziyād arrested al-Ḥusayn's agent, Muslim b. 'Aqīl, Ibn al-Ḥurr left al-Kūfah and encamped at Qaṣr Banī Muqātil (in the desert near present-day Ukhayḍir). In 61/681, al-Ḥusayn passed by 'Ubaydallāh b. al-Ḥurr's camp and called on him to help; Ibn al-Ḥurr refused (Ṭabarī, II, 305, 388–90), but offered al-Ḥusayn a swift horse on which to escape. Later, Ibn al-Ḥurr expressed his grief over the events at Karbalā' in a poem. In 67/686, he fought for Muṣ'ab against al-Mukhtār in the siege of al-Kūfah (Ṭabarī, II, 633–34).

His Death; the Circumstances That Brought It upon Him

According to Aḥmad b. Zuhayr—ʿAlī b. Muḥammad [al-Madāʾinī] —ʿAlī b. Mujāhid: ʿUbaydallāh b. al-Ḥurr was one of the best of his tribesmen[482] in righteousness, excellence, prayer, and exertion. After ʿUthmān was killed,[483] and conflict erupted between ʿAlī and Muʿāwiyah, he said, "Truly, God knows that I love ʿUthmān and will avenge him, now that he is dead." He therefore went to Syria and was on the side of Muʿāwiyah. (Mālik b. Misma' also went to Muʿāwiyah, being of similar opinion concerning the [766]
ʿUthmāniyyah.[484]) ʿUbaydallāh remained with Muʿāwiyah, was present with him at Ṣiffīn, and continued with him until ʿAlī (peace be upon him!) was killed.[485] After ʿAlī was killed, ʿUbaydallāh came to al-Kūfah. He went to his brothers and whoever had been active in the civil strife and said to them, "Men, I do not think anyone's standing aside will benefit him. We have been in Syria, and thus and so has happened in regard to Muʿāwiyah's enterprise." And the people said to him, "Thus and so has happened in regard to ʿAlī's enterprise." So he said, "Men, if we have the opportunity, throw off your restraint and take charge of your own affairs." They said, "We will meet." So they used to meet together concerning the matter.

When Muʿāwiyah died, the conflict erupted in the civil strife (*fitnah*) of Ibn al-Zubayr. ʿUbaydallāh said, "I do not think that Quraysh is doing the right thing. Where are the sons of free women?" Outlaws[486] of every tribe came to him, so that he had

---

482. The tribe of Juʿfī, to which he belonged, was a Yemeni tribe either allied to or a subdivision of the tribe of Madhḥij.

483. ʿUthmān, the third caliph, was killed in 35/656.

484. The ʿUthmāniyyah was the party that demanded that the murderers of ʿUthmān be punished. Muʿāwiyah, the governor of Syria, emerged as the leader of the party, based on his blood relationship to ʿUthmān (although he was not the next of kin).

485. The Battle of Ṣiffīn was in 38/657; ʿAlī was killed in 40/661.

486. The term *khalīʿ* referred to a man whose crimes had rendered him an outcast from his family, clan, or tribe. In effect, the tribe served notice that it would no longer protect such a man; if anyone wished to avenge himself on him for his crimes, he would no longer incur the wrath of the tribe for killing one of its members. Since in pre-Islamic Arabia the protection of a man's tribe was essential for survival, the *khalīʿ*'s life was in real danger. He could either

seven hundred skilled horsemen with him. "Give us your command," they said.

When 'Ubaydallāh b. Ziyād fled and Yazīd b. Mu'āwiyah died,[487] 'Ubaydallāh b. al-Ḥurr said to his young men, "Dawn has become visible to anyone who has eyes.[488] So if you want [to act, do it]." He went out to al-Madā'in and left no money that was brought from al-Jibāl province to the government but that he took it and took from it his stipend and the stipends of his companions. Then he said, "You have partners in this money in al-Kūfah, men who have a claim to it; but take the coming year's stipend in advance." To the official in charge of the treasury he wrote a quittance[489] for the money he had collected and began to range the rural districts (*kuwar*) in a similar manner.

[Al-Madā'inī] said: I asked ['Alī b. Mujāhid], "Was it his practice to help himself to people's money and that of merchants?" He said to me, "You do not know Abū al-Ashras.[490] By God, there
[767] was no Arab tribesman in the land more respectful toward free women, or more abstemious from unseemly behavior and wine drinking than he. All that demeaned him in people's eyes was his poetry, for he was one of the young men fondest of poetry."

'Ubaydallāh b. al-Ḥurr continued in this way until al-Mukhtār rose to power[491] and was informed of what he was doing in the

---

become a lone brigand, trusting to his own skill in eluding enemies, or he could band together with others in the same predicament.

487. After Yazīd b. Mu'āwiyah died in 64/683, 'Ubaydallāh b. Ziyād, the Umayyad governor of al-Baṣrah and al-Kūfah (he had been responsible for the death of al-Ḥusayn and the repression of the Kūfan Shī'īs), was forced to flee to Syria. See *EI*[1], s.v. 'Ubaid Allāh b. Ziyād.

488. Proverbial for a thing that has become altogether manifest. See Lane, *Lexicon*, I, 286, s.v. *bāna*; Freytag, II, 255; Maydānī, II, 39.

489. *Barā'ah*, a document stating that the person in question had fulfilled his duty and was under no further obligation. See ed. Leiden, *Glossarium*, p. CXXX.

490. Abu al-Ashras ("the most ill-natured, harsh, or severe") is the nickname of 'Ubaydallāh b. al-Ḥurr.

491. I.e., in the events of 66/685 in al-Kūfah. Cf. Dīnawarī, *Akhbār*, 304: "Al-Mukhtār wrote to 'Ubaydallāh b. al-Ḥurr al-Ju'fī, who was attacking and raiding in the region of al-Jabal, and said to him, 'You rebelled only in anger over al-Ḥusayn. We, too, are among those who are angry on his account. We have devoted ourselves to avenging his blood. Help us in the matter.' When 'Ubaydallāh made no reply, al-Mukhtār rode to 'Ubaydallāh's house in al-Kūfah, destroyed it, and ordered 'Ubaydallāh's wife to be arrested and imprisoned." The sequence of events in Dīnawarī is: arrest and imprisonment of 'Ubaydallāh's wife, 'Ubaydallāh's

Sawād. Al-Mukhtār ordered ʿUbaydallāh's wife, Umm Salamah al-Juʿfiyyah, to be imprisoned. Al-Mukhtār said, "By God, I will kill him or kill his companions." When ʿUbaydallāh b. al-Ḥurr learned of this, he came with his young men, entered al-Kūfah by night, broke the door of the prison, and brought out his wife and every woman and man who was in it. Al-Mukhtār sent some men to fight him, and he fought with them until he had left the city. When he got his wife out of prison, he recited:

Have you not known, Umm Tawbah, that I am
  the horseman who protects those of Madhḥij he is duty-bound to protect,
And that I came to the prison at the height of the forenoon[492]
  with young men, each of them a protector of what is inviolable, each of them fully armed?
As soon as the women came out of prison, there appeared to us
  a forehead like a sunbeam, unwrinkled,
And a smooth cheek, revealing a young woman beloved
  to us—may every rain cloud that approaches give her drink!
The only life for me is to visit you fearlessly,
  as was our habit before my warring and my rebelling.
You are the soul's object of solicitude and love: [768]
  Peace be upon you from a companion covered with scars!
Because of your imprisonment, I remained imprisoned, downcast,
  grieved by what you encountered thereafter.
By God, did you ever see a horseman like me,
  when they stormed the prison from every entry?
[A man] such as I will protect such [a woman] as you;
  I hold fast whenever a crisis does not loosen its grip.
For you I will fight them with the sword, that you may return
  to safety and a life abundant and plentiful.
If they surround me, I will charge them
  like the father of two lion cubs cornered in a thicket.

---

raid on the estate of ʿAmr b. Saʿīd al-Hamdānī, his rescue of his wife, and his fighting his way out of al-Kūfah.

492. Either there is a disparity between the poem (he came in the forenoon) and the associated prose text (he came by night), as is not uncommon in Arabic sources that cite poems within historical narratives, or (as seems implied in Dīnawarī) ʿUbaydallāh entered al-Kūfah by night and rescued his wife the following day.

I challenged Ibn Kāmil al-Shākirī to fight me,
but he turned away, galloping swiftly, not turning aside.
If they call out my name, I turn against them
horses generous in battle, most of them with hurting hoofs.[493]
No wonder Salmā, my wife, says,
"Ibn al-Ḥurr, truly you are a man who never withdraws from fighting!
Leave the men; do not fight them. Escape safely;
hasten with the horsemen—God guide you!—and go forth."
I hope, O best of women, to be seen
in the best state of one who has hopes; so hope you!
[769] How lovely it was when I said to Aḥmar of Ṭayyi'[494]
and to Ibn Khubayb, "The dawn has drawn near; journey forth!"
And when I said to this one, "Travel," to that one, "Depart,"
and to that one afterwards, "Saddle up!"

He began to harass al-Mukhtār's financial agents and partisans. [The tribe of] Hamdān arose with al-Mukhtār, burned Ibn al-Ḥurr's house, and sacked his estate at al-Jubbah and al-Budāt.[495] When he learned of this, he went to the estates of 'Abd al-Raḥmān b. Sa'īd b. Qays at Māh,[496] caused them to be plundered, and caused everything belonging to [the tribe of] Hamdān there to be plundered. Then he went to the Sawād and left no property belonging to any Hamdānī untaken. Concerning that, he said:

---

493. I.e., because he has driven them so hard.

494. Aḥmar of Ṭayyi' was one of Ibn al-Ḥurr's companions. See Ṭabarī, II, 388–390, and II, 775, below.

495. Al-Jubbah and al-Budāt (or al-Badāt) are two districts (*tassūj*) in the *sawād* of al-Kūfah (Yāqūt, *Mu'jam*, s.vv.). The Nahr al-Badāt was a canal that left the Kūfah branch of the Euphrates about a day's journey north of al-Kūfah and flowed south to the Great Swamp. See Le Strange, *Lands*, 74.

496. Two cities or districts had the name of Māh: Māh al-Baṣrah, the Nihāwand district, whose taxes were used for the support of the military population of al-Baṣrah, and Māh al-Kūfah, the city of Dīnawar in al-Jibāl, whose revenues were applied to the benefit of the citizens of al-Kūfah. Since 'Abd al-Raḥmān b. Sa'īd b. Qays (who, according to Dīnawarī, *Akhbār*, 302, had carried out al-Mukhtār's order to sack and destroy 'Ubaydallāh's house) was one of the *ashrāf* of al-Kūfah, the city of Dīnawar seems more likely. See *EI*², s.vv. Dīnawar and Māh al-Baṣra; Le Strange, *Lands*, 189.

Of the bulk of our property neither the liar[497]
    nor the blue-eyed[498] men of Hamdān have left anything but a remnant.
Is it right that Shākir should plunder my estates,
    and that Ibn Saʿīd's estate should be safe from me?
Have you not known, Umm Tawbah, that I
    am not listless when confronting the vicissitudes of fortune?
I tighten my belt for every adversity,
    and against every affliction I am exceedingly stalwart.
If I do not come to Shākir in the morning with a squadron
    and cure my sword's thirst with my own two hands—
(They destroyed my house and led my wife off [770]
    to their prison—the Muslims are my witnesses.
They gave her no time to tie her veil.
    O the marvel! Will fate avenge me?)
Then I am not Ibn al-Ḥurr,[499] if I do not suprise them
    with armored horsemen who attack like lions.
My horsemen are not cowards; I have urged them
    against an army numerous and well equipped.

This is [part of] a long poem.

[Continuing,] he said: He used to come to al-Madā'in and make the rounds of the Jūkhā district financial agents, taking whatever money they had, and then head toward al-Jibāl province. He continued in this manner until al-Mukhtār was killed. After al-Mukhtār had been killed, people said to Muṣʿab in his second governorship, "Ibn al-Ḥurr split with both [ʿUbaydallāh] b. Ziyād and al-Mukhtār. We fear he may attack the Sawād as he used to do." Muṣʿab therefore imprisoned him. Ibn al-Ḥurr said:

Who will inform the young men
    that a strong door and its keeper have come between them and their brother,
In a dwelling unpleasing?
    Whenever he stands up, fetters creak and respond to him.

---

497. I.e., al-Mukhtār.

498. In Arabic poetry, blue eyes are considered a defect: either a sign of poor vision (cataracts) or a sign of hostility, See Lane, *Lexicon*, III, 1228. Dīnawarī, *Akhbār*, 304, reads "the man."

499. Punning on the literal meaning of Ibn al-Ḥurr, "son of the free man."

On the leg above the heel there is something black, mute,
and strong; it contracts his steps and shortens them.
This did not happen because of a great crime I committed,
but a slanderer spread his lies.
[771] There is a course in the wide world;
for many a man his paths on it have been strait.
For man there is a lesson in fortune, time,
and the past, if ever vicissitudes occur.

ʿUbaydallāh [b. al-Ḥurr] asked some men from Madhḥij to go to Muṣʿab on his behalf. He sent to the eminent men of the tribe and said, "Go to Muṣʿab and speak to him by himself, for he has imprisoned me without a crime. Some liars have slandered me and made him afraid of things I would not do and that would not be my business." But he also sent word to some young men from Madhḥij, saying, "Gird on swords and take battle gear. I have sent some men to Muṣʿab to speak to him on my behalf. Stand at the door. If the men come out and he has accepted their intercession, interfere with no one; let your swords be covered by your garments."

The men from Madhḥij came, entered Muṣʿab's presence, and spoke to him. He accepted their intercession and released ʿUbaydallāh. Ibn al-Ḥurr had said to his companions, "If the men come out and Muṣʿab has not accepted their intercession, take the prison by force; I will help you from inside." When Ibn al-Ḥurr came out, he said to them, "Show your swords." They showed them; no one interfered with him, and he went to his home. Muṣʿab regretted having released him, for Ibn al-Ḥurr was openly disobedient. When men came to congratulate him, he said, "This matter[500] is meet only for such men as were your former caliphs. We see no one equal to them or like them among us, that we should allow him to conduct our affairs and grant him our sincere advice.[501] If it is only 'He who overcomes takes the spoil,'[502] why

500. Arabic *amr*, which means both "command," and "matter, thing," is used like Latin *res* in the phrase *res publica* to mean "state or commonwealth," and particularly the caliphate. Cf. Dozy, *Supplément*, I, 37.

501. The Arabic idiom, "grant sincere advice," is stronger than the English equivalent. It is regularly used by synecdoche to mean the entire loyalty of a man to his superior.

502. I.e., if the caliphate has become merely the prerogative of whoever has the

do we bind ourselves with allegiance (*bayʿah*) to them, when they are no braver than we in battle or wealthier than we? The Messenger of God charged us, "No obedience to a creature that involves disobeying the Creator!" After the four who have passed away,[503] we have seen no righteous imām or pious helper (*wazīr*); all of them have disobeyed and opposed [God]—strong as to this world and weak as to the next! Why should our honor be violated, when we are veterans of al-Nukhaylah, al-Qādisiyyah, Jalūlā', and Nihāwand?[504] We meet spearheads with our necks and swords with our faces, and then our right and merit go unacknowledged! Then fight for your wives. Whatever happens, there will be advantage in it for you. I hereby turn against them[505] and show them hostility. There is no strength but in God!" [772]

So ʿUbaydallāh b. al-Ḥurr made war on them and raided. To deal with him, Muṣʿab sent Sayf b. Hāni' al-Murādī, who said to ʿUbaydallāh, "Muṣʿab will give you the tax revenue of Bādūrayā,[506] on condition that you swear allegiance and become obedient to him." ʿUbaydallāh replied, "Don't I [already] have the tax revenue of Bādūrayā and other districts? I accept nothing, and on no condition will I trust them. But I see, young man"—Sayf was a young man at the time—"that you are an intelligent young fellow. Wouldn't you like to follow me, and I will make you rich?" Sayf refused.

When he left prison, Ibn al-Ḥurr said:

Kūfah is not my mother, nor is Baṣrah my father;
    neither does laziness deflect me from travel.

(Abū al-Ḥasan [al-Madā'inī] said the authorship of this verse is attributed to Suḥaym b. Wathīl al-Riyāḥī.)

---

strength to seize it by force. The expression is proverbial, see Freytag, II, 677 (Maydānī, II, 219).

503. I.e., the first four caliphs: Abū Bakr, ʿUmar, ʿUthmān, and ʿAlī.

504. Famous battles: At al-Nukhaylah in 41/661, Kūfan forces rescued Muʿāwiyah's Syrians from a band of Khārijites (Ṭabarī, II, 7–9). Al-Qādisiyyah and Jalūlā' were both sites of great Muslim victories over the Persians in 16/637. The Muslim victory at Nihāwand, in 21/641, effectively opened the Iranian plateau to Muslim penetration.

505. Literally, "I have turned towards them the outer side of the shield." The expression is a proverb meaning to become hostile to someone after reconciliation. See Freytag, II, 258 (Maydānī, II, 40).

506. Bādūrayā was a village on the west bank of the Tigris later incorporated into greater Baghdad. See Le Strange, *Lands*, 31.

Ibn al-Zubayr, do not think I am like a drowsy man
who, when he alights in a place, sleeps until he is told, "Go away."
If I do not incite to visit you horses that run grimly,
carrying their riders, may I not be called a man of judgment and valor.
[773] If you do not see raids against you from every side,
so that you speedily repent, O man,
May no chaste woman ever lay off her veil in my household,
and may I live only on vain hopes and excuses![507]

This is [part of] a long poem.

Muṣʿab sent al-Abrad b. Qurrah al-Riyāḥī with a band of men to fight him, but he was defeated by Ibn al-Ḥurr, who struck him a blow on the face. Then Muṣʿab sent against him Ḥurayth b. Zayd (or Yazīd), who challenged him to single combat, but ʿUbaydallāh b. al-Ḥurr killed him. Then Muṣʿab sent against him al-Ḥajjāj b. Jāriyah[508] al-Khathʿamī and Muslim b. ʿAmr, who met him at the Ṣarṣar canal,[509] but ʿUbaydallāh fought them and defeated them. Then Muṣʿab sent him men to offer him safety, gifts, and charge of any country he wanted; but he refused. He went to Narsā;[510] its *dihqān*,[511] Ṭīzjushnas, fled with the revenue of al-Fallūjah and, pursued by Ibn al-Ḥurr, went to ʿAyn al-Tamr,[512] where he took refuge with the forces of Bisṭām b. Maṣqalah b.

507. An oath to divorce his wife is implied. Such as oath was considered particularly strong.

508. Ms. "Ḥārithah," corrected by ed. Leiden, *Addenda*, p. DCLXXIII.

509. A canal that left the Euphrates about 10 miles south of al-Anbār, passed through the town of Ṣarṣar, just south of Baghdad, and flowed into the Tigris about 5 miles north of al-Madā'in. See Le Strange, *Lands*, 32, 35, 67.

510. Apparently a variant for the Nars canal (attributed to the Persian Narsā) that left the Sūrā channel of the Euphrates near al-Ḥillah. The districts between the main branch of the Euphrates and the Sūrā channel were called Upper and Lower Fallūjah. See Le Strange, *Lands*, 73f.

511. A *dihqān* was a member of the local class of Persian landlords in Iraq who administered subdistricts. See EI^2, s.v. Mss. Pet, O and Co give the first syllable of the name as Ṭīr-, but vary in dotting the remaining consonants.

512. ʿAyn al-Tamr was a town in a fertile depression on the border of the desert west of the Euphrates, some 60 miles northwest of al-Kūfah. Since it commanded the approach to al-Kūfah from the Western Desert, governors of al-Kūfah normally maintained a garrison there. See EI^2, s.v.; Yāqūt, *Muʿjam*, s.v.

Hubayrah al-Shaybānī, who was in charge of the town. Bisṭām and his forces went out and fought Ibn al-Ḥurr. Bisṭām's cavalry numbered one hundred and fifty horsemen. Challenged by Ibn al-Ḥurr to single combat, Yūnus b. Hāʿān al-Hamdānī from Khaywān[513] said, "The worst that fortune has in store is what it brings in the end. I never thought I would live until a man challenged me to single combat."[514] He met him in single combat, and Ibn al-Ḥurr struck him a blow that knocked the strength out of him; then they grappled, and both fell from their horses. Ibn al-Ḥurr took Yūnus's turban, tied his hands with it, and then rode off.

Al-Ḥajjāj b. Jāriyah al-Khathʿamī came to them. Al-Ḥajjāj attacked him, but ʿUbaydallāh also took him prisoner. Bisṭām b. Maṣqalah challenged al-Mujashshir[515] to single combat; they exchanged blows until each had wearied the other. When Ibn al-Ḥurr saw that Bisṭām was winning, he attacked Bisṭām. Bisṭām grappled with him and both fell on the ground. Ibn al-Ḥurr fell on Bisṭām's chest and took him captive. That day, he took many men captive. One man would say, "I was your companion on such and such a day"; another would say, "I dwelt among you"; and each of them sought to gain favor by what he thought would be to his advantage, so that he would be released. [774]

ʿUbaydallāh b. al-Ḥurr sent horsemen from among his companions under the leadership of Dalham al-Murādī to seek the *dihqān*. They found him and took the money before there was any fighting. Ibn al-Ḥurr said:

If I had four men like Jarīr,[516]
    I would go to the treasury in the morning and collect.
Muṣʿab and those with him would not frighten me.
    How excellent a young man is Ibn Mashjaʿah!

---

513. Khaywān was a town in Yemen. See Yāqūt, *Muʿjam*, s.v., and *Lisān*, s.v.

514. Cf. Balādhurī, *Ansab*, V, 295: "One of Bisṭām's men, Yūnus b. ʿĀhān by name, challenged Ibn al-Ḥurr to single combat. ʿUbaydallāh said—and it became proverbial, 'The worst that fortune has in store is what it brings in the end. I never thought I would live to see a man such as this one challenge me to single combat.'"

515. One of ʿUbaydallāh b. al-Ḥurr's men.

516. Jarīr b. Kurayb commanded Ibn al-Ḥurr's left wing (Balādhurī, *Ansāb*, V, 295).

Then 'Ubaydallāh went to Takrīt. Al-Muhallab's financial agent fled from Takrīt, and 'Ubaydallāh stayed there, collecting the revenue. Muṣ'ab sent al-Abrad b. Qurrah al-Riyāḥī and al-Jawn b. Ka'b al-Hamdānī with a thousand men, and al-Muhallab reinforced the two with Yazīd b. al-Mughaffal with five hundred men to fight him. A man from Ju'fī[517] said to 'Ubaydallāh, "A large number have come upon you; do not fight them," but he replied:

My kinsmen try to make me afraid of being killed:
but I shall die only when the appointed Decree[518] comes.
Perhaps, spears with their points will draw wealth near,
and we shall live as generous men; or [it may be that] we shall attack and be killed.[519]

Then he said to al-Mujashshir...,[520] gave him his banner, and
[775] sent Dalham al-Murādī forward with him. He fought them for two days, having three hundred men with him. Jarīr b. Kurayb was wounded; 'Amr b. Jundab al-Azdī and many of his horsemen were killed. At evening the two sides stopped fighting.

'Ubaydallāh left Takrīt and said to his companions, "I am taking you to 'Abd al-Malik b. Marwān." So they made ready; but then he said, "I fear I may depart from life without having frightened Muṣ'ab and his companions. Let us go back to al-Kūfah." [Continuing,] he said: He went to Kaskar,[521] banished its financial agent, and took its treasury. Then he went to al-Kūfah and encamped at Laḥḥām Jarīr.[522] Muṣ'ab sent 'Umar b. 'Ubaydallāh b. Ma'mar against him, and he fought with him. Ibn al-Ḥurr then

---

517. Ju'fī was Ibn al-Ḥurr's own tribe.

518. *Al-kitāb al-mu'ajjal,* literally, "the appointed book," or "the book whose time is appointed," i.e. the divine decree fixing the term of a man's life. The phrase occurs in Qur'ān 3:145.

519. Balādhurī, *Ansāb,* V, 296: "...and we shall live as generous men whom men ask for gifts and for whose generosity they hope." The Balādhurī version adds two lines: "Have you not seen that poverty brings contempt upon its people, and that in wealth there is eminence and adornment? If you do not venture upon what is fearful, you will never attain enough wealth to satisfy a friend and provide a surplus."

520. A word such as "Advance!" has apparently dropped out of the text (ed. Leiden, note).

521. See note 342.

522. Ibn al-Athīr, *Kāmil,* IV, 293, reads "Ḥammām Jarīr."

left for Dayr al-Aʿwar.[523] Muṣʿab sent Ḥajjār b. Abjar against him. When Ḥajjār was defeated, Muṣʿab heaped abuse on him, sent him back, and had Jawn b. Kaʿb al-Hamdānī and ʿUmar b. ʿUbaydallāh b. Maʿmar join forces with him. So they all fought Ibn al-Ḥurr. Many of Ibn al-Ḥurr's companions were wounded and their horses hamstrung. When al-Mujashshir, who carried Ibn al-Ḥurr's banner, was wounded, he gave the banner to Aḥmar of Ṭayyi'. Ḥajjār b. Abjar was beaten back, but wheeled round and returned to the fight. The two sides fought hard until evening. Ibn al-Ḥurr said:

If I had three men like young al-Mujashshir,
I would attack them [sc. the enemy] by night, not doubting.
He helped me the night of Dayr al-Aʿwar
with spear thrust and sword stroke, and at the crossing;
ʿUmar b. Maʿmar then would perish.

Ibn al-Ḥurr then left al-Kūfah.

Muṣʿab then wrote to Yazīd b. al-Ḥārith b. Ru'aym al-Shaybānī, who was at al-Madā'in, ordering him to fight Ibn al-Ḥurr. Yazīd sent forward his son Ḥawshab, who met ʿUbaydallāh b. al-Ḥurr at Bājisrā.[524] ʿUbaydallāh defeated him and killed some of his men. Ibn al-Ḥurr went and entered al-Madā'in, and [776]
Yazīd's forces took refuge in the stronghold. Then ʿUbaydallāh left. Muṣʿab dispatched al-Jawn b. Kaʿb al-Hamdānī and Bishr b. ʿAbdallāh al-Asadī against him. Al-Jawn encamped at Ḥawlāyā;[525] Bishr went to Tāmarrā,[526] and encountered Ibn al-Ḥurr. Ibn al-Ḥurr killed him, defeated his forces, and then met al-Jawn b. Kaʿb at Ḥawlāyā. ʿAbd al-Raḥmān b. ʿAbdallāh went out to fight him; Ibn al-Ḥurr attacked him, thrust him with a spear, killed him, and defeated and pursued his forces. Then Bushayr b. ʿAbd al-Raḥmān b. Bushayr al-ʿIjlī went out to fight him. They

523. Dayr al-Aʿwar lay north of al-Kūfah, approximately halfway to Karbalā'. See *EI*², s.v.

524. Bājisrā lay on the Nahrawān Canal, about 35 miles north of al-Madā'in. See Le Strange, *Lands*, 59.

525. Ḥawlāyā is located in the Nahrawān district (Yāqūt, *Muʿjam*, s.v.).

526. Tāmarrā was the name given to the Nahrawān Canal north of Bājisrā. See Le Strange, *Lands*, 59f.

met at Sūrā and fought hard. Bushayr then turned away from him, went back to his district (*ʿamal*), and said, "I have defeated Ibn al-Ḥurr." When what he had said reached Muṣʿab, the latter said, "He is one of those who like to be praised for what they have not done."

ʿUbaydallāh [b. al-Ḥurr] remained in the Sawād, raiding and collecting the tax revenues. Concerning this, Ibn al-Ḥurr said:

Ask Ibn Ru'aym about how I fight and take my stand
at the Hall of Khusraw,[527] not turning my back to them.
Distinguished [in war], I wheel round to charge them, and you see them
like goats that take to the rocks for fear of the wolf.
I attacked them by night in the stronghold of Khusraw son of Hurmuz
with bright whetted [swords] and dark [spears] from al-Khaṭṭ.[528]
I gave them spear thrusts and sword blows; you see them
seeking refuge from us in the middle of the night atop the stronghold.
[777] They seek refuge from me out of timorousness and fear,
as doves seek refuge from a hawk.

Then, among other things mentioned, ʿUbaydallāh b. al-Ḥurr joined ʿAbd al-Malik b. Marwān. After he had come to him, ʿAbd al-Malik sent him with ten men toward al-Kūfah, ordering him to advance toward it until the [Syrian] army joined him. ʿUbaydallāh set out with the men. Having reached al-Anbār,[529] he dispatched people to al-Kūfah to tell his companions of his coming and ask them to come out to him. When the Qays party[530] learned of this,

527. *Īwān Kisrā*, the great Sasanian ceremonial hall, located on the east bank of the Tigris at al-Madā'in. See EI^2, s.v. al-Madā'in.

528. Al-Khaṭṭ, a place in the Yamāmah (eastern Arabia) was proverbial for producing (or importing) good spears. See Lane, *Lexicon*, II, 760.

529. Al-Anbār, on the left bank of the Euphrates, is about 12 *farsakh*s (44.6 miles) in a westerly direction from Baghdad. It was an important crossing place on the Euphrates near the northernmost navigable canal connecting the Euphrates with the Tigris. See EI^2, s.v.

530. *Al-Qaysiyyah*: On the division of the Arab tribes in Syria and al-Jazīrah into two antagonistic groups, Kalb and Qays, and on the loyalty of the Qays to Ibn

they went to al-Ḥārith b. ʿAbdallāh b. Abī Rabīʿah, Ibn al-Zubayr's governor for al-Kūfah, and asked him to send an army with them, which he did. When they encountered ʿUbaydallāh, he fought them for a time. Then his horse drowned,[531] and he boarded a ferryboat. A local peasant[532] jumped on him and grabbed his arms; the others struck him with stones and cried out, "This is the man wanted by the Commander of the Faithful." The two men grappled with each other and drowned. They pulled ʿUbaydallāh b. al-Ḥurr out, cut off his head, and sent it to al-Kūfah and then to al-Baṣrah.[533]

According to Abū Jaʿfar [sc. al-Ṭabarī]: Another account of his death has also been given. ʿUbaydallāh b. al-Ḥurr is said to have died for the following reason: He used to visit Muṣʿab in al-Kūfah and saw the latter setting the people of al-Baṣrah ahead of him. He therefore is said to have written ʿAbdallāh b. al-Zubayr a *qaṣīdah*,[534] reproving Muṣʿab, and threatening to go over to ʿAbd al-Malik b. Marwān. In it he said:

Deliver a message to the Commander of the Faithful,
for I am not of an unseemly opinion trying to outwit him:

---

al-Zubayr, see note 11. Ibn al-Athīr, *Kāmil*, IV, 293f., adds that most of Ibn al-Ḥurr's men had gone ahead to raise support in al-Kūfah, leaving Ibn al-Ḥurr vulnerable.

531. Ms. O: "was hamstrung."

532. Literally, "a man from the *anbāṭ*," i.e. a Nabatæan, any of the Aramaic-speaking peasantry of Iraq.

533. Cf. the more detailed account in Ibn al-Athīr, *Kāmil*, IV, 294 (summarizing Balādhurī, *Ansāb*, V, 297): "They surrounded him, put his companions to flight, and tried unsuccessfully to take him prisoner. He allowed his companions to leave; they did so, and no one hindered them. He began to fight alone. A man from Bāhilah named Abū Kudyah attacked him, but Ibn al-Ḥurr hit him with a spear. They began to shoot arrows at him and crowded around him, but could not come near him. 'Are these arrows,' he would say, 'or are they spindles?' When the wounds had weakened him, he waded into a ferry there; he entered it, but his horse would not enter it. He boarded the boat, and the shipman took him to the middle of the Euphrates. The horsemen caught sight of him. There were some Nabatæan peasants with the shipman in the boat. The horsemen said to them, 'The man wanted by the Commander of the Faithful is in the boat. If he gets away from you, we will kill you.' Ibn al-Ḥurr jumped up to fling himself into the water, but a powerful man jumped him and grabbed his arms (his wounds were dripping blood). The rest of the men struck him with oars. When he saw that they wanted to take him to the Qays, he grabbed the man with him and threw himself with him into the water. Both of them drowned."

534. I.e., a long ode involving a stylized sequence of themes. See EI^2, s.v. Ḳaṣīda.

[778] Is it a matter of right that I be turned away and that Muṣʿab take
as his two helpers men I have been battling?
How, when I have sworn you my true allegiance,
is my right turned aside when I demand it?
I bestowed on you such a thing as is not to be disregarded;
I did good to you, when the rugged parts of the affair were difficult.
But when the kingdom shone brightly and enemies had submitted,
and when he had obtained his desire of the wealth of Iraq,
Muṣʿab turned away from me. Had it been anyone else,
I would not reproach him for what happened between us.
What has made me have an evil opinion of Muṣʿab is the fact that Muṣʿab
has shown himself the friend of all who bear malice toward us.
If you drive me away, I will not drink
when the water has been muddied, after [another] drinker has been favored with the clear!
A man receives only what God sends
to him and what the Writer has inscribed in the Book.
When I stand by the door, Muslim[535] is allowed in,
but the gatekeeper prevents me from entering the door.

This is [part of] a long poem.

He composed the following addressed to Muṣʿab when he was in his prison. ʿAṭiyyah b. ʿAmr al-Bakrī had been imprisoned with him. When ʿAṭiyyah was released, ʿUbaydallāh said:

I say to him, "Patience, ʿAṭiyyah;
it is prison only until God makes a way out."
[779] I see my fate as two kinds of day:
one day a wandering fugitive, one day crowned among kings.
Will you speak ill of my religion when I come to you,
but draw al-Bāhilī and Ḥashraj near because of religion?
Have you not seen that the face of the kingdom has been marred

535. I.e., Muslim b. ʿAmr al-Bāhilī, the father of Qutaybah b. Muslim. See Ibn al-Athīr, *Kāmil*, IV, 291.

and the *nab*ʿ trees of God's earth have become *ʿawsaj*
trees?[536]

This is [part of] a long poem.

The following was also composed to reprove Muṣʿab. He mentions how Muṣʿab took as a companion Suwayd b. Manjūf, who had a scanty beard.

For which deed of endurance[537] and which favor [they bestowed]
are Muslim and al-Muhallab made to go ahead of me?
And Ibn Manjūf is summoned ahead of me, as if he were
a gelding come to water when the asses go off to pasture.
The shaykh of Tamīm has a head like *thaghāmah*,[538]
and [the tribesmen of] ʿAylān are afraid of us, watching.
I have made the strongholds of Azd, stretching between Manbij[539]
and the *ghāf*[540] trees of the valley of Oman,
Lands from which our swords have banished the foe,
from which Ṣufrah[541] dwells remote, and to which he is a
stranger.

He also composed a *qaṣīdah* in which he satirized [the tribe of] Qays ʿAylān. In it he said:

I am a son of the Banū Qays; if you ask [780]
about Qays, you will find them uppermost among the tribes.
Have you not seen how the Qays, Qays ʿAylān,[542] have veiled
their beards and sold their arrows for spindles?
I continued to have hope in the Azd,[543] until I saw
that they fell short of their haughty houses.

---

536. The hard wood of the *nab*ʿ tree was used for arrows; the soft wood of the *ʿawsaj* (boxthorn) was used for women's spindles (Lane, *Lexicon*, V, 2042).

537. For a discussion of *balāʾ* ("steadfastness, deed of endurance, manly deed") see Bravmann, *The Spiritual Background of Early Islam*, 83ff.

538. *Thaghāmah*, a mountain plant, perhaps wormwood or hyssop, was proverbial for its whiteness. See Lane, *Lexicon*, I, 339.

539. Manbij is about 50 miles northeast of Aleppo in Syria.

540. The *ghāf* tree, which is said to be large, grows in sand, and has sweet fruit, is particularly associated with Oman, the original home of the Azd tribe. See Lane, *Lexicon*, VI, 2318.

541. I.e., al-Muhallab b. Abī Ṣufrah.

542. Qays, the purported ancestor of the tribe of Qays, received the nickname ʿAylān, either from his father or because his horse was no named (*Lisān*).

543. The Azd were a group of South Arabian tribes, some of whom migrated

Zufar b. al-Ḥārith then wrote to Muṣʿab, saying, "I took care of fighting Ibn al-Zarqā'[544] on your behalf, and now Ibn al-Ḥurr is satirizing Qays!"

Then a group of the Banū Sulaym took Ibn al-Ḥurr and made him a prisoner. For his part, he said, "I merely said:

Have you not seen how the Qays, Qays ʿAylān, have come
 to us and brought spears and parties of horsemen?"

One of their men, named ʿAyyāsh, killed him. Zufar b. al-Ḥārith[545] said:

When I saw that men were sons by a stepmother,[546]
 and every speaker slandered us beyond measure,
Our going with our swords toward death spoke for us,
 and the wrinkling of the vein of the places where one kicks the mount [to make it gallop].
Had Ibn al-Ḥurr asked, he would have been told that they[547]
 are Yemeni and that they are not bartered for spindles.
He would have been told that our swords are acquainted
 with necks from the top to the backbone.

---

to Iraq from Oman. See *EI*^{2}, s.v. Ṭabarī, II, 463, quotes these lines in connection with the tribal conflicts of 64/783 in al-Baṣrah. After Yazīd's death, the Umayyad governor of Iraq, ʿUbaydallāh b. Ziyād, was forced to flee to Syria. Before leaving, he appointed the leader of the Azd, Masʿūd b. ʿAmr, to serve as his deputy. Masʿūd was subsequently assassinated (by a Khārijite, but the Azd suspected the Banū Tamīm of having engineered the affair). Violence erupted between the Azd (and their ally, the Rabīʿah tribe of Bakr b. Wā'il) and Tamīm (with its Muḍar ally, Qays ʿAylān). After many deaths on both sides, the Azd agreed to accept blood money (*diyah*) from the Tamīm. Although such payments were an accepted way of ending tribal violence, they laid a group open to the charge of not being bold enough to exact vengeance in blood. The following additional lines in Ṭabarī, II, 463, make this explicit:

Shall Masʿūd be killed, and they not avenge him?
 The swords of Azd have become like sickles.
What good is there in blood-money that has bestowed humiliation upon the Azd,
 so that their clans are reviled in gatherings.

544. This pejorative epithet ("son of the blue-eyed woman") refers to Marwān b. al-Ḥakam. See Ibn al-Athīr, *Kāmil*, IV, 295; Ibn Ḥajar, *Tabṣīr*, 1469. On blue eyes as evil, see note 498.

545. On the poetry of the Qaysi leader Zufar b. al-Ḥārith al-Kilābī, see F. Sezgin, *GAS*, II, 339–40.

546. I.e., when they turned away from us and mistreated us.

547. I.e., our arrows.

ʿAbdallāh b. Ḥammām[548] said: [781]

Ibn al-Ḥurr, you chanted alone by yourself
the words of a man inebriated or tottering.
Do you remember tribesmen whose spears hurt you,
who protected their relations on the battlefield?
[The tribe of] Rabīʿah weeps because of what they encountered at their hands;
moreover, you are not the best among the kinsmen of Bakr.
Why did you not seek revenge for them with a Juʿfī,
since they are your people closely related, in previous years?
On the day of the multitude,[549] we left them humiliated,
taking refuge from our swords in the mimosa trees.
On the day of al-Nukhayl, ʿUmayr with his troops mixed with you,
and you did not rejoice over him when he did so.
On the day of Sharāḥīl, we cut off your noses;
on that day he did not act injuriously against us.
With the blade of the sword, we struck the crown of his head,
which had but recently known the services of the hairdresser.
If noses of Madhḥij have thereby been rubbed in the dust,[550]
so may hateful noses be humiliated and hated.

[Four Separate Banners at the Pilgrimage]

According to Abū Jaʿfar [sc. al-Ṭabarī]: In this year, four banners came to ʿArafāt.[551]

According to Muḥammad b. ʿUmar [al-Wāqidī]—Shuraḥbīl b.

---

548. ʿAbdallāh b. Ḥammām al-Salūlī lived mostly in al-Kūfah. Ṭabarī, II, 636–42, shows him as having been originally unsympathetic to the Shīʿah and as writing a panegyric of al-Mukhtār more or less to save his skin. Later, he became loyal to the Umayyads. See F. Sezgin, *GAS*, II, 324.

549. Possibly, "on the day (i.e., battle) of al-Tharī (a place name)."

550. "To rub someone's nose in the dust," means to humiliate him, the nose held high in the air being, in Arabic as in English, a sign of haughtiness. See Lane, *Lexicon*, III, 1113.

551. I.e., four separate groups of pilgrims, led by four standard-bearers, gathered at ʿArafāt for the *wuqūf* ("standing," or "station") that climaxes the Ḥajj (pilgrimage). In 68, the day of the *wuqūf*, 9 Dhū al-Ḥijjah, fell on July 15, 688. See *EI*², s.vv. ʿArafa and Ḥadjdj.

[782] ʿAwn—his father, who said: In the year 68, four banners stood at ʿArafāt: Ibn al-Ḥanafiyyah with his companions stood with a banner at Jabal[552] al-Mushāt; Ibn al-Zubayr stood with a banner at the present standing place of the imām; then Ibn al-Ḥanafiyyah led his companions forward so that they stood opposite Ibn al-Zubayr; behind these two was Najdah, the Ḥarūrī,[553] and the banner of the Banū Umayyah was to the left of the two. The first banner to return [from ʿArafāt] was that of Muḥammad b. al-Ḥanafiyyah; he was followed by Najdah, then by the banner of the Banū Umayyah, and then by the banner of Ibn al-Zubayr, with the people following it.

According to Muḥammad [b. ʿUmar al-Wāqidī]—Ibn Nāfiʿ—his father, who said: That evening, Ibn ʿUmar had begun to hurry back [from ʿArafāt] with Ibn al-Zubayr's party; but when Ibn al-Zubayr went slowly, after Ibn al-Ḥanafiyyah, Najdah, and the Banū Umayyah had gone past, Ibn ʿUmar said, "Ibn al-Zubayr is waiting, as was the custom of pre-Islamic times."[554] Then he rushed forward, and Ibn al-Zubayr rushed after him.

According to Muḥammad [b. ʿUmar al-Wāqidī]—Hishām b. ʿUmārah—Saʿīd b. Muḥammad b. Jubayr—his father, who said: Fearing there would be strife (*fitnah*), I went on foot to all of them. I went to Muḥammad b. ʿAlī at al-Shiʿb[555] and said, "Abū al-Qāsim, fear God; we are in a place of sacred rites and sacred territory, and the people are ambassadors of God to this house.[556]

---

552. For *jabal* ("mountain"), one should read *ḥabl* ("large sand dune"), as in the parallel text in Ibn Saʿd, *Ṭabaqāt*, V, 75 (and note).

553. I.e., the Khārijite. Because the Khārijites gathered at the town of Ḥarūrā' (ca. 2 miles from al-Kūfah) when they "seceded" (*kharaja*) from ʿAlī's army in opposition to the plan for arbitration between ʿAlī and Muʿāwiyah, they were called "Ḥarūriyyah" (sing. Ḥarūrī). See *EI*², s.v. Ḥarūrā'. Najdah's followers controlled large areas of al-Yamāmah (central Arabia) at this time. See note 385.

554. Pilgrims depart from ʿArafāt after sunset on the ninth of Dhū al-Ḥijjah and rush back to Mecca without delay. The parallel text in Ibn Saʿd, *Ṭabaqāt*, V, 76, makes it clear that Ibn ʿUmar left as soon as the sun set, according to what he considered to be the Prophet's Sunnah; Ibn al-Zubayr, on the other hand, was waiting for darkness to fall. On the *jāhiliyyah*, "time of ignorance," or pre-Islamic paganism, see *EI*², s.v. Djāhiliyya.

555. Al-Shiʿb ("the path between two mountains") was a watering place between al-ʿAqabah and al-Qāʿ, three miles from Mecca on the Mecca-Medina road (Yāqūt, *Muʿjam*, s.v.).

556. The term ambassadors (*wafd*, pl. of *wāfid*) normally has the sense of persons coming to a great man to bring gifts or ask assistance (Lane, *Lexicon*, VIII, 2955). "This house" refers to the Kaʿbah.

Do not spoil their pilgrimage for them." He replied, "By God, I do not want that. I will not stand in the way of anybody seeking to approach this house, and no pilgrim will be harmed by me. However, I am a man defending myself from Ibn al-Zubayr and what he seeks from me. I seek this thing[557] only so that two men may not oppose me in it. But go to Ibn al-Zubayr, and speak to him; and go to Najdah." Muḥammad [b. Jubayr] continued: I went to Ibn al-Zubayr and spoke to him as I had spoken to Ibn al-Ḥanafiyyah. He said, "I am a man on whom the people have agreed and to whom they have sworn allegiance. These men are people of dissent." I said, "I think restraint would be best for you." He said, "I will do it." [783]

Then I went to Najdah al-Ḥarūrī. I found him among his companions and found ʿIkrimah, the lad (*ghulām*) of Ibn ʿAbbās, with him. I said, "Ask permission for me to go in to see your master." Muḥammad [b. Jubayr] continued: ʿIkrimah went in, and he admitted me without delay. I entered, greeted him with respect, and spoke to him as I had spoken to the two other men. He said, "As for initiating fighting against anyone, no; but I will fight anyone who begins to fight." I said, "I think the two men do not want to fight you." Then I went to the party of the Banū Umayyah and spoke to them as I had spoken to the other men. They said, "Our position is that we will not fight anyone, unless he fights us." Among those banners, I saw no men more tranquil or peaceful in their return [to Mecca] than Ibn al-Ḥanafiyyah.

[Those in Office during the Year]

According to Abū Jaʿfar [sc. al-Ṭabarī]: In this year, Ibn al-Zubayr's governor in charge of Medina was Jābir b. al-Aswad b. ʿAwf al-Zuhrī. Ibn al-Zubayr's brother Muṣʿab was in charge of al-Baṣrah and al-Kūfah. Hishām b. Hubayrah was in charge of the judiciary of al-Baṣrah, and ʿAbdallāh b. ʿUtbah b. Masʿūd was in charge of the judiciary of al-Kūfah. ʿAbdallāh b. Khāzim al-Sulamī was in charge of Khurāsān, and ʿAbd al-Malik b. Marwān was in Syria.

557. *Amr*, see note 500.

The Events of the Year 69

(July 6, 688–June 24, 689)

[The Revolt and Death of ʿAmr b. Saʿīd in Damascus]

According to al-Wāqidī, ʿAbd al-Malik b. Marwān went out to ʿAyn Wardah[558] this year and made ʿAmr b. Saʿīd b. al-ʿĀṣ[559] his deputy over Damascus. The latter fortified himself there. When word of this reached ʿAbd al-Malik, he returned to Damascus and besieged him.

Thus said al-Wāqidī. It is also said that ʿAmr b. Saʿīd went out

558. ʿAyn Wardah ("Rose Spring") is another name for the city of Raʾs ʿAyn ("Spring-Head") in al-Jazīrah province on the upper Greater Khābūr River near the present Syrian-Turkish border. See *EI*², s.v. ʿAyn al-Warda; Yāqūt, *Muʿjam*, s.v.

559. Abū Umayyah ʿAmr b. Saʿīd b. al-ʿĀṣ b. Umayyah al-Umawī, known as al-Ashdaq, was an Umayyad governor and general. Governor of Mecca when Yazīd b. Muʿāwiyah became caliph (60/680), he was appointed governor of Medina the same year. Upon the death of Yazīd, ʿAmr was mentioned as a possible successor to Marwān; he was the caliph's nephew through his mother and was also related to him on his father's side. Marwān, however, manipulated his own sons into the succession. ʿAmr's resentment came out in his attempted coup under Marwān's successor. See *EI*², s.v. ʿAmr b. Saʿīd al-Ashdak.

with 'Abd al-Malik, and that when the latter was at Buṭnān Ḥabīb, 'Amr returned to Damascus and fortified himself there, whereupon 'Abd al-Malik returned to Damascus.

According to Hishām b. Muḥammad [al-Kalbī]—'Awānah b. al-Ḥakam, who said: After 'Abd al-Malik b. Marwān returned from Buṭnān Ḥabīb to Damascus, he remained in Damascus for a time and then set out for Qarqīsiyā',[560] where Zufar b. al-Ḥārith al-Kilābī was. 'Amr b. Sa'īd was with 'Abd al-Malik. While at Buṭnān Ḥabīb, 'Amr b. Sa'īd devised treachery, turned back by night—Ḥumayd b. Ḥurayth b. Baḥdal al-Kalbī and Zuhayr b. al-Abrad al-Kalbī were with him—and reached Damascus, where 'Abd al-Raḥmān b. Umm al-Ḥakam al-Thaqafī was in charge as 'Abd al-Malik's deputy. When he learned of 'Amr b. Sa'īd's return, 'Abd al-Raḥmān fled and left his district; 'Amr entered the city and took control of it and its treasuries. [784]

Someone other than the two previously mentioned authorities said that this episode took place in the year 70. He also said that 'Abd al-Malik's journey from Damascus was toward Iraq, aimed at Muṣ'ab b. al-Zubayr. 'Amr b. Sa'īd b. al-'Āṣ said to 'Abd al-Malik, "Behold, you are going out to Iraq. Your father promised this thing[561] to me after him. On that basis, I exerted myself for him; and my effort on his behalf is not hidden from you. Then grant this thing to me after you." 'Abd al-Malik gave him no response, so 'Amr left him and returned to Damascus. 'Abd al-Malik returned on his heels and reached Damascus.

Resumption of the account according to Hishām [b. al-Kalbī]—'Awānah, who said: Having taken control of Damascus, 'Amr looked for 'Abd al-Raḥmān b. Umm al-Ḥakam, but did not find

---

560. Qarqīsiyā, was in al-Jazīrah province, at the confluence of the Greater Khābūr and the Euphrates. See Yāqūt *Mu'jam*, s.v. 'Abd al-Malik's intention would have been to campaign against the pro-Zubayrid leader of the Qays, Zufar b. al-Ḥārith.

561. *Amr*, i.e., the caliphate. For the agreement reached at al-Jābiyah in 64/683 between the leaders of the Umayyad family and their supporters, proclaiming Marwān b. al-Ḥakam caliph on condition that his successors would be Khālid b. Yazīd b. Mu'āwiyah and 'Amr b. Sa'īd al-Ashdaq, see Ṭabarī, II, 474–76, summarized by Dixon, *Umayyad Caliphate*, 19. After his victory at Marj Rāhiṭ, Marwān maneuvered his son 'Abd al-Malik into the succession and excluded Khālid and 'Amr. See Dixon, 124ff., for this episode; also Buhl, "Die Krisis der Umajjadenherrschaft in Jahre 684," 50–64.

him. He therefore gave orders and had his house destroyed. The people gathered; ʿAmr ascended the pulpit, praised and extolled God, and said: "No one from Quraysh ever stood on this pulpit before me without asserting that his were a heaven and a hell, and that he would cause whoever obeyed him to enter the heaven, and whoever disobeyed him to enter the hell. But I tell you that heaven
[785] and hell are in the hand of God; nothing of that belongs to me, save that you have a claim to equal treatment[562] and a good stipend (*ʿaṭiyyah*) from me." Then he descended.

ʿAbd al-Malik arose in the morning, and ʿAmr b. Saʿīd was missing. He asked about him and was told what had happened. ʿAbd al-Malik therefore returned to Damascus; and behold, ʿAmr b. Saʿīd had covered [the wall of] Damascus with coarse haircloths.[563] ʿAbd al-Malik fought him there for several days. When ʿAmr b. Saʿīd sent out Ḥumayd b. Ḥurayth al-Kalbī in command of cavalry, ʿAbd al-Malik sent out Sufyān b. al-Abrad al-Kalbī against him. When ʿAmr b. Saʿīd sent out Zuhayr b. al-Abrad al-Kalbī, ʿAbd al-Malik sent out Ḥassān b. Mālik b. Baḥdal al-Kalbī against him.

According to Hishām [b. al-Kalbī]—ʿAwānah: One day, the two groups of horsemen stood facing each other. On the side of ʿAmr b. Saʿīd there was a man from [the tribe of] Kalb named Rajā' b. Sirāj. Rajā' said, "ʿAbd al-Raḥmān b. Sulaym, come out for single combat." ʿAbd al-Raḥmān, who was on the side of ʿAbd al-Malik, said, "He who vies with al-Qārah in archery has done them justice,"[564] and came forward to engage Rajā' in single combat. The two thrust at each other with spears. ʿAbd al-Raḥmān's stirrup

562. *Mu'āsāh*, "treating as an equal," implies generosity in sharing one's possessions with others. See Lane, *Lexicon*, I, 60. Parallel accounts say that ʿAmr's generosity drew the people of Damascus to his side. See Balādhurī, *Ansāb*, IV/1, 443 (authority of Abū Mikhnaf).

563. I.e., in preparation for a siege by ʿAbd al-Malik. The parallel text in Balādhurī (authority of Abū Mikhnaf and others) makes this clear: "He placed upon the wall of Damascus coarse haircloths, wood, coarse cotton cloth, and stuffed bedding and prepared for a siege" (Balādhurī, *Ansāb*, IV/1, 443).

564. Proverbial, see Freytag, II, 257 and *Lisān*, s.v. *qārah* (root *q-w-r*). According to the most likely explanation, the Qārah were a tribal group known as skilled archers. The saying originated when one of them gave his opponent choice of a contest in wrestling, running, or archery. When the opponent chose archery, the man, before hitting his opponent's heart with an arrow, replied with the saying, which became proverbial.

snapped, and Ibn Sirāj escaped from him. ʿAbd al-Raḥmān said, "By God, had the stirrup not snapped, you would have cast forth the figs[565] in your stomach." So there was no truce between ʿAmr and ʿAbd al-Malik.

When their fighting had gone on a long time, the women of Kalb came with their children and wept, saying to Sufyān b. al-Abrad [al-Kalbī] and [Ḥumayd b. Ḥurayth] b. Baḥdal al-Kalbī, "Why will you slay yourselves for the ruler of Quraysh?" Each of them swore he would not go back until his fellow went back. When they all had agreed to go back, they looked and found that Sufyān was older[566] than Ḥurayth. So they asked Ḥurayth, and he went back. ʿAbd al-Malik and ʿAmr then made peace and drew up a written document between them. ʿAbd al-Malik gave ʿAmr a promise of safety. This took place on the eve of Thursday.

According to Hishām [b. al-Kalbī]—ʿAwānah: Armed with a [786] black bow, ʿAmr b. Saʿīd went out with horsemen. He went forward and made his horse trample the ropes of ʿAbd al-Malik's tent. The ropes broke, and the tent fell. ʿAmr dismounted and sat down. ʿAbd al-Malik was furious and said to ʿAmr, "Abū Umayyah, armed with this bow, you resemble this tribe of Qays." "No," he replied, "I resemble someone better than they: al-ʿĀṣ b. Umayyah."[567] Then he rose up in anger, and the horsemen with him, until he entered Damascus.

ʿAbd al-Malik entered Damascus on Thursday and sent to ʿAmr, saying, "Give the men their provisions."[568] ʿAmr sent word to him, saying, "This is no city of yours; leave it." When Monday came—four days, that is, after ʿAbd al-Malik's entry into Damascus—he sent to ʿAmr, saying, "Come to me." (ʿAmr was at the home of his wife from the tribe of Kalb.) Now ʿAbd al-Malik had summoned Kurayb b. Abrahah b. al-Ṣabbāḥ al-Ḥimyarī[569] and consulted him in the matter of ʿAmr b. Saʿīd. Kurayb said to

565. Ed. Cairo emends to "straw."
566. Mss. O and Co, "greater."
567. ʿAmr's grandfather.
568. Arabic *arzāq*, plural of *rizq*, from Middle Persian *rōzik*, "daily allowance."
569. Kurayb b. Abrahah b. al-Ṣabbāḥ al-Ḥimyarī, a companion of the Prophet, was the chief of the Yemeni tribe of Ḥimyar in Syria during the days of Muʿāwiyah. He witnessed the Battle of Ṣiffīn, served in Egypt under the governor ʿAbd al-ʿAzīz b. Marwān, and lived to see al-Ḥajjāj's governorship of Iraq. He died in 75/694. See Ibn Hajar, *Iṣābah*, V, 641–43.

him, "In this matter,[570] Ḥimyar has been reduced to naught. I have no opinion for you on it. Neither my female nor my male camel is involved in this affair."[571] When ʿAbd al-Malik's messenger came to summon ʿAmr, the messenger found ʿAbdallāh b. Yazīd b. Muʿāwiyah at ʿAmr's house. ʿAbdallāh said to ʿAmr b. Saʿīd, "Abū Umayyah, you are dearer to me, by God, than my hearing and sight. I see that this man has sent word for you to go to him. My opinion is that you should not do it." ʿAmr said to him, "Why?" He replied, "Because Tubayʿ, the son of Kaʿb al-Aḥbār's wife,[572] said, 'Behold, a great descendant of Ismāʿīl shall return. He shall shut the gates of Damascus and go forth from it. Shortly thereafter he shall be killed.'" ʿAmr said to him, "By God, even if I were asleep, I would not fear that Ibn al-Zarqā'[573] would wake me. He is not the sort of person who would embolden himself to do that to me. Also, ʿUthmān b. ʿAffān came to me
[787] last night in a dream and clothed me with his shirt." Now ʿAbdallāh b. Yazīd was the husband of Umm Mūsā, the daughter of ʿAmr b. Saʿīd. ʿAmr said to the messenger, "Greet ʿAbd al-Malik, and tell him I will come to him this evening, God willing."

When it was evening, ʿAmr put on a sturdy coat of mail between a linen tunic[574] and a linen shirt and girded on his sword. At his home were his wife from the tribe of Kalb and Ḥumayd b. Ḥurayth b. Baḥdal al-Kalbī. As he rose to leave, he tripped on the carpet.

---

570. Parallel in Ibn al-Athīr, *Kāmil*, IV, 298: "in such a matter as this."

571. A proverb meaning, "I have nothing at stake in the affair." See Freytag, II, 499 (Maydānī, II, 144).

572. Tubayʿ, who settled in Ḥimṣ in Syria, is said to have passed on the lore of his stepfather, Kaʿb al-Aḥbār. The latter, a learned Yemeni Jew (his name means "Kaʿb of the scholars"), introduced many stories of Jewish origin into Islam and often appears as a foreteller of future events. He is said to have predicted the death of ʿUmar. The following anecdote illustrates his reputation, which apparently rubbed off on his stepson: "When the head of al-Mukhtār was brought to ʿAbdallāh b. al-Zubayr, he said, 'Nothing has happened under my rule but that Kaʿb told me about it. He mentioned, however, that a man from the tribe of Thaqīf would kill me; yet here lies the man's head before me!' Ibn al-Zubayr did not realize that al-Ḥajjāj, also from Thaqīf, lay in wait for him." (Ibn Ḥajar, *Iṣābah*, V, 650) See *ibid.*, I, 377, on Tubayʿ; Ibn Saʿd, *Ṭabaqāt*, VII, 452; and *EI*², s.v. Kaʿb al-Aḥbār.

573. A derogatory name for ʿAbd al-Malik ("son of the blue-eyed woman"). See notes 498 and 544.

574. *Qabā'*: "a kind of tunic, resembling the *qafṭān*, generally reaching to the middle of the shank, divided down the front, and made to overlap over the chest" (Lane, *Lexicon*, VIII, 2984).

Ḥumayd said to him, "By God, if you obey me, you will not go to him." His wife said the same to him, but he paid no attention to what they said and went out with a hundred of his *mawālī*. ʿAbd al-Malik had sent to the sons of Marwān, and they had gathered at his home. When ʿAbd al-Malik was informed that ʿAmr was at the gate, he ordered that those with him be barred; ʿAmr himself was admitted and entered. Thus, ʿAmr's companions remained barred at each gate, and ʿAmr entered the courtyard[575] of the house, having only a servant of his with him. ʿAmr turned his eyes toward ʿAbd al-Malik, and behold, around him were the sons of Marwān, and with them were Ḥassān b. Mālik b. Baḥdal al-Kalbī and Qabīṣah b. Dhu'ayb al-Khuzāʿī.[576] Seeing their assembly and sensing evil, ʿAmr turned to his servant and said, "Go quickly—alas for you!—to Yaḥyā b. Saʿīd[577] and tell him to come to me." Not having understood what he had said, the servant [788] said to him, "At your service!" So ʿAmr said to him, "Go away from me into God's burning and fire!"

ʿAbd al-Malik said to Ḥassān and Qabīṣah, "If you wish, arise and meet with ʿAmr in the house." Then ʿAbd al-Malik said to them, as if jesting, so that ʿAmr b. Saʿīd might feel at ease, "Which of you two has been longer [in office]?" Ḥassān said, "Qabīṣah, O Commander of the Faithful, has been longer in office than I." (Qabīṣah was in charge of the seal.) ʿAmr then turned to his servant and said, "Go quickly to Yaḥyā and command him to come to me." Not having understood what he had said, the servant said to him, "At your service!" So ʿAmr said, "Go away from me!"

After Ḥassān and Qabīṣah had gone out, ʿAbd al-Malik ordered the doors shut. ʿAmr entered. ʿAbd al-Malik greeted him, said, "Here, please,[578] Abū Umayyah," seated him on the couch with him, and began talking to him at length. Then he said, "Lad, take the sword from him." ʿAmr said, "We belong to God, O Commander of the Faithful!"[579] ʿAbd al-Malik said, "Do you desire to

---

575. The older sense of *qāʿah* is the courtyard of a house; later it comes to mean the main salon. It is not clear which meaning is intended here.

576. Qabīṣah was ʿAbd al-Malik's secretary (*kātib*); see below, Ṭabarī, II, 837.

577. Yaḥyā was ʿAmr's brother.

578. Literally, "God be merciful to you." But the English suggests something sinister; the Arabic has overtones of affection and intimacy.

579. Here, this expression is said in suprise and as a protest of good intentions.

sit with me wearing your sword?"—and he took the sword from him. They spoke for a time, and then ʿAbd al-Malik said to him, "Abū Umayyah!" He replied, "At your service, Commander of the Faithful!" ʿAbd al-Malik said, "When you threw off your allegiance to me, I swore an oath that if I laid eyes on you and had power over you, I would put you in shackles."[580] The sons of Marwān said to him, "Then will you release him, O Commander of the Faithful?" ʿAbd al-Malik replied, "Then I will release him. What [else] might I possibly do to Abū Umayyah?" The sons of Marwān said, "Carry out the oath of the Commander of the Faithful." ʿAmr said, "God has made your oath come true, O Commander of the Faithful." ʿAbd al-Malik took out a set of shackles from under his couch, tossed them toward ʿAmr, and said, "Lad, bind him in them." The servant lad got up and bound him in them. ʿAmr said, "For God's sake, Commander of the Faithful, do not make me go out in them before the chiefs of the people." ʿAbd al-Malik replied, "Craftiness, Abū Umayyah, even at the point of death?[581] No, by God; we would not make you go out in shackles before the chiefs of the people. And we will remove them from you in no other wise than upwards."

Thereupon, ʿAbd al-Malik gave ʿAmr a pull that made his mouth hit the couch, breaking his front tooth. ʿAmr said, "For God's sake, O Commander of the Faithful, may what moves you
[789] to break a bone of mine not be the commission of something even worse than that!" ʿAbd al-Malik said to him, "By God, if I knew that you would spare me if I spared you and that Quraysh would prosper, I would release you. But never have two men come together in a city in a situation like ours but one expelled the other." When ʿAmr saw that his tooth had been broken and realized what ʿAbd al-Malik planned to do, he said, "Will you commit treachery, Ibn al-Zarqāʾ?"

It has been said [by another authority]: When ʿAbd al-Malik

580. *Jāmiʿah*: a neck shackle to which were attached thongs to bind the hands to the neck. See Lane, *Lexicon*, II, 458.

581. A proverb, see Freytag, II, 680 (Maydānī, II, 220). ʿAbd al-Malik's allusion to ʿAmr's craftiness is clarified by the parallel in Balādhurī, *Ansāb*, IV/1, 445: "ʿAmr wanted to make a show of not wanting to go out only in order to entice ʿAbd al-Malik into sending him out. ʿAmr's supporters surrounding the palace would then free him."

pulled ʿAmr so that his tooth fell out, ʿAmr began to rub it. ʿAbd al-Malik said to him, "I see that your tooth is so important to you that you will never again be well disposed toward me." So he gave orders, and ʿAmr was beheaded.

Resumption of ʿAwānah's account: The muezzin announced the afternoon prayer. ʿAbd al-Malik went out to lead the people in worship and commanded ʿAbd al-ʿAzīz b. Marwān to kill ʿAmr. When ʿAbd al-ʿAzīz approached with the sword, ʿAmr said, "For the sake of God and kinship, do not carry out my murder yourself; let someone more distantly related than you take charge of it. So ʿAbd al-ʿAzīz threw away the sword and sat down. ʿAbd al-Malik, having prayed a quick prayer, entered [the palace again], and the doors were shut. People saw that when ʿAbd al-Malik came out, ʿAmr was not with him. They mentioned this to Yaḥyā b. Saʿīd, and he came with men and alighted at the gate of ʿAbd al-Malik; a thousand of ʿAmr's slaves were with him and many of his companions afterwards. Those who were with him began to shout, "Let us hear your voice, Abū Umayyah!" With Yaḥyā b. Saʿīd, [790]
Ḥumayd b. Ḥurayth and Zuhayr b. al-Abrad came forward, broke the door of the enclosure (*maqṣūrah*),[582] and attacked the men with swords. A slave of ʿAmr b. Saʿīd named Maṣqalah struck al-Walīd b. ʿAbd al-Malik a blow on the head. Ibrāhīm b. ʿArabī,[583] the official in charge of the *dīwān*,[584] carried [al-Walīd] away and brought him into the room where documents were kept.[585]

Having prayed, ʿAbd al-Malik came in and found ʿAmr alive. He said to ʿAbd al-ʿAzīz, "What prevented you from killing him?" He replied, "His beseeching me for the sake of God and kinship prevented me, so that I softened to him." ʿAbd al-Malik said to him, "God shame your piss-on-her-heels mother! You take

---

582. This term has several meanings. It is "the enclosure in a mosque where the prince sits" (Lane, *Lexicon*, VII, 2536). In Damascus, the public treasury was also called *maqṣūrah*; and any gatehouse or railing could also be given the name. A subsequent reference in ʿAwānah's account indicates that the *maqṣūrah* in the mosque is meant. See Dozy, *Supplément*, II, 366; Ṭabarī, II, 794.

583. Ms. Pet: "b. ʿAdī"; Balādhurī, *Ansāb*, IV/1, 448: "Ibn Arqam."

584. *Dīwān*, apparently from Middle Persian, meant a list or register, and, by extension, the administrative department or office in charge of maintaining such a register. See *EI*², s.v.

585. *Bayt al-qarāṭīs*: from *qirṭās*, papyrus (later, paper) or a rolled document. See Lane, *Lexicon*, VII, 2517; *EI*², s.v. Ḳirṭās.

after no one but her." ('Abd al-Malik's mother was 'Ā'ishah bint Mu'āwiyah b. al-Mughīrah b. Abī al-'Āṣ b. Umayyah; 'Abd al-'Azīz's mother was Laylā.[586] As Ibn al-Ruqayyāt said:[587]

That is Laylā's son, 'Abd al-'Azīz: at Bābilyūn[588]
his food bowls are full to overflowing.)[589]

'Abd al-Malik then said, "Lad, bring me the lance." He brought it.
[791] 'Abd al-Malik brandished it and thrust at 'Amr with it. When it did not penetrate, he did it again. It did not penetrate. He put his hand on 'Amr's arm and felt the coat of mail. Laughing, he said, "And wearing mail, too! Abū Umayyah, you really came prepared! Lad, bring me the sword that will not bend." He brought him his sword. 'Abd al-Malik gave orders: 'Amr was thrown down, and 'Abd al-Malik sat on his chest and cut his throat, saying:[590]

'Amr, if you do not cease reviling me and speaking
contemptuously of me,
I will strike you so that the owl will cry, "Give me drink!
Give me drink!"[591]

'Abd al-Malik shook with trembling, as has been said to befall a man if he kills a relative. 'Abd al-Malik was carried from 'Amr's chest and laid on his bed. He said, "Never have I seen the like of

586. Full name: Laylā bint Zabbān b. al-Aṣbagh al-Kalbī (Balādhurī, *Ansāb*, IV/1, 448).

587. 'Ubaydallāh b. Qays al-Ruqayyāt (nicknamed "al-Ruqayyāt" because he wrote love poetry to three women, each named Ruqayyah), a Qurayshi poet, was originally a partisan of Ibn al-Zubayr, but went over to the Umayyads after the death of Muṣ'ab and 'Abdallāh b. al-Zubayr and became a panegyrist for them. These lines are from a *qaṣīdah* praising 'Abd al-'Azīz b. Marwān. See *Aghānī*, IV, 162.

588. Often known as Babylon, this was the Roman fortress still to be seen at Old Cairo. Because the Arab garrison city of Fusṭāṭ was nearby, Bābilyūn (or Bābalyūn) could be used as a name for the capital of Arab Egypt. 'Abd al-'Azīz b. Marwān was governor of Egypt under Marwān and 'Abd al-Malik. See *EI*², s.v. Bābalyūn; Yāqūt, *Mu'jam*, s.v.

589. I.e., he is a generous host. The line is quoted in the *Lisān*.

590. The line is from a *qasīdah* by Dhū al-Iṣba' al-'Adwānī, a pre-Islamic poet. See *Aghānī*, III, 9.

591. According to pre-Islamic folklore, if a slain man was not avenged, his spirit became an owl that hovered at his grave and continued to cry "Give me drink!" until vengeance was taken. See *Lisān*, s.v. *hāmah*.

this: he was killed by someone who possessed this world and did not seek the hereafter."

Yaḥyā b. Sa'īd and those with him came into the house into the presence of the sons of Marwān. They reviled the sons of Marwān and their *mawālī* who were with them, and the latter fought with Yaḥyā and his companions. 'Abd al-Raḥmān b. Umm al-Ḥakam al-Thaqafī came. The head was given to him, and he threw it to the people. 'Abd al-'Azīz b. Marwān arose, took money in purses, and started throwing them to the people. When the people looked at the money and saw the head, they grabbed the money and dispersed.

It has been said that when 'Abd al-Malik b. Marwān went out to prayer, he commanded his servant lad Abū al-Zu'ayzi'ah[592] to kill 'Amr. The latter did so, and threw his head to the people and [792] 'Amr's companions.

According to Hishām [b. al-Kalbī]—'Awānah: It was related to me that 'Abd al-Malik ordered the money that had been thrown to the people to be collected; thus it all returned to the treasury.

On that day, Yaḥyā b. Sa'īd was hit on the head with a rock. 'Abd al-Malik ordered his bed taken out into the mosque. He left [the house] and sat down on it. Al-Walīd b. 'Abd al-Malik was missing, and 'Abd al-Malik started saying, "Woe unto you! Where is al-Walīd? By their father, if they have killed him, they have attained their revenge." Ibrāhīm b. 'Arabī al-Kinānī came to him and said, "Behold, al-Walīd is in my house. He has received a wound, but has not been harmed."

Yaḥyā b. Sa'īd was brought to 'Abd al-Malik, who ordered him killed. But 'Abd al-'Azīz [b. Marwān] stood before him and said, "May God make me your ransom, Commander of the Faithful! Will you kill [all] the Banū Umayyah in a single day?" So he ordered Yaḥyā to be imprisoned. Then 'Anbasah b. Sa'īd was brought, and he ordered him killed. But 'Abd al-'Azīz stood before him and said, "I ask you to remember God, Commander of the Faithful, in the matter of extirpating and destroying the Banū Umayyah." So he ordered 'Anbasah to be imprisoned. Then 'Āmir b. al-Aswad al-Kalbī was brought in. 'Abd al-Malik struck his

592. See below, Ṭabarī, II, 837, where Abū al-Zu'ayzi'ah is identified as a *mawlā* in charge of 'Abd al-Malik's correspondence bureau.

head with a cane rod he had, and said, "Will you fight against me on the side of ʿAmr? Will you take his side against me?" ʿĀmir said, "Yes, because ʿAmr honored me, and you despised me; he drew me close, and you drove me away; he brought me near, and you made me distant; he treated me well, and you wronged me. Therefore I took his side against you." ʿAbd al-Malik ordered him to be killed; but ʿAbd al-ʿAzīz stood up and said, "I ask you to remember God, Commander of the Faithful, concerning this my maternal uncle." So ʿAbd al-Malik gave him into his hands and ordered the sons of Saʿīd to be imprisoned.

Yaḥyā [b. Saʿīd] remained in prison for a month or more. Then
[793] ʿAbd al-Malik ascended the pulpit. Having praised and extolled God, he asked the people's advice about putting him to death. One preacher among the people stood up and said, "Do snakes bear anything but snakes? By God, we think you should kill him, because he is a hypocrite, an enemy." Then ʿAbdallāh b. Masʿadah al-Fazārī stood up and said, "Commander of the Faithful, Yaḥyā is the son of your paternal uncle. You know how closely he is related. They did what they did, and you did to them what you did; and you do not feel safe with them. Yet, I do not think you should kill them. Make them go to your enemy: if they are killed, their affair will have been taken care of for you by the hand of others; if they return safely, you will consider what to do with them." ʿAbd al-Malik took his advice. He sent out the family of Saʿīd and had them go to Muṣʿab b. al-Zubayr. When they came to him, Yaḥyā b. Saʿīd went before him. Ibn al-Zubayr said to him, "You escaped, but your tail was plucked."[593] "By God," replied Yaḥyā, "the tail still has its hair!"

ʿAbd al-Malik sent to ʿAmr's wife from the tribe of Kalb, saying, "Send me the peace agreement I wrote for ʿAmr." She said to his messenger, "Go back and tell him that I wrapped that agreement in his shrouds with him so that with it he might call you to task before his Lord."

ʿAmr b. Saʿīd and ʿAbd al-Malik both traced their descent to Umayyah. ʿAmr's mother, Umm al-Banīn, the daughter of al-Ḥakam b. Abī al-ʿĀṣ, was ʿAbd al-Malik's paternal aunt.

---

593. Proverbial for someone who narrowly escapes death; see Freytag, II, 201 (Maydānī, II, 14); *Lisān*, s.v. *h-s-s*.

According to Hishām [b. al-Kalbī]—'Awānah: What happened between 'Abd al-Malik and 'Amr was an old feud. The mother of the two sons of Sa'īd was Umm al-Banīn. 'Abd al-Malik and Mu'āwiyah were the two sons of Marwān. When they [all] were lads, they constantly used to go to Umm Marwān b. al-Ḥakam al-Kināniyyah[594] and talk at her home. With 'Abd al-Malik and Mu'āwiyah, one of their black servant lads used to go out also. Whenever they came to her, Umm Marwān used to prepare food for them and bring it to them, placing a bowl in front of each man separately. She was continually stirring up quarrels between Mu'āwiyah b. Marwān and Muḥammad b. Sa'īd, and between 'Abd al-Malik and 'Amr b. Sa'īd. As a result, they used to fight with each other and cut each other, sometimes not talking with each other. Umm Marwān used to say, "If these two have no intelligence, those two have." Such was her custom, whenever they came to her, until she had implanted rancor in their hearts. [794]

It has been mentioned [by another authority] that 'Abdallāh b. Yazīd al-Qasrī (Abū Khālid) was with Yaḥyā b. Sa'īd when he entered the mosque, broke the door of the enclosure, and fought with the sons of Marwān. When 'Amr was killed and his head brought out to the people, 'Abdallāh and his brother Khālid rode away and reached Iraq. He remained with the sons of Sa'īd who were with Muṣ'ab, until unity[595] was established under 'Abd al-Malik. 'Abdallāh b. Yazīd's eye had been put out at the Battle of Marj [Rāhiṭ];[596] he had been on the side of Ibn al-Zubayr, fighting the Banū Umayyah. After the establishment of unity, he went before 'Abd al-Malik, and [the latter] asked, "How are you, family of Yazīd?" 'Abdallāh replied, "Disgrace! disgrace!"[597] 'Abd al-

---

594. I.e., Marwān's mother, who was from the tribe of Kinānah.

595. *Jamā'ah*: "a gathering together," especially the unity or concord of the Islamic community after civil strife (ed. Leiden, *Glossarium*, p. CLXX; Dozy, *Supplément*, I, 215). The reference is to the year 73/692, the restoration of a single caliphal authority over all Muslims after the death of Ibn al-Zubayr.

596. Fought in 64/683, between Marwān and the supporters of Ibn al-Zubayr, it ended with a complete defeat for the latter. See EI^2, s.v.

597. Accepting the emendation *khizyan khizyan* proposed by ed. Leiden, *Glossarium*, p. CLXXXVII. Mss. O and Co read *ḥizban ḥizban* ("party by party"); C reads *ḥarban ḥarban* ("war! war!"); and the editor's original emendation was *ḥurabā'a ḥurabā'a* ("despoiled! despoiled!").

Malik said, "That is for what your hands have forwarded: God is never unjust unto His servants."[598]

According to Hishīm [b. al-Kalbī]—ʿAwānah: The sons of ʿAmr b. Saʿīd came before ʿAbd al-Malik after the establishment of
[795] unity. They were four: Umayyah, Saʿīd, Ismāʿīl, and Muḥammad. When he beheld them, ʿAbd al-Malik said to them, "You are men of a noble family.[599] You have always seen yourselves as having some preeminence over all your kin, albeit one that God has not given you. What took place between your father and me was nothing new; it was inveterate in the souls of your ancestors against our ancestors in pre-Islamic times." Umayyah b. ʿAmr, who was their eldest, found himself unable to speak; he was the noblest and most intelligent of them. So Saʿīd b. ʿAmr, the middle in age, stood up and said, "O Commander of the Faithful, now that God has brought Islam and destroyed former things, promising Paradise, and warning of the Fire, why do you reproach us with something that happened in pre-Islamic times? As for what transpired between you and ʿAmr, ʿAmr was your paternal cousin, and you know best what you did. ʿAmr has arrived before God—'and God suffices for a reckoner.'[600] By my life, if you punish us for what happened between him and you, the interior of the earth were better for us than its surface!" ʿAbd al-Malik was much softened toward them, and said, "Your father made me choose between his killing me or my killing him; so I chose his death over my own. But you—how I long for you! How linked I am to you in kinship, and how mindful of your right!" So he rewarded them well, showed them favor, and drew them close.

It has been mentioned: One day, Khālid b. Yazīd b. Muʿāwiyah said to ʿAbd al-Malik, "The strange thing about you and ʿAmr b. Saʿīd is how you took him off guard and killed him." ʿAbd al-Malik said:

I drew him near me, that his mind might be calm,
    and that I might leap upon him with the assault of a man firm and masterful,

598. Qur'ān 22:10. If the reading *khizyan khizyan* is correct, ʿAbd al-Malik is answering an allusion to Qur'ān 22:9 with an allusion to the following verse.

599. Arabic, *ahlu baytin*: "people of a [distinguished, noble] household."

600. Qur'ān 4:6 and 33:39.

In anger and in defense of my religion:
the bungler's way is not like the way of the man who does things right!

According to ʿAwānah: A man met Saʿīd b. ʿAmr b. Saʿīd in Mecca and said to him, "By the Lord of this House,[601] there was no one like your father among the kinsmen![602] But he attempted to wrest from his kin what they had in their hands, and so he perished." [796]

Al-Wāqidī says that only the siege between ʿAbd al-Malik b. Marwān and ʿAmr b. Saʿīd took place in the year 69. ʿAmr b. Saʿīd fortified himself in Damascus; ʿAbd al-Malik returned from Buṭnān Ḥabīb and besieged him, but his killing of ʿAmr took place in the year 70.

[A Khārijite Killed at the Pilgrimage]

During this year, at al-Khayf of Minā,[603] a Khārijite proclaimed the slogan, "Judgment belongs to none but God!"[604] He was killed at al-Jamrah.[605]

According to Muḥammad b. ʿUmar [al-Wāqidī]—Yaḥyā b. Saʿīd b. Dīnār—his father, who said: I saw him draw his sword at al-Jamrah. They were a group, but God restrained their hands. He came forward from among them and proclaimed, "Judgment belongs to none but God!" The people turned upon him and killed him.

---

601. I.e., the Kaʿbah.

602. I.e., the Umayyad family.

603. Literally, "the sloping land [between the mountains and the bottom of the valley] at Minā": At Minā the pilgrims gather from the tenth to the thirteenth of Dhū al-Ḥijjah. On the first day, the ʿĪd al-Aḍḥā sacrifice is performed; the following days are days of visiting and social relations before returning to Mecca. See *EI*², s.v. Ḥadjdj.

604. The slogan of the Khārijites when they rejected mediation between ʿAlī and Muʿāwiyah by two men, Abū Mūsā al-Ashʿarī and ʿAmr b. al-ʿĀṣ; see note 40.

605. Al-Jamrah, literally, "the heap of pebbles," is a construction called "Jamrat al-ʿAqabah" near the western exit from the valley of Minā. Pilgrims throw seven stones, now interpreted as stoning the Devil. See *EI*², s.vv. Ḥadjdj and al-Djamra.

[Those in Office during the Year]

ʿAbdallāh b. al-Zubayr led the pilgrimage this year. His governor in charge of the garrison cities of al-Kūfah and al-Baṣrah this year was his brother Muṣʿab b. al-Zubayr. Shurayḥ [b. al-Ḥārith al-Kindī] was in charge of the judiciary of al-Kūfah. Hishām b. Hubayrah was in charge of the judiciary of al-Baṣrah. ʿAbdallāh b. Khāzim was in charge of Khurāsān.

The Events of the Year 70

(June 25, 689—June 14, 690)

[ʿAbd al-Malik and the Byzantines]

In this year, the Byzantines arose and gathered an army against the Muslims in Syria. For fear of what he might do to the Muslims, ʿAbd al-Malik made peace with the Byzantine emperor, on terms that every Friday he would deliver a thousand dīnārs to him.[606]

[Muṣʿab b. al-Zubayr Visits Mecca]

According to Muḥammad b. ʿUmar [al-Wāqidī]: During this year, Muṣʿab b. al-Zubayr went to Mecca, bringing a great deal of money, which he divided among his kinsmen and others. He brought many horses and camels and much baggage. He sent much money to ʿAbdallāh b. Ṣafwān, Jubayr b. Shaybah, and ʿAbdallāh b. Muṭīʿ, [797]
and he slaughtered many fattened camels.

606. Cf. Balādhurī, *Ansāb*, V, 299–300.

[Those in Office during the Year]

ʿAbdallāh b. al-Zubayr led the pilgrimage this year. His governors in charge of the garrison cities during this year were his agents of the previous year in charge of finances[607] and the judiciary.

607. *Maʿāwin* seems here to be used generally for "financial matters, taxes." See Dozy, *Supplément*, II, 192; and note 446, above.

The Events of the Year 71

(June 15, 690–June 3, 691)

Among these events was ʿAbd al-Malik b. Marwān's going to Iraq to fight Muṣʿab b. al-Zubayr. According to what some have said, ʿAbd al-Malik used to continue drawing closer to Muṣʿab until he arrived at Buṭnān Ḥabīb, while Muṣʿab would go out to Bājumayrā.[608] When winter set in, each of them would go back to his encampment; then they would return [to the war]. As ʿAdī b. Zayd b. ʿAdī b. al-Riqāʿ al-ʿĀmilī said:[609]

By my life, our horsemen took to the desert
in the vicinity of the Tigris because of Muṣʿab.
When the hypocrite of the people of Iraq

---

608. ʿAbd al-Malik encamped at Buṭnān Ḥabīb, near Qinnasrīn, in Syria; Muṣʿab at Bājumayrā, near Takrīt, at the southern border of al-Jazīrah (Yāqūt, *Muʿjam*, s.v. Bājumayrā).

609. ʿAdī b. Zayd b. [Mālik] b. ʿAdī b. al-Riqāʿ al-ʿĀmilī: Syrian poet and panegyrist of the Umayyad caliphs Yazīd b. Muʿāwiyah and al-Walīd b. ʿAbd al-Malik. Lines of the poem, with variants, are found in *Aghānī*, XVII, 165; Balādhurī, *Ansāb*, V, 342; and Dīnawarī, *Akhbār*, 317; see also F. Sezgin, *GAS*, II, 321f.

was reproved, but was not made to return [from his evil
ways],
We advanced toward him under a man possessing might to repel
his enemies,
who gives little thought to those who are absent.
They brandish [spears], each of them long-shafted,
the blade and the tip of the shaft close-fitted.
[798] Their shouts as they advance seem like
the crying of the sand grouse of a fruitful land.
Before us went one whose face was bright,
and whose character and origins were noble.
He was aided by us, and we were helped by him:
he whom God helps will not be overcome.

[Khālid b. ʿAbdallāh Raises Support for ʿAbd al-Malik in al-Baṣrah]

According to ʿUmar b. Shabbah—ʿAlī b. Muḥammad [al-Madā'inī], who said: ʿAbd al-Malik came from Syria intending to fight Muṣʿab. (This happened prior to this year, in the year 70.) With him was Khālid b. ʿAbdallāh b. Khālid b. Asīd. Khālid said to ʿAbd al-Malik, "If you send me to al-Baṣrah and have a few horsemen follow me, I hope to subdue it for you." ʿAbd al-Malik sent him. Khālid arrived there clandestinely with his *mawālī* and close associates, and stayed at the home of ʿAmr b. Aṣmaʿ al-Bāhilī.

According to ʿUmar [b. Shabbah]—Abū al-Ḥasan [ʿAlī b. Muḥammad al-Madā'inī]—Maslamah b. Muḥārib: ʿAmr b. Aṣmaʿ gave Khālid protection and sent a message to ʿAbbād b. al-Ḥuṣayn, who was in charge of Ibn Maʿmar's police. (Whenever Muṣʿab left al-Baṣrah, he made ʿUbaydallāh b. ʿUbaydallāh b. Maʿmar his deputy over the city. ʿAmr b. Aṣmaʿ hoped that ʿAbbād b. al-Ḥuṣayn would pledge allegiance to him.) The message was as follows: "I have given Khālid protection, and would like you to know it so that you can back me." ʿAmr's messenger reached ʿAbbād as the latter was dismounting from his horse. ʿAbbād said to [the messenger], "Tell him, 'By God, before I even take off my horse's saddlecloth, I will come to [take] you with horsemen!'" ʿAmr therefore said to Khālid, "I will not deceive you: ʿAbbād will be upon us at any moment. No, by God; I cannot protect you. Stay, instead, with Mālik b. Misma'."

According to Abū Zayd ['Umar b. Shabbah]—Abū al-Ḥasan ['Alī b. Muḥammad al-Madā'inī]: It is also said that Khālid stayed at the home of 'Alī b. Aṣma', and that 'Abbād was informed of this. 'Abbād then sent word to him, saying, "I am coming to [take] you." [799]

According to 'Umar [b. Shabbah]—'Alī b. Muḥammad [al-Madā'inī]—Maslamah and 'Awānah: Khālid galloped out of the house of Ibn Aṣma', with a thin linen shirt on him, his thighs uncovered, and his feet out of the stirrups. When he reached Mālik, he said, "I have been forced to turn to you. Give me protection." He said yes. He went out with his son and sent messengers to the Bakr b. Wā'il and Azd. The first banner that came to him was that of the Banū Yashkur.[610] 'Abbād came with horsemen; the two sides stood facing each other, but there was no fighting between them. The next morning, they went to Jufrat Nāfi' b. al-Ḥārith (it later came to be known as Jufrat Khālid).[611] With Khālid were men from the Banū Tamīm who had come to him; among them were Ṣa'ṣa'ah b. Mu'āwiyah, 'Abd al-'Azīz b. Bishr, and Murrah b. Maḥkān, with a number of their tribesmen. Khālid's forces were known as "Jufriyyah," referring to al-Jufrah; Ibn Ma'mar's forces were known as "Zubayriyyah." Among the Jufriyyah were 'Ubaydallāh b. Abī Bakrah, Ḥumrān [b. Abān], and al-Mughīrah b. al-Muhallab. Among the Zubayriyyah was Qays b. al-Haytham al-Sulamī, who used to hire men to fight on his side. Once, when a man demanded his salary from him, he said, "Tomorrow I will give it to you." Therefore, Ghaṭafān b. Unayf, one of the Banū Ka'b b. 'Amr,[612] said:

O little bells,[613] how badly you have decided!
The cash is a debt [due later], while the fighting is [due] right now;

---

610. The Banū Yashkur were affiliated with the tribe of Bakr b. Wā'il.

611. *Jufrah* means a wide, round hole in the ground. *Jufrat Nāfi'* means "the *jufrah* of Nafi'"; *Jufrat Khālid* means "the *jufrah* of Khālid. Yāqūt, *Mu'jam*, s.v. Jufrah, mentions such a place in al-Baṣrah, but gives no exact location.

612. The Banū Ka'b b. 'Amr were affiliated with the tribe of Tamīm.

613. Besides the explanation given below, there is an ironic reference to the

And you are at the gate, passing the night in pleasant
conversation and delaying.[614]

(Qays used to caparison the neck of his horse with little bells.)
[800] The commander of the horsemen of the Banū Ḥanẓalah[615] was ʿAmr b. Wabarah al-Quḥayfī.[616] He had slaves whom he used to hire out at thirty [dirhams] a man each day; he in turn would give them ten apiece. So someone said to him:

How badly you have decided, O Ibn Wabarah!
You are given thirty, and you give ten.

Al-Muṣʿab sent Zaḥr b. Qays al-Juʿfī to reinforce Ibn Maʿmar with a thousand men. To reinforce Khālid, ʿAbd al-Malik sent ʿUbaydallāh b. Ziyād b. Ẓabyān, but the latter was unwilling to enter al-Baṣrah and sent Maṭar b. al-Taw'am as a messenger. When the latter came back to him and told him that the men had dispersed, he rejoined ʿAbd al-Malik.

According to Abū Zayd [ʿUmar b. Shabbah]—Abū al-Ḥasan [ʿAlī b. Muḥammad al-Madā'inī]—a shaykh from the Banū ʿArīn[617]—al-Sakan b. Qatādah, who said: They fought with each other twenty-four days. Mālik [b. Mismaʿ's] eye was hit, and he wearied of battle. Envoys went between them (Yūsuf b. ʿAbdallāh b. ʿUthmān b. Abī al-ʿĀṣ [was one of them]),[618] and Ibn Maʿmar made peace with Mālik on condition that he would make Khālid leave al-Baṣrah and would be guaranteed safety. Mālik therefore made Khālid leave al-Baṣrah. Fearing, however, that al-Muṣʿab would not approve ʿUbaydallāh [b. ʿUbaydallāh b. Maʿmar's] promise of safety, Mālik went to Tha'j.[619] Speaking about Mālik

---

proverbial expression, "He hangs bells on his neck," meaning "He imperils or endangers himself, and is a bold man." See Lane, *Lexicon*, II, 438, s.v. *juljul*.

614. Ms. Pet: "while you are fat, delaying." Balādhurī, *Ansāb*, IV/1, 468 (also on authority of al-Madā'inī): "and you are stingy of giving, miserly."

615. The Banū Ḥanẓalah were affiliated with the tribe of Tamīm.

616. The name is given thus in Mss. O, B and Co; Pet "al-Juʿayfī"; C "al-ʿUjayfī" (agreeing with Balādhurī, *Ansāb*, IV/1, 468).

617. The Banu ʿArīn were affiliated with the tribe of Tamīm.

618. The bracketed words are from the parallel text in Balādhurī, *Ansāb*, IV/1, 469.

619. Tha'j (or Thāj) was "a village of the Bakr b. Wā'il tribe in the Yamāmah" (Balādhurī, *Ansāb*, IV/1, 464, on authority of Abū Mikhnaf). Yāqūt, *Muʿjam*, s.v., places it in Baḥrayn, which included the mainland area opposite the island. The

and about how the Tamīmiyyah[620] had joined him and Khālid,[621] al-Farazdaq said:[622]

I marvel at tribesmen whose father was Tamīm,
and the places where their camels kneel are great among the Banu Saʿd.[623]
They were the most powerful of men, before they went
to the Azd, with their beards yellow, and to Mālik.
What do you think of Muṣʿab, the son of the Apostle [of the Prophet],[624] [801]
when he bares his teeth, not laughing?
We banished Mālik from his lands,[625]
and we put out his eye with short spears.

According to Abū Zayd [ʿUmar b. Shabbah]—Abū al-Ḥasan [ʿAlī b. Muḥammad al-Madāʾinī]—Maslamah: When ʿAbd al-Malik returned to Damascus, Muṣʿab's only concern was al-Baṣrah.[626] He hoped to overtake Khālid there, but he found that the latter had already left and that Ibn Maʿmar had guaranteed the safety of the men, most of whom had stayed, though some of them, fearing Muṣʿab, had left. Muṣʿab therefore became angry with Ibn Maʿmar, swore he would never confer favor upon him,

---

name survives in a town about 90 miles northwest of Dhahrān in Saudi Arabia. At the time of Mālik's flight, it was under the control of the Khārijite Najdah b. ʿĀmir, thus out of the reach of Ibn al-Zubayr (See Balādhurī, *Ansāb*, XI, 146).

620. *Tamīmiyyah* means "party of Tamīm."

621. The poem can be found in the *Dīwān* of al-Farazdaq (ed. Boucher, 157; ed. Dār Ṣādir, Beirut, II, 57).

622. Al-Farazdaq (Abū Firās Hammām b. Ghālib b. Ṣaʿṣaʿah) was a poet of the Banū Dārim clan of the tribe of Tamīm. He was born in al-Baṣrah ca. 20/641 and died there in 110/738. See EI^2, s.v. al-Farazdak.

623. The Banū Saʿd were a division of the Tamīm.

624. Muṣʿab's father, al-Zubayr b. al-ʿAwwām, was known as *al-Ḥawārī* (from Ethiopic *ḥawaryā*, "apostle") because of his closeness to Muḥammad (first-cousin) and because he had been one of the early converts to Islam who took refuge for a time in Ethiopia to escape persecution. See EI^2, s.v. Ḥawārī.

625. *Dīwān*, "our lands."

626. Cf. parallel in Balādhurī, *Ansāb*, IV/1, 470 (on authority of al-Madāʾinī): "After allegiance had been sworn to Muṣʿab, and ʿAbd al-Malik had returned to Damascus because of ʿAmr al-Ashdaq, Muṣʿab's only concern was al-Baṣrah." Similarly, in the Abū Mikhnaf account (Balādhurī, *loc. cit.*, 463–464), ʿAbd al-Malik's preoccupation with the revolt of ʿAmr in Damascus freed Muṣʿab from worry about the north and allowed him to turn his attention to al-Baṣrah.

and sent a messenger to the Jufriyyah, abusing and rebuking them.

According to Abū Zayd [ʿUmar b. Shabbah]: Al-Madāʾinī and other Baṣran relaters of historical narratives assert that [Muṣʿab] sent for them and they were brought to him. Turning to ʿUbaydallāh b. Abī Bakrah, he said, "Son of a stray![627] You are nothing but the son of a bitch that the dogs mounted one after another, so that she whelped ruddy, and black, and blond—from each sire a pup resembling it. Your father was nothing but a slave who came to the Messenger of God from the stronghold of al-Ṭāʾif.[628] Then you gave testimony, claiming that Abū Sufyān[629] whored with your mother. By God, if I live, I will indicate your correct ancestry!" Then he summoned Ḥumrān, and said, "Son of a Jewess! You are nothing but a Nabatæan peasant brought as a captive from ʿAyn al-Tamr." Then he said to al-Ḥakam b. al-Mundhir b. al-Jārūd, "Son of a knave! Do you know who you are and who al-Jārūd was? Al-Jārūd was nothing but a peasant on Ibn Kāwān Island,[630] a Persian who crossed over to the [Arabian] coast and
[802] affiliated with the ʿAbd al-Qays. No, by God; I know of no tribe harboring more evil than they. Then he married his sister to al-Mukaʿbir,[631] the Persian, and he never obtained any honor greater than that. These, O son of Qubādh, are her children." Then ʿAbdallāh b. Faḍālah al-Zahrānī was brought. Muṣʿab said, "Are you not descended from the people of Hajar, and then from the people of Samāhīj?[632] By God, I will sent you back to your

627. See Ibn Qutaybah, *Maʿārif*, ed. Wüstenfeld (Göttingen, 1850), 147 [ed. Leiden note].

628. The city of al-Ṭāʾif lies in the mountains about 40 miles southeast of Mecca. See *EI*[1], s.v.; Yāqūt, *Muʿjam*, s.v.

629. Abū Sufyān was the head of the Banū Umayyah during the lifetime of Muḥammad. An opponent of Islam for most of his life, he was not converted until very late. See *EI*[2], s.v.

630. Ibn Kāwān Island is the large island now known as Qeshm, off the coast of Fārs Province, north of the Strait of Hormuz. See *EI*[2], s.v. Ḳishm.

631. In Ṭabarī, I, 985 this nickname is explained as meaning "the Cutter." It was given to one of the agents of the Sasanian monarch Khusraw Anūshirwān (ruled 531–79), the son of Qubādh I (ruled 498 or 499–531), because of his habit of cutting off arms and legs among the Arabs.

632. Hajar was the main city of al-Baḥrayn (but on the Arabian mainland, since al-Baḥrayn in earlier times included the area on the mainland now known as al-Ḥasā); Samāhīj was an island between al-Baḥrayn and the Oman coast. See *EI*[2], s.v. Baḥrayn; Yāqūt, *Muʿjam*, s.vv. On the people of Hajar as descended from prostitutes brought from al-Ahwāz and the Sawād, see the story in Ṭabarī, I, 985f.

relatives!" Then 'Alī b. Aṣma' was brought. Muṣ'ab said, "Sometimes a slave of the Banū Tamīm, and sometimes claiming relation to Bāhilah?" Then 'Abd al-'Azīz b. Bishr b. Ḥannāṭ was brought. Muṣ'ab said, "Son of a man reviled! Didn't your uncle steal a she-goat during the time of 'Umar, who ordered him taken to have [his hand] cut off? But, by God, the only person who has been roughly treated is the one who married your sister!" (His sister was married to Muqātil b. Misma'.) Then Abū Hāḍir al-Asadī was brought. Muṣ'ab said, "Son of a woman from Iṣṭakhr! What have you to do with the *ashrāf*? You are merely descended from people of Qaṭar, an interloper among the Banū Asad, with not a relative or kinsman among them." Then Ziyād b. 'Amr was brought. Muṣ'ab said, "Son of a man from Kirmān! You are nothing but a peasant from the people of Kirmān. You crossed into Fārs and became a sailor. What do you have to do with fighting? You are more adept at pulling hawsers." Then 'Abdallāh b. 'Uthmān b. Abī al-'Āṣ was brought. Muṣ'ab said to him, "Will you say all sorts of things against me, when you are a peasant from the people of Hajar? Your father went to al-Ṭā'if—they take in anyone who flocks to them and take pride in him. But, by God, I will send you back to those from whom you came originally." Then Shaykh b. al-Nu'mān was brought. Muṣ'ab said, "Son of a knave! You are nothing but a peasant from the people of Zandaward.[633] Your mother ran away, and your father was killed; his [803]
sister was married by a man from the Banū Yashkur and gave birth to two lads, and the two of them incorporated you into their family tree."

Then he beat them a hundred strokes each, shaved their heads and beards, razed their houses, exposed them to the sun three days, forced them to divorce their wives, and kept their children away on expeditions. He paraded the men around al-Baṣrah and made them swear not to marry free women.

Muṣ'ab sent Khidāsh b. Yazīd[634] al-Asadī to seek those companions of Khālid who had fled. He overtook Murrah b. Maḥkān[635] and seized him. Murrah said:

633. Zandaward was a town in Iraq near the site of Wāsiṭ (Yāqūt, *Mu'jam*, s.v.).

634. Mss. O, B, and Co read: "b. Marthad."

635. Murrah b. Maḥkān al-Sa'dī was a poet of the Sa'd clan of the tribe of Tamīm. See F. Sezgin, *GAS*, II, 402.

Banū Asad, if you kill me, you will make war
with Tamīm, when war, having broken out, spreads rapidly.
Banū Asad, do you have any leniency,
to excuse me if the shoe made me slip?
Let enemies not think that if I become absent from them
and little fire can be elicited from me, my war has abated,
[And that] you will walk the ways safely, Khidāsh,
When the spears have drunk once of my [blood] and drunk again.

But Khidāsh had him brought near and killed him. (Khidāsh was in charge of Muṣʿab's police at the time.) Also, Muṣʿab ordered Sinān b. Dhuhl, one of the Banū ʿAmr b. Marthad, to raze the house of Mālik b. Mismaʿ. Muṣʿab took what was in Mālik's house; among the things he took was a slave girl who bore him ʿUmar b. Muṣʿab.

[ʿAbd al-Malik Attacks Muṣʿab; the Death of Muṣʿab][636]

[804] [Continuing,] he said: Muṣʿab stayed in al-Baṣrah until he went to al-Kūfah. He remained in al-Kūfah until he went out to fight ʿAbd al-Malik. ʿAbd al-Malik encamped at Maskin.[637] ʿAbd al-Malik wrote to the people of Iraq who had been partisans of his father Marwān;[638] all of them responded to him, and as a condition each one asked him for the governorship of Iṣbahān, which he conferred upon all of them. Among them were: Ḥajjār b. Abjar, al-Ghaḍbān b. al-Qabaʿtharā, ʿAttāb b. Warqāʾ, Qaṭan b. ʿAbdallāh al-Ḥārithī, Muḥammad b. ʿAbd al-Raḥmān b. Saʿīd b. Qays, Zaḥr

636. Additional material can be found in Balādhurī, *Ansāb*, V, 331–355; *Aghānī*, XVII, 161–67; Ibn al-Athīr, *Kāmil*, IV, 323–336.

637. Maskin was a district along the Dujayl canal, north of Baghdad, and west of the Tigris River (Le Strange, *Lands*, 51, 81; Yāqūt, *Muʿjam*, s.v.).

638. Arabic, *al-Marwāniyyah*. *Aghānī*, XVII, 162, preserves a fuller text of al-Madāʾinī's account: "Then ʿAbd al-Malik wrote to the Kūfan and Baṣran *ashrāf*, inviting them to him, and raising their hopes. They responded to him, stipulated conditions for him, and asked for governorships. When forty of them asked for the governorship of Iṣbahān, ʿAbd al-Malik said to his companions in amazement, 'Alas, what is this Iṣbahān?'" One should compare a series of reports in Balādhurī, *Ansāb*, V, 232–33, where Iraqi *ashrāf* take the initiative in inviting ʿAbd al-Malik to come to Iraq.

b. Qays, and Muḥammad b. ʿUmayr.[639] Muḥammad b. Marwān was in charge of ʿAbd al-Malik's vanguard, ʿAbdallāh b. Yazīd b. Muʿāwiyah was in charge of his right wing, and Khālid b. Yazīd was in charge of his left wing. Muṣʿab, whom the people of al-Kūfah had failed to aid, advanced toward him.

According to ʿUrwah b. al-Mughīrah b. Shuʿbah, who said: Muṣʿab came marching out. He was leaning on the mane of his horse, looking right and left at the men. His eye fell on me. "ʿUrwah," he said, "come to me." I went over to him. "Tell me about al-Ḥusayn b. ʿAlī," he said, "how he acted in refusing to submit to the judgment of Ibn Ziyād and in resolving to fight." And he said:[640]

They who are in al-Ṭaff,[641] of the family of Hāshim,
shared their property, and so set the example, to the
generous, of the sharing of property.

[Continuing,] he said: So I knew he would not turn away until he was killed.

According to Muḥammad b. ʿUmar [al-Wāqidī]—ʿAbdallāh b. Muḥammad b. ʿAbdallāh b. Abī Qurrah—Isḥāq b. ʿAbdallāh b. Abī Farwah—Rajā' b. Ḥaywah, who said: After he had killed ʿAmr [805]
b. Saʿīd, ʿAbd al-Malik put his hand to the sword and killed those who opposed him. When he decided to go to fight Muṣʿab, Syria and its people having become his possession, he addressed the people and commanded them to make ready to march against Muṣʿab. The chiefs of the Syrians came to him one after the other; while not opposing what he wanted to do, they wanted him to remain and send the armies forward: if they won, well and good; if they did not win, he would aid them with the armies; for they feared for the people that if he were killed in his encounter with Muṣʿab, there would be no king after him.[642]

---

639. Ms. Pet adds: "b. ʿUṭārid." From Ṭabarī, II, 806f. and Balādhurī, *Ansāb*, V, 341, it appears that these men went over to ʿAbd al-Malik during the fighting.

640. The verse is attributed to Sulaymān b. Qattah (*Aghānī*, XVII, 165). It is quoted and translated in Lane, *Lexicon*, I, 87.

641. Karbalā', where al-Ḥusayn was killed, was located in the region known as al-Ṭaff. See note 213 (Ṭabarī, II, 686).

642. An alternate translation: "there would be no kingdom after him."

They said, "O Commander of the Faithful, you should stay where you are and send a man from your family as commander of these armies, dispatching him to fight Muṣʿab." ʿAbd al-Malik said, "This affair can be handled only by a man from Quraysh who has good judgment. I might perchance send someone who has bravery, but not good judgment. But I find in my soul that I am discerning in war, and brave with the sword, if I am forced to use it. Muṣʿab is with[643] a family of bravery. His father was the bravest of Quraysh. He, too, is brave, but he has no knowledge of war and likes ease. With him there are men who will oppose him; with me there men who will give me sincere advice."

So ʿAbd al-Malik went and encamped at Maskin, and Muṣʿab went to Bājumayrā. ʿAbd al-Malik wrote to his supporters among the people of Iraq. Ibrāhīm b. al-Ashtar took ʿAbd al-Malik's letter, sealed and unread, and gave it to Muṣʿab, who asked, "What is in it?" Ibrāhīm replied, "I have not read it." Muṣʿab read it: ʿAbd al-Malik was inviting Ibn al-Ashtar to his side and offering him the governorship of Iraq. Ibn al-Ashtar said to Muṣʿab, "From no one has he had less to hope for than from me. He has written to all your companions as he has written to me. Heed me concerning
[806] them, and cut off their heads!" "Then," said Muṣʿab, "their tribesmen will not be loyal to us." Ibn al-Ashtar said, "Then load them with irons, send them to the White [Palace] of Khusrāw,[644] and imprison them there. Put in charge of them someone who will cut off their heads if you are defeated. If you are victorious, you can bestow them on their tribesmen as a favor." "Abū al-Nuʿmān," said Muṣʿab, "I am too preoccupied to attend to that. God have mercy on Abū Baḥr:[645] as if foreseeing our present plight, he warned me about the treachery of the people of Iraq."

According to ʿUmar [b. Shabbah]—Muḥammad b. Sallām [al-

643. Alternate reading in Ibn al-Athīr, *Kāmil*, IV, 323: "from."

644. The White Palace was the old Sasanian royal residence at al-Madā'in. It was located about a mile to the north of the Great Ceremonial Hall (*Īwān Kisrā*). See Le Strange, *Lands*, 34; *EI*², s.v. al-Madā'in.

645. Abū Baḥr is al-Aḥnaf b. Qays. According to Ibn al-Athīr, *Kāmil*, IV, 324, the leader of the Tamīm in al-Baṣrah accompanied Muṣʿab's army to al-Kūfah, where he died. Cf. the fuller version of al-Aḥnaf's words (Balādhurī, *Ansāb*, V, 337–38): "Do not meet any foe while relying on the people of Iraq; for, like a prostitute who wants a new lover every day, they want a new commander every day."

Jumaḥī][646]—ʿAbd al-Qāhir b. al-Sarī, who said: The people of Iraq intended to betray Muṣʿab. But Qays b. al-Haytham said, "Woe unto you! Do not cause the Syrians to come among you. By God, if they taste your life, they will expropriate your dwellings from you. By God, I have seen the chief of the Syrians at the gate of the caliph, rejoicing if the latter sent him on a mission. I have seen us on summer expeditions, one of us in charge of a thousand camels, while each of their chieftains went raiding on his horse, with his provisions behind him."[647]

[Continuing,] he said: When the two armies drew near to each other at Dayr al-Jāthalīq,[648] in the Maskin district, Ibrāhīm b. al-Ashtar advanced and attacked Muḥammad b. Marwān, making him give way. Then ʿAbd al-Malik b. Marwān sent out ʿAbdallāh b. Yazīd b. Muʿāwiyah, who drew near to Muḥammad b. Marwān. The fighters closed with each other. Muslim b. ʿAmr al-Bāhilī was killed.[649] Also killed were Yaḥyā b. Mubashshir, one of the Banū Thaʿlabah b. Yarbūʿ, and Ibrāhīm b. al-Ashtar. ʿAttāb b. Warqāʾ, who was in charge of the horsemen on the side of Muṣʿab, fled.[650] Then Muṣʿab said to Qaṭan b. ʿAbdallāh al-Ḥārithī, "Abū ʿUthmān, forward with your horsemen!" "I do not think it advis- [807]
able," he replied. "Why?" said Muṣʿab. Qaṭan said, "I do not want [the tribesmen of] Madhḥij killed for nothing." Then Muṣʿab said to Ḥajjār b. Abjar, "Abū Usayd, forward with your banner!" "Toward this dirty crowd?" he replied. "By God," said Muṣʿab,

---

646. Abū ʿAbdallāh Muḥammad b. Sallām al-Jumaḥī was a literary historian who died in 231/845 or 232 in Baghdad; see *EI*², s.v. Ibn Sallām al-Djumaḥī.

647. The wealth of Iraq and the poverty of Syria are being compared. Cf. the reading in Balādhurī, *Ansāb*, V, 244–45: "I have seen us on summer expeditions; *the provisions of* one of us were on many camels, while one of them [i.e., the Syrians] would go raiding with his provisions behind him [i.e., on the saddle of his own horse]."

648. Dayr al-Jāthalīq means "the monastery of the Catholicos" (the head of the Nestorian Christians). See *EI*², s.v. Dayr al-Djāthalīḳ.

649. He was in charge of Ibn al-Ashtar's right wing. According to *Aghānī*, XVII, 164, and Balādhurī, *Ansāb*, V, 341–42, he was carried away wounded and managed to obtain a guarantee of safety for his children from ʿAbd al-Malik before he died. His son, Qutaybah b. Muslim, served the Umayyads loyally and greatly extended Muslim territory in Central Asia.

650. According to Balādhurī, *Ansāb*, V, 338, the flight was intentional. ʿAttāb had sworn allegiance to ʿAbd al-Malik and had promised to betray Muṣʿab. Suspecting treachery, Ibn al-Ashtar asked Muṣʿab not to rely on ʿAttāb, but Muṣʿab disregarded the warning.

"your hesitating to go toward it smells worse and is more vile!" Then he made a similar request of Muḥammad b. ʿAbd al-Raḥmān b. Saʿīd b. Qays, who replied, "I do not see that anyone has done it, so that I should do it!" Muṣʿab said, " O Ibrāhīm! And today I have no Ibrāhīm!"

According to Abū Zayd [ʿUmar b. Shabbah]—Muḥammad b. Sallām, who said: When Ibn Khāzim was told of Muṣʿab's going to fight ʿAbd al-Malik, he said, "Is ʿUmar b. ʿUbaydallāh b. Maʿmar with him?" The response was, "No, he has made him his agent in charge of Fārs." Ibn Khāzim said, "Then is al-Muhallab b. Abī Ṣufrah with him?" The response was, "No, he has made him his agent in charge of al-Mawṣil."[651] Ibn Khāzim said, "Then is ʿAbbād b. al-Ḥuṣayn with him?" The response was, "No, he has made him deputy in charge of al-Baṣrah." Ibn Khāzim then said, "And I am in Khurāsān":

Take me and drag me away, O she-hyena; rejoice
over the flesh of a man whose helper was not present today.

Muṣʿab said to his son, ʿĪsā b. Muṣʿab, "Mount, my son, and ride with your companions to your uncle in Mecca. Tell him what the people of Iraq have done. Leave me, for I am a dead man." His son said, "By God, never will I [go to] tell Quraysh about you. If you wish, go to al-Baṣrah, for they are in a state of unity (*jamāʿah*); or go to join the Commander of the Faithful." Muṣʿab said, "By God, let Quraysh not say that I fled because of what Rabīʿah did when they failed to help, so that I entered the sanctuary of Mecca
[808] in defeat. Rather, I will fight. If I am killed, the sword is no shame, and flight is neither my habit nor my nature. But if you want to go back, go back and fight." So he went back and fought until he was killed.

---

651. Similarly in Balādhurī, *Ansāb*, V, 345. See below (Ṭabarī II, 821), where al-Muhallab receives the news of Muṣʿab's death while he is campaigning against the Khārijites in Khūzistān. One report in Balādhurī states that Muṣʿab wanted al-Muhallab (who was governor of al-Mawṣil) to help fight ʿAbd al-Malik, but the people of al-Baṣrah refused to march unless al-Muhallab were recalled from al-Mawṣil and sent to Khūzistān fight the Khārijites and prevent them from making incursions into Iraq. (Balādhurī, *Ansāb*, V, 332, 335–36; *ibid.*, XI, 123–24; cf. Ibn al-Athīr, *Kāmil*, IV, 332.)

According to ʿAlī b. Muḥammad [al-Madāʾinī]—Yaḥyā b. Ismāʿīl b. Abī al-Muhājir—his father: ʿAbd al-Malik, by way of his brother Muḥammad b. Marwān, sent a message to Muṣʿab, saying, "Your cousin will give you a guarantee of safety." Muṣʿab said, "A man like me leaves this place either victor or vanquished."

According to al-Haytham b. ʿAdī—ʿAbdallāh b. ʿAyyāsh—his father, who said: As we were standing with ʿAbd al-Malik b. Marwān during his fight with Muṣʿab, Ziyād b. ʿAmr [al-ʿAtakī][652] came up to him and said, "O Commander of the Faithful, Ismāʿīl b. Ṭalḥah was a good protector[653] to me; rarely did Muṣʿab intend me harm but he warded it from me. If you think it good, grant him safety despite his offense." ʿAbd al-Malik said, "He is safe." Ziyād, who was an extremely large man, went between the two battle lines and shouted, "Where is Abū al-Bakhtarī Ismāʿīl b. Ṭalḥah?" The latter having come forward, Ziyād said, "I want to say something to you." So he drew near until the necks of their horses touched. (Men [going into battle] used to use doubled up garment edges as belts.)[654] Ziyād put his hand into Ismāʿīl's belt and plucked him—he was a thin man—from his saddle. Ismāʿīl said, "Abū al-Mughīrah, I beseech you; this is not loyalty to Muṣʿab." Ziyād said, "I would rather have this than see you slain tomorrow."

After Muṣʿab had refused to accept the guarantee of safety, Muḥammad b. Marwān called to ʿĪsā b. Muṣʿab and said to him, "O son of my brother, do not cause your own death. You have a [809] guarantee of safety." Muṣʿab, too, said to him, "Your uncle has guaranteed your safety; go to him." But he said, "Let the women of Quraysh not say that I delivered you to be slain." "Then go forward before me," said Muṣʿab, "and I will reckon upon obtain-

---

652. Tribal *nisbah* from Balādhurī, *Ansāb*, V, 341.

653. *Jāru sidqin*, implying faithful carrying out of the obligations of *jiwār* (the granting of protection).

654. The meaning of *bi-al-ḥawāshī al-maḥshuwwah* is unclear. Most likely, a man going into battle gathered up the bottom of his shirt and tucked it under a belt of doubled material. See Dozy, *Supplément*, I, 292. Cf. Ṭabarī, II, 629: "Ibn al-Ashtar took the bottom of his tunic (*qabāʾ*), lifted it up, tucked it under a red belt he was wearing made of the edges of cloaks, and tightened the belt over it—he had covered his coat of mail with the tunic." The suggestion of ed. Leiden, *Glossarium*, p. DXVIII, that in the time of ʿAbd al-Malik, "stuffed intestines" were used as belts, seems farfetched.

ing [a reward from God] through you."[655] So he fought before him until he was killed.

Muṣʿab was wounded by an arrow shot. Zā'idah b. Qudāmah saw him and attacked. Crying "Vengeance for al-Mukhtār," he struck him with a spear, and threw him to the ground. ʿUbaydallāh b. Ziyād b. Ẓabyān dismounted by him and cut off his head, saying, "He killed my brother, al-Nābi' b. Ziyād." ʿUbaydallāh brought the head to ʿAbd al-Malik b. Marwān, who rewarded him with a thousand dinars. These he refused to take, saying, "I did not kill him out of obedience to you; I killed him to avenge what he did to me. I do not take money for carrying a head." And he left it with ʿAbd al-Malik.[656]

The vendetta that ʿUbaydallāh b. Ziyād b. Ẓabyān mentioned as the reason for his killing Muṣʿab was as follows: In one of his terms as governor, Muṣʿab appointed Muṭarrif b. Sīdān al-Bāhilī, a member of the Banū Ji'āwah, to be in charge of his police.

According to ʿUmar b. Shabbah—Abū al-Ḥasan al-Madā'inī and Makhlad b. Yaḥyā b. Ḥāḍir: Al-Nābi' b. Ziyād b. Ẓabyān and a man of the Banū Numayr were brought to Muṭarrif, after the two had committed highway robbery. Muṭarrif killed al-Nābi', and flogged the Numayrī and released him. Then ʿUbaydallāh b. Ziyād b. Ẓabyān gathered a group of men (this was after Muṣʿab had removed Muṭarrif from al-Baṣrah and set him in charge of al-Ahwāz) and went out to attack Muṭarrif. The two sides met and took their stand with a river between them. Muṭarrif crossed over to ʿUbaydallāh b. Ziyād b. Ẓabyān, and the latter gave him a quick spear thrust and killed him. Muṣʿab then sent Mukram b. Muṭarrif to pursue Ibn Ẓabyān. Mukram went as far as ʿAskar
[810] Mukram,[657] which therefore took its name from him, but did not

655. The expression *aḥtasib-ka*, "I reckon you for myself," is explained by Lane, *Lexicon*, II, 565: "*Iḥtasaba waladahū*. . . is said when one has lost by death an adult child or son or daughter; meaning 'He prepared, or provided, in store for himself, a reward, by his patience on the occasion of his being afflicted and tried by the death of his adult child.'"

656. Cf. the report in Balādhurī, *Ansāb*, V, 333 (repeated 340): "As ʿUbaydallāh placed the head before ʿAbd al-Malik, the latter bowed down. Later, ʿUbaydallāh used to say, 'Never have I regretted anything as much as I regret not having cut off ʿAbd al-Malik's head at that time, thereby giving people relief. I would have killed the two kings of the Arabs in a single day.'" ʿAbd al-Malik's reaction when these words were reported to him is given in Balādhurī, *Ansāb*, XI, 202.

657. ʿAskar Mukram (the name means Mukram's Camp, but Yāqūt says this

find Ibn Ẓabyān. After his brother had been killed, Ibn Ẓabyān joined ʿAbd al-Malik. Mentioning this, al-Baʿīth al-Yashkurī said after the death of Muṣʿab:[658]

When we saw that the leaders of the enterprise (*amr*) were
 spiritless,
 and that necks were about to become hindquarters,[659]
We held steadfast to God's command (*amr*), until He should set
 matters right;
 and we approved of no governor but one from Umayyah.
We killed Muṣʿab and the son of Muṣʿab:
 the clansman of Asad[660] and al-Nakhaʿī the Yemenite.[661]
Death's eagle passed by Muslim[662] from us;
 it sank its tooth[663] into him, and he was slain.
We made [Muṭarrif] Ibn Sīdān drink an overflowing cup
 that satisfied us: the best part of the matter is what gives
 satisfaction.

According to Abū Zayd [ʿUmar b. Shabbah]—ʿAlī b. Muḥammad [al-Madāʾinī], who said: Ibn Ẓabyān passed Muṭarrif's daughter in al-Baṣrah. Someone said to her, "This is the man who killed your father." She said, "For the sake of God, my father [met his death]." But Ibn Ẓabyān said:

Not for the sake of God did your father meet his end,
 but for the sake of money.

---

alludes to another Mukram) was a city in Khūzistān province, about 35 miles northeast of Ahwāz, where the Dujayl River was joined by the waters of the Masruqān Canal. See *EI*², s.v.; Yāqūt, *Muʿjam*, s.v., and Le Strange, *Lands*, 237.

658. Verses three and four can be found in *Aghānī*, XVII, 164, where they are attributed to Yazīd b. al-Riqāʿ, the brother of ʿAdī b. al-Riqāʿ, with a note that some attribute them to al-Baʿīth al-Yashkurī.

659. The metaphor is drawn from horsemanship. The leaders of the state are compared to the chest (*ṣadr*, pl. *ṣudūr*) of a spiritless horse that holds its head low and is about to turn tail (i.e., turn its neck in the direction of its hindquarters). Cf. Lane, *Lexicon*, I, 314, s.v. *tawālī*.

660. Muṣʿab and his brother ʿAbdallāh were members of the Banū Asad b. ʿAbd-al-ʿUzzā b. Quṣayy (a clan of Quraysh). See Ibn al-Athīr, *Kāmil*, IV, 254.

661. I.e., Ibrāhīm b. al-Ashtar al-Nakhaʿī.

662. I.e., Muslim b. ʿAmr al-Bāhilī (*Aghānī*, XVII, 164; Balādhurī, *Ansāb*, V, 341–42).

663. Variant in *Aghānī*, XVII, 164: "talon."

[811] After Muṣʿab had been killed, ʿAbd al-Malik b. Marwān summoned the people of Iraq to allegiance, and they swore allegiance to him. Muṣʿab was killed at a canal called al-Dujayl,[664] at Dayr al-Jāthalīq. After he was killed, ʿAbd al-Malik ordered him and his son ʿĪsā to be buried.

According to al-Wāqidī—ʿUthmān b. Muḥammad—Abū Bakr b. ʿUmar—ʿUrwah, who said: When Muṣʿab was killed, ʿAbd al-Malik said, "Bury him: by God, of old there was respect between us and him, but this kingdom is a barren thing."[665]

According to Abū Zayd [ʿUmar b. Shabbah]—Abū Nuʿaym [al-Faḍl b. Dukayn]—ʿAbdallāh b. al-Zubayr Abū Abī Aḥmad—ʿAbdallāh b. Sharīk al-ʿĀmirī, who said: As I was standing beside Muṣʿab b. al-Zubayr, I took a letter out of my tunic for him, and said to him, "This is ʿAbd al-Malik's letter." He said, "[Do] what you want." [Continuing,] he said: Then one of the Syrians came, entered his camp, and took out a slave girl. She shouted, "Alas my humiliation!" Muṣʿab looked at her and then paid no further attention to her.

[Continuing,] he said: Muṣʿab's head was brought to ʿAbd al-Malik. He looked at it and said, "When will Quraysh nourish the like of you?" And two [men] in Medina were talking to Ḥubbā,[666] when someone told them that Muṣʿab had been killed. She said, "May his slayer perish!" Told that ʿAbd al-Malik b. Marwān had killed him, she said, "My father [as ransom] for the slayer and the slain!" [Continuing,] he said: Later, when ʿAbd al-Malik made

---

664. The Dujayl Canal left the Euphrates at the village of al-Rabb (north of al-Anbār), watered the districts of Maskin and Qatrabbul, and flowed into the Tigris at Baghdad. See Yāqūt, *Muʿjam*, s.v.

665. "Barren" (*ʿaqīm*) is applied not only to things that bring forth no offspring, and are therefore unprofitable, but also to things that destroy. Thus, in Qurʾān 51:41, the tribe of ʿĀd is destroyed by a wind that is called *ʿaqīm*. Lane, *Lexicon*, V, 2117, quotes this saying of ʿAbd al-Malik, together with the paraphrase given by various Arabic lexicographers, as follows: "Dominion is a condition in which, or in the seeking of which, relationship profits not, nor friendship: for a man will slay his son, if he fear him, and his father, for dominion; or because, in seeking it, the father will be slain, and the son, and the brother, and the paternal uncle; or because, in it, the ties of relationship are severed by slaughter and by undutiful conduct." See also Freytag, II, 685 (Maydānī, II, 222).

666. Ḥubbā al-Madīniyyah was a society woman from Medina. Her home was a gathering place for young men of Quraysh. See Balādhurī, *Ansāb*, XI, 186.

the pilgrimage, Ḥubbā approached him and said, "Did you kill your fellow tribesmen Muṣʿab?" He replied: [812]

Whoever tastes war, finds its taste
bitter, and it leaves him in a rough country.[667]

And Ibn Qays al-Ruqayyāt said:[668]

A slain man resting at Dayr al-Jāthalīq
has bequeathed shame and humiliation to the two garrison cities.
Bakr b. Wā'il was not loyal to God,
neither was Tamīm steadfast in the encounter.
Had he been a tribesman of Bakr,[669] there would have gathered round him
squadrons whose ardor rises to the boil and lasts.
But the obligation to defend was neglected; [813]
on that day there was no generous Muḍar tribesman among [the squadrons].
God reward with infamy any Kūfan there
and any Baṣran of them: whoever does what is blameworthy is to be blamed.
Sons [of one father with us, but] of different mothers, they left our backs uncovered,
though we were of pure and genuine stock among them.
If we are destroyed, they will not remain after us;
[only] for someone who possesses honor is there inviolable territory among the Muslims.

According to Abū Jaʿfar [sc. al-Ṭabarī]: It has been said that the events I have mentioned—Muṣʿab's death, and the war between him and ʿAbd al-Malik—took place in the year 72, and that the affair of Khālid b. ʿAbdallāh b. Khālid b. Asīd and his going to al-

667. The verse is by the pre-Islamic poet Abū Qays b. al-Aslat and is quoted in *Aghānī*, XV, 160, 161. For "leaves him," the variants "imprisons him," and "makes him kneel down," are recorded.

668. Lines of this elegy for Muṣʿab are quoted in various other sources; cf. *Aghānī*, XVII, 165; Balādhurī, *Ansāb*, V, 342; Dīnawarī, *Akhbār*, 319; *Dīwān*, 300ff.

669. For "a Bakrī," the version quoted in Yāqūt, *Muʿjam*, s.v. Dayr al-Jāthalīq, reads, "with Qays"; another version reads, "a Qaysī" [ed. Leiden note].

Baṣrah on behalf of ʿAbd al-Malik took place in 71.[670] Muṣʿab was killed in [the month of] Jumādā II.[671]

[ʿAbd al-Malik Enters al-Kūfah]

According to al-Wāqidī, ʿAbd al-Malik b. Marwān entered al-Kūfah this year and distributed the districts[672] of Iraq and the garrison cities of al-Kūfah and al-Baṣrah among his financial agents. However, Abū al-Ḥasan [al-Madāʾinī] mentions that this took place in the year 72.

According to ʿUmar [b. Shabbah]—ʿAlī b. Muḥammad [al-Madāʾinī], who said: Muṣʿab was killed on Tuesday, the thirteenth day of Jumādā I or II, of the year 72.[673]

[814] When ʿAbd al-Malik came to al-Kūfah, according to what has been mentioned, he encamped at al-Nukhaylah. Then he called on the people to swear allegiance. Quḍāʿah[674] came. When he saw a small number, ʿAbd al-Malik said, "People of Quḍāʿah, how did you remain safe from Muḍar, in spite of your small number?" ʿAbdallāh b. Yaʿlā al-Nahdī said, "We are stronger than they and more able to defend ourselves." "By means of whom?" he asked. "By means of those of us who are on your side, Commander of the Faithful," he replied. Then Madhḥij and Hamdān[675] came. ʿAbd al-Malik said, "With these men there, I think no one will accomplish anything in al-Kūfah." Then Juʿfī[676] came. When ʿAbd al-Malik looked at them, he said, "People of Juʿfī, you have covered and hidden the son of one of your tribeswomen." (He

---

670. This is the chronology of al-Madāʾinī and of Abū Mikhnaf. See *Aghānī*, XVII, 161 (al-Madāʾinī), and Balādhurī, *Ansāb*, XI, 26 (Abū Mikhnaf).

671. Dixon, *Umayyad Caliphate*, 134, gives reasons for preferring 72. Jumādā II of 72 began on October 30, 691. Dīnawarī, *Akhbār*, 319, reads: "on Thursday, the middle day of Jumādā I, 72."

672. *Aʿmāl*, pl. of *ʿamal*, "units of fiscal administration for collecting taxes" (Morony, *Iraq*, 528).

673. 13 Jumādā I corresponds to October 12, 691; 13 Jumādā II corresponds to November 11, 691. There is a problem in that neither date fell on a Tuesday, according to the Wüstenfeld-Mahler tables.

674. Quḍāʿah (of which the Banū Kalb were the most prominent subdivision) was usually placed among the Yemeni tribes, although some genealogists placed it among the northern tribes. See *EI*², s.v. Ḳuḍāʿa.

675. Madhḥij and Hamdān were both Yemeni tribes; see *EI*², s.vv.

676. Juʿfī was a Yemeni tribe related to Hamdān or to Madhḥij (*Lisān*).

meant Yaḥyā b. Sa'īd b. al-'Āṣ.) They said, "Yes." "Hand him over," he said. "When he is safe!" they said. "And you make conditions, too?" he said. One of them said, "By God, it is not out of ignorance of your right that we make conditions; rather, we presume upon you as a child presumes upon his father." "By God," he said, "how excellent a tribe you are! Truly, you have been skilled horsemen in pre-Islamic times and in Islam. He is safe." They brought him. (His *kunyah* was Abū Ayyūb.) Looking at him, 'Abd al-Malik said, "Abū Qabīḥ![677] Having thrown off allegiance to me, with what face will you look toward your Lord?" "With the face He created," he said, and swore allegiance. Then he turned to go. Looking at the back of his head, 'Abd al-Malik said, "What a man he is! What a knower he is!" (He meant of the Arabic language.)[678]

According to 'Alī b. Muḥammad [al-Madā'inī]—al-Qāsim b. Ma'n and other(s)—Ma'bad b. Khālid al-Jadalī, who said: Then we tribesmen of 'Adwān[679] came forward to him. [Continuing,] he said: We put forward a handsome, comely man, and I remained in the rear. (Ma'bad was ugly.) 'Abd al-Malik said, "Who [are they]?" The scribe said, "'Adwān." 'Abd al-Malik said:[680]

Bring an excuse for the tribe 'Adwān: [815]
 they were the serpents of the earth,[681]
But they acted wrongfully against each other
 and were not regardful of each other.[682]

---

677. As a nickname, "Abū Qabīḥ" means "man with an ugly [face]," or, "doer of an ugly [deed]."

678. For the expression *ibn zawmalah*, "one who is knowledgeable, expert in a matter," see ed. Leiden, *Glossarium*, p. CCLXXIX. *Addenda*, p. DCLXXIV, indicates that one should read *'arabiyyah* (Arabic language), rather than *gharībah* (strange, i.e., a knower of strange things). If one accepts the emendation, this is one of the earliest examples of the the word *'arabiyyah* in this sense. Cf. Balādhurī, *Ansāb*, V, 353, and note.

679. The tribal genealogy is 'Adwān b. 'Amr b. Qays 'Aylān b. Muḍar (*Lisān*).

680. The verses are by the poet Dhū al-Iṣba' al-'Adwānī. See *Aghānī*, III, 2, 4; and F. Sezgin, *GAS*, II, 297f.

681. "Serpents of the earth," meaning "cunning, guileful, malignant, or mischievous, and strong, not neglecting to take blood-revenge." See Lane, *Lexicon*, V, 1986, where the first two lines of the poem are explained.

682. The tribe of 'Adwān was rent by internal wars in which Dhū al-Iṣba' took part. In the *Aghānī* version, the next verse, not quoted by 'Abd al-Malik, is: "So they became subjects of talk, with [people] raising and lowering their voices."

Of them were chieftains
and those who fully repay actions.[683]

Then he went up to the handsome man and said, "Go on!" "I don't know," he replied. So I said from behind him:

And of them is an arbiter who decrees,
and what he decrees is not annulled.
And of them are those who give the pilgrimage the signal to proceed,[684]
according to custom and obligation.
From the time they are born, they grow up
with the best of pure lineage.[685]

[Continuing,] he said: Leaving me, 'Abd al-Malik turned to the handsome man and said, "Who is it [who composed the lines]?" "I don't know," he said. So I said from behind him, "Dhū al-Iṣba'!" [Continuing,] he said: Turning to the handsome man, 'Abd al-Malik said, "And why was he called Dhū al-Iṣba'?"[686] "I don't know," he said. So I said from behind him, "Because a snake bit his toe and he cut it off."[687] Then he turned to the handsome man and said, "What was his [real] name?" "I don't know," he said. So I said from behind him, "Ḥurthān b. al-Ḥārith!" Then 'Abd al-Malik turned to the handsome man and said, "From which [clan] of you was he?" "I don't know," he said. So I said from behind him, "Banū Nājī!" 'Abd al-Malik said:

---

683. *Qarḍ,* literally "loan," is to be taken here in the figurative sense of any good or bad act for which men reward or requite each other. See Lane, *Lexicon,* VII, 2516, and *Lisān,* s.v.

684. The line is explained in *Aghānī,* III, 4: "Giving permission, or a signal, for the pilgrimage to pass on [from 'Arafāt] belonged to the tribe of Khuzā'ah; but then the tribe of 'Adwān took it from them, and it came into the hands of one of their tribesmen called Abū Sayyārah, of the Banū Wābish b. Zayd b. 'Adwān.... Abū Sayyārah used to give the pilgrims the signal to proceed by going in front of them on his donkey, and addressing them...."

685. The *Aghānī* and Mss. C and Pet give a different text: "When they beget, they produce noble sons, with the best of pure lineage."

686. *Dhū al-Iṣba'* means "the man with the finger, or toe."

687. The text in *Aghānī* reads, "and it [i.e., the toe or finger] dried up."

Away with the Banū Nājī and your creating discord among
them![688]
and do not make your eyes follow what is perishing.
Whenever I say a kind word, to create harmony among them, [816]
Wuhayb says, "I will not make peace with that one."
So he became like the back of an ass, his hump cut off;
the children surround him, humpbacked, kneeling.[689]

Then he turned to the handsome man and said, "How much is your military stipend (*ʿaṭā'*)?" "Seven hundred [dirhams]," he said. ʿAbd al-Malik said to me, "At how much are you?" "Three hundred," I said. Turning to the two scribes, he said, "Deduct four hundred from this one's stipend and add it to this one's." So I came back at a stipend of seven hundred, and he at three hundred!

Then Kindah[690] came. ʿAbd al-Malik looked at ʿAbdallāh b. Isḥāq b. al-Ashʿath and commended him to his brother Bishr [b. Marwān], saying, "Make him one of your companions." Dāwūd b. Qaḥdham came with two hundred tribesmen from Bakr b. Wā'il, wearing Davidic tunics (after his name).[691] He sat down with ʿAbd al-Malik on his couch,[692] and ʿAbd al-Malik turned to him. Then he arose, and they arose with him. Following them with his gaze, ʿAbd al-Malik said, "Those evildoers! By God, had their leader not come to me, not one of them would have given me obedience."

Then, as some have said, he put Qaṭan b. ʿAbdallāh al-Ḥārithī in charge of al-Kūfah for forty days; then he removed him and appointed Bishr b. Marwān. ʿAbd al-Malik ascended the pulpit of al-Kūfah and preached, saying: "If ʿAbdallāh b. al-Zubayr were

---

688. Alternate reading: "As for the Banū Nājī, do not mention them . . ." (*Aghānī*, III, 3).

689. *Aghānī*: "So he became like the back of a stallion; he goes slowly toward the enemy, humpbacked, kneeling."

690. Kindah was a tribal group of South Arabian origins that had led a powerful confederation in pre-Islamic times. The grandfather of the ʿAbdallāh mentioned here was the Kindī chief al-Ashʿath b. Qays, who had led his tribe's delegation to Medina to accept Islam and had later fought at Ṣiffīn on the side of ʿAlī. See *EI*², s.v. Kinda.

691. *Aqbiyah* (pl. of *qabā'*) *dāwūdiyyah*, i.e., chain mail: according to Qur'ān 343:10–11, David was the inventor of mailed coats.

692. *Sarīr* is also used for a throne.

a caliph, as he asserts, he would come out and share his substance equally [with his supporters];[693] he would not plant his tail[694] in the sanctuary of Mecca." Then he said, "I have appointed Bishr b. Marwān your governor, and have commanded him to deal well with those who are obedient, but severely with those who dis-
[817] obey. Heed him and obey." He appointed Muḥammad b. ʿUmayr as his governor (*ʿāmil*) in charge of Hamadhān, and Yazīd b. Ruwaym in charge of al-Rayy.[695] He distributed governors, but he did not keep his promise to anyone who had imposed upon him as a condition the governorship (*wilāyah*) of Iṣbahān. Then he said, "Bring me those evildoers who spoiled Syria and corrupted Iraq." Someone said, "The heads of their tribes have granted them protection." "Does anyone," he replied, "grant protection against me?" Now ʿAbdallāh b. Yazīd b. Asad had taken refuge with ʿAlī b. ʿAbdallāh b. ʿAbbās, with whom Yaḥyā b. Maʿyūf al-Hamdānī had also taken refuge. Al-Hudhayl b. Zufar b. al-Ḥārith and ʿAmr b. Yazīd al-Ḥakamī took refuge with Khālid b. Yazīd b. Muʿāwiyah. ʿAbd al-Malik guaranteed their safety, and they came out of hinding.

According to Abū Jaʿfar [sc. al-Ṭabarī]: In this year ʿUbaydallāh b. Abī Bakrah and Ḥumrān b. Abān contended with each other for leadership (*riyāsah*) in al-Baṣrah.

According to ʿUmar b. Shabbah—ʿAlī b. Muḥammad [al-Madāʾinī], who said: When al-Muṣʿab was killed, Ḥumrān b. Abān and ʿUbaydallāh b. Abī Bakrah arose and contended with each other for the governance (*wilāyah*) of al-Baṣrah. Ibn Abī Bakrah said, "I am wealthier than you: I expended [my wealth]

693. *Āsā bi-nafsihī*, "share equally with himself," i.e., he would share the lot of his supporters. The words "with his supporters," are supplied from Balādhurī, *Ansāb*, XI, 29f. Cf. the words of ʿAbdallāh b. al-Zubayr's son refusing to flee to save himself: "What a bad son I should be if I did not make myself share equally with you, so that what befalls you will befall me." (Balādhurī, *Ansāb*, XI, 74).

694. The metaphor is taken from the locust, which inserts its tail into the ground to lay its eggs. The expression means "to remain fixed in a place" (Lane, *Lexicon*, VI, 2246).

695. Hamadhān and Rayy are both in Jibāl province. Hamadhān is the modern Hamadān; Rayy is only a few miles from modern Tehran. See Le Strange, *Lands*, 215–17. Balādhurī, *Ansāb*, V, 354, argues that *Ḥawshab b.* Yazīd b. Ruwaym must have been appointed governor of Rayy, since Yazīd was killed before the death of Muṣʿab.

for Khālid's forces at the battle of al-Jufrah." Someone said to Ḥumrān, "You lack strength against Ibn Abī Bakrah. Seek help from ʿAbdallāh b. al-Ahtam; if he helps you, Ibn Abī Bakrah will not have strength against you." Ḥumrān did so, and prevailed over al-Baṣrah, with Ibn al-Ahtam in charge of its police. Ḥumrān had standing in the eyes of the Banū Umayyah.

According to Abū Zayd [ʿUmar b. Shabbah]—Abū ʿĀṣim al-Nabīl, who said: A man spoke to me and said that a bedouin Arab shaykh arrived and, seeing Ḥumrān, asked, "Who is that?" They said, "Ḥumrān." He said, "I once saw him when his cloak[696] had slipped from his shoulder, and Marwān and Saʿīd b. al-ʿĀṣ hastened to him, each striving to be the first to straighten it."

According to Abū Zayd [ʿUmar b. Shabbah]—Abū ʿĀṣim [al-Nabīl], who said: I told this to one of the sons of ʿAbdallāh b. ʿĀmir, and he said, "My father told me that Ḥumrān put out his [818]
leg, and Muʿāwiyah and ʿAbdallāh b. ʿĀmir each strove to be first to massage it."

[Khālid b. ʿAbdallāh Becomes Governor of al-Baṣrah]

In this year, ʿAbd al-Malik sent Khālid b. ʿAbdallāh as governor of al-Baṣrah.

According to ʿUmar [b. Shabbah]—ʿAlī b. Muḥammad [al-Madāʾinī], who said: Ḥumrān remained in charge of al-Baṣrah a short while. Ibn Abī Bakrah left and went to ʿAbd al-Malik in al-Kūfah after the death of Muṣʿab. Then ʿAbd al-Malik appointed Khālid b. ʿAbdallāh b. Khālid b. Asīd to be in charge of al-Baṣrah and its fiscal districts. Khālid sent ʿUbaydallāh b. Abī Bakrah as his deputy in charge of al-Baṣrah. When ʿUbaydallāh came to Ḥumrān, the latter said, "Have you come? Would that you had not come!" So Ibn Abī Bakrah was in charge of al-Baṣrah until Khālid arrived.

According to what al-Wāqidī asserts, ʿAbd al-Malik returned to Syria this year.

---

696. *Ridāʾ*, a single piece of cloth worn draped over the shoulders (Lane, *Lexicon*, III, 1072).

[Ibn al-Zubayr's Governors during This Year]

[Continuing,] he said: In [this year], Ibn al-Zubayr removed Jābir b. al-Aswad b. ʿAwf from Medina and made Ṭalḥah b. ʿAbdallāh b. ʿAwf his governor there.

[Continuing,] he said: Ṭalḥah was Ibn al-Zubayr's last governor of Medina. [He remained] until Ṭāriq b. ʿAmr, ʿUthmān's *mawlā*, arrived there. Ṭalḥah then fled, and Ṭāriq stayed in Medina until ʿAbd al-Malik wrote to him [confirming him as governor].

[The Pilgrimage]

According to al-Wāqidī, ʿAbdallāh b. al-Zubayr led the pilgrimage this year.

[Ibn al-Zubayr's Sermon after the Death of Muṣʿab][697]

According to Abū Zayd [ʿUmar b. Shabbah]—Abū Ghassān Muḥammad b. Yaḥyā—Muṣʿab b. ʿUthmān, who said: When news of Muṣʿab's death reached ʿAbdallāh b. al-Zubayr, he arose among the people and said: "Praise be to God! His are the creation and the command.[698] He gives the kingdom to whom He will, and withdraws the kingdom from whom He will; He exalts whom
[819] He will, and abases whom He will.[699] Verily, God does not abase him on whose side is the right, though he were but a single man; neither does He exalt him whose friend is Satan and his party, though all mankind were on his side. Truly, there has come to us from Iraq a report that has both saddened us and made us rejoice. The death of Muṣʿab—God's mercy upon him!—has been reported to us. What caused us to rejoice was our knowledge that his death was a testimony[700] on his behalf. What saddened us was

697. Parallel accounts can be found in Balādhurī, *Ansāb*, V, 347–48, and *Aghānī*, XVII, 166. Both accounts note that Ibn al-Zubayr refrained from mentioning his brother's death for several days after it had become common knowledge in Mecca, and that when he finally spoke, deep emotion was visible on his face.

698. Qur'ān 7:54.

699. Cf. ibid., 3:26.

700. *Shahādah*, which also means "martyrdom."

the fact that separation from a beloved kinsman brings a pang of grief that the lover feels at the time of affliction. Afterwards, however, the man of judgment turns to a fitting patience and noble endurance. If I have been afflicted by the death of Muṣʿab, I have been afflicted by that of al-Zubayr previously; neither am I free of affliction in regard to ʿUthmān. Muṣʿab was only one servant among God's servants, one helper among my helpers. Verily, the people of Iraq, people of treachery and hypocrisy, handed him over and sold him for a very low price. If he has been slain, we, by God, do not die in our beds[701] like the sons of Abū al-ʿĀṣ, none of whom died in war either in pre-Islamic times or in Islam. We die a sudden death by spears or under the shadow of swords. The present world is but a loan from the Supreme King, whose authority does not pass away, and whose dominion does not perish. If it turns its face toward me, I do not take it like a man whose head is turned and who exults immoderately; if it turns its back, I do not weep over it like an abject man confounded by fear. I say this, and ask God's forgiveness for myself and for you."

[ʿAbd al-Malik's Banquet at al-Khawarnaq]

[ʿUmar b. Shabbah] also mentions that ʿAbd al-Malik, having killed Muṣʿab and entered al-Kūfah, ordered a great deal of food [820] prepared and brought to al-Khawarnaq,[702] and issued a general invitation. So the people entered and took their seats. When ʿAmr b. Ḥurayth al-Makhzūmī[703] entered, ʿAbd al-Malik said, "Come to me, and sit on my couch." And he seated him with him. Then he said, "What food that you have eaten do you like best and think most delicious?" "Roast young kid," he said, "nicely sea-

701. Cf. the vivid touch added in the version given in Balādhurī, *Ansāb*, V, 348: "We do not die in our beds of indigestion (*ḥabajan*)." The unusual word refers to the fatal indigestion camels suffer when they graze too much on a certain plant, and alludes to the gluttony and hedonism of the Banū Marwān. Cf. ed. Leiden, *Addenda*, p. DCLXXIV.

702. See note 466.

703. He had been Muṣʿab's deputy for al-Kūfah while Muṣʿab was fighting at Maskin. He had apparently gone over to ʿAbd al-Malik under the influence of his letters. See Balādhurī, *Ansāb*, V, 351.

soned and well cooked." "That's nothing!" said ʿAbd al-Malik. "What do you think of a suckling lamb, carefully scalded and well cooked, [so tender that when] you pull its hind leg toward you, you make its front leg follow, one that has been nourished on equal parts of milk and butter?" The tables were brought, and they ate. ʿAbd al-Malik b. Marwān said, "How pleasant our life is! If only anything lasted![704] But, as the ancient poet said:

Everything new, O Umaymah, goes toward decay;
 and every man will some day become a has-been.

When he finished eating, ʿAbd al-Malik toured the palace. He said to ʿAmr b. Ḥurayth, "Whose is this house?" and "Who built this house?"[705] ʿAmr told him, and ʿAbd al-Malik said:

Everything new, O Umaymah, goes toward decay;
 and every man will some day become a has-been.

Then he went to his sitting place and reclined, saying:

[821] Work with deliberation, for you are mortal;
 and toil [only] for yourself, O man.
What was, now that it has past, seems as if it had never been;
 and what is seems as if it had already passed away.

---

704. A similar conversation on the theme of mutability is reported to have taken place between al-Nuʿmān, the original builder of al-Khawarnaq, and his vizier. One day, al-Nuʿmān, who was a cruel and evil ruler, looked out from his palace at the lush gardens and plentiful waters. He asked his vizier whether he had ever seen such a sight. The vizier replied, "No, if it only were to last!" Surprised, al-Nuʿmān asked, "And what lasts?" "What is in God's presence in the hereafter," replied the vizier. "And how can one obtain it?" asked al-Nuʿmān. "By your leaving the world, worshiping God, and seeking what is His." Al-Nuʿmān, it is said, left his palace and became an ascetic that very night. See Ibn al-Faqīh, *Kitāb al-buldān*, 177–78. The story is said to have been told to ʿAbd al-Malik's son Hishām at al-Khawarnaq. See *Aghānī*, II, 35–36, where ʿAdī b. Zayd's poem on the *Ubi Sunt!* theme is quoted.

705. Cf. the parallel in Balādhurī, *Ansāb*, V, 352, where ʿAbd al-Malik can see the various mansions of al-Kūfah from al-Khawarnaq and asks about them. However, since Arabic *bayt* can mean either a separate house or a chamber within a larger building (Lane, *Lexicon*, I, 280), he may have been asking about who added various rooms to the palace. Cf. the report in Ibn al-Faqīh, *Kitāb al-buldān*, 178 (on the authority of al-Haytham b. ʿAdī), that any governor who came to al-Kūfah would expand or renovate the palace of al-Khawarnaq. In Balādhurī, ʿAbd al-Malik apparently asks about both subjects.

According to al-Wāqidī, ʿAbd al-Malik conquered Qaysāriyyah[706] in this year.

---

706. Qaysāriyyah (Caesarea) is about 25 miles south of Haifa on the Mediterranean coast. Umayyad preoccupation with Ibn al-Zubayr had given the Byzantines an opportunity to attack and damage Qaysāriyyah and ʿAsqalān. Once secure in power, ʿAbd al-Malik rebuilt and fortified the two places, along with other coastal points such as Acre and Tyre. See *EI*[2], s.v. Ḳaysāriyya; Balādhurī, *Futūḥ*, 143.

The Events of the Year 72

(June 4, 691–May 22, 692)

According to Abū Jaʿfar [sc. al-Ṭabarī]: Among these events were those involving the Khārijites and those involving al-Muhallab b. Abī Ṣufrah and ʿAbd al-ʿAzīz b. ʿAbdallāh b. Khālid b. Asīd.

[ʿAbd al-Malik and the Khārijites]

According to Hishām b. Muḥammad [al-Kalbī]—Abū Mikhnaf—Ḥaṣīrah b. ʿAbdallāh [b. al-Ḥārith al-Azdī] and Abū Zuhayr [al-Naḍr b. Ṣāliḥ] al-ʿAbsī: After eight months of extremely hard fighting between the Azāriqah and al-Muhallab at Sūlāf, it was reported to them that Muṣʿab b. al-Zubayr had been killed. The news reached the Khārijites before it reached al-Muhallab and his forces. The Khārijites therefore called to them, saying, "Will you not tell us what you say about Muṣʿab?" They replied, "An imām of right guidance!" The Khārijites said, "Then he is your friend in the present world and the world to come?" "Yes," they replied. The Khārijites said, "And you are his friends while you are alive and when you are dead?" They replied, "And we are his friends alive and dead." The Khārijites said, "Then what do you say about

ʿAbd al-Malik b. Marwān?" "He is the son of the Accursed One," they replied. "We are quit of him, leaving him to God. In our sight, shedding his blood is more licit than shedding yours." The Khārijites said, "Then you are quit of him in the present world and the world to come?" "Yes," they replied, "just as we are quit of you." The Khārijites said, "And you are his enemies while you are alive and when you are dead?" "Yes," they said, "we are enemies of him, even as we are enemies of you." The Khārijites said, "Your imām Muṣʿab has been killed by ʿAbd al-Malik b. Marwān, and we think that tomorrow you will make ʿAbd al-Malik your imām, although now you declare yourselves quit of [822] him and curse his father." "You lie," they said, "you enemies of God!"

On the morrow, when the death of Muṣʿab became evident to them, al-Muhallab had the men swear allegiance to ʿAbd al-Malik b. Marwān. The Khārijites then came to them and said, "What say you about Muṣʿab?" "You enemies of God," they said, "we will not tell you what we say about him." For they did not want to give the lie to themselves before them. The Khārijites said, "You told us yesterday that he was your friend in the present world and the world to come, and that you were his friends alive and dead. Then tell us what you say about ʿAbd al-Malik." "He is our imām and caliph," they said, for having sworn allegiance to him, they found no way to avoid saying this. The Azāriqah said, "Enemies of God! Yesterday you were asserting that you were quit of him in the present world and the world to come and claimed that you were his enemies alive and dead, and today he is your imām and caliph! Now that your imām whom you used to declare your friend has been killed, which of the two is the legitimate one? Which is the rightly guided one, and which is the one that strays?" "You enemies of God," they said, "we were satisfied with the former, while he was the manager of our affairs; and we are satisfied with the latter, even as we were with the former." The Khārijites said, "No, by God; but you are brothers of the devils, friends of the evildoers, and slaves of the present world."

ʿAbd al-Malik b. Marwān sent Bishr b. Marwān to be in charge of al-Kūfah and Khālid b. ʿAbdallāh b. Khālid b. Asīd to be in charge of al-Baṣrah. When Khālid arrived, he established al-Muhallab in charge of the taxes (*kharāj*) and special revenue (*maʿūnah*) of al-

Ahwāz,[707] and sent ʿĀmir b. Mismaʿ to be in charge of Sābūr, Muqātil b. Mismaʿ to be in charge of Ardashīr Khurrah,[708] Mismaʿ b. Mālik b. Mismaʿ to be in charge of Fasā and Darābjird,[709] and al-Mughīrah b. al-Muhallab to be in charge of Iṣṭakhr.

Khālid b. ʿAbdallāh sent to Muqātil and dispatched him with an army to the area of ʿAbd al-ʿAzīz [b. ʿAbdallāh]. ʿAbd al-ʿAzīz went out seeking the Azāriqah. The latter descended upon him from the direction of Kirmān, until they reached Darābjird, and
[823] he traveled toward them. Qaṭarī [b. al-Fujāʾah] sent nine hundred horsemen with Ṣāliḥ b. Mikhrāq, who marched with them until he met ʿAbd al-ʿAzīz, who was traveling with his men by night, not in battle array, and put the men to flight. Muqātil b. Mismaʿ dismounted and fought until he was killed. ʿAbd al-ʿAzīz b. ʿAbdallāh fled, and his wife, the daughter of al-Mundhir b. al-Jārūd, was taken. She was offered to the highest bidder, and her price reached one hundred thousand [dirhams], for she was beautiful. One of her kinsmen, a Khārijite leader named Abū al-Ḥadīd al-Shannī, feeling that his honor was at stake, said, "Step aside! So I see this idolatress[710] has indeed tempted you." And he beheaded her. People claim that he then went to al-Baṣrah and was seen by the family of al-Mundhir, who said, "By God, we do not know whether we should praise you or blame you." He used to say, "I did it only out of zeal and indignation."

ʿAbd al-ʿAzīz made his way to Rāmhurmuz.[711] Someone went and informed al-Muhallab about him, and the latter sent one of

---

707. Cf. Ibn al-Athīr, *Kāmil*, IV, 342: "When Khālid arrived [in al-Baṣrah], al-Muhallab was fighting the Azāriqah. [Khālid] put him in charge of the taxes and special revenues of al-Ahwāz, and sent his own brother, ʿAbd al-ʿAzīz b. ʿAbdallāh, to fight the Khārijites; and [Khālid] sent Muqātil b. Mismaʿ with him." The motive behind Khālid's decision to take matters into his own hands is not clear; it may have been personal jealousy of al-Muhallab (Dixon, *Umayyad Caliphate*, 176).

708. Ardashīr Khurrah (Shīrāz was later its chief town) was one of the five districts into which the province of Fārs was divided. See Le Strange, *Lands*, 248.

709. Darābjird was the chief town of the southeastern district of Fārs, to which it gave its name. Fasā lay about 30 miles west of Darābjird.

710. *Mushrikah*, literally, "[woman] who associates [other beings with God]," hence a polytheist or idolater, one outside the Islamic community. There may be an allusion to Qurʾān 2:221, "Do not marry idolatresses."

711. Rāmhurmuz lay in Khūzistān province, about 70 miles (three days' march) east of Ahwāz. See Le Strange, *Lands*, 243, 247.

the shaykhs from among his tribesmen,[712] a horseman of his, to ʿAbd al-ʿAzīz, saying, "Go to him; if he has retreated in defeat, console him, and tell him he has done nothing that men before him have not done. Tell him that the armies will soon reach him, and that God will strengthen and help him." The man came and found ʿAbd al-ʿAzīz encamped with about thirty men,[713] downcast and sad. The Azdī greeted him, informed him that he was al-Muhallab's messenger, told him what he had been commanded to say, and proposed that he mention to him whatever need he had. Then he returned to al-Muhallab and told him the news. Al-Muhallab said to him, "Go now to Khālid in al-Baṣrah, and tell [824] him the news." "Am I to go to him," he said, "and tell him that his brother has been routed? By God, I will not!" Al-Muhallab said, "By God, no one but you shall go to him: you were the one who saw him face to face, and you were my messenger to him." The man said, "Then he will guide you, O Muhallab, if he goes to him this year and then departs."[714] Al-Muhallab said, "As for you, by God, you feel safe from me; but, by God, if you were with anyone else, and he sent you on a march, you would leave in a hurry!" The man turned to him and said, "You think you are doing us a favor by your forbearance! By God, we more than repay you! Do you not know that we expose ourselves to death on your behalf and protect you from your enemies? By God, if we were with someone who behaved foolishly[715] toward us and sent us to march off on his affairs, and then needed our fighting and aid, we would put him between ourselves and our enemy and protect ourselves by means of him." Al-Muhallab said, "You are right; you are right." Then he called a young man from Azd who was with him, and sent him to tell Khālid the news about his brother. The young Azdī tribesman came to Khālid, who was surrounded by men and who was wearing a green coat (*jubbah*) and a green

712. As mentioned below, the man was from the tribe of Azd.

713. Mss. O, B, and Co: horsemen.

714. The meaning is not clear, and there are a number of textual variants. The word translated, "he will guide you," can, with a change of vowels, mean "he will bestow a gift on you." For, "if he goes," Ms. O reads, "if you go."

715. *Yajhalu*, from *jahila*, to be ignorant, behave with foolishness (*jahl*), is the opposite of behaving with forbearance (*ḥilm*), and implies roughness, even violent disregard for the right.

bordered shawl (*miṭraf*), and greeted him. Khālid returned the greeting and asked, "What has brought you?" "May God make you prosper!" he said. "Al-Muhallab has sent me to report to you what I have seen with my own eyes." "And what have you seen?" asked Khālid. "I saw 'Abd al-'Azīz at Rāmhurmuz," he said, "defeated." "You are lying," said Khālid. "No," he said, "by God, I have not lied or said anything but the truth to you. If I am a liar, take my life; but if I am telling the truth, give me—God make you prosper!—your coat and scarf!" Khālid said, "Alas! What an easy thing you have asked! You have contented yourself, despite
[825] the great stake if you are lying, with a small stake, if you are telling the truth." Khālid imprisoned him, but ordered him to be treated well; finally, it became clear to him that the men had been defeated. Khālid then wrote to 'Abd al-Malik, as follows:

> To proceed: I am informing the Commander of the Faithful—may God grant him honor!—that I sent 'Abd al-'Azīz b. 'Abdallāh to seek the Khārijites. They met him in Fārs. The two sides fought very hard, and 'Abd al-'Azīz was defeated when the men abandoned him. Muqātil b. Misma' was killed, and the remnants of the army went to al-Ahwāz. I have wanted to inform the Commander of the Faithful about this, that I may receive his opinion and command, and may make myself subject to it, God willing. Peace be with you, and the mercy of God!

'Abd al-Malik then wrote to him:

> To proceed: Your messenger has brought your letter in which you inform me of your having sent your brother to fight the Khārijites and of the defeat of those who were defeated and the death of those who were killed. I asked your messenger where al-Muhallab was, and he told me that he was your agent in charge of al-Ahwāz. What bad judgment it is when you send your brother, a rustic[716] from the people of Mecca, to fight, and retain by your

716. *A'rābī*, usually means bedouin, as opposed to sedentary, but as ed. Leiden, *Glossarium*, p. CCCLV, notes, it is often used abusively ("rustic"). Cf. Ṭabarī, II, 590: *mā ahlu Makkata illā a'rāb* ("The people of Mecca are nothing but rustics").

> side, collecting taxes, al-Muhallab, who is fortunate in judgment, good in management, skillful and experienced in war—a man of war, and the son of men of war! See that he[717] hastens with the men, so that you meet them in al-Ahwāz and beyond al-Ahwāz. I have sent to Bishr to have him reinforce you with an army of Kūfans. When you encounter your enemy, deal with them according to no plan until you take it to al-Muhallab and consult him about it, God willing. Peace be with you, and the mercy of God!

Khālid was distressed that ʿAbd al-Malik had faulted his judgment in sending his brother and neglecting al-Muhallab, and that, not approving of his independent judgment, he had said, "Submit it to al-Muhallab and ask his advice about it." [826]

ʿAbd al-Malik wrote to Bishr b. Marwān:

> To proceed: I have written to Khālid b. ʿAbdallāh commanding him to hasten toward the Khārijites. Dispatch five thousand men to him, and send as their commander one of your men that you approve of. When they have completed this campaign of theirs, you are to send them off to al-Rayy to fight their enemies, man their frontier garrisons (*masāliḥ*), and collect their tribute (*fay'*), until their tour of duty ends and you recall them and send others in their place.

Bishr ordered the Kūfans to furnish five thousand troops and sent ʿAbd al-Raḥmān b. Muḥammad b. al-Ashʿath in command of them, saying, "When you complete this campaign of yours, go to al-Rayy." And he wrote him a writ of appointment for the place.

Khālid led out the Baṣrans and arrived in al-Ahwāz; ʿAbd al-Raḥmān b. Muḥammad came with the Kūfan contingent and met them in al-Ahwāz. The Azāriqah approached the city of al-Ahwāz and the camp of the troops. Al-Muhallab said to Khālid b. ʿAbdallāh, "I see many boats here. Gather them for yourself, for I think

717. The Leiden editor suggests amending to "you," to maintain consistency of pronouns, but this shift of persons is not uncommon.

the enemy will surely burn them." Indeed, it was only a short time before a group of Khārijite horsemen quickly advanced toward them and burned them. Khālid b. ʿAbdallāh sent al-Muhallab to command his right wing, and Dāwūd b. Qaḥdham of the Banū Qays b. Thaʿlabah to command his left wing. Passing by ʿAbd al-Raḥmān b. Muḥammad, who had not dug a trench, al-Muhallab said to him, "Brother, what is preventing you from digging a trench?" "By God," he replied, "they are more insignificant to me than a camel's fart!"[718] [Al-Muhallab] said, "Do not think them insignificant, son of my brother; they are the beasts of prey of the
[827] Arabs. I will not leave until you make a trench for yourself." He did so. When the Khārijites learned of what ʿAbd al-Raḥmān b. Muḥammad had said about them, that they were "more insignificant to him than a camel's fart," their poet said:

O seeker of the right, do not be lured[719] by hope:
separating you from what you desire is the limit of the term [of your life].
Work on behalf of your Lord, and ask Him for His reward;
know that the fear of Him is the best deed.
Attack the effeminate ones who caparison themselves in mail of Median steel,
that they may be saluted tomorrow morning with a camel's fart.

They remained encamped for about twenty nights. Then Khālid advanced his men toward the enemy. The latter, seeing something that frightened them—the number of men and their state of preparation—started to withdraw. Khālid's men became emboldened against them: the horsemen charged them, and he advanced toward them. The enemy withdrew, as if on the defensive, turning away, and thinking they did not have strength to fight the entire force. Khālid b. ʿAbdallāh had Dāwūd b. Qaḥdham follow them with an army of Baṣrans. Khālid returned to al-Baṣrah, ʿAbd al-Raḥmān b. Muḥammad went to al-Rayy, and al-Muhallab remained in al-Ahwāz. Khālid b. ʿAbdallāh wrote to ʿAbd al-Malik:

---

718. Proverbial, see Freytag, II, 891 (Maydānī, II, 303–4).
719. The unusual verb *istahwā* recalls Qur'ān 6:71: "Like one lured to bewilderment in the earth by Satans. . . ."

> To proceed: I am informing the Commander of the Faithful—may God make him prosper!—that I went out to fight the Azāriqah, who have turned away from the faith and withdrawn from the governance of the Muslims. We met at the city of al-Ahwāz, hastened toward each other, and fought as hard as men have ever fought. Then God sent down His help upon the believers and Muslims and made His enemies retreat. The Muslims followed them, killing them, while the enemy could neither prevent it nor find safety. God made what was in their camp [828] booty (*fay'*) for the Muslims. Then I made Dāwūd b. Qaḥdham follow them. If God so wills, He will destroy them and uproot them. Peace be with you!

When this letter reached ʿAbd al-Malik, he wrote to Bishr b. Marwān:

> To proceed: Send from you a brave man skilled in war, with four thousand horsemen, and let them go to Fārs in search of the renegades; for Khālid has written to me, informing me that he has sent Dāwūd b. Qaḥdham to seek them. Command the man you send not to disobey Dāwūd b. Qaḥdham, if the two of them meet, for the disagreement of men among themselves is help to the enemy against them. Peace be with you!

Bishr b. Marwān sent ʿAttāb b. Warqāʾ with four thousand Kūfan horsemen. They went out, met Dāwūd b. Qaḥdham in the territory of Fārs, and followed in pursuit of the enemy, until the horses of most of the men perished, and they themselves were overcome by fatigue and hunger. The bulk of the two armies returned on foot to al-Ahwāz.

Concerning the defeat of ʿAbd al-ʿAzīz and his abandonment of his wife, Ibn Qays al-Ruqayyāt of the Banū Makhzūm said:[720]

ʿAbd al-ʿAzīz, you disgraced your entire army,
and left them lying on every road:

720. *Dīwān* (ed. Rhodokanakis), 293–94.

Either dying of thirst,
or cut to pieces and slain among the men.
Why didn't you remain steadfast, fighting beside the martyr,
Muqātil [b. Misma']?[721]
For you came back, your strength undone, in the evening;
[829] You left your army with no commander over them
(return with lasting shame in life!);
And you forgot your wife, when she was led away a captive,
making eyes weep as she cried aloud and wailed.

There occurred in this year the rebellion of the Khārijite Abū Fudayk from the Banū Qays b. Tha'labah, who seized al-Baḥrayn and killed Najdah b. 'Āmir al-Ḥanafī.[722] Faced by both the affair of Qaṭarī [b. Fujā'ah's] descent upon al-Ahwāz and the affair of Abū Fudayk, Khālid b. 'Abdallāh sent his brother, Umayyah b. 'Abdallāh, in command of a large army to fight Abū Fudayk. Abū Fudayk, however, defeated him, took a slave girl of his, and made her his own. Umayyah rode one of his horses and reached al-Baṣrah in three days. Khālid wrote to 'Abd al-Malik about his condition and that of the Azāriqah.

['Abd al-Malik Sends al-Ḥajjāj to Fight Ibn al-Zubayr]

In this year, 'Abd al-Malik sent al-Ḥajjāj b. Yūsuf to Mecca to fight 'Abdallāh b. al-Zubayr. The following reason is given for his sending al-Ḥajjāj, rather than someone else, against him:[723] When 'Abd al-Malik was about to return to Syria, al-Ḥajjāj b. Yūsuf stood before him and said, "O Commander of the Faithful, I dreamed I had taken 'Abdallāh b. al-Zubayr and flayed him; so send me to him and put me in charge of fighting him." 'Abd al-Malik therefore sent him with a large army of Syrians, and he

721. The line plays on the literal meaning of the name Muqātil, "a fighting [person]."

722. See Balādhurī, *Ansāb*, XI, 142ff. for further accounts of the downfall of Najdah and the rise of Abū Fudayk b. Thawr.

723. Cf. the report in Dīnawarī, *Akhbār*, 319, that while at al-Kūfah, 'Abd al-Malik placed Qudāmah b. Maẓ'ūn in charge of the army sent to attack Ibn al-Zubayr but replaced Qudāmah with al-Ḥajjāj upon his return to Syria.

went and arrived at Mecca. ʿAbd al-Malik had written to the Meccans offering a guarantee of safety if they became obedient to him.

According to al-Ḥārith [b. Muḥammad][724]—Muḥammad b. Saʿd[725]—Muḥammad b. ʿUmar [al-Wāqidī]—Muṣʿab b. Thābit[726] [830] —Abū al-Aswad[727]—ʿAbbād b. ʿAbdallāh b. al-Zubayr, who said: When Muṣʿab b. al-Zubayr was killed, ʿAbd al-Malik b. Marwān sent al-Ḥajjāj b. Yūsuf against Ibn al-Zubayr in Mecca. Al-Ḥajjāj left with two thousand men from the Syrian army during Jumādā of the year 72.[728] He did not turn toward Medina, but traveled along the Iraq road[729] and encamped at al-Ṭāʾif.[730] He kept sending detachments to ʿArafah in the area outside the sacred territory (*ḥaram*);[731] Ibn al-Zubayr also sent a detachment, and the two sides fought there. Ibn al-Zubayr's horsemen were always defeated, while al-Ḥajjāj's horsemen returned victorious. Al-Ḥajjāj then wrote to ʿAbd al-Malik, asking his permission to besiege Ibn al-Zubayr and enter the sacred territory against him. He told ʿAbd al-Malik that the vehemence of Ibn al-Zubayr's strength had abated and that most of his forces had dispersed, leaving him. He

---

724. Al-Ḥārith b. Muḥammad b. Abī Usāmah Abū Muḥammad al-Tamīmī, a Baghdadi *muḥaddith* and historian (b. 186/802, d. 282/895), was a pupil of al-Wāqidī and a teacher of al-Ṭabarī. See F. Sezgin, *GAS*, I, 160, 300.

725. Abū ʿAbdallāh Muḥammad b. Saʿd b. Manīʿ al-Baṣrī al-Zuhrī, called "Kātib al-Wāqidī" ("al-Wāqidī's secretary") was born in al-Baṣrah in 168/784, and died in Baghdad in 230/845. A pupil of al-Wāqidī, his monumental *Kitāb al-ṭabaqāt al-kabīr* contains biographies of the Prophet, his companions, and their descendants to the year 230. See ibid., I, 300f.

726. Muṣʿab b. Thābit b. ʿAbdallāh al-Asadī d. 157/773. See ibid., I, 285.

727. Abū al-Aswad Muḥammad b. ʿAbd al-Raḥmān b. Nawfal b. al-Aswad al-Asadī, d. 131/748 or 137, was the foster-son of ʿUrwah b. al-Zubayr (the brother of ʿAbdallāh and Muṣʿab b. al-Zubayr). See ibid., I, 248f.

728. In the year 72, Jumādā I began on September 30, and Jumādā II on October 30, 691. The parallel account in Balādhurī, *Ansāb*, V, 357, notes that other authorities placed the number of men at 3,000 or 5,000.

729. The pilgrim roads from Iraq to Mecca began at al-Baṣrah and al-Kūfah and came together at Dhāt ʿIrq. Medina was reached by a branch road going west from the main route. See Le Strange, *Lands*, 83–4.

730. Cf. Balādhurī, *Ansāb*, V, 257 (from ʿAwānah), where ʿAbd al-Malik explicitly commands al-Ḥajjāj to avoid any attack that would endanger the Kaʿbah; instead, he was to block the roads and starve out Ibn al-Zubayr.

731. Mecca and its immediate environs are a *ḥaram*, sacred territory in which no fighting is permitted. ʿArafah, to which the pilgrims proceed on the 9th of Dhū al-Ḥijjah, lies outside the Meccan *ḥaram*. See EI^2, s.v. ʿArafa.

asked ʿAbd al-Malik to reinforce him with men. Al-Ḥajjāj received ʿAbd al-Malik's reply.[732] ʿAbd al-Malik wrote to Ṭāriq b. ʿAmr, commanding him, with the soldiers of the army he had with him, to join al-Ḥajjāj. Ṭāriq marched with five thousand of his men and joined al-Ḥajjāj. Al-Ḥajjāj's arrival in al-Ṭā'if took place in Shaʿbān of the year 72.[733] At the beginning of Dhū al-Qaʿdah,[734] al-Ḥajjāj left al-Ṭā'if, encamped at Bi'r Maymūn,[735] and besieged Ibn al-Zubayr. Al-Ḥajjāj led the pilgrimage this year, since Ibn al-Zubayr was besieged.

Ṭāriq [b. ʿAmr's] arrival in Mecca took place on the new moon of Dhū al-Ḥijjah.[736] Al-Ḥajjāj[737] did not circumambulate the Kaʿbah, nor did he go to it in pilgrim's garb (*iḥrām*).[738] He wore a sword, but did not approach women or use perfume until ʿAbdallāh b. al-Zubayr was killed. Ibn al-Zubayr sacrificed camels in Mecca on the day of sacrifice, but neither he nor his companions performed the pilgrimage that year, because they did not stand at ʿArafah.

[831] According to Muḥammad b. ʿUmar [al-Wāqidī]—Saʿīd b. Muslim b. Bābak—his father, who said: I made the pilgrimage in the year 72. We came to Mecca and entered it from the upper part of the city. We found the forces of al-Ḥajjāj and Ṭāriq between al-Ḥajūn[739] and Bi'r Maymūn. We circumambulated the Kaʿbah and [went between] Ṣafā and Marwah.[740] Then al-Ḥajjāj led the

---

732. According to Balādhurī, *Ansāb*, V, 358 (from ʿAwānah), ʿAbd al-Malik at this point told al-Ḥajjāj to do whatever he thought best. Al-Ḥajjāj proceeded to set up a trebuchet and bombard Mecca. Another report in Balādhurī (from Wāqidī) states that the bombardment was halted during the pilgrimage only at the pleading of ʿAbdallāh b. ʿUmar and resumed immediately afterwards (ibid., 360). Ṭabarī's brief account of the siege omits many details to be found in Balādhurī, *Ansāb*, V, 358ff.

733. Shaʿbān of 72 began on December 28, 691.

734. Dhū al-Qaʿdah of 72 began on March 25, 692.

735. Yāqūt locates Bi'r Maymūn ("Maymūn's Well") in the higher part of the city of Mecca. There is evidence placing it between the Great Mosque and Minā, on the main road to Iraq. See *EI*², s.v.; Yāqūt, *Muʿjam*, s.v.

736. Dhū al-Ḥijjah of 72 began on April 24, 692.

737. The parallel in Balādhurī, *Ansāb*, V, 360, makes it clear that al-Ḥajjāj is meant. The sentence about Ṭarīq's arrival is parenthetical.

738. For a description of the garment worn by pilgrims, see *EI*², s.v. Iḥrām.

739. Al-Ḥajūn is a hill in Mecca where a cemetery was located (Yāqūt, *Muʿjam*, s.v.).

740. After circumambulating the Kaʿbah seven times upon arrival in Mecca,

pilgrimage: I saw him making the station at the hills of ʿArafah, on horseback, wearing a coat of mail and a neck protector.[741] Then he went back. I saw him turn off toward Biʾr Maymūn. He did not circumambulate the Kaʿbah. His men were armed. I saw that they had a great deal of food, and I saw a caravan coming from Syria carrying food: biscuit, barley meal, and flour. I saw that his forces had plenty to eat. We bought biscuit from some of them for a dirham, and it satisfied us—we were a party of three—until we reached al-Juḥfah.[742]

According to Muḥammad b. ʿUmar [al-Wāqidī]—Muṣʿab b. Thābit—Nāfiʿ, a *mawlā* of the Banū Asad, who was knowledgeable about the civil strife (*fitnah*) of Ibn al-Zubayr, who said: Ibn al-Zubayr was besieged the night of the new moon of Dhū al-Qaʿdah in the year 72.

[ʿAbd al-Malik and ʿAbdallāh b. Khāzim]

In this year, ʿAbd al-Malik wrote to [ʿAbdallāh] Ibn Khāzim al-Sulamī, summoning him to swear allegiance, and assigning him Khurāsān as a means of subsistence (*ṭuʿmah*) for seven years.

According to ʿAlī b. Muḥammad [al-Madāʾinī]—al-Mufaḍḍal b. Muḥammad, Yaḥyā b. Ṭufayl, and Zuhayr b. Hunayd (some of whom report more than the others): Muṣʿab b. al-Zubayr was killed in the year 72, while ʿAbdallāh b. Khāzim was at Abrashahr,[743] fighting Baḥīr b. Warqāʾ al-Ṣuraymī of Ṣuraym[744] b. al-Ḥārith. ʿAbd al-Malik b. Marwān then wrote to Ibn Khāzim by [832]
way of Sawrah b. Ashyam al-Numayrī, saying, "Khurāsān is yours for seven years, provided that you swear allegiance to me." Ibn Khāzim replied to Sawrah, "But for the fact that I would thereby

---

pilgrims traverse the distance between the hills of Ṣafā and Marwah in a rite called *saʿy*. See EI^2, s.v. Ḥadjdj.

741. *Mighfar*: a piece of mail that is worn under the helmet and that hangs down to protect the neck. See Lane, *Lexicon*, VI, 2274f.

742. Al-Jūḥfah was a large town, the fourth stage on the road between Mecca and Medina (Yāqūt, *Muʿjam*, s.v.).

743. Abrashahr was an alternate name for Naysābūr (Persian, Nīshāpūr), one of the major cities of Khurāsān, now located in northeastern Iran. See Le Strange, *Lands*, 383.

744. Also vocalized Ṣarīm, this was a subdivision of Tamīm. See Ibn al-Athīr, *Kāmil*, IV, 345.

stir up trouble between the Banū Sulaym and the Banū ʿĀmir, I would kill you! Now eat this page!" So he ate it. [Continuing,] he said: Abū Bakr b. Muḥammad b. Wāsiʿ said it was Sawādah b. ʿUbaydallāh al-Numayrī who delivered ʿAbdallāh b. Khāzim's writ of appointment. Another person said that ʿAbd al-Malik sent Sinān b. Mukammil al-Ghanawī to Ibn Khāzim, and wrote to him, saying, "Khurāsān is yours as an assigned means of subsistence (*ṭuʿmah*)." Ibn Khāzim said to him, "'Abū al-Dhibbān'[745] only sent you because you are from Ghanī, and he knows I will not kill a man from Qays. Now eat his letter!"

[Continuing,] he said: ʿAbd al-Malik wrote to Bukayr b. Wishāḥ, a member of the Banū ʿAwf b. Saʿd (he was Ibn Khāzim's deputy in charge of Marw), appointing him to the governorship of Khurāsān, making him promises, and raising his hopes. So Bukayr b. Wishāḥ threw off his allegiance to ʿAbdallāh b. al-Zubayr and propagandized for ʿAbd al-Malik b. Marwān. The people of Marw responded favorably to him. When Ibn Khāzim learned of this, he feared that Bukayr would lead the people of Marw against him, and that the people of Marw and of Abrashahr would join forces against him. He therefore left Baḥīr and went toward Marw, intending to go to his son in Tirmidh.[746] Baḥīr followed him and overtook him at a village called in Persian Shāhmīghad, eight *farsakhs* from Marw. [Continuing,] he said: Ibn Khāzim fought with Baḥīr. A *mawlā* of the Banū Layth said: "I was in a dwelling close to the place where the men fought. When the sun rose, the two armies rushed at each other, and I began to hear sword blows.
[833] As the day advanced, the sounds became softer—because of the advancing of the day, I thought. When I had prayed the noon prayer—or a little before noon—I went out. A man from the Banū Tamīm met me. I said, 'What is the news?' He said, 'I have killed the enemy of God, Ibn Khāzim. Here he is!' Behold, he was being carried on a mule; they had tied a rope to his loins and a stone, and had balanced him with it on the mule."

745. The epithet, meaning, "man of flies," was applied to a man with foul breath, from which ʿAbd al-Malik was said to suffer. See Balādhurī, *Ansāb*, XI, 152–53.

746. Tirmidh (modern Termez, on the Soviet-Afghan border), lay on the Oxus River (modern Amu Darya), about 300 miles east of Marw, and was the most important town of the Ṣaghāniyān district. See Le Strange, *Lands*, 440–41; *EI*[1], s.v.

[Continuing,] he said: The man who killed Ibn Khāzim was Wakīʿ b. ʿUmayrah al-Qurayʿī, called Ibn al-Dawraqiyyah.[747] Baḥīr b. Warqāʾ, ʿAmmār b. ʿAbd al-ʿAzīz al-Jushamī, and Wakīʿ fought Ibn Khāzim by turns, thrust him with spears, and threw him down. Wakīʿ sat on his chest and killed him. A certain governor asked Wakīʿ, "How did you kill Ibn Khāzim?" He replied, "I subdued him with the end of the spear shaft. After he was thrown down, I sat on his chest. He tried to get up but could not. I said, 'Vengeance for Dawīlah!'" (Dawīlah was a full brother of Wakīʿ who had been previously killed in some other fighting.) "He spat out phlegm in my face, and said, 'God curse your father! Will you kill the leader[748] of Muḍar to avenge your brother, a peasant not worth a handful of date pits?' (He may have said, '[a handful of] earth.') I never saw anyone with more spirit[749] than he when at the point of death." [Continuing,] he said: One day, Ibn Hubayrah mentioned this report and said, "That, by God, is courage!"

[Continuing,] he said: As soon as Ibn Khāzim was killed, Baḥīr sent a man from the Banū Ghudānah to inform ʿAbd al-Malik b. Marwān of Ibn Khāzim's death, but did not send the head. Bukayr b. Wishāḥ, with the people of Marw, came to Baḥīr and his men after Ibn Khāzim had been killed. Bukayr wanted to take Ibn Khāzim's head, but Baḥīr forbade him; Bukayr therefore hit him with a stick, took the head, and bound and imprisoned Baḥīr. [834]
Bukayr sent the head to ʿAbd al-Malik, and wrote informing him that it was he who had killed Ibn Khāzim. When the head was brought before him, ʿAbd al-Malik summoned the Ghudānī tribesman, Baḥīr's messenger, and asked, "What is this?" "I don't know," he replied. "I did not leave the men until Ibn Khāzim had been killed."

A man from the Banū Sulaym said:

O night we spent in Naysābūr! Give back to me
the morning—woe unto you!—or brighten.

747. I.e., son of the woman from Dawraq (a town in Khūzistān). See Le Strange, *Lands*, 242.

748. Literally, "the ram (*kabsh*) of Muḍar." The ram, as leader of the flock, was used figuratively for the leader of an army, a tribe, etc. See Lane, *Lexicon*, VI, 2588f.

749. Literally, "with more saliva (*rīq*)." See Lane, *Lexicon*, III, 1203.

Its stars were slow-moving, languid;
as if its firmament had been in the hands of a cupbearer.
Umm Zayd reviles time's accidents:
but have you any way of changing [time's] accidents?
[Time's accidents] have ignored my honor; they have turned away from me
for the present world's brief term.
Had horsemen from Sulaym been present
the morning the wounded lion was surrounded,
Generous men would have taken the field around him,
and grave would the vengeance have been in the search for retaliation.
Now barking dogs remain:
after you there is no [lion's] roar on earth.

[Those in Office during the Year]

Al-Ḥajjāj b. Yūsuf took charge of leading the pilgrimage this year. The governor of Medina for ʿAbd al-Malik was Ṭāriq [b. ʿAmr], the *mawlā* of ʿUthmān; and of al-Kūfah, Bishr b. Marwān. ʿUbaydallāh b. ʿAbdallāh b. ʿUtbah b. Masʿūd was in charge of its judiciary. Khālid b. ʿAbdallāh b. Khālid b. Asīd was governor of al-Baṣrah, and Hishām b. Hubayrah was in charge of its judiciary. Some say that ʿAbdallāh b. Khāzim al-Sulamī was governor of Khurāsān; others say it was Bukayr b. Wishāḥ. Those who say that ʿAbdallāh b. Khāzim was in charge of Khurāsān in the year 72
[835] assert that ʿAbdallāh b. Khāzim was killed only after ʿAbdallāh b. al-Zubayr had been killed; that ʿAbd al-Malik wrote to ʿAbdallāh b. Khāzim, summoning him to obedience, and offering him Khurāsān as an assigned means of subsistence (*ṭuʿmah*) for ten years, only after ʿAbdallāh b. al-Zubayr had been killed, and that ʿAbd al-Malik sent Ibn al-Zubayr's head to him. When ʿAbdallāh b. al-Zubayr's head arrived, ʿAbdallāh b. Khāzim swore he would never render obedience to ʿAbd al-Malik; calling for a basin, he washed the head of Ibn al-Zubayr, anointed it with spices, shrouded it, prayed over it, and then sent it to the family of ʿAbdallāh b. al-Zubayr in Medina; and he made the messenger eat ʿAbd al-Malik's letter, saying, "If you were not a messenger, I would kill you." Some say he cut off the man's arms and legs and beheaded him.

A Chapter in Which We Mention the Secretaries since the Beginning of Islam[750]

Hishām [b. al-Kalbī] and others relate that the first Arab who wrote[751] in Arabic was Ḥarb b. Umayyah b. ʿAbd Shams, and that the first person to write in Persian was Bīwarasb,[752] who lived in the time of Idrīs.[753] The first person who distinguished the orders of secretaries and elucidated their ranks was Luhrasb b. Kāwghān b. Kaymūs.[754]

It is related that Abarwīz[755] said to his secretary, "Language consists of four divisions: asking for something, asking about something, commanding something, and informing about something. These are the four supports of discourses. If one seeks a [836]
fifth, it will not be found; if one of the four is subtracted, [the supports] will not be complete. If you seek, be gentle; if you ask, be brisk;[756] if you command, be firm; and if you inform, be precise."

Abū Mūsā al-Ashʿarī said: "The first who said, 'To proceed,'[757]

---

750. The following section, which is inserted in Mss. O, B, and Co, is not found in Mss. Pet and C, or in Ibn al-Athīr. In Ms. Co, a marginal note reads: "An addition which [is not] from the original." At the end of the section, there is a note: "[Here ends] the chapter; one returns [to the words of] Abū Jaʿfar [al-Ṭabarī]"—(ed. Leiden, note). The material can be found fleshed out with many anecdotes in the *Kitāb al-wuzarāʾ wa-al-kuttāb*, by al-Jahshiyārī (d. 331/942; German translation by J. Latz, *Das Buch der Wezire*).

751. *Kataba*, "he wrote," can also mean, "he was a *kātib*," i.e. a scribe or secretary (in the professional sense).

752. Bīwarasb or Bēwarasb (the name means "Myriad Horses"), also known as al-Azdahāq or Zahhāk, was a legendary king of Iran, a monstrous tyrant said to have reigned a thousand years. See Ṭabarī, I, 201–10.

753. A prophet named Idrīs is mentioned in Qurʾān 19:56 and 21:85. Islamic tradition identifies him with the Biblical Enoch. See *EI*², s.v.; Bell and Watt, *Introduction to the Qurʾān*, 28 and note.

754. Luhrasb/Luhrasp was the fourteenth king to rule over Iran in the Shāhnāma. He was the father of Gushtasp, during whose reign Zoroaster appeared. See Ṭabarī, I, 645ff.

755. The Persian form is Aparwēz (older) or Parvīz (modern). Ed. Leiden vocalizes, Abrawīz. He was Khusraw II, ruled 590–627.

756. Variant in *al-ʿIqd*: be clear.

757. *Ammā baʿdu*, literally, "As for afterwards." In letters, homilies, and other formal compositions, this formula marks the end of the introductory matter (usually an elaboration of the praise of God and the Prophet) and the beginning of the subject proper.

was David. This is the 'separation of the speech'[758] God mentions in reference to him." Al-Haytham b. 'Adī said: "The first who said, 'To proceed' was Quss b. Sā'idah al-Iyādī."[759]

Those who were secretaries to the Prophet: 'Alī b. Abī Ṭālib and 'Uthmān b. 'Affān used to write down the revelation. If they were absent, Ubayy b. Ka'b and Zayd b. Thābit wrote it. Khālid b. Sa'īd b. al-'Āṣ and Mu'āwiyah b. Abī Sufyān used to write in his presence concerning his affairs. 'Abdallāh b. al-Arqam b. 'Abd Yaghūth and al-'Alā' b. 'Uqbah used to write among the people concerning their affairs. 'Abdallāh b. al-Arqam often wrote to kings from the Prophet.

'Uthmān, Zayd b. Thābit, 'Abdallāh b. al-Arqam, 'Abdallāh b. Khalaf al-Khuzā'ī, and Ḥanẓalah b. al-Rabī' were secretaries to Abū Bakr.

Zayd b. Thābit and 'Abdallāh b. al-Arqam were secretaries for 'Umar b. al-Khaṭṭāb. 'Abdallāh b. Khalaf al-Khuzā'ī, father of Ṭalḥah al-Ṭalḥāt, was in charge of the *dīwān* of al-Baṣrah. Abū Jabīrah b. al-Ḍaḥḥāk al-Anṣārī was 'Umar's secretary in charge of the *dīwān* of al-Kūfah. 'Umar b. al-Khaṭṭāb said to his secretaries and governors:[760] "Power to perform an office lies in your not putting off today's task until tomorrow; for if you do, tasks will come at you from every direction, and you will not know which
[837] one you should take up first. He was the first who drew up *dīwān* registers among the Arabs in Islam.

Marwān b. al-Ḥakam was secretary to 'Uthmān. 'Abd al-Malik was his secretary for the *dīwān* of Medina; Abū Jabīrah al-Anṣārī was in charge of the *dīwān* of al-Kūfah. Abū Ghaṭafān b. 'Awf b. Sa'd b. Dīnār of the Banū Duhmān of Qays 'Aylān also was

---

758. *Faṣl al-khiṭāb*: In Qur'ān 38:20, David is said to have been given wisdom and *faṣl al-khiṭāb*. The phrase is usually translated in a more general sense—"speech decisive" (Arberry), "decisive speech" (Pickthall)—but Abū Mūsā al-Ash'arī apparently thought it meant quite literally the formula used to separate the preliminary invocations of God from the body of a speech.

759. Quss b. Sā'idah was a legendary figure of Arab antiquity said to have been the greatest orator among all the tribes. He is always said to have been a monotheist, sometimes to have been a Christian, or even a bishop of Najrān. The youthful Muḥammad is supposed to have heard him at the fair of 'Ukāẓ. See *EI*², s.v. Ḳuss b. Sā'ida; Nicholson, *Literary History*, 135–56.

760. *'Ummāl*, pl. of *'āmil*, "[fiscal] agent, governor."

secretary to him, as were Ahyab, his *mawlā*, and Ḥumrān [b. Abān], his *mawlā*.

Saʿīd b. Nimrān al-Hamdānī, who later was in charge of the judiciary of al-Kūfah for Ibn al-Zubayr,[761] was secretary to ʿAlī. ʿAbdallāh b. Masʿūd was also his secretary. It is said that ʿAbdallāh b. Jubayr was his secretary. ʿUbaydallāh b. Abī Rāfiʿ was also his secretary. (There is disagreement about Abū Rāfiʿ's name; some say it was Ibrāhīm, some Aslam, some Sinān, and some ʿAbd al-Raḥmān).

Muʿāwiyah's secretary in charge of correspondence was ʿUbayd b. Aws al-Ghassānī. His secretary in charge of the tax bureau (*dīwān al-kharāj*) was Sarjūn b. Manṣūr al-Rūmī.[762] ʿAbd al-Raḥmān b. Darrāj, a *mawlā* of Muʿāwiyah, also was secretary to him. ʿUbaydallāh b. Naṣr b. al-Ḥajjāj b. ʿAlā' al-Sulamī was in charge of one of his *dīwāns*.

Al-Rayyān b. Muslim was secretary to Muʿāwiyah b. Yazīd.[763] His secretary in charge of the *dīwān* was Sarjūn. It is said that Abū al-Zuʿayziʿah was also his secretary.

Qabīṣah b. Dhu'ayb b. Ḥalḥalah al-Khuzāʿī, whose *kunyah* was Abū Isḥāq, was secretary to ʿAbd al-Malik. His secretary in charge of the correspondence bureau (*dīwān al-rasā'il*) was his *mawlā*, Abū al-Zuʿayziʿah.

Al-Qaʿqāʿ b. Khālid (or Khulayd) al-ʿAbsī was secretary to al-Walīd.[764] His secretary for the tax bureau was Sulaymān b. Saʿd al-Khushanī; his *mawlā* Shuʿayb al-ʿUmānī was in charge of the registry department (*dīwān al-khātam*); his *mawlā* Janāḥ was [838] in charge of the correspondence department; and his *mawlā* Nufayʿ b. Dhu'ayb was in charge of income-yielding properties (*mustaghallāt*).[765]

Sulaymān b. Nuʿaym al-Ḥimyarī was secretary to Sulaymān.[766]

---

761. See Ṭabarī, II, 537.

762. The father of St John of Damascus. See Hitti, *History of the Arabs*, 245–46.

763. Note the omission of the reign of Yazīd b. Muʿāwiyah. Muʿāwiyah b. Yazīd b. Muʿāwiyah ruled briefly in 64/683.

764. Al-Walīd b. ʿAbd al-Malik ruled from 86/705 to 96/715.

765. *Mustaghall*, pl. *mustaghallāt*, included any income-generating property: cultivated land, houses, markets, mills, etc. See Dozy, *Supplément*, II, 220; Shaban, *Islamic History*, II, 17.

766. Sulaymān b. ʿAbd al-Malik ruled from 96/715 to 99/717.

The secretary of Maslamah [b. 'Abd al-Malik][767] was his *mawlā* Samī'. Al-Layth b. Abī Ruqayyah, the *mawlā* of Umm al-Ḥakam bint Abī Sufyān, was in charge of the correspondence department; Sulaymān b. Sa'd al-Khushanī was in charge of the tax bureau; Nu'aym b. Salāmah, a *mawlā* of Yemenites from Palestine, was in charge of the registry department. (Some say that Rajā' b. Ḥaywah was in charge of the seal.)

Al-Mughīrah b. Abī Farwah[768] was secretary to Yazīd b. al-Muhallab.[769]

Al-Layth b. Abī Ruqayyah, the *mawlā* of Umm al-Ḥakam bint Abī Sufyān, and Rajā' b. Ḥaywah were secretaries to 'Umar b. 'Abd al-'Azīz.[770] Ismā'īl b. Abī Ḥakīm, the *mawlā* of al-Zubayr, was also secretary to him. In charge of the tax bureau was Sulaymān b. Sa'd al-Khushanī, who was succeeded by Ṣāliḥ b. Jubayr al-Ghassānī (some say al-Ghudanī) and 'Adī b. al-Ṣabāḥ b. al-Muthannā, whom al-Haytham b. 'Adī mentioned as being one of his chief secretaries.

Before Yazīd b. 'Abd al-Malik[771] became caliph, his secretary was a man named Yazīd b. 'Abdallāh. Then he made Usāmah b. Zayd al-Salīḥī secretary.

Sa'īd b. al-Walīd b. 'Amr b. Jabalah al-Kalbī, [called] al-Abrash,[772] and having the *kunyah* Abū Mujāshi', was secretary to Hishām.[773] Naṣr b. Sayyār was in charge of the Khurāsān tax bureau for Hishām. Among [Hishām's] secretaries at al-Ruṣāfah[774] was Shu'ayb b. Dīnār.

---

767. Maslamah b. 'Abd al-Malik was a great military leader. Under Sulaymān, he besieged Constantinople (98/716–17). During the reign of Yazīd b. 'Abd al-Malik (101–5/720–24), he suppressed a major revolt by Yazīd b. al-Muhallab in Iraq and became its governor. See *EI*^{2}, s.v.

768. Read "b. Abī Qurrah." See Latz, *Das Buch der Wezire*, 97, note.

769. Yazīd b. al-Muhallab was appointed governor of Iraq by Sulaymān in 96/715. Two years later, the governorship of Khurāsān was also given to him.

770. 'Umar b. 'Abd al-'Azīz ruled from 99/717 to 101/720.

771. Yazīd b. 'Abd al-Malik ruled from 101/720 to 105/724.

772. Speckled, or perhaps, freckled.

773. Hishām b. 'Abd al-Malik ruled from 105/724 to 125/743.

774. Al-Ruṣāfah ("the Causeway," according to Le Strange; Yāqūt calls the derivation of the name unclear) was the desert palace Hishām built 4 leagues from al-Raqqah in al-Jazīrah province to escape from the plague. See Le Strange, *Lands*, 106; Yāqūt, *Mu'jam*, s.v.

Bukayr b. al-Shammākh was secretary to al-Walīd b. Yazīd.[775] Sālim, the *mawlā* of Sa'īd b. 'Abd al-Malik, was in charge of the correspondence department. Also among his secretaries was 'Abdallāh b. Abī 'Amr (some give his name as 'Abd al-A'lā b. Abī 'Amr). 'Amr b. 'Utbah was in charge of the caliphal residence.[776] [839]

'Abdallāh b. Nu'aym was secretary to Yazīd b. al-Walīd, [called] "the Reducer."[777] 'Amr b. al-Ḥārith, a *mawlā* of the Banū Jumaḥ, was in charge of his registry department; Thābit b. Sulaymān b. Sa'd al-Khushanī (some say al-Rabī' b. 'Ar'arah al-Khushanī) was in charge of his correspondence department; and al-Naḍr b. 'Amr, a Yemeni, was in charge of taxes and the bureau of the small seal for him.

The secretary of Ibrāhīm b. al-Walīd[778] was Ibn Abī Jum'ah, who was in charge of the *dīwān* in Palestine for him.[779] The people swore allegiance to Ibrāhīm (b. al-Walīd), except the inhabitants of Ḥimṣ, who swore allegiance to Marwān b. Muḥammad al-Ja'dī.

The secretaries of Marwān [b. Muḥammad][780] were 'Abd al-Ḥamīd b. Yaḥyā, *mawlā* of al-'Alā' b. Wahb al-'Āmirī, Muṣ'ab b. al-Rabī' al-Khath'amī, and Ziyād b. Abī al-Ward. 'Uthmān b. Qays, *mawlā* of Khālid al-Qasrī, was in charge of the correspondence department. Also among his secretaries were Makhlad b. Muḥammad b. al-Ḥārith, called Abū Hāshim, and Muṣ'ab b. al-

775. Al-Walīd b. Yazīd ruled from 125/743 to 126/744.

776. For this meaning of *ḥaḍrah*, "presence," see Dozy, *Supplément*, I, 298.

777. *Al-Nāqiṣ*: Yazīd b. al-Walīd ruled for six months in 126/744. "His first act was to abolish the increase of the stipends to the Syrian troops granted by his predecessor" (Shaban, *Islamic History*, I, 155). He also curtailed large-scale public works—therefore the epithet.

778. Ibrāhīm b. al-Walīd succeeded his brother Yazīd and reigned for four months in 126/744, though his rule was not acknowledged by all factions. See Shaban, *Islamic History*, I, 160.

779. A name appears to have fallen out of Ṭabarī's text. Al-Jahshiyārī reads: "The secretary of Ibrāhīm was Ibrāhīm b. Abī Jum'ah. Thābit b. Nu'aym al-Judhāmī was in charge of the *dīwān* of Palestine." If the text of Ṭabarī was originally similar, one can explain why in the next sentence Ibrāhīm is identified as "b. al-Walīd," i.e., the caliph, not Ibrāhīm b. Abī Jum'ah, his secretary. See Latz, *Das Buch der Wezire*, 118–19.

780. Marwān b. Muḥammad succeeded to the throne in 127/744 and ruled until the fall of the Umayyad line in 132/750.

Rabīʿ al-Khathʿamī, called Abū Mūsā. ʿAbd al-Ḥamīd b. Yaḥyā had a distinguished reputation for eloquence. Among his poetry that has been anthologized is the following:[781]

Something that will not return has departed;
 something that will not go away has taken its place.
How I grieve for the successor who has taken up its abode!
 How I grieve for the predecessor who has departed!
I weep much over the one, and for the other I weep
 like a despondent woman bereft:
She weeps much because of a son of hers who has cut [the bond of relationship],
 and she weeps for a son of hers that has tied it fast.[782]
[840] In her innermost heart she never ceases
 from tears and weeping.
The errors of youth's intoxication have come to an end;
 fear of God has driven away falsehood's deviation.

The secretary of Abū al-ʿAbbās[783] was Khālid b. Barmak. Abū al-ʿAbbās entrusted his daughter Rayṭah to Khālid b. Barmak so that the latter's wife, Umm Khālid bint Yazīd, might nurse her while she was breast-feeding a daughter of Khālid's named Umm Yaḥyā; and Umm Salamah, the wife of Abū al-ʿAbbās, nursed Umm Yaḥyā, the daughter of Khālid, while she was breast-feeding her daughter Rayṭah. Ṣāliḥ b. al-Haytham, a *mawlā* of Rayṭah bint Abī al-ʿAbbās, was in charge of the correspondence department.

The secretary of Abū Jaʿfar al-Manṣūr[784] was ʿAbd al-Malik b. Ḥumayd, the *mawlā* of Ḥātim b. al-Nuʿmān al-Bāhilī, a Khurāsānian. Hāshim b. Saʿīd al-Juʿfī and ʿAbd al-Aʿlā b. Abī Ṭalḥah of the Banū Tamīm were his secretaries in Wāsiṭ. It is said that

781. The first four lines are quoted in Ibn Nubātah, *Sarḥ al-ʿuyūn*, 241, where the second line has an interesting variation: "How I grieve for one who, having progeny, arrives! How I grieve for one preceding who has departed!" The metaphor of gray hair or old age as "having progeny" is powerful, but is not in the line as given in al-Ṭabarī.

782. I.e., one son who by departing has cut the ties and another who by remaining has tied them fast.

783. Abū al-ʿAbbās ʿAbdallāh b. Muḥammad, known as al-Saffāḥ, the first caliph of the ʿAbbāsid line, ruled from 132/749 to 136/754.

784. Abū Jaʿfar, known as al-Manṣūr, ruled from 136/754 to 158/775.

Sulaymān b. Makhlad was a secretary to Abū Jaʿfar. Among [the verses] that Abū Jaʿfar used to quote was the following:

Nothing relieves the mind like a firm decision,
when some matter has been present too long in the mind.

Also among his secretaries were al-Rabīʿ, and ʿUmārah b. Ḥamzah, who was among the most distinguished men. The following is by him:

Never complain about a time when you enjoyed sound health:
in bodily health there is wealth!
Suppose you were the imām:[785] could you profit
from the present world's ease if you were sick?

And he used to quote the words of the slave of the Banū al-Ḥasḥās:

Is the eye's tear shed because of Umayyah?
If only that had been known of you before today!
Let your eye not weep: time is full of change;
in it, friend from friend departs.

The secretary of al-Mahdī[786] was Abū ʿUbaydallāh; Abān b. Ṣadaqah was in charge of his correspondence department, and [841]
Muḥammad b. Ḥamīd the Secretary was in charge of his military *dīwān* (*dīwān al-jund*). There was also Yaʿqūb b. Dāwūd, whom he appointed to be in charge of his vizierate and affairs. The following is by him:

I marvel greatly at the changing of affairs—
now what one likes, now what one dislikes!
Time plays with men;
to it belong turns that run their course.

The following is by [Yaʿqūb b. Dāwūd's] son, ʿAbdallāh b. Yaʿqūb, whose [sons] Muḥammad and Yaʿqūb were both excellent poets:

Gray hair checked my vehemence and passion;
from my eyelids it drew a copious flow of tears.
Desiring to hide its visible appearance

785. I.e., the caliph, in his capacity as leader of the Islamic community.
786. Al-Mahdī, the third ʿAbbāsid caliph, ruled from 158/775 to 169/785.

from my eyes, I tried something hopeless:
I colored what time had colored.
My coloring did not last, but time's coloring lasted.
Do not go so far away, O proud vigor of youth,
from which I departed in years gone by!
What I have retained from those days
is but as dreams that come by night.

The following is by his father:

Divorce the present world with a threefold divorce,[787]
and take to wife another.
The world is an unfaithful wife
who cares not who comes to her.

After him, al-Mahdī appointed al-Fayḍ b. Abī Ṣāliḥ vizier. He was a generous man.

The secretaries of Mūsā al-Hādī[788] were ʿUbaydallāh b. Ziyād b. Abī Laylā and Muḥammad b. Ḥamīd. One day, al-Mahdī asked ʿUbaydallāh's father about the poems of the Arabs; so he compiled
[842] them for him. And he said, "The wisest of them is the saying of Ṭarafah b. al-ʿAbd":[789]

I see that the grave of the avaricious man, stingy with his property,
is like the grave of the erring man who wastes [his property] in idleness.
You see two heaps of dirt on which there are
mute slabs of hard stone.
I see that death chooses the generous, and selects
the best of the tenacious niggard's property.
I see life as a treasure that diminishes each night:
and what the days and time diminish becomes spent.

---

787. In Islamic law, the formula of divorce must be repeated three times before witnesses. Hence, the expression, "a threefold divorce," came to be applied to anything done irrevocably.

788. Al-Mahdī's son, Mūsā b. Muḥammad, took the throne name of al-Hādī, and ruled from 169/785 to 170/786.

789. Ṭarafah b. al-ʿAbd was a pre-Islamic poet. The lines are from his *Muʿallaqah* (see *Dīwān*, 31–32), one of a collection of seven long pre-Islamic poems made by Ḥammād al-Rāwiyah, a famous reciter of ancient poetry who died ca. 156/772.

By your life, [I swear that] death, even when it does not hit the
young man,
is like a tether that has been left loose, but its end is in hand!

Also, his saying:

I see both of us: each one's friend wishes
that what has slipped away from us might come back.
Thing was [joined] to thing; but time,
which returns to separate what it joined, has separated it.

Also, the saying of Labīd:[790]

Indeed, you ask a man what he seeks:
whether it is a serious matter that must be accomplished, or
error and vanity.
Verily, everything but God is vanity,
and every pleasure must inevitably pass away.
I see that men know not what is destined for them:
yea, every man of sound judgment makes entreaty to God.

Also, the saying of al-Nābighah al-Jaʿdī:[791]

Long was my acquaintance with youthful vigor and those who
have it;
and I encountered fearful things that turn one's locks white.
But I never found brothers to be other than companions,
and I never found kin to be other than places of abode.
Do you not know how I have been afflicted by the loss of
Muḥārib,[792]
and how today neither I nor you have anything of him?

Also, the saying of Hudbah b. Khashram:[793]

---

790. Labīd b. Rabīʿah, the latest of the Muʿallaqāt poets, is said to have abjured poetry after his conversion to Islam and to have died early in the reign of Muʿāwiyah. See Nicholson, *Literary History*, 119–21; F. Sezgin, *GAS*, II, 126–27.

791. Al-Nābighah al-Jaʿdī (Ḥibbān b. Qays) was born before Islam, but lived most of his life as a Muslim and died in 65/684. The last line of the poem is found in the *Ḥamāsah* of Abū Tammām, a famous early anthology of pre-Islamic and early Islamic poetry. See F. Sezgin, *GAS*, II, 245–47; M. Nallino, *Le Poesie di an-Nābiġah al-Ǧaʿdī* (Rome, 1953), 122, 124.

792. Muḥārib was the poet's son. The line is addressed to his wife.

793. Hudbah b. Khashram was a poet from the tribe of ʿUdhrah, known for

I am not overly joyful if time gladdens me,
nor am I impatient of its shifting changes.
[843] I do not seek evil when evil[794] leaves me alone,
but when I am forced to do evil, I do it.
People do not know the truth about destiny:
Destiny will never offer them relief from what they dislike.
Destiny has a share in a young man's family and inherited possessions,
like the notching of the cutter that separates.

Also, the saying of Ziyādah b. Zayd,[795] which ʿAbd al-Malik b. Marwān used to quote:

He remembered Umaymah from afar and returned
to her after copious and long weeping.
Truly, the man who has experienced destiny and who does not fear
the shifting of its mornings and evenings lacks understanding.
Are not destiny and the days as you see [them to be]:
loss of wealth, or parting from a beloved?
Of all that is to come you are the kinsman;
but you are no kinsman of anything that has gone away.
Something remote, while it is coming, is not like something [rapidly] approaching;
neither is a past joy nearby.[796]

Also, the saying of Ibn Muqbil:[797]

When she saw how youth's vigor had altered, she wept for it:
and gray hair is the worst of these alterations.
Men's care is life; but I think

its "chaste" love poetry. See Ibn Qutaybah, *al-Shiʿr wa-al-shuʿarā'*, 434–38; F. Sezgin, *GAS*, II, 265–66.

794. *Sharr*, meaning both "evil" and "violence."

795. Another poet from the tribe of ʿUdhrah. See F. Sezgin, *GAS*, II, 266.

796. Another possible translation: "There is nothing far that does not come, as if it were rapidly advancing; neither is a past joy nearby." The version in Ibn Qutaybah, *al-Shiʿr wa-al-shuʿarā'*, 437–38, reads: "All that is coming and going to occur is not remote; neither is a past joy nearby."

797. The lines are also attributed to al-Akhṭal, cf. al-Mubarrad, *Kāmil*, 3:14.

long life only increases weariness.
If you are in need of treasures, you will find
no treasure like good works.

Yaḥyā b. Khālid [b. Barmak] served as [al-Hādī's] vizier; his son, Ja'far b. Yaḥyā b. Khālid, served as al-Rashīd's[798] vizier. Among his attractive sayings is: "Writing is the badge of wisdom; by it, wisdom's beads are separated and its scattered parts are strung together." Thumāmah said: "I said to Ja'far b. Yaḥyā, 'What is clarity (*bayān*)?' He said, 'That the word encompass your meaning, communicate your intention, be free of ambiguity, and not require that one call on the aid of thought to gather its intention.'" Al-Aṣma'ī[799] said: "I heard Yaḥyā b. Khālid say, 'The present world is vicissitude; wealth is a loan. We have an example in those who were before us; and in us there will be a lesson to those who come after us.'"

We will name the remaining secretaries of the 'Abbāsids when we reach the 'Abbāsid dynasty, God willing!

---

798. Hārūn al-Rashīd ruled from 170/786 to 193/809.

799. Al-Aṣma'ī (d. 213/828) was a philologist active at the court of Hārūn al-Rashīd. See *EI*², s.v.; Nicholson, *Literary History*, 345.

[844]

The Events of the Year 73

(May 23, 692–May 12, 693)

Among major events was the death of ʿAbdallāh b. al-Zubayr.

A Description of [the Death of Ibn al-Zubayr]

According to al-Ḥārith [b. Muḥammad]—Muḥammad b. Saʿd—Muḥammad b. ʿUmar [al-Wāqidī]—Isḥāq b. Yaḥyā—ʿUbaydallāh b. al-Qibṭiyyah, who said: The war between Ibn al-Zubayr and al-Ḥajjāj took place for six months and seventeen nights in the hollow[800] of Mecca.

According to Muḥammad b. ʿUmar [al-Wāqidī]—Muṣʿab b. Thābit—Nāfiʿ, a *mawlā* of the Banū Asad knowledgeable about the civil unrest (*fitnah*) of Ibn al-Zubayr, who said: Ibn al-Zubayr was besieged the night of the new moon of Dhū al-Qaʿdah in the year 72; he was killed on the seventeenth of Jumādā I in the year

800. *Baṭn*, the central part of the valley in which Mecca is built. See *EI*², s.v. Makka.

73.[801] Al-Ḥajjāj besieged Ibn al-Zubayr for eight[802] months and seventeen nights.

According to al-Ḥārith [b. Muḥammad]—Muḥammad b. Saʿd—Muḥammad b. ʿUmar [al-Wāqidī]—Isḥāq b. Yaḥyā—Yūsuf b. Māhak, who said: I saw the trebuchet (*manjanīq*)[803] with which [stones] were being hurled. The sky was thundering and lightning, and the sound of thunder and lightening rose above that of the stones, so that it masked it. The Syrians considered this ominous [845] and withheld their hands. But al-Ḥajjāj, having lifted the skirt of his tunic and tucked it into his belt, picked up the trebuchet stone and loaded it. "Shoot," he said; and he himself shot with them. [Continuing,] he said: During the morning, a thunderbolt struck and was followed by a second, killing twelve of his men. The Syrians became discouraged, but al-Ḥajjāj said, "Men of Syria, do not consider this extraordinary. I am a native of Tihāmah:[804] these are the thunderbolts of Tihāmah. Behold, victory has come! Rejoice; the enemy will be afflicted even as you have been." The next day, there was lightning, and a number of Ibn al-Zubayr's men were struck. Al-Ḥajjāj said, "Don't you see that they are being hit? You are in a state of obedience; they are in a state of disobedience."[805]

Thus, the war between Ibn al-Zubayr and al-Ḥajjāj continued until shortly before Ibn al-Zubayr's death, by which time the latter's companions had separated themselves from him and most

---

801. I.e., the siege began on March 25, 692, and Ibn al-Zubayr was killed on October 4, 692.

802. Thus in the text, despite the fact that the period from Dhū al-Qaʿdah to Jumādā I is only six months. The parallel passage in Balādhurī, *Ansāb*, V, 368, reads: "He was killed on a Tuesday in Jumādā II in the year 73. The siege lasted six months and seventeen nights. . . . Ibn al-Zubayr was killed when he was seventy-three years old." Dīnawarī, *Akhbār*, 321 has: "Tuesday, the seventeenth of Jumādā II in the year 73."

803. For a description of the siege engine, a traction trebuchet, see *EI*^{2}, s.v. Mandjanīḳ.

804. Tihāmah is the Red Sea coastal plain of the Arabian peninsula.

805. Cf. the account in Balādhurī, *Ansāb*, V, 362 (from ʿAwānah), where al-Ḥajjāj not only gives the naturalistic explanation that thunderstorms are frequent in Tihāmah, but adds: "Let what you see not frighten you. When the ancients used to sacrifice, a fire would be sent down to consume it; and that was a sign that the sacrifice had been accepted."

of the people of Mecca had gone out to al-Ḥajjāj under a promise of safety.

According to al-Ḥārith [b. Muḥammad]—[Muḥammad] b. Sa'd—Muḥammad b. 'Umar [al-Wāqidī]—Isḥāq b. 'Abdallāh—al-Mundhir b. Jahm al-Asadī, who said: I saw Ibn al-Zubayr the day he was killed. His companions had separated themselves from him, and those on his side had abandoned him in large numbers and had started going out to al-Ḥajjāj: finally, about ten thousand went out to him. It is also mentioned that Ibn al-Zubayr's two sons, Ḥamzah and Khubayb, were among those who left him and went out to al-Ḥajjāj. They received a promise of safety for themselves from [al-Ḥajjāj].

Then Ibn al-Zubayr went to see his mother, Asmā'.[806] According to Muḥammad b. 'Umar [al-Wāqidī]—Abū al-Zinād—Makhra-
[846] mah b. Sulaymān al-Wālibī: When he saw how the people were forsaking him, Ibn al-Zubayr went to see his mother. "Mother," he said, "the people have forsaken me, even my two sons and my family. With me there remain only a few people who do not have the endurance to defend themselves more than a short time. The enemy, however, will grant me whatever I desire from this present world. What is your advice?" She said, "You, my son, know yourself best. If you know you are right and have been advocating what is right, persevere for it, for your companions have been killed while in the right. Do not enable the young men (*ghilmān*) of the Banū Umayyah to make sport of you.[807] But If you only desire the present world, what a bad servant [of God] you are!—you have undone yourself and undone those who were killed fighting on your side. For you to say, 'I was right, but when my companions grew feeble, I became weak,' is not what free men or men of religion do. How long is your stay in this world? Death is better!"

Ibn al-Zubayr approached and kissed her head, saying, "This, by God, is what I think. I swear by Him to Whom I have been sum-

---

806. She was the daughter of Abū Bakr.

807. Cf. another version of this scene (Balādhurī, *Ansāb*, V, 364), in which Ibn al-Zubayr spells out his fear that after killing him, the Syrians may mutilate his body and crucify it. Al-Ḥajjāj is reported to have exposed the headless body of Ibn al-Zubayr on a cross (ibid., 368–70).

moning men until this very day, I have not inclined to the present world or loved life in it. Only indignation on behalf of God, that His sacred territory not be profaned, moved me to come out [to do what I did].[808] But I wanted to know your mind; and you have increased my firmness of belief. Behold, mother, I shall be killed this very day. Let your grief not be great. Submit to God's command. For your son intended to do nothing dishonorable or indecent: he did not act unjustly in applying God's ordinance, he betrayed no trust, and he intended to wrong no Muslim or confederate.[809] When informed of wrongdoing on the part of my agents, I never approved; rather, I disapproved of it. I have never preferred [847] anything to the approval of my Lord. O God, I do not say this to justify myself by myself—Thou knowest me best! I say it to comfort my mother, that she may endure my loss with patience." His mother said, "I pray God that I may endure your loss with good patience, if you precede me; and if I precede you, may there be [patient endurance] of my loss. Go out, that I may see how your cause proceeds." He said, "God grant you a good reward, mother. And do not cease praying for me before and after." She said, "I will never cease. Whoever may have been killed while in error, you will have been killed while in the right!" Then she said, "O God, have mercy on this long night vigil, this weeping and thirst in the midday summer heat of Medina and Mecca, and on his piety toward his father and me. O God, I have yielded him to Thy command concerning him, and am content with what Thou hast decreed; reward me for ʿAbdallāh with the reward of those who are patient and thankful." According to Muṣʿab b. Thābit: She survived him by only ten days—some say five.

According to Muḥammad b. ʿUmar [al-Wāqidī]—Mūsā b. Yaʿqūb b. ʿAbdallāh—his paternal uncle, who said: When Ibn al-Zubayr went before his mother, he was wearing a mailed coat and a protective head covering (*mighfar*). He stood and greeted her, then drew near, took her hand, and kissed it. She said, "This is farewell; do not be far away!"[810] Ibn al-Zubayr said, "I have come

---

808. *Khurūj* ("coming out") also has the sense of "rebel."

809. *Muʿāhid*: a non-Muslim who has a treaty of protection from the Muslims. See Lane, *Lexicon*, V, 2184.

810. *Baʿuda*, "to be/go far away," is used in elegies as a euphemism for "die."

to say farewell. I think this is the last day that will pass for me of this world. Know, mother, that if I am killed, I am only flesh; what is done to me will not harm me." She said, "You are right, my son. Persevere in your firm belief, and do not give Ibn Abī ʿAqīl[811] power over you. Come near me, so that I can bid you
[848] farewell." He came near her, kissed her, and embraced her. When she felt[812] the chain mail, she said, "This is not the action of someone who intends what you intend." He said, "I put on this chain mail only to give you strength." The old woman said, "It gives me no strength." So he took it off. Then he rolled up his sleeves, gathered up the bottom of his shirt (there was a coat [*jubbah*] of mixed silk and wool[813] under the shirt), and tucked the bottom of it into his belt, while his mother said, "Put on your garments with the skirts tucked up!"[814] Then Ibn al-Zubayr left, saying:

I, when I know my day [has come], bear it with patience;
others, when they know [theirs has come], find fault.

Hearing what he had said, the old woman said, "Be steadfast, by God, God willing! Your [fore]father[s] are Abū Bakr and al-Zubayr, and your [grand]mother Ṣafiyyah bint ʿAbd al-Muṭṭalib."[815]

According to al-Ḥārith [b. Muḥammad]—Ibn Saʿd—Muḥammad b. ʿUmar [al-Wāqidī]—Thawr b. Yazīd—a shaykh from Ḥimṣ who was present at Ibn al-Zubayr's battle with the Syrians, who said: I saw him on Tuesday. We men of Ḥimṣ would go up against him in groups of five hundred by a gate that was ours, which we would enter, and which no one but us would enter. He

---

The fuller version of the scene given by Balādhurī, *Ansāb*, V, 364, implies another meaning: "Be/go not far away, save from the fire [of hell]." I.e., may you be close to heaven.

811. I.e., al-Ḥajjāj, so named after his grandfather.

812. Cf. Balādhurī, *Ansāb*, V, 365 (from Abū Mikhnaf). She was blind and therefore was not aware of the chain mail until she embraced her son.

813. *Khazz* refers to a mixture of silk and wool, sometimes to (coarsely woven?) silk. See Lane, *Lexicon*, II, 731.

814. I.e., "Be ready to act with vigor." See Lane, *Lexicon*, IV, 1595.

815. Through his mother, Asmāʾ bint Abī Bakr, ʿAbdallāh b. al-Zubayr was the grandson of Abū Bakr, the first caliph. Through his father, al-Zubayr b. al-ʿAwwām, he had as his grandmother the Prophet's aunt, Ṣafiyyah bint ʿAbd al-Muṭṭalib.

came out to meet us by himself, coming after us when we were retreating from him. I have not forgotten a *rajaz* poem of his:

I, when I know my day [has come], bear it with patience—
only the free man knows his two days!
Others, when they know [theirs has come], find fault.

I said, "By God, you are a man free and noble!" I have seen him standing in the lowest part of the hollow. No one would approach him, so that we thought he would not be killed.

According to al-Ḥārith [b. Muḥammad]—Ibn Saʿd—Muḥam- [849]
mad b. ʿUmar [al-Wāqidī]—Muṣʿab b. Thābit—Nāfiʿ, a *mawlā* of the Banū Asad, who said: I saw the gates[816] filled with Syrians on Tuesday, and Ibn al-Zubayr's forces gave up the watch stations.[817] The enemy outnumbered them and set men, a commander, and troops from one country at every gate: troops from Ḥimṣ held the gate facing the door of the Kaʿbah; troops from Damascus held the Banū Shaybah Gate; troops from the Jordan held the Ṣafā Gate; troops from Palestine held the Banū Jumaḥ Gate; and troops from Qinnasrīn held the Banū Sahm Gate. Al-Ḥajjāj and Ṭāriq b. ʿAmr were together between the lowest part of the hollow (*al-Abṭaḥ*) and al-Marwah. Ibn al-Zubayr would attack sometimes in one area, sometimes in another: it was as if he were a lion in a thicket, the men not venturing to attack him. He would assault the troops holding a gate and would dislodge them, while reciting the *rajaz* verse:

I, when I know my day [has come], bear it with patience—
only the free man knows his two days!

Then he would shout, "Abū Ṣafwān![818] What a victory, if only there were men for it!

If my opponent were one man, I would take care of him!"[819]

Ibn Ṣafwān said, "Yes, by God, and a thousand, too!"

---

816. I.e., the gates of the Great Mosque.
817. *Maḥāris*, pl. of *maḥras*, see Dozy, *Supplément*, I, 270.
818. Abū Ṣafwān is ʿAbdallāh b. Ṣafwān b. Umayyah al-Jumaḥī. For his death in the fighting, see below, Ṭabarī, II, 852.
819. The verse is by Duwayd b. Zayd. See Ibn Sallām, *Ṭabaqāt al-shuʿarāʾ*, 32.

According to al-Ḥārith [b. Muḥammad]—Ibn Sa'd—Muḥammad b. 'Umar [al-Wāqidī]—Ibn Abī al-Zinād and Abū Bakr b. 'Abdallāh b. Muṣ'ab—Abū al-Mundhir,[820] and also according to Nāfi', a *mawlā* of the Banū Asad, both of whom said: The morning of Tuesday, the seventeenth of Jumādā I, in the year 73, al-Ḥajjāj
[850] seized the gates from Ibn al-Zubayr. Ibn al-Zubayr had spent most of the night praying. Then he sat with his legs braced against his belly with the shoulder belts of his sword[821] and slept lightly. He awoke at dawn and said, "Give the call to prayer, Sa'd." The latter thereupon gave the call to prayer beside the *Maqām*.[822] Ibn al-Zubayr performed the ablutions and prayed the two prostrations of the morning (*fajr*) prayer. Then he came forward. The muezzin gave the second call to prayer.[823] Ibn al-Zubayr led his companions in prayer, and recited the Sūra of the Pen,[824] word by word. Then, having pronounced the salutation,[825] he stood up, praised and extolled God, and said, "Uncover your faces, so that I can look [at you]." (They had on neck protectors [*mighfar*] and turbans.) When they had uncovered their faces, he said, "Family of al-Zubayr, if you give yourselves up willingly for me, we shall be people of a distinguished house among the Arabs. We shall have been extirpated for the sake of God, but no calamity will have afflicted us. And now, O family of al-Zubayr, let sword blows not frighten you. Whenever I have been present at a battle field, I have been carried away wounded from among the slain; and I have found the treatment of sword wounds to be worse than the pain of the sword's blow. Guard your swords as you guard your faces. I know of no man who ever broke his sword and saved his life. If a man loses his sword, he is as defenseless as a woman. Pay no attention to the glittering swords; let each man engage his adversary. Let no question about me distract you, and do not say, 'Where is 'Abdal-

820. Abū al-Mundhir is Hishām b. Muḥammad al-Kalbī (ed. Leiden, *Addenda*, p. DCLXXV).

821. For a description of this posture, called *iḥtibā'*, see Lane, *Lexicon*, II, 507.

822. On the Station (*Maqām*, or *Maqām Ibrāhīm*), see note 239.

823. The *iqāmah*, which is given just before the commencement of public prayer. See Dozy, *Supplément*, II, 432.

824. Sūra 68 of the Qur'ān.

825. Each of the five daily prayers ends with a twofold salutation ("Peace be upon you, and the mercy of God") addressed to the guardian angels.

lāh b. al-Zubayr?' But if anyone asks about me, I am in the front ranks:[826]

The time has come for Ibn Salmā not to remain,
but to meet destiny, whichever way he turn.
I will not buy life at the cost of disgrace,
nor climb a ladder for fear of death.[827]

Attack, with God's blessing!" then he attacked [the enemy] and got as far as al-Ḥajūn. A brick was hurled at him and struck him [851]
in the face; he was shaken by it, and his face began bleeding. When he felt the warmth of the blood flowing on his face and beard, he said:[828]

Not on our heels do our wounds bleed:
on the front of our feet the blood is visible!

Then [the enemy] gathered together against him.

[Continuing,] both said: An insane freedwoman (*mawlāh*) of ours cried out, "Alas for the Commander of the Faithful!" [Continuing,] both said: She had seen him where he fell. She pointed him out to them, and so he was killed. He was wearing garments of a mixture of silk and wool.

When the news reached al-Ḥajjāj, he prostrated himself. Together with Ṭāriq b. ʿAmr, he went and stood over him. Ṭāriq said, "Women have borne none manlier than he." Al-Ḥajjāj said, "Will you praise one who disobeys the Commander of the Faithful?" "Yes," said Ṭāriq, "he has freed us from blame; were it not for this, we would have no excuse.[829] We have been besieging him for

---

826. The lines, from a poem by al-Ḥuṣayn b. al-Ḥumām, can be found in the *Mufaḍḍaliyyāt* (no. 12), 230–31, where the first line reads: "There restrains Ibn Salmā [from love of this world] the fact that he will not remain, but will meet destiny. . . ."

827. Balādhurī, *Ansāb*, V, 367 (from Abū Mikhnaf and ʿAwānah) reports that Ibn al-Zubayr's remaining supporters suggested that he climb onto the roof of the Kaʿbah while they fought around the building to the death in his defense—hence the reference to "climbing a ladder."

828. The line, part of a *qaṣīdah* by the pre-Islamic poet al-Ḥuṣayn b. al-Ḥumām, can be found in the *Ḥamāsah*, 93. It puns on the fact that in Arabic "heel" (*ʿaqib*) has the same root as "to turn on one's heels, retreat" (*aʿqaba*), while "foot" (*qadam*) shares the same root as "To go forward, be bold" (*aqdama*).

829. The idea is that by his bravery, Ibn al-Zubayr has made praise of him allowable even for the followers of ʿAbd al-Malik.

seven months. He had no defensive trench,[830] no fortress, no stronghold; yet he held his own against us as an equal, and even got the better of us whenever we met with him." Their words were reported to ʿAbd al-Malik, who declared Ṭāriq right.

According to ʿUmar [b. Shabbah]—Abū al-Ḥasan [al-Madā'inī]—his authorities, one of whom said: It is as if I could still see Ibn al-Zubayr when he had killed a young black lad. He struck him, hamstringing him, and as he continued his attack on him, he said, "Patience, son of Ham! In such situations the noble endure patiently."

According to al-Ḥārith [b. Muḥammad]—Ibn Saʿd—Muḥammad b. ʿUmar [al-Wāqidī]—ʿAbd al-Jabbār b. ʿUmārah—ʿAbd-
[852] allāh b. Abī Bakr b. Muḥammad b. ʿAmr b. Ḥazm, who said: Al-Ḥajjāj sent the heads of Ibn al-Zubayr, ʿAbdallāh b. Ṣafwān, and ʿUmārah b. ʿAmr b. Ḥazm to Medina, where they were displayed; then they were taken to ʿAbd al-Malik b. Marwān. Al-Ḥajjāj entered Mecca and received the oath of allegiance to ʿAbd al-Malik b. Marwān from the [members of] Quraysh there.

According to Abū Jaʿfar [sc. al-Ṭabarī]: In this year, ʿAbd al-Malik appointed Ṭāriq, the *mawlā* of ʿUthmān, governor of Medina. He served as its governor for five months.

Bishr b. Marwān died this year, according to al-Wāqidī. Others say that his death took place in the year 74.

[ʿAbd al-Malik and the Khārijites]

Also in this year, according to what is mentioned, ʿAbd al-Malik sent ʿUmar b. ʿUbaydallāh b. Maʿmar to fight Abū Fudayk, ordering him to call up anyone he wanted from the two garrison cities to go with him. ʿUmar b. ʿUbaydallāh went to al-Kūfah and called up its people; ten thousand answered his call. Then he went to al-Baṣrah and called up its people; ten thousand answered his call.[831] Having issued them their provisions and given them their stipends, ʿUmar b. ʿUbaydallāh marched forth with them. He placed the Kūfans, led by Muḥammad b. Mūsā b. Ṭalḥah, on the right wing; he placed the Baṣrans, led by his brother's son, ʿUmar b. Mūsā b. ʿUbaydallāh, on the left wing; and he placed

830. Mss. O, B, and Co read, "army," instead of "defensive trench."
831. This sentence is omitted in Mss. O, B, and Co.

his horsemen in the middle. When they reached al-Baḥrayn, ʿUmar b. ʿUbaydallāh lined up his forces. He put the foot soldiers in front: they held short lances (*rimāḥ*) that they set in the ground, and they shielded themselves with saddle pads. Abū Fudayk and his forces attacked like a single man and routed ʿUmar b. ʿUbay- [853] dallāh's left wing, so that all scattered except al-Mughīrah b. al-Muhallab, Maʿn b. al-Mughīrah, Mujjāʿah b. ʿAbd al-Raḥmān, and the most skillful fighters. The latter turned to the ranks of the Kūfans, who held fast. ʿUmar b. Mūsā b. ʿUbaydallāh was left wounded. He was among the slain and had been badly wounded. When the Baṣrans saw that the Kūfans had not fled, they felt ashamed and returned to the fight, although they had no commander. When they reached the wounded ʿUmar b. Mūsā b. ʿUbaydallāh, they carried him, until they brought him into the camp of the Khārijites. There was a great deal of straw there. They set fire to it, and the wind turned against the Khārijites. The Kūfans and Baṣrans attacked, plundered their camp, killed Abū Fudayk, and besieged them in al-Mushaqqar.[832] The Khārijites submitted to judgment. According to what has been mentioned, ʿUmar b. ʿUbaydallāh put about six thousand of them to death and took eight hundred captive. They found Umayyah b. ʿAbdallāh's slave girl pregnant by Abū Fudayk. Then they returned to al-Baṣrah.

[Bishr b. Marwān Becomes Governor of al-Baṣrah]

In this year, ʿAbd al-Malik removed Khālid b. ʿAbdallāh from al-Baṣrah and appointed his [own] brother, Bishr b. Marwān, its governor. Thus, the governorship of both it and al-Kūfah came to be his. When Bishr was appointed governor of al-Baṣrah in addition to al-Kūfah, he went to al-Baṣrah and left ʿAmr b. Ḥurayth as his deputy in charge of al-Kūfah.

[Campaigns against the Byzantines]

In this year, Muḥammad b. Marwān campaigned during the summer and defeated the Byzantines. ʿUthmān b. al-Walīd's attack

832. Al-Mushaqqar was an ancient fortress in al-Baḥrayn. See Yāqūt, *Muʿjam*, s.v.

on the Byzantines in the region of Armenia is said to have taken place in this year. He had four thousand men, the Byzantines sixty thousand, but he defeated them and killed many of them.

[Those in Office during the Year]

During this year, the pilgrimage was led by al-Ḥajjāj b. Yūsuf,
[854] who was in charge of Mecca, Yemen, and al-Yamāmah. According to al-Wāqidī, Bishr b. Marwān was in charge of al-Kūfah and al-Baṣrah; others say that Bishr b. Marwān was in charge of al-Kūfah, and that Khālid b. ʿAbdallāh b. Khālid b. Asīd was in charge of al-Baṣrah. Shurayḥ b. al-Ḥārith was in charge of the judiciary of al-Kūfah, and Hishām b. Hubayrah was in charge of the judiciary of al-Baṣrah. Bukayr b. Wishāḥ was in charge of Khurāsān.

Bibliography of Cited Works

Aghānī. See al-Iṣbahānī.
al-ʿAlī, Ṣāliḥ Aḥmad. "Minṭaqat al-Kūfah." *Sumer* 21 (1965): 229–251.
al-Aʿshā Hamdān. *Dīwān*. Edited by R. Geyer under the title *Gedichte von Abû Baṣîr Maimûn ibn Qais al-Aʿšâ, nebst Sammlungen von Stücken anderer Dichter des gleichen Beinamens*. E.J.W. Gibb Memorial Series, New Series, VI. London: 1928.
al-Balādhurī. *Ansāb al-ashrāf*. Volume IV, part 1. Edited by Iḥsān ʿAbbās. Wiesbaden: 1979. Volume V. Edited by S. D. F. Goitein. Jerusalem: 1936. Vol. XI. Edited by W. Ahlwardt under the title *Anonyme arabische Chronik*. Greifswald: 1883.
———. *Futūḥ al-buldān*. Edited by M. J. de Goeje. Leiden: 1866.
Bell, Richard. *Bell's Introduction to the Qur'ān*. Revised and enlarged by W. Montgomery Watt. Edinburgh: 1970.
Blachère, Régis, M. Chouémi, and C. Denizeau. *Dictionnaire arabe-français-anglais*. Paris: 1967.
Bravmann, M. M. *The Spiritual Background of Early Islam: Studies in Ancient Arab Concepts*. Leiden: 1972.
Buhl, F. "Die Krisis der Umajjadenherrschaft im Jahre 684." *Zeitschrift für Assyriologie* 27 (1912): 50–64.
al-Dīnawarī, Abū Ḥanīfah Aḥmad b. Dāwūd. *Kitāb al-akhbār al-ṭiwāl*. Edited by Ignace Kratchkovsky. Leiden: 1912.
Dixon, ʿAbd al-Ameer ʿAbd. *The Umayyad Caliphate 65–86/684–705 (A Political Study)*. London: 1971.
Djaït, Hichem. *Al-Kūfa, naissance de la ville islamique*. Paris: 1986.
Dozy, R. *Supplément aux dictionnaires arabes*. 2 vols. Leiden: 1881. Reprinted Beirut: 1968.
al-Farazdaq. *Dīwān*. Edited by R. Boucher. Paris: 1870. Edited by Karam al-Bustānī, Beirut: n.d.

Freytag, G. W. *Arabum Proverbia*. 2 vols. Bonn: 1838–43.

Goutta, Guido Edler von. *Der Aġānīartikel über 'Aʿšā von Hamdān*. Ph.D. Dissertation, Freiburg I. B. Kirchhain N.-L.: 1912.

von Grunebaum, Gustav E. *Muhammadan Festivals*. Chicago, 1951. Reprinted London: 1976.

Hahn, Peter. *Surâqa b. Mirdâs: Ein schiitischer Dichter aus der Zeit des zweiten Bürgerkrieges (63–75 d.H.)*. Ph.D. Dissertation, Erlangen. Göttingen: 1938.

Hitti, Philip K. *History of the Arabs*. 10th ed. New York: 1970.

Husayn, S. M. "The Poems of Surâqah b. Mirdâs al-Bâriqî—An Umayyad Poet." *Journal of the Royal Asiatic Society* (1936): 475–490, 605–628.

Ibn ʿAbd Rabbih. *al-ʿIqd al-farīd*. Edited by Aḥmad Amīn et al. Cairo: 1367/1948.

Ibn al-Athīr, ʿIzz al-Dīn. *al-Kāmil fī al-Ta'rīkh*. Edited by C. J. Tornberg. 12 vols. Leiden: 1870.

Ibn Durayd, Muḥammad b. al-Ḥasan. *Kitāb al-ishtiqāq*. Edited by ʿAbd al-Salām Muḥammad Hārūn. Cairo: 1378/1958.

Ibn al-Faqīh al-Hamadhānī. *Kitāb al-buldān*. Edited by M. J. de Goeje. Bibliotheca Geographorum Arabicorum, Vol. V. Leiden: 1885. Translated by Henry Massé under the title *Abrégé du livre des pays [Mukhtaṣar kitāb al-buldān]*. Damascus: 1973.

Ibn Ḥajar al-ʿAsqalānī. *al-Iṣābah fī tamyīz al-ṣaḥābah*. Edited by ʿAlī Muḥammad al-Bijāwī. 8 vols. Cairo: n.d. [1970].

———. *Tabṣīr al-muntabih bi-taḥrīr al-mushtabih*. Edited by ʿAlī Muḥammad al-Bijāwī and Muḥammad ʿAlī al-Najjār. Cairo: 1964.

———. *Tahdhīb al-tahdhīb*. Hyderabad, 1325/1907. Reprinted Beirut: 1968.

Ibn Hishām. *Sīrat al-Nabī*. Edited by Muḥammad Muhyī al-Dīn ʿAbd al-Ḥamīd. 4 vols. Cairo: 1971–72.

Ibn Khurradādhbih. *Kitāb al-masālik wa-al-mamālik*. Edited by M. J. de Goeje. Bibliotheca Geographorum Arabicorum. Vol. VI. Leiden: 1889.

Ibn Manẓūr. *Lisān al-ʿArab*. 6 vols. Cairo: 1981.

Ibn [Isḥāq] al-Nadīm, Muḥammad. *Kitāb al-fihrist*. Edited and translated by Bayard Dodge under the title *The Fihrist of al-Nadīm*. 2 vols. New York: 1970.

Ibn Nubātah, Jamāl al-Dīn. *Sarḥ al-ʿuyūn fī sharḥ risālat Ibn Zaydūn*. Edited by Muḥammad Abū al-Faḍl Ibrāhīm. Cairo: 1964.

Ibn Qays al-Ruqayyāt, ʿUbaydallāh. *Dīwān*. Edited by N. Rhodokanakis as *Der Dīwān des ʿUbaid-Allāh ibn Ḳais ar-Ruḳajjāt*. In *Sitzungsberichte der Wiener Akademie der Wissenschaften*, Phil-Hist. Klasse, CXLIV (1901).

Ibn Qutaybah. *Kitāb al-maʿārif*. Cairo: 1969.

———. *Kitāb al-shiʿr wa-al-shuʿarāʾ*. Edited by M. J. de Goeje. Leiden: 1904.

Ibn Rustah, Abū ʿAlī Aḥmad b. ʿUmar. *Kitāb al-aʿlāq al-nafīsah*. Edited by M. J. de Goeje. Bibliotheca Geographorum Arabicorum. Vol. VII. Leiden: 1892.

Ibn Saʿd, Muḥammad. *Kitāb al-ṭabaqāt al-kubrā*. Edited by E. Sachau *et al*. Leiden: 1905. Also Beirut: 1978.

Ibn Sallām al-Jumaḥī. *Ṭabaqāt al-shuʿarāʾ*. Edited by M. M. Shākir. Cairo: 1394/1974.

al-Iṣbahānī, Abū al-Faraj. *Kitāb al-aghānī*. Edited by Ibrāhīm al-Abyārī. 31 vols. Cairo: 1969.

Jafri, S. Husain M. *Origins and Early Development of Shiʿah Islam*. London and New York: 1979.

al-Jahshiyārī. See Latz.

al-Khaṭīb al-Baghdādī, Abū Bakr Aḥmad b. ʿAlī. *Taʾrīkh Baghdād*. 14 vols. Cairo: 1931.

Kohlberg, Etan. "Abū Turāb." *BSOAS* 41 (1978): 347–52.

Lane, Edward William. *An Arabic-English Lexicon*. London: 1863–93. Reprinted Beirut: 1968.

Latz, Josef. *Das Buch der Wezire und Staatssekretäre von Ibn ʿAbdūs Al-Ǧahšiyārī: Anfänge und Umaiyadenzeit*. Ph.D. Dissertation, Bonn. Bonn: 1958.

Le Strange, G. *The Lands of the Eastern Caliphate*. Cambridge: 1905. Reprinted Lahore: 1977.

Lisān. See Ibn Manẓūr.

Madelung, Wilferd. "ʿAbd Allāh b. al-Zubayr and the Mahdī." *JNES* 40 (1981): 291–305.

al-Maydānī. *Majmaʿ al-amthāl*. Cairo: 1959.

Miskīn al-Dārimī. *Dīwān*. Edited by ʿAbdallāh al-Jubūrī and Khalīl Ibrāhīm al-ʿAṭiyyah. Baghdad: 1970.

Morony, Michael G. *Iraq after the Muslim Conquest*. Princeton: 1984.

al-Mubarrad. *al-Kāmil*. Cairo: 1356/1937.

al-Mufaḍḍal al-Ḍabbī. *al-Mufaḍḍaliyyāt*. With commentary by al-Tabrīzī. Edited by ʿAlī Muḥammad al-Bijāwī. 3 vols. Cairo: 1977.

Nicholson, Reynold A. *A Literary History of the Arabs*. Cambridge: 1907. Reprinted Cambridge: 1969.

Qurʾān. Verses are numbered according to the Egyptian national edition. The translation, with modifications, is based on A. J. Arberry, *The Koran Interpreted*. London: 1955.

Rotter, G. "Die historischen Werke Madāʾinī's in Ṭabarī's Annalen." *Oriens* 23–24 (1974): 103–133.

Schacht, Joseph. *An Introduction to Islamic Law.* Oxford: 1964.

Schoeler, Gregor. "Die Frage der schriftlichen oder mündlichen Überlieferung der Wissenschaften im frühen Islam." *Der Islam* 62 (1985): 201–230.

Sezgin, Fuat. *Geschichte des Arabischen Schrifttums.* Band I. *Qur'ānwissenschaften, Ḥadiṯ, Geschichte, Fiqh, Dogmatik, Mystik bis ca. 430 H.* Leiden: 1967. Band II. *Poesie bis ca. 430 H.* Leiden: 1975.

Sezgin, Ursula. *Abū Miḫnaf: Ein Beitrag zur Historiographie der umaiyadischen Zeit.* Leiden: 1971.

Shaban, M. A. *Islamic History: A New Interpretation.* Vol. I. *A.D. 600–750.* Cambridge: 1971. Vol. II. *A.D. 750–1055.* Cambridge: 1976.

al-Shahrastānī. *al-Milal wa-al-niḥal.* Edited by ʿAbd al-Laṭīf Muḥammad al-ʿAbd. Cairo: 1977.

Shaked, Shaul. "From Iran to Islam: On Some Symbols of Royalty." *Jerusalem Studies in Arabic and Islam* 7 (1986): 75–91.

al-Ṭabarī, Abū Jaʿfar Muḥammad. *Ta'rīkh al-rusul wa-al-mulūk.* Edited by M. de Goeje *et al.* under the title *Annales quos scripsit Abu Djafar...at-Tabari.* 14 vols. Leiden: 1879–1901. Edited by Muḥammad Abū al-Faḍl Ibrāhīm. 10 vols. Cairo: 1967.

Ṭarafah b. al-ʿAbd. *Dīwān.* Edited by Max Seligsohn. Paris: 1901.

ʿUmar b. Abī Rabīʿah. *Dīwān.* Edited by Muḥammad Muḥyī al-Dīn ʿAbd al-Ḥamīd. Beirut: n.d.

al-Yaʿqūbī. *Kitāb al-buldān.* Edited by M. J. de Goeje. Bibliotheca Geographorum Arabicorum. Vol. VII. Leiden: 1892.

Yāqūt b. ʿAbdallāh al-Ḥamawī. *Muʿjam al-buldān.* Edited by Muḥammad Amīn al-Khānijī and Shaykh Aḥmad b. al-Amīn al-Shanqīṭī. 8 vols. Cairo: 1323/1906.

Index

The index contains all proper names of persons, places, and tribal and other groups, as well as topographical data, occurring in the introduction, the text, and the footnotes. As far as the footnotes are concerned, however, only those names that belong to the medieval or earlier periods are listed, and some terms that occur in footnotes in a purely explanatory context have been omitted in the index.

The definite article al- *and the abbreviations b. (*ibn, *"son of") and bt. (*bint, *"daughter of") have been disregarded for the purposes of alphabetizing. Where a name occurs in both the text and the footnotes on the same page, only the page number is given.*

A

Aaron, family of 70
Abān b. al-Nuʿmān b. Bashīr 111
Abān b. Ṣadaqah 219
Abarwīz 213
ʿAbbād b. ʿAbdallāh b. al-Zubayr (*rāwī*) 207
ʿAbbād b. al-Ḥuṣayn al-Ḥabaṭī 46–48, 87, 89, 90, 93, 100, 101, 106–7, 115, 117, 172–73, 182
al-ʿAbbās b. ʿAlī b. Abī Ṭālib 40
ʿAbbās b. Sahl b. Saʿd 56–57
ʿAbbāsid revolution xvi
ʿAbbāsids, secretaries of 223
ʿAbd al-Aʿlā b. Abī ʿAmr. *See* ʿAbdallāh b. Abī ʿAmr
ʿAbd al-Aʿlā b. Abī Ṭalḥah 218
ʿAbd al-ʿAzīz b. ʿAbdallāh b. Khālid b. Asīd 198, 200–3, 205; wife of (daughter of al-Mundhir b. al-Jārūd) 200, 205–6
ʿAbd al-ʿAzīz b. Bishr. b. Ḥannāṭ 119, 173, 177
ʿAbd al-ʿAzīz b. Marwān 161–64
ʿAbd al-Ḥamīd b. Yaḥyā (*mawlā* of ʿAlāʾ b. Wahb al-ʿĀmirī) 217–18
ʿAbd al-Jabbār b. ʿUmārah (*rāwī*) 232
ʿAbd al-Mālik b. Abī Zurʿah 44
ʿAbd al-Malik b. Ashāʾah al-Kindī 95
ʿAbd al-Malik b. al-Ḥārith b. al-Ḥakam b. Abī al-ʿĀṣ 55

'Abd al-Malik b. Ḥumayd (*mawlā* of Ḥātim b. al-Nu'mān al-Bāhilī) 218
'Abd al-Malik b. Marwān (caliph), xiii–xvi, 2 n. 6, 3, 53, 55, 109–10, 121, 134, 144, 146, 147, 153, 154–67, 169, 171–72, 174, 175, 178–97, 199, 202–12, 214, 222, 232–33; secretaries to 215
'Abd al-Mu'min b. Shabath b. Rib'ī 17
'Abd al-Qāhir b. al-Sarī (*rāwī*) 181
'Abd al-Qays (tribe) 33, 42, 46 n. 180, 47–48, 176; fifth of 87, 93; Mosque of 19
'Abd Rabbih al-Sulamī 8
'Abd al-Raḥmān b. 'Abdallāh (half-brother of Ibrāhīm b. al-Ashtar) 76, 83, 145
'Abd al-Raḥmān b. Abī Ji'āl 127
'Abd al-Raḥmān b. Abī Khushkārah al-Bajalī 33
'Abd al-Raḥmān b. Abī 'Umayr al-Thaqafī (*rāwī*) 91
'Abd al-Raḥmān b. Abī al-Zinād (*rāwī*) 230
'Abd al-Raḥmān b. 'Aqīl b. Abī Ṭālib 34
'Abd al-Raḥmān b. al-Ash'ath 115
'Abd al-Raḥmān b. Darrāj (*mawlā* of Mu'āwiyah) 215
'Abd al-Raḥmān b. Mikhnaf b. Sulaym al-Azdī 13–14, 17, 18, 22, 28, 87, 100, 102, 130
'Abd al-Raḥmān b. Muḥammad b. al-Ash'ath 100, 106–8, 116, 203–4
'Abd al-Raḥmān b. Sa'īd b. Qays al-Hamdānī 3–5, 12, 14, 18, 22, 29, 30, 138–39; House of 102
'Abd al-Raḥmān b. Ṣalkhab 33
'Abd al-Raḥmān b. Shurayḥ al-Shibāmī 93
'Abd al-Raḥmān b. Sulaym 156–57
'Abd al-Raḥmān b. 'Ubayd Abū al-Kanūd (*rāwī*) 26
'Abd al-Raḥmān b. Umm al-Ḥakam al-Thaqafī 155–56, 163
'Abd al-Raḥmān b. 'Uthmān b. Abī Zur'ah al-Thaqafī 44
'Abdallāh b. Abī 'Amr 217
'Abdallāh b. Abī Bakr b. Muḥammad b. 'Amr b. Ḥazm (*rāwī*) 232
'Abdallāh b. Aḥmad b. Shabbawayh (*rāwī*) 69, 71, 72, 81
'Abdallāh b. al-Ahtam 193
'Abdallāh b. 'Āmir [b. Kurayz] 118, 193; son of 193
'Abdallāh b. 'Amr al-Nahdī 94
'Abdallāh b. al-Arqam b. 'Abd Yaghūth 214
'Abdallāh b. 'Aṭiyyah al-Laythī (*rāwī*) 45
'Abdallāh b. 'Ayyāsh al-Mantūf (*rāwī*) 183
'Abdallāh b. Dabbās 31
'Abdallāh b. Dajājah al-Ḥanafī (father of Ṭarafah and Ṭarrāf) 105
'Abdallāh b. Ḍamrah al-'Udhrī 7–8
'Abdallāh b. Faḍālah al-Zahrānī 176
'Abdallāh b. Ḥamlah al-Khath'amī 6, 9
'Abdallāh b. Ḥammām al-Salūlī 151
'Abdallāh b. Ḥayyah al-Asadī 67
'Abdallāh b. Isḥāq b. al-Ash'ath 191
'Abdallāh b. Ja'dah b. Hubayrah b. Abī Wahb al-Qurashī al-Makhzūmī 36, 93, 94, 103
'Abdallāh b. Jubayr 215
'Abdallāh b. Kāmil al-Shākirī 18–20, 32, 32, 35, 37, 40–42, 44, 88, 89, 92, 138
'Abdallāh b. Khalaf al-Khuzā'ī 214
'Abdallāh b. Khāzim al-Sulamī 62–67, 121, 153, 168, 182, 209–12
'Abdallāh b. Mas'adah al-Fazārī 164
'Abdallāh b. Mas'ūd 215
'Abdallāh b. al-Mubārak (*rāwī*) 69, 71, 81
'Abdallāh b. Muḥammad b. 'Abdallāh b. Abī Qurrah (*rāwī*) 179
'Abdallāh b. Muslim b. 'Aqīl 42
'Abdallāh b. Muṭī' 10 n. 46, 11 n. 52, 12 n. 54, 45, 48 n. 192, 53, 54, 169
'Abdallāh b. Nawf al-Hamdānī 68, 73, 99
'Abdallāh b. Nu'aym 217
'Abdallāh b. Qays al-Khawlānī 33
'Abdallāh b. Qurād al-Khath'amī 9, 19, 85, 92, 95, 106

ʿAbdallāh b. Sabīʿ 16
ʿAbdallāh b. Ṣafwān b. Umayyah al-Jumaḥī 169, 229, 232
ʿAbdallāh b Ṣalkhab 33
ʿAbdallāh b. Shaddād al-Jushamī 37, 92, 106–7
ʿAbdallāh b. Sharīk al-ʿĀmirī 186
ʿAbdallāh b. Sharīk al-Nahdī 20, 22, 99
ʿAbdallāh b. ʿUmar 112, 152
ʿAbdallāh b. ʿUmayr al-Laythī 119
ʿAbdallāh b. ʿUqbah al-Ghanawī 43
ʿAbdallāh b. ʿUrwah al-Khathʿamī 43
ʿAbdallāh b. Usayd b. al-Nazzāl al-Juhanī 31–32
ʿAbdallāh b. ʿUtbah b. Masʿūd 121, 153
ʿAbdallāh b. ʿUthmān b. Abī al-ʿĀṣ 177
ʿAbdallāh b. Wahb b. ʿAmr 33
ʿAbdallāh b. Wahb b. Anas al-Jushamī. *See* ʿAbdallāh b. [Anas b.] Wahb b. Naḍlah al-Jushamī
ʿAbdallāh b. [Anas b.] Wahb b. Naḍlah al-Jushamī 88–89
ʿAbdallāh b. Warqāʾ al-Asadī 8
ʿAbdallāh b. Warqāʾ b. Junādah al- Salūlī 78–79
ʿAbdallāh b. Yaʿlā al-Nahdī 188
ʿAbdallāh b. Yaʿqūb 219
ʿAbdallāh b. Yazīd b. Asad al-Qasrī Abū Khālid 165, 192
ʿAbdallāh b. Yazīd b. Muʿāwiyah 158, 179, 181
ʿAbdallāh b. al-Zubayr xiii–xvi, 3, 12, 48, 53–56, 59–62, 66–67, 71, 72, 83, 89, 104, 111, 115, 118–21, 122, 135, 147, 152–53, 158 n. 572, 165, 168, 170, 182, 185, 191, 194–95, 206–9, 210, 212, 215, 224–32
ʿAbdallāh b. al-Zubayr Abū Abī Aḥmad (*rāwī*) 186
ʿAbdallāh b. Zuhayr al-Salūlī 76
ʿAbīdah b. Hilāl 131
al-Abrad b. Qurrah al-Riyāḥī 142, 144
al-Abrash. *See* Saʿīd b. al-Walīd
Abrashahr. *See* Naysābūr
Abū al-ʿAbbās. *See* al-Saffāḥ
Abū ʿAbd al-Aʿlā al-Zubaydī (*rāwī*) 42
Abū ʿAbdallāh al-Jadalī 59–61, 98; house of 19
Abū al-Aḥrās al-Murādī 98
Abū al-Aḥwaṣ al-Jushamī 76, 113
Abū ʿAlqamah al-Khathʿamī (*rāwī*) 110
Abū ʿAmrah. *See* Kaysān
Abū al-ʿĀṣ, sons of 195
Abū al-Ashras. *See* ʿUbaydallāh b. al-Ḥurr
Abū ʿĀṣim al-Nabīl (*rāwī*) 193
Abū al-Aswad Muḥammad b. ʿAbd al-Raḥmān b. Nawfal al-Asadī (*rāwī*) 207
Abū Baḥr. *See* al-Aḥnaf
Abū Bakr (caliph) 228; secretaries to 214
Abū Bakr b. ʿAbdallāh b. Muṣʿab (*rāwī*) 230
Abū Bakr b. Mikhnaf 126–27
Abū Bakr b. Muḥammad b. Wāsiʿ 210
Abū Bakr b. ʿUmar (*rāwī*) 186
Abū Bilāl, house of 35
Abū Dāwūd, Mosque of 19
Abū al-Dhibbān ("man of flies," i.e., ʿAbd al-Malik) 210
Abū Fudayk b. Thawr 206, 232–33
Abū Ghassān Muḥammad b. Yaḥyā (*rāwī*) 194
Abū Ghaṭafān b. ʿAwf b. Saʿd b. Dīnār 214
Abū al-Ḥadīd al-Shannī 200
Abū Hāḍir al-Asadī 177
Abū al-Ḥārith al-Kindī 98
Abū al-Ḥasan. *See* al-Madāʾinī
Abū Hāshim. *See* Makhlad b. Muḥammad
Abū Hurayrah b. Shurayḥ, 131–32
Abū Isḥāq. *See* al-Mukhtār
Abū Jabīrah b. al-Ḍaḥḥāk al-Anṣārī 214
Abū Jaʿfar. *See* al-Ṭabarī
Abū Jaʿfar al-Manṣūr. *See* al-Manṣūr
Abū Jaʿfar Muḥammad b. ʿAlī 37
Abū Janāb al-Kalbī (*rāwī*) 16, 109
Abū al-Jārūd [Ziyād b. al-Mundhir] (*rāwī*) 41
Abū Kudyah al-Bāhilī 147 n. 533
Abū Mikhnaf Lūṭ b. Yaḥyā b. Saʿīd b. Mikhnaf al-Azdī (*rāwī*) 4, 6–9, 11–

13, 16–17, 23–24, 26–34, 36, 38, 41–42, 44, 51, 53, 55, 57, 59, 67, 69, 72–73, 74, 79–82, 85–86, 90–91, 95, 98–99, 101, 108–10, 112, 120, 123, 126, 128–30, 133, 188 n. 670, 198
Abū Muḥammad al-Hamdānī (*rāwī*) 24 n. 97. *See* Yūnus b. Abī Isḥāq
Abū Mujāshiʿ. *See* Saʿīd b. al-Walīd
Abū al-Mukhāriq al-Rāsibī (*rāwī*) 120, 123
Abū al-Mundhir (*rāwī*) 230. *See* Hishām b. Muḥammad
Abū Mūsā al-Ashʿarī 29, 118, 213
Abū al-Muʿtamir 60–61
Abū Nuʿaym al-Faḍl b. Dukayn (*rāwī*) 186
Abū al-Qalūṣ 20–21
Abū al-Rabīʿ al-Salūlī (*rāwī*) 129
Abū Rawq (*rāwī*) 29, 108
Abū Ṣādiq (*rāwī*) 79
Abū al-Sāʾib Salm b. Junādah (*rāwī*) 29, 49
Abū Saʿīd al-Ṣayqal (*rāwī*) 6, 32, 74
Abū Ṣāliḥ. *See* Sulaymān [b. Ṣāliḥ]
Abū al-Ṣalt al-Taymī (*rāwī*) 6, 32, 74
Abū Sufyān b. Ḥarb 176
Abū Turāb ("Dusty," epithet for ʿAlī b. Abī Ṭālib) 77
Abū ʿUbaydallāh (secretary to al-Mahdī) 219
Abū Umāmah 73
Abū Umayyah. *See* ʿAmr b. Saʿīd
Abū Yazīd b. ʿĀṣim al-Azdī 125
Abū Yūsuf (*rāwī*) 57
Abū Zayd. *See* ʿUmar b. Shabbah
Abū al-Zinād [ʿAbdallāh b. Dhakwān] (*rāwī*) 226
Abū al-Zuʿayziʿah (*mawlā*) 163, 215
Abū al-Zubayr [Al-Arḥabī] (*rāwī*) 95
Abū al-Zubayr b. Kurayb al-Shibāmī 21, 30
Abū Zuhayr al-ʿAbsī. *See* al-Naḍr b. Ṣāliḥ
Abū Zurʿah b. Masʿūd 44
ʿĀd 87
Ādharbayjān 51, 118
ʿAdī b. Ḥātim al-Ṭāʾī Abū Ṭarīf 40–41
ʿAdī al-Ribāb. *See* Banū ʿAdī
ʿAdī al-Riqāʿ 185 n. 658
ʿAdī b. al-Ṣabāḥ b. al-Muthannā 216
ʿAdī b. Zayd b. ʿAdī b. al-Riqāʿ al-ʿĀmilī 171
ʿAdwān (tribe) 189
aḥbār, pl. of *ḥabr* ("Jewish scholar") 52 n. 216. *See also* Kaʿb al-Aḥbār; Tubayʿ
ahl al-bayt ("people of the Prophet's family") 39 n. 159
ahl al-siyar ("biographers") 121 n. 435
Aḥmad b. Shabbawayh (*rāwī*) 69, 71
Aḥmad b. Zuhayr (*rāwī*) 45, 135
Aḥmar b. Hadīj al-Hamdānī al-Fāyishī 30, 95
Aḥmar b. Shumayṭ al-Bajalī al-Aḥmasī 18, 20, 21, 37, 87–92, 115
Aḥmar of Ṭayyiʾ 138, 145
Aḥmas, Mosque of 18
al-Aḥnaf b. Qays 47–51, 66, 87, 93, 117, 119, 180
al-Ahwāz 119, 123–25, 133, 184, 200, 202–6
Ahyab (*mawlā* of ʿUthmān) 215
ʿĀʾishah bt. Khalīfah b. ʿAbdallāh al-Juʿfiyyah (wife of al-Ḥusayn b. ʿAlī) 24
ʿĀʾishah bt. Muʿāwiyah b. al-Mughīrah b. Abī al-ʿĀṣ b. Umayyah (mother of ʿAbd al-Malik) 162
al-Akhnas b. Sharīq, house of family of 18
al-Akhṭal (poet) 222 n. 797
al-ʿAlāʾ b. ʿUqbah 214
al-ʿAlāʾ b. Wahb al-ʿĀmirī 217
ʿAlī b. ʿAbdallāh b. ʿAbbās 192
ʿAlī b. Abī Tālib (caliph) xiv, 1 nn. 1 and 2, 8 n. 40, 21, 36, 72, 78, 81, 113–14, 135, 214; Chair of 44, 68–73; secretaries to 215. *See also* Abū Turāb; Shīʿah
ʿAlī b. Aṣmaʿ 173, 177
ʿAlī b. Ḥarb al-Mawṣilī (*rāwī*) 113
ʿAlī b. al-Ḥusayn 38, 42
ʿAlī b. Mālik al-Jushamī 76, 78

ʿAlī b. Muḥammad. *See* al-Madāʾinī
ʿAlī b. Mujāhid (*rāwī*) 135, 136
al-ʿAliyah. *See* Highlanders
ʿAlqamah b. Marthad (*rāwī*) 113
ʿĀmir b. al-Aswad al-Kalbī (*rāwī*), 45
ʿĀmir b. Mismaʿ 200
ʿĀmir b. Sharāḥīl al-Shaʿbī (*rāwī*) 23, 49, 82, 84
ʿAmmār b. ʿAbd al-ʿAzīz al-Jushamī 211
amr ("command") 140 n. 500, 153, 155 n. 561, 185
ʿAmr b. Aṣmaʿ al-Bāhilī 172–73
ʿAmr b. al-Ḥajjāj al-Zubaydī 15, 23–24
ʿAmr b. Ḥanẓalah 65
ʿAmr b. al-Ḥārith (*mawlā* of Banū Jumaḥ) 217
ʿAmr b. Ḥurayth al-Makhzūmī 195–96; Bath of 19
ʿAmr b. Jundab al-Azdī 144
ʿAmr b. Mālik Abū Kabshah al-Qaynī (*rāwī*) 8
ʿAmr b. Saʿīd b. al-ʿĀṣ Abū Umayyah al-Ashdaq xv, 154–67, 175, n. 626, 179; sons of 166; wife from tribe of Kalb 158–59, 164
ʿAmr b. Sarḥ (*mawlā* of al-Zuhayr, *rāwī*) 84
ʿAmr b. Ṣubayḥ al-Ṣudāʾī 42 n. 169, 43–44
ʿAmr b. Tawbah 15
ʿAmr b. ʿUtbah 217
ʿAmr b. Wabarah al-Quḥayfī 174
ʿAmr b. Yazīd al-Ḥakamī 192
ʿAmrah bt. Abī Mūsā al-Ashʿarī (wife of al-Sāʾib b. Mālik) 103
ʿAmrah bt. al-Nuʿmān b. Bashīr al-Anṣārī 111–12
Anas b. ʿAmr al-Azdī 17
ʿAnazah (tribe) 32, 40
al-Anbār 146
ʿAnbasah b. Saʿīd 163
Angels 28–29, 36
Anṣār 111
Arab (as ethnic group) 13, 22, 55, 56, 65, 92, 104, 112, 116, 126, 230
aʿrābī ("rustic") 202 n. 716
Arabic (language) 8
ʿArafah 207–9; Day of 7
ʿArafāt 151–52
Ardashīr Khurrah 200
Ark of the Covenant 70–71
Armenia 118, 234
Arrajān 124
Arwā (mother of ʿUthmān) 21
al-ʿĀṣ b. Umayyah 157
al-Aʿsar al-Shākirī 21
Aʿshā Hamdān (poet) 33, 35, 50, 71, 73, 90–91, 96–97
al-Ashajj, 96 n. 360. *See* al-Ashʿath b. Qays
al-Ashʿath (village) 44
al-Ashʿath b. Dhuʾayb 63
al-Ashʿath b. Qays al-Kindī 96, 106 n. 394, 191
ashrāf, sg. *sharīf* ("tribal dignitaries") xiv, 10–13, 19, 28, 31, 82, 85, 88, 106, 108, 177, 178 n. 638
ʿĀṣim b. ʿAbdallāh al-Azdī 95
ʿĀṣim b. Qays b. Ḥabīb al-Hamdānī 5
ʿAskar Mukram 184
Asmāʾ bt. Abī Bakr (mother of ʿAbdallāh b. al-Zubayr) 226–28
Asmāʾ b. Khārijah 130
al-Aṣmaʿī 223
al-Aswad b. Jarād al-Kindī 67
al-Aswad b. Saʿīd 107
ʿ*aṭāʾ* ("military stipend") 11 n. 50, 120, 191
ʿAtīk (clan of al-Azd) 47 n. 190
ʿAṭiyyah b. ʿAmr al-Bakrī 148
ʿAttāb b. Warqāʾ 130–33, 178, 181, 205
ʿAwānah b. al-Ḥakam (*rāwī*) 2–3, 84, 155–57, 161, 163, 165–67, 173
ʿAwf b. ʿAmr al-Jushamī 95
ʿAylān, 149 n. 542. *See* Qays ʿAylān
ʿAyn al-Tamr 142, 176
ʿAyn (al-) Wardah 2, 154; Battle of 2 n. 8, 45
ʿAyūf bt. Mālik b. Nahār b. ʿAqrab (wife of Khawalī b. Yazīd al-Aṣbaḥī) 35
ʿAyyāsh (father of ʿAbdallāh b. ʿAyyāsh, *rāwī*) 183
ʿAyyāsh b. Jaʿdah al-Jādalī 56–57

ʿAyyāsh b. Khāzim al-Hamdānī al-Thawrī 95
ʿAyyāsh al-Sulamī 150
Azāriqah xv, 122–34, 198–206
Azd (tribe) 14, 22, 47 n. 190, 48, 93, 123, 127, 149, 173, 175, 201; fifth of 87, 93
al-Azdahāq 213 n. 752. *See* Bīwarasb

B

Bāb al-Jisr 16
Bābilyūn 162
Badr, Battle of 27, 28 n. 114
Bādurayā 141
Baghdād 127 n. 455
Bāhilah (tribe) 177
Baḥīr b. Warqā' al-Ṣuraymī 209–11
al-Baḥrayn 119, 176 n. 632, 206, 233 n. 832
al-Baʿīth al-Yashkurī (poet) 185
Bajīlah (tribe) 14, 17, 89, 90
Bājisrā 145
Bājumayrā 70, 171, 180
Bakr. *See* Bakr b. Wā'il
Bakr b. Wā'il (tribe) 15 n. 65, 32 n. 134, 47 n. 190, 48, 126, 151, 173, 187, 191; fifth of 87, 93. *See also* Rabīʿah
al-Balādhurī, *Ansāb al-ashrāf* xiv–xv, xvii, 3 n. 17, 9 n. 43, 17 n. 75, 22 n. 85, 24 n. 94, 31 n. 127, 32 n. 133, 36 n. 149, 43 nn. 170 and 172, 47 n. 192, 48 n. 195, 49 nn. 198, 200, and 203, 50 nn. 205 and 207, 55 n. 219, 56 n. 223, 61 n. 236, 67 n. 258, 72 n. 281, 75 n. 284, 80 n. 303, 83 n. 309, 85 n. 318, 88 n. 328, 94 n. 349, 102 nn. 382 and 383, 104 n. 385, 111 nn. 406–8, 117 n. 422, 118 nn. 424 and 426, 119 n. 430, 120 n. 432, 122 n. 436, 127 n. 455, 134 n. 481, 143 nn. 514 and 516, 144 n. 519, 147 n. 533, 156 nn. 562 and 563, 160 n. 581, 161 n. 583, 162 n. 586, 169 n. 606, 171 n. 609, 174 nn. 616 and 619, 175 n. 626, 178 nn. 636 and 638, 179 n. 639, 180 n. 645, 181 nn. 647 and 649–50, 182 n. 651, 183 n. 652, 184 n. 656, 185 n. 662, 186 n. 666, 187 n. 668, 188 n. 670, 189 n. 678, 192 nn. 693 and 695, 194 n. 697, 195 nn. 701 and 703, 196 n. 705, 206 n. 722, 207 nn. 728 and 730, 208 nn. 732 and 737, 210 n. 745, 225 nn. 802 and 805, 226 n. 807, 228 nn. 810 and 812, 231 n. 827; *Futūḥ al-buldān* 197 n. 706
Banāt Talā 6, 9
Banū ʿAbd (tribe) 33
Banū ʿAbd Shams (clan of Quraysh) 46
Banū ʿAdī (tribe) 46, 66
Banū ʿĀmir (tribe) 210
Banū ʿAmr b. Marthad (tribe) 178
Banū ʿArīn (clan of Tamīm) 174
Banū Asad (tribe) 15 n. 65, 43, 67, 177, 178, 185, 209, 224, 229, 230; fourth of Madhhij and 5
Banū Asad b. Khuzaymah (tribe) 102, *See* Banū Asad
Banū ʿAwf b. Saʿd (tribe) 210
Banū Ḍabbah (tribe) 103, 116
Banū Ḍubayʿah (clan of Bakr b. Wā'il) 32
Banū Duhmān (clan of Qays ʿAylān) 34–35, 214; Mosque of 34
Banū Ghudānah (tribe) 211
Banū Ḥanīfah (tribe) 105
Banū Ḥanẓalah (clan of Tamīm) 11 n. 52, 174
Banū al-Ḥasḥas, slave of (poet) 219
Banū Jadhīmah b. Mālik, Street of (al-Kūfah) 102
Banū Jiʿāwaḥ (tribe) 184
Banū Jumaḥ (clan of Quraysh) 217; Gate of (Mecca) 229
Banū Kaʿb b. ʿAmr (clan of Tamīm) 173
Banū Kalb. *See* Kalb; Quḍāʿah
Banū Layth (tribe) 210
Banū Makhzūm (clan of Quraysh) 205; Mosque of (al-Kūfah) 101
Banū Nahd (clan of Hamdān) 22, 71

Banū Nājī (clan of ʿAdwān) 190, 191
Banū Numayr (tribe) 184
Banū Qasiyy, 52 n. 215. *See* Thaqīf
Banū Qays b. Thaʿlabah (tribe) 204, 206
Banū Saʿd (clan of Tamīm) 65, 175
Banū Sahm Gate (Mecca) 229
Banū Shaybah Gate (Mecca) 229
Banū Sulaym (clan of Qays ʿAylān) 65, 150, 210–12
Banū Tamīm (tribe) 15 n. 65, 46, 47 n. 192, 48, 60, 62–66, 87, 149, 173–75, 177, 178, 187, 209 n. 744, 210, 218; fifth of 87, 93; fourth of Tamīm and Hamdān 5, 68. *See also* Muḍar; Tamīmiyyah
Banū Taymallāh b. Thaʿlabah (tribe) 111
Banū Thaʿlabah b. Yarbūʿ (tribe) 181
Banū Umayyah (Umayyad family, clan of Quraysh) xiii–xvi, 1 n. 6, 12, 21 n. 83, 152–53, 163–65, 176 n. 629, 185, 193, 226
Banū Yashkur (clan of Bakr b. Wāʾil) 173, 177
barāʾah ("quittance") 136 n. 489
Bārʿītā 74
Bāsār 63, 65
al-Baṣrah xiii–xv, 2 n. 7, 25, 28, 31, 43, 45–50, 53–55, 67, 83–87, 115, 118–21, 122–25, 130, 133–34, 141, 153, 168, 170, 172–78, 182, 184, 185, 188, 192–93, 199–203, 204, 206, 212, 232–34; bridge of 47; dīwān of 214; *fayḍ* ("estuary") of 119; judiciary of 67, 121, 153, 168, 170, 212, 234; mosque of 46, 47, 84; people of 13, 25, 90–93, 99, 102, 107, 147, 187, 203–4, 232–33; provision depot (*madīnat al-rizq*) 46–47; treasury of 120
baṭn ("hollow") of Mecca 224, 229
bayʿah ("oath of allegiance") 55, 59–60, 87, 89, 110, 133, 141, 186, 188–89, 199, 209, 232
bayān ("clarity") 223
Bayt al-Qarāṭīs ("document room") 161
badāʾ (doctrine attributed to al-Mukhtār) 99 n. 371
Bilāl, house of 102. *See also* Abū Bilāl
Biʾr al-Jaʿd 34
Biʾr Maymūn 208–9
Bishr b. ʿAbdallāh al-Asadī 145
Bishr b. Jarīr b. ʿAbdallāh 14, 18
Bishr b. Marwān (brother of ʿAbd al-Malik) 191–92, 199, 203, 205, 212, 232–34
Bishr b. Ṣawt al-Qābiḍī Abū Asmāʾ 34
Bisṭām b. Maṣqalah b. Hubayrah al-Shaybānī 142–43
Bīwarasb 213
al-Budāt 138
Bujayr b. ʿAbdallāh al-Muslī 105–8
Bukayr b. al-Shammākh 217
Bukayr b. Wishāḥ 210–12, 234
Bunānah bt. Abī Yazīd b. ʿĀṣim al-Azdī 125–26
burnus ("hood") 32 n. 132
Bushayr b. ʿAbd al-Raḥmān b. Bushayr al-ʿIjlī 145
al-Buṭayn al-Laythī 98
Buṭnān Ḥabīb 134, 155, 167, 171
Buṭnān al-Ṭīn 134. *See* Buṭnān Ḥabīb
Byzantine emperor 169
Byzantines 169, 197 n. 706, 233–34

C

Caesarea. *See* Qaysāriyyah
Camel, Battle of the 50
Catholicos (head of Nestorian Christians) 181 n. 648
Chair of ʿAlī. *See* ʿAlī b. Abī Ṭālib, Chair of
Children of Israel 69, 70, 78
Christians 129. *See also* Catholicos
Civil War, Second xiii, xvi

D

Dabāhā 128
Ḍabbah. *See* Banū Ḍabbah

Dabīrā 128
al-Ḍaḥḥāk b. Qays al-Fihrī 3
al-Dajjāl 52
Dalham al-Murādī 143, 144
Damascus xv, 134, 154–64, 167, 175, 229
Dār al-Siqāyah 102
Dārā 83
Darābjird 200
David, King 214; Davidic tunics (chain mail) 191
Dawīlah b. ʿUmayrah al-Qurayʿī 211
Dawmah bt. ʿAmr (mother of al-Mukhtār) 102
Dāwūd b. Qaḥdham, 191, 204–5
Daylamites 33 n. 137, 90, 107
Dayr ʿAbd al-Raḥmān b. Umm al-Ḥakam 68, 128; bridge of 68
Dayr Abī Mūsā 5
Dayr al-Aʿwar 145
Dayr al-Jāthalīq xv, 181, 186, 187
al-Dhabbāḥīn Street 46
Dhāt ʿIrq 60
Dhū al-Iṣbaʿ al-ʿAdwānī (poet) 189–90
dihqān 119 n. 430, 142–43
al-Dīnawarī, *al-Akhbār al-ṭiwāl* xvii, 8 n. 39, 11 n. 52, 24 n. 94, 25 n. 98, 75 n. 285, 80 n. 303, 83 n. 309, 86 n. 321, 100 n. 374, 104 n. 387, 112 n. 411, 134 n. 481, 136 n. 491, 137 n. 492, 138 n. 496, 139 n. 498, 171 n. 609, 187 n. 668, 188 n. 671, 206 n. 723, 225 n. 802
Dirham (*mawlā* of the Banū Nahd) 22
dīwān ("military roll") 11 n. 50, 161, 214, 215, 217; institution by ʿUmar 214. See also *dīwān al-jund*, etc.
dīwān al-jund ("military dīwān") 219
dīwān al-kharāj ("tax bureau") 215–17
dīwān al-khātam ("registry department") 159, 215–17
dīwān al-khātam al-ṣaghīr ("bureau of the small seal") 217
dīwān al-rasāʾil ("correspondence department") 215–19
ḍuʿafāʾ ("the poor") 27
al-Dujayl Canal 186
Dukhtanūs 51
durūb, pl. of *darb* ("barricades") 101 n. 378
Duwayd b. Zayd (poet) 229 n. 819

E

Egypt 162 n. 588
Enoch. *See* Idrīs
Euphrates River 18, 78, 91, 92, 110, 115

F

Fāʾish (clan of Hamdān) 30
al-Fallūjah 142
al-Farazdaq (poet) 175
Fārs 86, 122–24, 177, 182, 200 nn. 708 and 709, 202, 205
farsakh 25 n. 103
Fartanā 62
Fasā 200
faṣl al-khiṭāb ("separation of the speech") 214
Fāṭimah (daughter of the Prophet) 1 n. 2, 32, 78
fayʾ ("permanent booty") 11–13, 203, 205
al-Fayḍ b. Abī Ṣāliḥ 220
Fifth. *See khums*
fitnah ("civil strife") 61, 135, 152, 209, 224
Fourth. *See rubʿ*
Fuḍayl b. Khadīj al-Kindī (*rāwī*) 67–69, 80, 81, 91, 101, 128
Furāt b. Ḥayyān al-ʿIjlī, house of 103
al-Furāt b. Zaḥr b. Qays al-Juʿfī 22, 24
Fusṭāṭ 162 n. 588

G

al-Ghaḍbān b. al-Qabaʿtharā 178
Ghanī (tribe) 43, 210
Ghaṭafān b. Unayf 173
Ghaylān b. Salamah b. Muʿattib al-

Thaqafī (poet) 104–5
Ghazwān b. Jaz' al-ʿAdawī 63
ghulām, pl. *ghilmān* 24, 64, 153, 226
Golden Calf 69

H

Ḥabbān b. ʿAlī (*rāwī*) 49
Ḥabīb b. Budayl (*rāwī*) 85
Ḥabīb b. Munqidh al-Thawrī 67–68
Ḥabl al-Mushāt 152 n. 552
al-Hādī (caliph), secretaries to 220–23
ḥaḍrah ("caliphal residence") 217
Ḥadrah b. ʿAbdallāh al-Azdī (*rāwī*) 128
Ḥaḍramawt 35, 131
Ḥafṣ b. ʿUmar b. Saʿd 38–39
Hajar 176, 177
al-Ḥajjāj b. ʿAlī al-Bāriqī (*rāwī*) 28
al-Ḥajjāj b. Ḥārithah. *See* al-Ḥajjāj b. Jāriyah
al-Ḥajjāj b. Jāriyah al-Khathʿamī 142–43
al-Ḥajjāj b. Nāshib al-ʿAdawī 62, 64
al-Ḥajjāj b. Yūsuf xv, 109, 115, 126, 158 n. 572, 206–9, 212, 224–26, 228–32, 234
Ḥajjār b. Abjar Abū Usayd 15, 23, 30, 145, 178, 181
al-Ḥajūn 208, 231
al-Ḥakam b. Hishām b. ʿAbd al-Raḥmān (*rāwī*) 44, 72
al-Ḥakam b. al-Mundhir b. al-Jārūd 176
Ḥakīm b. Ṭufayl al-Ṭāʾī al-Sinbisī 40
Ham, son of 232
Hamadhān 192
Ḥamal b. Mālik al-Muḥāribī 32
Haman 84
Hamdān (tribe) 8 n. 39, 14, 21, 29–30, 35, 50, 55, 56, 68, 71 n. 279, 82–83, 89, 95, 108, 114, 138–39, 188. *See also* Banū Nahd; Banū Tamīm, fourth of Tamīm and Hamdān; Khārif; Nāʿiṭ; Sabīʿ; Shākir; Shibām; Wādiʿah
Ḥammām Aʿyan 11, 69, 88
Ḥammām Jarīr. *See* Laḥḥām Jarīr
Ḥammām ʿUmar 37
al-Ḥamrāʾ 8 n. 39, 33 n. 137
Ḥamzah b. ʿAbdallāh b. al-Zubayr 118–20, 226
Hāni' b. Qays 60, 61
Ḥanẓalah b. al-Rabīʿ 214
Ḥaram ("sacred precinct" around Mecca) 60, 192, 207, 227
Ḥarb b. Umayyah b. ʿAbd Shams 213
al-Ḥarīsh b. Hilāl (poet) 66
al-Ḥārith b. [ʿAbdallāh b.] Abī Rabīʿah al-Qurashī al-Makhzūmī al-Qubāʿ 46–48, 54, 55 n. 219, 67, 83–84, 120, 122, 126–28, 130, 133, 147
al-Ḥārith b. Ḥaṣīrah (*rāwī*) 79
al-Ḥārith b. Muḥammad (*rāwī*) 207, 224–26, 228–30, 232
Ḥarmalah b. Kāhil 43
Ḥarūrāʾ 92, 97, 99, 152 n. 553; Battle of 83
Ḥarūrī (Khārijī) 152
al-Ḥasan b. Ḥammād (*rāwī*) 49
al-Ḥasan b. Kathīr (*rāwī*) 81
al-Ḥasan b. Rushayd al-Jūzjānī (*rāwī*) 62
Hāshim, family of 179
Hāshim b. Saʿīd al-Juʿfī 218
Ḥashraj 148
Ḥaṣīrah b. ʿAbdallāh b. al-Ḥārith al-Azdī (*rāwī*) 98, 99, 130, 198
Ḥassān b. Fā'id al-ʿAbsī 15, 20
Ḥassān b. Mālik b. Baḥdal al-Kalbī 156, 159
Ḥātim b. al-Nuʿmān al-Bāhilī 218
al-Ḥawārī ("the Apostle") 175. *See* al-Zubayr b. al-ʿAwwām
Ḥawlāyā 145
Ḥawshab al-Bursumī 44, 68, 73
Ḥawshab b. Yazīd b. al-Ḥārith b. Ruwaym 102, 145–46, 192 n. 695
al-Haytham b. ʿAdī (*rāwī*) 183, 214, 216
al-Haytham b. al-Aswad al-Nakhaʿī 36
Ḥayyān b. ʿAlī. *See* Ḥabbān
al-Hibyāṭ b. ʿUthmān b. Abī Zurʿah al-Thaqafī 44
Highlanders (people of al-ʿĀliyah) 67 n. 261, 94; fifth of 87, 93

Ḥijāz xiii–xiv, 2, 84, 104
Ḥimṣ 217, 228, 229
Ḥimyar (tribe) 157 n. 569, 158
Hind bt. Asmā' (wife of 'Ubaydallāh b. Ziyād) 80
Hind bt. al-Mutakallifah al-Nā'iṭiyyah 98–99
al-Ḥīrah 1 n. 3, 111; Canal 92
Hishām (caliph), secretaries to 216
Hishām b. 'Abd al-Raḥmān al-Thaqafī (*rāwī*) 44, 72, 91
Hishām b. Hubayrah 67, 121, 153, 168, 211, 234
Hishām b. Muḥammad al-Kalbī (*rāwī*) 2, 4, 14, 51, 53, 59, 67, 72, 74, 81, 85, 98, 120, 123, 126, 155–57, 163, 165–66, 198, 213
Hishām b. 'Umārah (*rāwī*) 152
Ḥubaysh b. Duljah al-Qaynī 2
Ḥubbā 186–87
Ḥubshī b. Junādah 79
Ḥuḍayn b. al-Mundhir 30
Hudbah b. Khashram (poet) 221–22
al-Hudhayl b. Zufar b. al-Ḥārith 192
Ḥujr b. 'Adī al-Kindī, nephew of 35; house of 45
Ḥumayd b. Ḥurayth b. Baḥdal al-Kalbī 75, 155–59, 161
Ḥumayd b. Muslim (*rāwī*, poet) 22, 33–34
Ḥumaydah bt. 'Umar b. Sa'd (poetess) 38
Ḥumrān b. Abān (*mawlā* of 'Uthmān) 173, 176, 192–93, 215
Ḥunayn, Battle of 28
Ḥuraqah (clan) 31
Ḥurayth b. Baḥdal al-Kalbī 157
Ḥurayth b. Zayd (or Yazīd) 142
Ḥurthān b. al-Ḥārith. *See* Dhū al-Iṣba'
al-Ḥusayn b. 'Alī b. Abī Ṭālib xiii, xiv, 1, 21–24, 27, 31–35, 38–41, 43, 52, 60–62, 77–78, 81. *See also* Shī'ah; al-Ṭaff; Tawwābūn
al-Ḥuṣayn b. al-Ḥumām (poet) 231 nn. 826 and 828
al-Ḥuṣayn b. Numayr al-Sakūnī 78, 80–81

I

Ibn 'Abbās 153
Ibn 'Abī 'Aqib al-Laythī (poet) 43
Ibn Abī Jum'ah. *See* Ibrāhīm b. Abī Jum'ah
Ibn Abī al-Zinād. *See* 'Abd al-Raḥmān b. Abī al-Zinād
Ibn A'tham al-Kūfī, *Kitāb al-futūḥ* xvii
Ibn 'Ayyāsh al-Mantūf. *See* 'Abdallāh b. 'Ayyāsh
Ibn Baḥdal 75
Ibn al-Dawraqiyyah. *See* Wakī'
Ibn Hubayrah. *See* Hishām b. Hubayrah
Ibn al-Kalbī. *See* Hishām b. Muḥammad
Ibn Kāwān Island 176
Ibn Khubayb 138
Ibn Ma'mar. *See* 'Ubaydallāh b. 'Ubayd [allāh]
Ibn Mashja'ah 143
Ibn Muqbil (poet) 222
Ibn Nāfi' (*rāwī*) 152
Ibn Nawf al-Hamdānī. *See* 'Abdallāh b. Nawf
Ibn Nubātah, *Sarḥ al-'uyūn* 218
Ibn Qays al-Ruqayyāt. *See* 'Ubaydallāh b. Qays
Ibn al-Ruqayyat. *See* 'Ubaydallāh b. Qays
Ibn Sa'd. *See* Muḥammad b. Sa'd
Ibn Salmā 231
Ibn Uqayṣir al-Quḥāfi al-Khath'amī 9
Ibn al-Zarqā' (i.e., 'Abd al-Malik b. Marwān) 158, 160
Ibn Ziyād. *See* 'Ubaydallāh b. Ziyād
Ibrāhīm b. 'Abd al-Raḥmān al-Anṣārī (*rāwī*) 79
Ibrāhīm b. Abī Jum'ah 217
Ibrāhīm b. 'Arabī al-Kinānī 161, 163
Ibrāhīm b. al-Ashtar al-Nakha'ī xiv, 4 n. 20, 10–11, 14–18, 20, 67–69, 74–83, 88, 109–10, 118, 128, 130, 134, 180–82, 185
Ibrāhīm b. Sulaymān al-Ḥanafī (*rāwī*) 113

Ibrāhīm b. al-Walīd (caliph), secretaries of 217
Īdhaj 133
Idrīs (prophet) 213
Ignorance, Time of. *See* Jāhiliyyah
Iḥrām ("pilgrim's garb") 208
ʿIkrimah (*ghulām* of Ibn ʿAbbās) 153
ʿIkrimah b. Ribʿī 30; house of 101
Imām xvi, 2 n. 9, 77, 110, 141, 198–99; Standing Place of (at ʿArafāt) 152
ʿImrān b. Khālid 32
Indian steel, sword of 98
Iram 87
Iraq xiv–xv, 2–3, 55, 74, 109, 122, 148, 155, 165, 171, 188, 192, 194; people of, and ʿAbd al-Malik 178, 180–82, 186, 195; Iraq road 207
ʿĪsā b. Muṣʿab b. al-Zubayr 182–86
Iṣbahān 123, 124, 130–33, 178, 192
al-Iṣbahānī, Abū al-Faraj, *Kitāb al-aghānī* xvii
Isḥāq b. ʿAbdallāh b. Abī Farwah (*rāwī*) 179, 226
Isḥāq b. [Muḥammad b.] al-Ashʿath 14, 18
Isḥāq b. Yaḥyā b. Ṭalḥah (*rāwī*) 69–70, 224–25
Ismāʿīl, "great descendant of" 158
Ismāʿīl b. Abī Ḥakīm (*mawlā* of al-Zubayr) 216
Ismāʿīl b. Abī al-Muhājir (*rāwī*) 183
Ismāʿīl b. ʿAmr b. Saʿīd 166
Ismāʿīl b. Nuʿaym (*rāwī*) 55
Ismāʿīl b. Ṭalḥah b. ʿUbaydallāh Abū al-Bakhtarī 70, 131, 183
isnād ("chain of authorities") 6 n. 31
Iṣṭakhr 124, 177, 200
Iyās b. Shurayḥ 126

J

Jabal al-Mushāt 152
jabbānah ("tribal cemetery") 14 n. 60, 34. *See* Jabbānat Banī Salūl, etc.
Jabbānat Banī Salūl 15, 16
Jabbānat Bishr 14
Jabbānat Kindah 14, 100
Jabbānat Mikhnaf 14
Jabbānat Murād 15, 100
Jabbānat al-Sabīʿ 14, 16–19, 21, 24, 27, 29, 31, 40, 67, 100
Jabbānat al-Ṣāʾidiyyīn, 100–1
Jābir b. al-Aswad b. ʿAwf al-Zuhrī 153, 194
al-Jābiyah, agreement of 155 n. 561
Jaʿdah b. Hubayrah b. Abī Wahb al-Makhzūmī 70, 72
Jaʿfar b. Yaḥyā b. Khālid b. Barmak 223
Jāhiliyyah ("Time of Ignorance") 12, 152
al-Jahshiyārī, *Kitāb al-wuzarāʾ wa-al-kuttāb* 213 n. 750
Jalūlāʾ, Battle of 141
jamāʿah ("unity") 165–66, 182
al-Jamrah 167
al-Janad 27
Janāḥ (*mawlā* of al-Walīd) 215
Janb (tribe) 42
Jarīr b. Kurayb 143, 144
al-Jārūd 176
Jawbar 129
al-Jawn b. Kaʿb al-Hamdānī 144, 145
Jay 130 n. 467. *See* Iṣbahān
Jayhān b. Mashjaʿah al-Ḍabbī 62, 65
al-Jazīrah xiv, 3, 34, 43, 75, 82, 83, 110, 118, 133
al-Jazzār (nickname of Muṣʿab b. al-Zubayr) 84
Jerusalem 81
Jews 120, 158 n. 572
al-Jibāl 108, 109, 136, 139
jihād ("holy war") 78
al-Jisr al-Akbar ("Great Bridge") 87, 124
John of Damascus, St 215 n. 762
Jordan, troops from 229
Jubayr al-Ḥaḍramī 14
Jubayr b. Shaybah 169
al-Jubbah 138
Juʿfī (tribe) 135 n. 482, 144, 151, 188
Jufrat Khālid 173, 193
Jufrat Nāfiʿ b. al-Ḥārith 173
Jufriyyah 173, 176

Juhaynah (tribe) 34; Mosque of (al-Kūfah) 101
al-Juḥfah 209
Jūkhā 5, 125, 139
jumzān 23
Jundabs of Azd 72
al-Jundu'ī 21

K

Ka'b b. Abī Ka'b al-Khath'amī 12–13, 14, 18
Ka'b al-Aḥbār 158
Ka'bah 110, 152, 167, 207 n. 730, 208–9, 229, 231 n. 827; *Rukn* ("Corner of") 61
kāfir ("unbeliever") 125
kāfirkūbāt ("clubs") 61
Kāhil (tribe) 60
Kalb (tribe) 3 n. 11, 15 n. 65, 75, 156–58, 164, 188 n. 674. *See also* Quḍā'ah
al–Kalbāniyyah 25
al-Kallā' 46
Karbalā' 1 n. 2, 52 n. 213, 179 n. 641. *See also* al-Ṭaff
Kardam b. Marthad b. Najabah al-Fazārī 125
Karkh 127
Kaskar 91, 144
Kathīr b. Ismā'īl al-Kindī 88
Kaysān Abū 'Amrah (*mawlā* of 'Uraynah) 25–26, 35, 37–38, 88
Kaysāniyyah 25 n. 101
Khalī' ("outlaw") 135
Khālid b. 'Abdallāh b. Khālid b. Asīd 172–75, 177, 187, 193, 199–206, 212, 233, 234
Khālid b. Barmak 218
Khālid b. Sa'īd b. al-'Āṣ 214
Khālid b. Yazīd b. Mu'āwiyah 155 n. 561, 166, 179, 192
Khālid b. Yazīd al-Qasrī (brother of 'Abdallāh b. Yazīd al-Qasrī) 165
Khalīfah al-A'war (*mawlā* of Banū 'Adī) 46
al-Khallālīn (section of al-Baṣrah) 46
kharāj ("taxes") 86, 199
Khārif (clan of Hamdān) 71
Khārijites xv–xvi, 104 n. 385, 123–34, 152 n. 553, 167, 182 n. 651, 198–200, 202–6, 232–33. *See also* Azāriqah; Ḥarūrī; *Muḥakkimūn*; Nāfi' b. al-Azraq; Najdiyyah; Qaṭarī
al-Kharrārah 129
Khashabiyyah 50, 59–62, 94 n. 349
Khath'am (tribe) 14, 43, 89, 95
al-Khaṭṭ (source of spears) 146
Khawalī b. Yazīd al-Aṣbaḥī 35; wife of 35
al-Khawarnaq 129, 195–96
al-Khayf 127 n. 457, 167
Khaywān 143
Khāzir River 74–75, 80, 82, 88
Khidāsh b. Yazīd al-Asadī 177–78
Khubayb b. 'Abdallāh b. al-Zubayr 226
khums, pl. *akhmās* ("fifth," division of Baṣran army) 87, 93. *See* 'Abd al-Qays, fifth of; al-Azd, fifth of; Bakr b. Wā'il, fifth of; Highlanders, fifth of; Banū Tamīm, fifth of
Khunays, Crossroads of 102
Khurāsān 62–66, 67, 121, 153, 168, 182, 209–12, 234; tax bureau of 216
Khurshādh Canal 91
Khusraw, son of Hurmuz 146; *Īwān* ("ceremonial hall") 146; White Palace of 180
Khūzistān 182 n. 651
Kindah (tribe) 44 n. 175, 95, 191; fourth of Rabī'ah and Kindah 5, 67
Kirmān 123, 124, 133, 177, 200
Kisrā. *See* Khusraw
al-Kūfah xiii–xv, 1, 3, 5, 6, 10–24, 27–45, 48, 53, 54, 59, 67, 82, 83, 85–88, 91–92, 98, 100–9, 111, 113–14, 116–18, 120, 121, 122, 126, 128, 130, 135–37, 141, 144–47, 153, 168, 170, 178, 187, 188–91, 193, 195, 199, 212, 232–34; *dīwān* of 214; mosque of

92, 101, 109, 113; judiciary of 121, 153, 168, 212, 215, 234; market of 17, 102; Palace of 92, 95, 100–4, 116; people, troops of 60, 78, 90, 93, 94, 99, 102, 130, 179, 187, 203, 205, 232, 233
al-Kunāsah 15, 18, 30, 67, 100
Kurayb b. Abrahah b. al-Ṣabbāḥ al-Ḥimyarī 157
al-Kuwayfah 91 n. 338

L

Labīd (poet) 221
Laḥḥām Jarīr 144
Lane of the Baṣrans (al-Kūfah) 102
Laylā bt. Qumāmah al-Muzaniyyah 98
Laylā bt. Zabbān b. al-Aṣbagh al-Kalbī (mother of ʿAbd al-ʿAzīz b. Marwān) 162
al-Layth b. Abī Ruqayyah (*mawlā* of Umm al-Ḥakam) 216
liḥāf (woman's outer garment) 101
Luhrasb b. Kāwghān b. Kaymūs 213

M

Maʿadd 27
Maʿbad b. Khālid al-Jadalī 69–70, 189
al-Madā'in 5, 10, 82, 103, 122, 125, 127, 130, 136, 139, 145, 180. *See also* Khusraw, *Īwān*; Khusraw, White Palace of; Sābāṭ
al-Madā'inī, Abū al-Ḥasan ʿAlī b. Muḥammad (*rāwī*) 2 n. 5, 45, 59, 62, 84, 116, 135, 136, 141, 172–76, 183–84, 185, 188–89, 192, 193, 209, 232
al-Madhār xv, 88–90, 115
Madhḥij (tribe) 15, 83, 137, 140, 151, 181, 188; fourth of Madhḥij and Asad 5, 67
Madīnat al-Rizq. *See* al-Baṣrah, provision depot
Māh 138
al-Mahbadhān, Bath of 22
Mahdī 39, 40 n. 160, 60
al-Mahdī (caliph), secretaries to 219–20
Makhlad b. Muḥammad b. al-Ḥārith Abū Hāshim 217
Makhlad b. Yaḥyā b. Ḥāḍir (*rāwī*) 184
Makhramah b. Sulaymān al-Wālibī (*rāwī*) 226
Mālik b. ʿAmr Abū Nimrān al-Nahdī 20, 32, 92, 94–95
Mālik b. Aʿyan al-Juhanī (*rāwī*) 31
Mālik b. al-Ḥārith al-Nakhaʿī al-Ashtar (father of Ibrāhīm b. al-Ashtar) 10 n. 46, 83
Mālik b. Mismaʿ al-Bakrī Abū Ghassān 48–49, 87, 93, 120, 135, 173–75, 178
Mālik b. al-Mundhir 87, 93
Mālik b. al-Nusayr al-Baddī 31
Maʿn b. al-Mughīrah 233
Manbij 149
Manīʿ b. al-ʿAlā' al-Saʿdī (*rāwī*) 51
manjanīq ("trebuchet") 208 n. 732, 225
al-Manṣūr, Abū Jaʿfar (caliph) 218–19; secretaries to 218–19
Maqām Ibrāhīm ("Station of Abraham") 61, 230
maqṣūrah ("enclosure") 161, 165
Mardānshāh 119
Marj Rāhiṭ, battle of 3, 155 n. 561, 165
Marjānah (mother of ʿUbaydallāh b. Ziyād) 77–78, 81–82
Marw 62 n. 247, 210–11
Marwah 208, 229
Marwān b. al-Ḥakam (caliph) xiv, 2–3, 75, 104, 150, 154 n. 559, 155 n. 561, 178, 193, 214; family, sons of 75, 126, 159–60, 163, 165
Marwān b. Muḥammad al-Jaʿdī (caliph) 217; secretaries to 217
Marwāniyyah 178
masāliḥ ("frontier garrisons") 203
Maskin 178, 180–81
Maslamah b. ʿAbd al-Mālik 216; secretary to 216
Maslamah b. Muḥārib (*rāwī*) 59, 66,

172, 173, 175
Maṣqalah (slave of ʿAmr b. Saʿīd b. al-ʿĀṣ) 161
Masʿūd b. ʿAmr al-Azdī 150 n. 543
Maṭar (servant of Qafal family) 111
Maṭar b. al-Taw'am 174
maʿūnah, pl. *maʿāwin* ("special grant") 124, 170, 199
mawālī, sg. *mawlā* ("client") 11–13, 50, 55, 77, 85, 86, 88–89, 95, 97, 107, 117, 159, 163, 172; street of (al-Baṣrah) 46
al-Mawṣil 3–4, 6, 74, 82, 83, 118, 123, 133, 182
maysir (game) 96
Mecca xiii, xv, 53–56, 59–62, 84, 119, 120, 151–53, 167, 169, 182, 192, 202, 206–9, 224–32, 234; gates 229, 230; Mosque of 61. *See also* Ḥaram
Medina xiii, 2 n. 7, 53, 55–56, 58, 67, 120, 153, 186, 194, 207, 212, 227, 232; *dīwān* of 214; fourth of 5, 67. *See also* Ṭaybah; Wādī al-Qurā
millah ("religious community") 107
Minā 167
al-Mirbad 47, 64
al-Mishraqī [al-Ḍaḥḥāk b. ʿAbdallāh] (*rāwī*) 26, 80, 82
Miskin b. ʿĀmir b. Unayf al-Dārimī (poet) 51
Misma' b. Mālik b. Misma' 200
Moses 84; family of 70
Muʿādh b. Hāni' b. ʿAdī al-Kindī (nephew of Ḥujr b. ʿAdī) 35
Muʿāwiyah b. Abī Sufyān (caliph) xiii, 2 n. 6, 3 n. 11, 8 n. 40, 135, 193, 214; secretaries to 215
Muʿāwiyah b. Marwān 165
Muʿāwiyah b. Qurrah al-Muzanī 90
Muʿāwiyah b. Yazīd (caliph) xiii, 2 n. 6; secretaries to 215
Muḍar (tribal group) 15, 17–18, 20, 30, 49, 50, 65, 70, 187, 188, 211
al-Mufaḍḍal b. Muḥammad (*rāwī*) 209
al-Mughīrah b. Abī Farwah (or Abī Qurrah) 216
al-Mughīrah b. al-Muhallab 173, 200, 233
al-Muḥakkimūn 8
al-Muhallab b. Alī Ṣufrah 86–87, 89–90, 92–94, 100–2, 110, 118, 123, 133–34, 144, 149, 182, 198–204
Muḥammad (Prophet) 1 n. 2, 27, 77, 78, 87, 89, 110, 112, 114, 115, 141; family of 23, 31–32, 37, 39, 44, 53, 58, 60, 71, 78, 82, 87, 89, 104, 114, 176; secretaries to 214
Muḥammad b. Abān (*rāwī*) 113
Muḥammad b. ʿAbd al-Raḥmān b. Saʿīd b. Qays al-Hamdānī 102, 108, 116, 178, 182
Muḥammad b. ʿAbdallāh b. Khāzim al-Sulamī 62, 65, 66
Muḥammad b. ʿAbdallāh b. Yaʿqūb 219
Muḥammad b. ʿAmmār b. Yasīr 31
Muḥammad b. ʿAmr b. Saʿīd b. al-ʿĀṣ 166
Muḥammad b. al-Ashʿath b. Qays al-Kindī Abū Qāsim 12, 44, 85–86, 90, 93, 95, 96–97, 100, 116
Muḥammad b. Barrād (*rāwī*) 29
Muḥammad b. Ḥamīd the Secretary 219–20
Muḥammad b. al-Ḥanafiyyah xiv, 1 n. 1, 13, 15, 38–39, 53, 58–62, 98–99, 100 n. 374, 114 n. 415, 152–53. *See also* Mahdī
Muḥammad b. al-Ḥārith 130
Muḥammad b. Jubayr (*rāwī*) 152, 153
Muḥammad b. Marwān (brother of ʿAbd al-Malik) 179, 181, 183, 233
Muḥammad b. Mikhnaf b. Sulaym (*rāwī*) 126
Muḥammad b. Mūsā b. Ṭalḥah 232
Muḥammad b. Qays 60
Muḥammad b. Saʿd al-Zuhrī Abū ʿAbdallāh (*rāwī*) 207, 224, 225–26, 228–30, 232; *Kitāb al-ṭabaqāt al-kabīr* xvii
Muḥammad b. al-Sā'ib al-Kalbī (*rāwī*) 2 n. 4, 98

Muḥammad b. al-Sa'ib b. Mālik al-Ash'arī 103–4
Muḥammad b. Sa'īd b. al-'Āṣ 165
Muḥammad b. Sallām al-Jumaḥī (*rāwī*) 180–81, 182
Muḥammad b. 'Umar. *See* al-Wāqidī Muḥammad b. 'Umar
Muḥammad b. 'Umayr b. 'Uṭārid 18, 51, 130, 179, 192
Muḥammad b. Yūsuf (*rāwī*) 112
Muḥārib, son of the poet Labīd 221
al-Muḥillūn, -īn ("shedders of innocent blood") 57
al-Mujālid b. Sa'īd (*rāwī*) 23, 49
al-Mujashshir 143–45
Mujjā'ah b. 'Abd al-Raḥmān 233
al-Muka'bir 176
al-Mukhtār b. Abī 'Ubayd b. Mas'ūd al-Thaqafī Abū Isḥāq xiv–xvi, 1, 3–5, 10–20, 22–25, 27–46, 48–56, 58–61, 67–70, 72–73, 77, 81–83, 85–96, 97 n. 362, 100–7, 109, 111, 114, 115–18, 120, 136–39, 158 n. 572, 184
Mukram b. Muṭarrif b. Sīdān al-Bāhilī 184
al-Mundhir b. Ḥassān b. Ḍirār al-Ḍabbī 116
al-Mundhir b. Jahm al-Asadī (*rāwī*) 226
al-Mundhir b. al-Jārūd, daughter of 200; family of 200
Muqātil b. Misma' al-Bakrī 93, 177, 200, 202, 206
Murrah b. Maḥkān 173, 177
Murrah b. Munqidh b. al-Nu'mān al-'Abdī 42
Mūsā b. 'Abdallāh b. Khāzim al-Sulamī 63–65
Mūsā b. Abī Mūsā al-Ash'arī 73
Mūsā b. 'Āmir Abū al-Ash'ar al-Juhanī al-'Adawī (*rāwī*) 4, 7–8, 9, 31, 34–36, 38, 53, 72–73
Mūsā b. Ya'qūb b. 'Abdallāh (*rāwī*) 227
Muṣ'ab b. al-Rabī' al-Khath'ami Abū Mūsā 217–18
Muṣ'ab b. Thābit (*rāwī*) 207, 209, 224, 227, 229
Muṣ'ab b. 'Uthmān (*rāwī*) 194
Muṣ'ab b. al-Zubayr xv, 25, 28, 42–44, 55, 66, 83–94, 98–112, 115–21, 122–26, 131, 133, 139–50, 153, 155, 164, 165, 168, 169, 171–72, 174–88, 192–95, 198–99, 207, 209
Musāfir b. Sa'īd b. Nimrān al-Nā'iṭī 38, 54, 93, 108–9
al-Mushaqqar (fortress in al-Baḥrayn) 233
mushrikah ("idolatress") 200
Muslim b. 'Abdallāh al-Ḍabābī (*rāwī*) 24, 26
Muslim b. 'Amr al-Bāhilī 142, 148–49, 181, 185
Muslim b. 'Aqīl b. Abī Ṭālib 78 n. 293
Muslim b. Bābak (*rāwī*) 208
mustaghallāt ("income-yielding properties") 215
Muṭarrif b. Sīdān al-Bāhilī 184–85; daughter of 185
al-Mutawakkil b. 'Abdallāh al-Laythī (poet) 52, 72
al-Muthannā b. Mukharribah al-'Abdī 45–48, 55
Muzāḥim b. Mālik 76

N

Nabatæan 10, 147, 176
al-Nābi' b. Ziyād b. Ẓabyān 184–85
al-Nābighah al-Ja'dī (poet) 221
al-Naḍr b. 'Amr 217
al-Naḍr b. Ṣāliḥ Abū Zuhayr al-'Absī (*rāwī*) 11, 30, 67, 128, 130, 133, 198
Nāfi' (*mawlā* of Banū Asad, *rāwī*) 209, 229–30
Nāfi' b. al-Azraq 122 n. 437
Nahd. *See* Banū Nahd
Nahr al-Baṣriyyīn Canal 115
Nahrawān Districts 125
Nā'iṭ (clan of Hamdān) 29
al-Najaf 113, 114
Najdah b. 'Āmir al-Ḥanafī al-Ḥarūrī 104, 119 n. 431, 152–53, 206. *See also* Najdiyyah

Najdiyyah, 119
Nakhaʿ (tribe) 18 n. 77, 75
Narsā 142
Nāshiṭ mountain pass 133
Naṣībīn 82–83
nāṣir ("helper, avenger") 31 n. 128
Naṣr b. Sayyār 216
Naʿthal (nickname for ʿUthmān) 114
Naysābūr 209–11
Nihāwand, battle of 141
Nīshāpūr. *See* Naysābūr
Nuʿaym b. Salāmah (*mawlā*) 216
Nufayʿ b. Dhu'ayb (*mawlā* of al-Walīd) 215
al-Nukhayl, Day of 151
al-Nukhaylah 128, 141, 188
al-Nuʿmān (builder of al-Khawarnaq) 129 n. 466, 196 n. 704
al-Nuʿmān b. ʿAwf b. Abī Jābir al-Azdī 5
al-Nuʿmān b. Ṣuhbān al-Jarmī al-Rāsibī 22

O

Oman 149

P

Palestine 216; *dīwān* of 217; troops from 229
Parvīz. *See* Abarwīz
Persepolis. *See* Iṣṭakhr
Persians 8 n. 39, 11 n. 49, 13, 33, 38, 91, 116, 176. *See also* al-Ḥamrā'
Pharaoh 78, 84
Pilgrimage 59, 66, 121, 151–53, 168, 170, 187, 194, 208–9, 212, 234

Q

Qabīṣah b. Dhu'ayb b. Ḥalḥalah al-Khuzāʿī Abū Isḥāq 159, 215
al-Qādisiyyah 32, 44, 85; Battle of 141; Canal 92
Qafal family of Banū Taymallāh b. Thaʿlabah 111
al-Qaʿqāʿ b. Khālid al-ʿAbsī 215
al-Qārah 156
Qarqīsiyā' 155
qaṣīdah 147, 149
al-Qāsim b. Maʿn (*rāwī*) 189
al-qāsiṭīn ("deviators") 68
Qasiyy, 38
Qaṭan b. ʿAbdallāh al-Ḥārithī Abū ʿUthmān 178, 181, 191; Bath of 19
Qaṭar 177
Qaṭarī b. al-Fujā'ah 133, 200, 206
Qays ʿAylān (tribe) 3, 15, 16, 75, 149, 150, 157, 210, 214; party (*Qaysiyyah*) 146–47
Qays b. al-Haytham al-Sulamī 46–48, 87, 93, 173–74, 181
Qays b. Mālik 61
Qays b. Saʿīd 107
Qays b. Ṭahfah al-Nahdī 67
Qaysāriyyah 197
Qaysiyyah. *See* Qays ʿAylān, party
Qeshm Island. *See* Ibn Kāwān Island
qiblah 107, 112
Qinnasrīn 134; troops from 229
Quʿayqiʿān (mountain) 119
al-Qubāʿ. *See* al-Ḥārith b. [ʿAbdallāh b.] Abī Rabīʿah
Qubādh 176
Quḍāʿah (tribe) 188. *See also* Kalb
Qudāmah b. Ḥawshab (*rāwī*) 12
Qudāmah b. Maẓʿūn 206 n. 723
Qur'ān 28 n. 114, 71, 77, 89, 99, 110, 114, 125, 214, 230; passages quoted 7, 20, 28, 30, 34, 37, 38, 49 n. 200, 59, 61, 68, 70, 71 n. 278, 78, 84, 98–99, 100, 102, 110, 144 n. 518, 166, 194, 214; Sūra of the Pen 230
Quraysh (tribe) 38, 71, 135, 156, 157, 160, 180, 182, 183, 186, 232; meteor of (ʿUmar b. Saʿd b. Abī Waqqāṣ) 51
qurrā' ("Qur'ān reciters") 17

Qurrah b. ʿAlī b. Mālik al-Jushamī 78
Qūsān Canal 91
Quss b. Sāʿidah al-Iyādī 214
al-Quṣṣāṣ ("storytellers"), Mosque of 19
Qutaybah b. Muslim 181 n. 649

R

al-Rabīʿ (secretary to al-Manṣūr) 219
al-Rabīʿ b. ʿArʿarah al-Khushanī 217
Rabīʿah (tribal group) 15, 20, 30, 49, 50, 81, 93, 151, 182; fourth of Rabīʿah and Kindah 5; fourth of Kindah and 67
Rabīʿah b. al-Mukhāriq al-Ghanawī 6–9
Rabīʿah b. Nājid, slave woman of 125, 126
Rabīʿah b. Tharwān al-Ḍabbī 15
Rādhān districts 6
Rajāʾ b. Ḥaywah (*rāwī*) 179, 216
Rajāʾ b. Sirāj 156–57
Rajaz poetry 80, 128, 131, 228–29
Rāmhurmuz 200, 202
Raqabah b. al-Ḥurr 62, 64
al-Raqīm 56
Raʾs ʿAyn. *See* ʿAyn (al-)Wardah
Raʾs al-Jālūt, bridges of 68
al-Rashīd (caliph) 223
al-Rawḥāʾ 37
Rayṭah (daughter of Caliph al-Saffāḥ) 218
Rayṭah bt. Yazīd 126
al-Rayy 192, 203, 204
al-Rayyān b. Muslim 215
Razīn ʿAbd al-Salūlī 88
Razīn b. al-Mutawakkil al-Bakrī 126
Riddah, War of 106
Rifāʿah b. Qumāmah al-Muzanī 98
Rifāʿah b. Shaddād b. ʿAwsajah al-Fityānī 17, 21, 22
rubʿ, pl. *arbāʿ* ("fourth," division of Kūfan army) 5 n. 24. *See* Madhḥij, fourth of Madhḥij and Asad; Medina, fourth of; Banū Tamīm, fourth of Tamīm and Hamdān; Rabīʿah, fourth of Kindah and
rumḥ ("spear length") 20 n. 82
al-Ruṣāfah 216
al-Ruwāʿ bt. Iyās b. Shurayḥ al-Hamdānī 126

S

Sabaʾiyyah 13, 70, 71
al-Sabakhah 15, 22, 46, 99–100
Sābāṭ 14, 15, 82, 125
Sabīʿ (clan of Hamdān) 129. *See also* Jabbānat al-Sabīʿ
Sābūr 123, 124, 200
Sādamāh. *See* Sātīdamā
Ṣafā 208; Gate (Mecca) 229
al-Saffāḥ, Abū al-ʿAbbās (caliph) 218; secretaries to 218
Ṣafiyyah bt. ʿAbd al-Muṭṭalib (grandmother of ʿAbdallāh b. al-Zubayr) 228
Ṣafiyyah bt. Abī ʿUbayd (sister of al-Mukhtār) 112 n. 409
al-Sāʾib b. Mālik al-Ashʿarī 33, 37, 82, 93, 98, 103–4
Saʿīd b. ʿAbd al-Raḥmān b. Ḥassān b. Thābit (poet) 112
Saʿīd b. ʿAmr b. Saʿīd b. al-ʿĀṣ 166–67
Saʿīd b. al-ʿĀṣ 193
Saʿīd b. Dīnār (*rāwī*) 167
Saʿīd b. Muḥammad b. Jubayr (*rāwī*) 152
Saʿīd b. Munqidh al-Hamdānī al-Thawrī 92–93, 95, 116 n. 421
Saʿīd b. Muslim b. Bābak (*rāwī*) 208
Saʿīd b. Nimrān al-Hamdānī 215
Saʿīd b. al-Walīd b. ʿAmr b. Jabalah al-Kalbī al-Abrash Abū Mujāshiʿ 216
sajʿ (rhymed prose) 4 n. 21, 99 n. 370
al-Sakan b. Qatādah (*rāwī*) 174
Sakīnah 71
Ṣāliḥ b. al-Haytham (*mawlā* of Rayṭah

bt. Abī al-ʿAbbās) 218
Ṣāliḥ b. Jubayr al-Ghassānī (or al-Ghudanī) 216
Ṣāliḥ b. Masʿūd al-Khathʿamī 58–59
Ṣāliḥ b. Mikhrāq 127, 200
Sālim (*mawlā* of Saʿīd b. ʿAbd al-Mālik) 217
Salīm b. Yazīd al-Kindī 95
Ṣalkhab 33
Salmā (wife of ʿUbaydallāh b. al-Ḥurr) 138
Salmān b. Ḥimyar al-Thawrī al-Hamdānī 56, 57, 83
Samāhīj 176
Samīʿ (*mawlā* of Maslamah b. ʿAbd al-Mālik) 216
Saqar 49, 50
Saqaṭ ("section of rubbish dealers," al-Baṣrah) 47
ṣarafān 23
al-Ṣarāt 128, 129; bridge of 130
Sarjūn b. Manṣūr al-Rūmī 215
Ṣarṣar Canal 142
Ṣaʿṣaʿah b. Muʿāwiyah 173
Sātīdamā 25
Sawād 10, 108, 109, 137–39, 146
Sawādah b. ʿUbaydallāh al-Numayrī 210
Sawrah b. Ashyam al-Numayrī 209
Sayf b. Hāniʾ al-Murādī 141
al-Saylaḥīn 92
Secretaries 213–23
Shabath b. Ribʿī al-Tamīmī 11–13, 15, 16–17, 18, 20, 70, 83, 85, 128, 130
Shabath Road (al-Kūfah) 95
al-Shaʿbī. *See* ʿĀmir b. Sharāḥīl
Shaddād b. ʿAbdallāh b. Shaddād al-Jushamī 107
Shaddād b. al-Mundhir (brother of Ḥuḍayn) 30
Shahm b. ʿAbd al-Raḥmān al-Juhanī (*rāwī*) 34
Shāhmīghad 210
Shākir (clan of Hamdān) 16, 71 n. 280, 72, 89, 102, 139
Shamir b. Dhī al-Jawshan 12, 15, 16, 24–26
Sharāf 23
Sharāḥīl, day of 151
sharīf. *See ashrāf*
Sharīk b. Jadīr al-Taghlibi 80–81
Shaykh b. al-Nuʿmān 177
Shīʿah xiii–xiv, xvi, 1 n. 1, 2, 18 n. 78, 36, 39–41, 53, 77, 90, 98. *See also* ʿAlī b. Abī Ṭālib; Kaysāniyyah; Khashabiyyah; Muḥammad b. al-Ḥanafiyyah; al-Mukhtār; Sabaʾiyyah; Turābiyyah
al-Shiʿb 152
Shiʿb ʿAlī 62
Shibām (clan of Hamdān) 18–21, 29, 71–72, 89, 102
Shiḥr 27
Shuʿayb b. Dīnār 216
Shuʿayb al-ʿUmānī (*mawlā* of al-Walīd) 215
Shuʿbah b. Ẓahīr al-Nahshalī 62, 64
shūrā ("consultation") 89
Shuraḥbīl b. ʿAwn (*rāwī*) 151–52
Shuraḥbīl b. Dhī Buqlān al-Nāʿiṭī al-Hamdānī 29
Shuraḥbīl b. Dhī al-Kalāʿ 78, 81
Shuraḥbīl b. Wars al-Hamdānī 55–57
Shurayḥ b. al-Ḥārith al-Kindī 168, 234
shurṭah ("picked troops," "police") 36, 57, 71, 77, 79, 80, 82, 83, 111
Ṣiffīn, battle of 81 n. 305, 94, 135
Simāk b. Yazīd 129
Sinān b. Anas 43
Sinān b. Dhuhl 178
Sinān b. Mukammil al-Ghanawī 210
Sinjār 83
Siʿr b. Abī Siʿr al-Ḥanafī 5, 7, 30, 32
Slave(s) 8, 11–13, 24, 88, 89, 92, 117
Smiths, Street of the (al-Kūfah) 102
Ṣudāʾ (tribe) 43
Sufyān b. al-Abrad al-Kalbī 156, 157
Sufyān b. al-Sāʾib b. Mālik al-Ashʿarī 98
Sufyān b. Yazīd b. al-Mughaffal al-Azdī 76, 79, 81
Suḥaym b. Wathīl al-Riyāḥī (poet) 141
Sūlāf 134, 198
Sulaym b. Yazīd al-Kindī 92, 93

Sulaymān [b. Ṣāliḥ] (*rāwī*) 69, 71, 81
Sulaymān b. ʿAbd al-Malik (caliph), secretaries to 215
Sulaymān b. Abī Rāshid (*rāwī*) 33
Sulaymān b. Makhlad 219
Sulaymān b. Muḥammad al-Ḥaḍramī (*rāwī*) 14
Sulaymān b. al-Muḥtafiz al-Māzinī (brother of Bishr) 66
Sulaymān b. Nuʿaym al-Ḥimyarī 215
Sulaymān b. Saʿd al-Khushanī 215, 216
Sulaymān b. Ṣurad 2 n. 8, 40 n. 160, 45. *See also* Tawwābūn
Sunnah of the Prophet 89, 110
Sūrā 5, 16, 146
Surāqah b. Mirdās al-Bāriqī (poet) 22, 23, 27–29, 83, 127
Ṣuraym b. al-Ḥārith (clan of Tamīm) 209
Suwayd b. Ghaflah (*rāwī*) 113
Suwayd b. Manjūf 149
Suwayd b. Riʾāb al-Shannī 48
Syria xiv–xv, 2, 84, 104, 109, 110, 121, 134, 135, 153, 169, 172, 179, 181, 192, 193, 206, 209; Syrians, Syrian army xvi, 10, 13, 55, 67, 70, 74, 78, 107–10, 179, 181, 186, 207, 225, 228–29

T

al-Ṭabarī Abū Jaʿfar Muḥammad b. Jarīr (*rāwī*) 1, 45, 53, 59, 62, 66, 69, 115, 116, 134, 147, 151, 153, 187, 192, 198, 232; text of *Taʾrīkh* xvi–xvii
al-Ṭaff 52, 179
al-Ṭāʾif 176, 177, 207, 208
Takrīt 3–4, 144
Ṭalḥah b. ʿAbdallāh b. ʿAwf 194
Ṭalḥah al-Ṭalḥāt [b. ʿAbdallāh b. Khalaf al-Khuzāʿī] 214
Tāmarrā 145
Ṭamastān Bridge 124
Tamīm. *See* Banū Tamīm; Tamīmiyyah
Tamīmiyyah 175
al-Tammārīn (section of al-Kūfah) 15
Ṭarafah b. al-ʿAbd (poet) 220
Ṭarafah b. ʿAbdallāh b. Dajājah al-Ḥanafī 105
Ṭāriq b. ʿAmr (*mawlā* of ʿUthmān) 194, 208, 212, 229, 231–32
Ṭarrāf b. ʿAbdallāh b. Dajājah al-Ḥanafī 105
Tawwābūn 2, 40 n. 160, 45
Ṭaybah (Medina) 58
Thābit b. Nuʿaym al-Judhāmī 217 n. 779
Thābit b. Sulaymān b. Saʿd al-Khushanī 217
Thaʾj 174
Thaqīf (tribe) 52 n. 215, 115, 158 n. 572. *See also* Qasiyy
Thawr (clan of Hamdān) 83, 89
Thawr b. Yazīd 228
Thumāmah [b. Ashras] 223
Tigris River 97, 125, 171
Tihāmah 225
Ṭījushnas 142
Tirmidh 210
Ṭīzanābādh 85
Trebuchet. *See manjanīq*
Tubayʿ, son of Kaʿb al-Aḥbār's wife 158
al-Ṭufayl b. ʿĀmir 60
Ṭufayl b. Jaʿdah b. Hubayrah 69–70, 72
al-Ṭufayl b. Laqīṭ 75, 76
al-Ṭufayl b. Mirdās al-ʿAmmī (*rāwī*) 62
ṭuʿmah ("means of subsistence, grant") 63, 131, 209–10, 212
Turābiyyah 77 n. 289. *See also* Abū Turāb
Turks 64, 90, 107

U

ʿUbayd b. Aws al-Ghassānī 215
ʿUbayd b. Mālik al-Ashʿarī (brother of al-Sāʾib) 98
ʿUbaydallāh b. ʿAbdallāh b. ʿUtbah b. Masʿūd 212

'Ubaydallāh b. Abī Bakrah 173, 176, 192–93
'Ubaydallāh b. Abī Rāfi' 215
'Ubaydallāh b. 'Alī b. Abī Ṭālib 100, 115
'Ubaydallāh b. al-Ḥurr xv, 100–2, 116–17, 134–51
'Ubaydallāh b. Nājiyah al-Shibāmī 42
'Ubaydallāh b. Naṣr b. al-Ḥajjāj b. 'Alā' al-Sulamī 215
'Ubaydallāh b. Qays al-Ruqayyāt (poet) 162, 187, 205
'Ubaydallāh b. al-Qibṭiyyah (*rāwī*) 224
'Ubaydallāh b. 'Ubayd[allāh] b. Ma'mar 118, 120, 172–75
'Ubaydallāh b. Ziyād xiv, 2–3, 6, 9, 10, 18 n. 78, 67, 70, 74–78, 80–83, 109, 136, 139, 150 n. 543, 179. *See also* Marjānah
'Ubaydallāh b. Ziyād b. Abī Laylā 220
'Ubaydallāh b. Ziyād b. Ẓabyān 174, 184–85
'Ubaydallāh b. Zuhayr al-Sulamī 81
Ubayy b. Ka'b 214
'Udhrah (tribe) 221, 222 n. 795
'Umar b. 'Abd al-'Azīz (caliph), secretaries to 216
'Umar b. 'Abd al-Raḥmān b. al-Ḥārith b. Hishām al-Makhzūmī 45, 53–54
'Umar b. 'Abdallāh al-Nahdī 92
'Umar b. Abī Rabī'ah al-Qurashī (poet) 111
'Umar b. al-Khaṭṭāb (caliph) 177, 214; secretaries to 214
'Umar b. Mikhnaf 22
'Umar b. Mūsā b. 'Ubaydallāh b. Ma'mar al-Taymī '232–33
'Umar b. Muṣ'ab b. al-Zubayr 178
'Umar b. Sa'd b. Abī Waqqāṣ 18, 36–39, 51 n. 211
'Umar b. Shabbah Abū Zayd (*rāwī*) 84, 116, 118–19, 172–76, 180, 182, 184–86, 188, 192–95, 232
'Umar b. 'Ubaydallāh b. Ma'mar al-Taymī 87, 89, 92–93, 123–25, 144–45, 182, 232–33
'Umārah b. 'Amr b. Ḥazm 232
'Umārah b. Ḥamzah 219
Umaymah 196
'Umayr (at battle of al-Nukhayl) 151
'Umayr b. al-Ḥubāb al-Sulamī 75–76, 78–80
'Umayr b. Ṭāriq 60
'Umayr b. Ziyād (*rāwī*) 29
Umayyads, Umayyad family, Umayyah. *See* Banū Umayyah
Umayyah b. 'Abdallāh b. Khālid b. Asīd 206; slave girl of 233
Umayyah b. 'Amr b. Sa'īd b. al-'Āṣ 166
Umm al-Banīn bt. al-Ḥakam b. Abī al-'Āṣ 164–65
Umm al-Ḥakam bt. Abī Sufyān 216
Umm Hāni' bt. Abī Ṭālib (sister of 'Alī and mother of Ja'dah b. Hubayrah) 72
Umm Khālid bt. Yazīd (wife of Khālid b. Barmak) 218
Umm Kulthūm bt. al-Faḍl b. al-'Abbās b. 'Abd al-Muṭṭalib 73
Umm Marwān b. al-Ḥakam al-Kināniyyah 165
Umm Mūsā bt. 'Amr b. Sa'īd b. al-'Āṣ 158
Umm Salamah (wife of Caliph Abū al-'Abbās al-Saffāḥ) 218
Umm Salamah al-Ju'fiyyah Salmā Umm Tawbah (wife of 'Ubaydallah b. al-Ḥurr) 137–39
Umm Tawbah. *See* Umm Salamah al-Ju'fiyyah
Umm Thābit bt. Samurah b. Jundab al-Fazārī (wife of al-Mukhtār) 44, 103, 111
umm walad (slave woman who has borne a child to her master) 125
Umm Yaḥyā (daughter of Khālid b. Barmak) 218
Umm Yazīd bt. Simāk b. Yazīd 129
Umm Zayd 212
ummah ("community") 59
Upper Ustān 126
'Uqbah al-Asadī (poet) 117

Uqbah b. 'Ashīrah al-Shannī 48
'Uqbah b. Ṭāriq al-Jushamī 16
'Uraynah. *See* Kaysān
'Urwah [b. al-Zubayr] (*rāwī*) 186, 207 n. 727
'Urwah b. al-Mughīrah b. Shu'bah (*rāwī*) 179
al-'Uryān b. al-Haytham b. al-Aswad al-Nakha'ī 36–37
Usāmah b. Zayd al-Salīḥī 216
'Uthmān b. 'Affān (caliph) 21, 114, 118, 135, 158, 195, 214, 232; secretaries to 214–15
'Uthmān b. Bishr b. al-Muḥtafiz al-Muzanī (or al-Māzinī) 62–63, 66
'Uthmān b. Khālid b. Usayr al-Duhmānī al-Juhanī 34–35
'Uthmān b. Muḥammad (*rāwī*) 186
'Uthmān b. Qays (*mawlā* of Khālid al-Qasrī) 217
'Uthmān b. al-Walīd 233–34
'Uthmāniyyah 135
'Uyaynah b. Asmā' 80

W

Wādī al-Qurā 53, 55–56
Wādi'ah (tribe) 19, 22
Wāfid b. Abī Yāsir (*rāwī*) 84
Wahbīl (clan of Nakha') 75, 98
Wakī' b. 'Umayrah al-Quray'ī 211
al-Walīd b. 'Abd al-Mālik (caliph) 161, 163; secretaries to 215
al-Walīd b. 'Uqbah b. Abī Mu'ayṭ, house of 79
al-Walīd b. Yazīd (caliph), secretaries to 217
al-Wāqidī Muḥammad b. 'Umar (*rāwī*) 115–16, 120, 151–52, 154, 167, 169, 179, 186, 188, 193–94, 197, 207–9, 224–30, 232, 234
Wāqiṣah 23
Ward b. al-Falaq al-'Anbarī 62, 66
Warqā' b. 'Āzib al-Asadī al-Nakha'ī 5, 7, 10, 79, 81, 98
Warrād (*mawlā* of Banū 'Abd Shams) 46–47
wars (ointment) 33
waṣī ("legatee") 114
Wāsiṭ 91, 218
Wāzi' b. al-Sarī (*rāwī*) 17
wazīr ("helper") xiv, xvi, 1 n. 1, 141
wijādah 2 n. 4

Y

Yaḥyā b. Abī 'Īsā (*rāwī*) 98
Yaḥyā b. Ḍamḍam 103
Yaḥyā b. Ismā'īl b. Abī al-Muhājir (*rāwī*) 183
Yaḥyā b. Khālid b. Barmak 223
Yaḥyā b. Ma'yūf al-Hamdānī 192
Yaḥyā b. Mubashshir 181
Yaḥyā b. Sa'īd b. al-'Āṣ 159, 161, 163–65, 189
Yaḥyā b. Sa'īd b. Dīnār (*rāwī*) 167
Yaḥyā b. Sa'īd b. Mikhnaf al-Azdī (father of Abū Mikhnaf, *rāwī*) 13, 126
Yaḥyā b. Ṭufayl (*rāwī*) 209
al-Yamāmah 104, 234
Ya'qūb b. 'Abdallāh b. Ya'qūb 219
Ya'qūb b. Dāwūd 219
Yasār (*mawlā* of Abū Bakr b. Mikhnaf) 127
Yazīd b. 'Abd al-Malik (caliph), secretaries to 216
Yazīd b. 'Abdallāh 216
Yazīd b. Anas b. Kilāb al-Asadī 4–7, 9–11
Yazīd b. al-Ḥārith b. [Yazīd b.] Ru'aym al-Shaybānī 15, 23, 30, 130, 131 n. 467, 145
Yazīd b. Mu'āwiyah (caliph) xiii, 2 n. 6, 3 n. 11, 136
Yazīd b. al-Mughaffal 144
Yazīd b. al-Muhallab, secretary to 216
Yazīd b. al-Riqā' (poet) 185 n. 658
Yazīd b. Ruwaym 192
Yazīd b. Sharāḥīl al-Anṣārī 38, 98
Yazīd b. 'Umayr b. Dhī Murrān al-Hamdānī 21

Yazīd b. al-Walīd (caliph), secretaries to 217
Yemen 234; Yemenis, people of Yemen 15–18, 20, 23, 24, 30, 38
Yūnus b. Abī Isḥāq (*rāwī*) 16, 24, 27, 129
Yūnus b. Hāʿān (or ʿĀhān) al-Hamdānī 143
Yūnus b. ʿImrān 60–61
Yūsuf b. ʿAbdallāh b. ʿUthmān b. Abī al-ʿĀṣ 174
Yūsuf Canal 92
Yūsuf b. Māhak (*rāwī*) 225
Yūsuf b. Yazīd (*rāwī*) 86

Z

Ẓabyān b. ʿUmārah (or ʿUthmān) al-Tamīmī 38, 60–61
Zahhāk. *See* Bīwarasb
Zaḥr b. Qays al-Juʿfī 14, 18, 22, 100, 102, 174, 178–79
Zā'idah b. Qudāmah 54, 184
Zamzam 59–61
Zandaward 177
Zayd b. Ruqād al-Janbī 42, 43 n. 172
Zayd b. Thābit 214
al-Zayyātīn [Street] (al-Kūfah) 105
Zirbī (*ghulām*) 24
Ziyād (?) 117
Ziyād b. Abī Laylā (father of ʿUbaydallāh b. Ziyād b. Abī Laylā) 220
Ziyād b. Abī al-Ward 217
Ziyād b. ʿAmr al-ʿAtakī al-Azdī Abū al-Mughīrah 47–49, 87, 93, 177, 183
Ziyād b. Mālik of Banū Ḍubayʿah 32
Ziyād b. Sumayyah (i.e., Ziyād b. Abī Sufyān, called Ziyād b. Abīhi) 35 n. 146, 45
Ziyādah b. Zayd (poet) 222
al-Zubayr b. al-ʿAwwām (father of ʿAbdallāh b. al-Zubayr) 84, 175, 195, 228; family of 58, 109, 110, 112, 230
al-Zubayr b. Khuzaymah al-Khathʿamī 9
al-Zubayr b. al-Māḥūz 123, 125, 131, 133
Zubayriyyah 173
Zufar b. al-Ḥārith al-Kilābī 150, 155
Zuhayr b. al-Abrad al-Kalbī 155, 156, 161
Zuhayr b. Dhu'ayb al-ʿAdawī 62–66
Zuhayr b. Hunayd (*rāwī*) 209

www.ingramcontent.com/pod-product-compliance
Lightning Source LLC
Chambersburg PA
CBHW020642230426
43665CB00008B/287
* 9 7 8 0 7 9 1 4 0 2 2 2 1 *